Protestant Modernity

Protestant Modernity

Weber, Secularisation, and Protestantism

Anthony J. Carroll, S.J.

University of Scranton Press
Scranton and London

Library of Congress Cataloging-in-Publication Data

Carroll, Anthony J., 1965–
Protestant modernity: Weber, secularisation, and Protestantism/Anthony J. Carroll.
p. cm.
Includes bibliographical references.
ISBN 978-1-58966-163-9 (pbk.)
1. Christianity and the social sciences—History of doctrines. 2. Weber, Max, 1864–1920—Influence. 3. Religion and sociology. 4. Christian sociology. 5. Secularisation. 6. Protestant churches—Doctrines. I. Title.
BR115.S57C37 2007
306.6'804—dc22

2007043804

Distribution:
University of Scranton Press
Chicago Distribution Center
11030 S. Langley
Chicago, IL 60628

PRINTED IN THE UNITED STATES OF AMERICA

To Joseph and Margaret Carroll

Contents

Acknowledgements

This book has been a long time in the making. That it exists at all is due to the love, support, and critique of many people. It began as a doctoral dissertation at the University of Frankfurt am Main under the patient guidance of my supervisor Professor Dr. Dr. Matthias Lutz-Bachmann. His encouragement during my years of study in Germany enabled me to find my own voice and to survive the ups and down of working on a doctorate. I thank him for his generosity and great kindness to me. Many friends and colleagues in Frankfurt also should be thanked for their love and support, especially Gisela Watts for reading through the original manuscript and for her corrections.

Since my return to England, many people have contributed in different ways to this book. Special thanks go to my family, friends, and communities who have put up with a recluse during many stages of the writing. My thanks go to Dr. Laurence Paul Hemming, Dean of Research at Heythrop College, University of London, for his encouragement to publish and for putting me in touch with Mr. Jeff Gainey, Director of the University of Scranton Press, who, has been consistently encouraging, patient, and kind.

Thanks also are due to my colleagues at Heythrop College for their support and encouragement of this work, especially Dr. Michael Kirwan, S.J., who made helpful comments on both the introduction and conclusion. I would like especially to thank my colleagues in the Heythrop Institute for Religion, Ethics, and Public Life who, under the directorship of Dr. James Hanvey, S.J., have been a source of both support and stimulation. I thank Dr. Hanvey for his comments on part of the manuscript and for his encouragement to bring it to completion. I thank also Moyra Tourlamain, who read through the entire manuscript and corrected many of my convoluted turns of phrase and put them into better English, and Rebekah O'Keeffe who did some final proofreading.

I would like to thank Dr. James Sweeney, C.P., Head of Pastoral and Social Studies at Heythrop College, for reading and commenting upon the manuscript and for pointing out a number of errors. Those that remain are entirely my responsibility. My thanks also go to the two anonymous readers at Scranton University Press who made very important suggestions for how the dissertation could be turned into a book. I also thank Professor David Chalcraft for his helpful bibliographical comments, and Árpád Horváth for the beautiful photograph of Frankfurt am Main which adorns the cover.

I owe a special word of thanks to the Sisters of the Assumption who, at a crucial stage, provided me with a quiet refuge in order to bring this book to completion.

I also thank my Jesuit communities in Frankfurt and London for their support and stimulation over the time of writing, and especially both Fr. David Smolira, S.J., and Fr. Michael Holman, S.J., Jesuit Provincials during the time of writing.

I dedicate this book to my deceased parents, Joseph and Margaret Carroll, who would certainly have seen the funny side, and who gave me more than I can say.

Introduction

When I have some free time, I like to go walking in the countryside. Invariably, on such occasions, the walk is punctuated by coming across some old buildings. Two types tend to predominate. The first is a pub: a welcome place to stop and refresh oneself after the exertions of walking. The second is a church. Although far from being an expert in ecclesiastical architecture, almost instinctively I, or one of my walking companions, will say: "this is a Protestant Church," "this is a Catholic Church," or "this is an Orthodox Church." Would that it were so easy to detect the confessional influences that have shaped the architecture of social theory! This work aims to highlight just such a confessional influence on Weber's thought, hence the title: "Protestant Modernity."[1]

The subject of this work is the social theory of Max Weber, a giant of early sociology and rightly classified as one of the "founding fathers" of the discipline, who has significantly influenced a multitude of later social thinkers. In treating Max Weber as the subject, I focus on his work according to two closely related dimensions. The first is a reconstruction of the theory of secularisation present in his works. The second is a positioning of this theory within the architecture of its Protestant heritage.[2]

The objective of reconstructing Weber's account of secularisation is quite simple. For many years I heard it described, together with that of Émile Durkheim, as a central source of "classical secularisation" theory.[3] Moreover, in attending academic conferences, I would hear it said that "Weber's theory of secularisation is clearly outdated," or "Empirical evidence now shows conclusively that Weber's theory of secularisation is wrong." My problem and, in fact, embarrassment after many years spent reading Weber, was that I did not really understand exactly what Weber's theory of secularisation was. Was it simply his thesis on Protestantism and capitalism? Perhaps it was the big idea behind his collected works on the sociology of religion. Or was it rather to do with his methodological writings? Then again, was it in his political writings? Moreover, when I came to study later social theorists such as Jürgen Habermas, Anthony Giddens, Alain Touraine, and Niklaus Luhmann, I noticed that each of them used Weber in their own theories of modernity and society and would consider his theory of secularisation to be an *a priori* of modern social theory. So what exactly is it? The more that I read Weber, the more it became clear to me that only through an exegesis of Weber's writings would I find an answer to my question. Chapters 3 and 4 are this exegesis.

In reading through Weber's major writings with the systematic intention of reconstructing his theory of secularisation, I was not unaware of the difficulties facing someone offering an interpretation of Weber's corpus. In Chapter 2, I review the history of attempts to find the interpretative key to Weber's work and also provide the background necessary to understand Weber in his social, political, religious, and intellectual context.

Sometimes the most basic questions are the hardest to answer. Chapter 1 looks at just such a question: What is meant by secularisation? In looking at Weber's theory of secularisation, I quickly became aware that not only did I not know what Weber's theory was; I did not know what secularisation was. This first chapter answers this question at a number of different levels. First, it situates the question of secularisation within its historical context. I thus begin this chapter by looking at the modern experience of secularisation ushered in by the French Revolution. This leads on to a consideration both of the ideas important in shaping and expressing the secular worldview of modern times and of secularisation at the level of European society. This chapter considers secularisation and secularisation theory at historical, intellectual, and social levels and introduces the reader to debates that are currently raging on both sides of the Atlantic concerning the meaning and even the very existence of the process of secularisation. This first chapter has no pretension to being exhaustive but, rather, sketches a panorama against which Weber's own work can be seen to make an important contribution to thinking about religion and society.

The second dimension of this work, situating Weber's theory of secularisation within its Protestant heritage, runs throughout Chapters 2 to 5. In drawing out hermeneutical judgements conditioning Weber's sociological typology, theological sources shaping Weber's arguments, biographical material influencing Weber's own intellectual and emotional character, and the historical situation of the newly formed German nation state, the importance of the Protestant heritage of Weber's theory of secularisation is demonstrated. Whilst this dimension is present throughout Chapters 2 to 5, Chapter 5 is entirely devoted to it and brings out some of the definitive aspects of Protestantism that helped shape Weber's views. In the earlier chapters, I make it clear in my exegesis how particular works of Weber trade on their Protestant heritage. The effect of this exegetical work is cumulative and builds up to a crescendo in Chapter 5.

Taken together, these two dimensions form the basic idea of this book: that Weber's theory of secularisation narrates a Protestant account of modernity. Because secularisation has been, until recently, an uncontested motif of accounts of modernity, and Weber's own account has influenced many of the leading theorists of modernity, demonstrating the Protestant heritage of Weber's account has significant implications. Highlighting the Protestant metanarrative[4] that informs it inevitably puts a question mark over the confessional neutrality of other theories that depend on Weber's account.

Yet, a word of caution is in order. I am not arguing that everything in Weberian sociology can be explained by reference to its Protestant heritage. To do so would be simplistic and exaggerated. Rather, my purpose here is to systematically highlight how this Protestant heritage has shaped Weber's own theory of secularisation, and so to make explicit the importance of confessional influences on his work. Contemporary social theory is in danger of projecting current confessional ecumenism or even irrelevance onto previous generations. Even a cursory knowledge of nineteenth- and early twentieth-century German history reveals the shortsightedness of such a position when it comes to understanding Weber's work.

In making explicit the Protestant metanarrative inscribed on Weber's theory of secularisation, the importance of religious confession in shaping the very architecture of early social theory is made apparent. It also raises the question of how a social theory influenced by Protestantism might differ from, say, one influenced by Catholicism or Islam. This book is not the place to answer that question. Here, I limit myself to Weber and the Protestant influences that shaped his theory of secularisation. But what does it mean to say that Weber's theory of secularisation is structured by its Protestant architecture?

In my almost intuitive recognition of the confession of a Christian church from its architecture, reconstruction of tacit knowledge reveals a whole series of fascinating things about the significance of confession for ecclesiastical architecture.[5] Protestant churches tend to be more spartan, less colourful and full of images, and to have fewer side chapels and altars. Clearly, the sixteenth-century shift from Catholic to Protestant forms of worship and the centrality of the principle of *sola scriptura* resulted in the removal of the images of saints, the Blessed Virgin Mary, and devotional statues of Jesus from churches, as the Protestant emphasis on the Word and preaching gradually replaced the focus on the eucharistic sacrifice of the Mass. Protestant churches were designed to enable the congregation to see and hear the preacher of the Word, whilst for the Catholic at the time it might have been enough to see the priest's elevation of the Host during the consecration. As a result, Protestant churches took the form of open halls, sometimes with extra seating in the galleries in order to listen to the preacher as he broke the Word open for the congregation. As Protestantism developed, British Nonconformist chapels were built as a bare and highly efficient preaching space, with the traditional east end altar being replaced by the pulpit and clerk's desks. Although medieval monastic architecture, such as that of the Cistercians or Carthusians, reflected the austerity of the life of these orders, the advent of parish churches and chapels in such austere Protestant style makes even an intuitive grasp of ecclesiastical architecture and its underlying theology sufficient to detect differences between the confessions.

In leading the reader into the architecture of Weber's work, I hope to make the confessional influences on his theory of secularisation equally apparent to the reader. Clearly, the structures and the symbols manifesting these confessional differences differ in church architecture and social theory. Nevertheless, the underlying ideas are unsurprisingly similar: the non-sacramental conception of reality resulting from the separation of grace from nature; the separation of asceticism and mysticism; the opposition of faith and reason; the emphasis on the universal vocation of all believers as against the special vocation of the priesthood and religious life; the exclusive emphasis on biblical authority over against the hierarchical authority of the tradition of the Church; the emphasis on charisma over against institutional authority; the Two-Kingdoms doctrine of Luther over against the interpenetration of the earthly and the heavenly realms; the separation of contemplation and action; the opposition of law and spirit; the opposition of politics and religion; the opposition to a realised eschatology in the ecclesiological and sacramental form in favour of an eschatological withdrawal from the world; and the opposition of secular positive law to substantive natural law.

All these components of the Protestant architecture of Weber's theory of secularisation will be elucidated during the exegesis of his major texts. Little by little, the structure of Weber's architecture will become apparent as the reader walks through the cathedral-like edifice of Weber's works.

Notes

1. A number of scholars have noticed the influence of Protestantism on Weber's thought. See, for example, Midgley (1983). I am grateful to Professor David J. Chalcraft for bringing this work to my attention, Merton (1993), and Gane (2004): 163 n. 7.

2. The importance of Puritanism in secularisation previously has been noted in both popular and scholarly studies. For an excellent popular study, see Armstrong (2004), and on a more scholarly level,

see Marty and Appleby (eds.) (1991): 1–65, 142–196, and Marty and Appleby (eds.) (1995): 155–178.

3. A recent example of this can be found in Norris and Inglehart (2004).

4. By metanarrative, I mean the basic framework or general narrative in which Weber's account of secularisation and modernity is told.

5. For an interesting study of the influence of Protestantism on modern architecture, see Brett (2004).

List of Abbreviations

Weber's Works

AJ *Das antike Judentum.* In *GARS* III.

GARS *Gesammelte Aufsätze zur Religionssoziologie.* (1988) [1920, 1921]. Edited by Marianne Weber. Tübingen: J.C.B. Mohr (Paul Siebeck). UTB Editions in Three Volumes.

GASW *Gesammelte Aufsätzte zur Sozial- und Wirtschaftsgeschichte.* (1988) [1924]. Edited by Marianne Weber. Tübingen: J.C.B. Mohr (Paul Siebeck). UTB Edition.

GAW *Gesammelte Aufsätze zur Wissenschaftslehre.* (1988) [1922]. Edited by Johannes Winckelmann, 7th ed. Tübingen: J.C.B. Mohr (Paul Siebeck), UTB Edition.

GPS *Gesammelte Politische Schriften.* (1988) [1921]. Edited by Johannes Winckelmann, 5th ed. Tübingen: J.C.B. Mohr (Paul Siebeck), UTB Edition.

MWG *Max Weber Gesamtausgabe.* (1984–continuing). Tübingen: J.C.B. Mohr (Paul Siebeck).

PE *Die protestantische Ethik und der "Geist" des Kapitalismus.* (2000) [1904–1905, 1920]. Edited and introduced by Klaus Lichtblau and Johannes Weiß. Weinheim: Beltz Athenäum.

PS *Die protestantischen Sekten und der Geist des Kapitalismus.* In *GARS* I.

WEWR *Die Wirtschaftsethik der Weltreligionen.* In *GARS* I.

WuG	*Wirtschaft und Gesellschaft.* (1972) [1921, 1922]. 5th revised ed. Student edition. Directed by Johannes Winkelmann. Tübingen: J.C.B. Mohr (Paul Siebeck).
Einleitung:	In *Die Wirtschaftsethik der Weltreligionen, GARS* I: 237–275.
Objektivität:	*Die "Objektivität" sozialwissenschaflicher und sozialpolitischer Erkenntnis,* in *GAW*: 146–214.
Politik:	*Politik als Beruf,* in *GPS*: 505–560.
Vorbemerkung:	In *GARS* I: 1–16.
Wissenschaft:	*Wissenschaft als Beruf,* in *GAW*: 582–613.
Zwischenbetrachtung:	*Zwischenbetrachtung: Theorie der Stufen und· Richtungen religiöser Weltablehnung,* in *GARS* I: 536–573.

The original date of publication is shown in square brackets.

CHAPTER 1

Historical and Systematic Aspects of Modern Secularisation

For some time now the Western theory of secularisation has been closely tied to the narrative of the emergence of modern society.[1] One might summarise this narrative in the following way: due to a constellation of factors such as the rise of new scientific methods, the political and legal settlements of the seventeenth-century wars of religion, the invention of new forms of political and economic theory, and the religious and cultural changes associated with the Reformation, the Renaissance, and the French Revolution, society went through a process of modernisation.[2] This process involved a transition from the feudal society of medieval Christendom to a modern capitalist secular society.[3] Societal modernisation was brought about through the functional differentiation of sectors of society which had previously been fused together in an undifferentiated whole.[4] The separation of the domains of politics into the apparatus of the state and its legitimation through various forms of democratic sovereignty, and of the economy into a network of interacting markets based on the freedom of the individual to buy and sell, produced the capitalist societies of the modern period. This development is further understood as the separation of a public sphere of the political engagement of citizens in the formation of public opinion from a private sphere of personal interests. In this model, religion is considered to be a private interest, and adherence to a particular "brand," or none, is considered to be similar to the decision to buy one product over another. The decline and eventual elimination of religion from society, which is sometimes understood to be the logical consequence of this modernisation, is thus seen to be a result of loss of interest in this product or the discovery of a better one to perform its functions.[5] Seen thus, religion does not play, and indeed is often forbidden to play, a role in the formation of public opinion in the public sphere.[6]

The history of the retreat of religion from public life is a long and complicated story that can only be sketched in this chapter. Nevertheless, any adequate investigation into the complexity of theories of secularisation should be informed by this history so as to shape its systematic endeavours by coherence to and correspondence with the actual events of history.[7] I thus begin this consideration of the historical and systematic aspects of modern secularisation by turning to the events that would send shock waves around the world in the modern era and would significantly shape the ways in which religion and public life have been thought about until recently.

The French Revolution and Modern Secularisation

The most significant event for the modern history of secularisation is without doubt the French Revolution. The major decisions taken at that time, the *Declaration of the Rights of Man and the Citizen*, and the *Civil Constitution*, have shaped the modern period and the relationship between religion and society right up to the present day. The old order, referred to in French as the *ancien regime*, was characterised by the confessional nature of the State. That is to say, just as an individual confessed allegiance to a religion, so also did the State have an official religion, which its citizens shared. The application of the principle of *Cuius regio, eius religio* (whose district it is, his religion it is), an ancient principle dating back to the time of Emperor Constantine, had put an end to the confessional disputes between the forces of the Holy Romanm Emperor, Charles V, and the force of the Schmalkaldic League with the signing of the Peace of Augsburg in 1555 and, later, settled the religious wars in seventeenth-century Europe. Britain, however, was an exception to this rule.[8] There, the 1707 Act of Union, which forged the British nation, meant that Queen Anne was the Supreme Governor of the Church of England but simply a member of the Church when in Scotland.[9] Yet the principle was universally accepted that the unity of faith in a land structured the relations between religion and society.

The beginnings of religious toleration had somewhat modified this principle in countries such as Britain and Hungary, but the revocation of the Edict of Nantes in 1685, which had granted toleration to Protestants in France, illustrated the continuing fragility of the idea of religious toleration before the French Revolution. It would be the lasting legacy of the French Revolution to initiate the process of the separation of creed and citizenship that characterises the modern history of secularisation.[10] Nineteenth-century Europe would continue this process of separating religion from society and would develop its own theories of history to justify this process.

Thus, in Article X of the *Declaration of the Rights of Man and the Citizen*, which was adopted by the Constituent Assembly on August 26, 1789, the way was set for the dissociation of creed and citizenship that would be later adopted by other European nations. The French Revolution ended both a tradition of identifying the State with a particular religion and the historic link between Catholicism and political society in France. Article X stressed that no citizen should be harassed for the opinions that they held, even for their religious opinions. Thus, religious opinions were placed on a par with all personal choices and would no longer be a *sine qua non* for the civil and political rights associated with citizenship. As a logical consequence, the Assembly granted Jews and Protestants complete citizenship in 1791.

The separation of society from religion, an important part of the modern concept of secularisation, should not, however, be traced back simply to this one act of the Constituent Assembly. The members of the Assembly were themselves still deeply rooted in the conviction of "one nation, one faith" and would have considered it unthinkable not to have begun their anniversary celebrations of the taking of the Bastille and the remodelling of the institutions of France with a Mass celebrated by the bishop delegate of the Assembly, accompanied by 300 priests. As René Rémond argues, this clearly shows that the idea of the separation of religion and politics was still very foreign at the time of the Revolution, even to the elected members of the French National Assembly.[11]

French society also emerged out of the royalist tradition and presumed that the rights and privileges of the monarchy should now pass to the people. Just as the kings had chosen their own bishops and priests, the people should now have the same right. The Civil Constitution of the Clergy, passed in 1790, thus reformed the structures of the Church in France, including the boundaries of dioceses, which were henceforth to be based on the Departments, and gave the people the right to elect bishops and priests through their Assembly. This finally galvanised the pope of the time, Pius VI, to issue his letter of March 10, 1791, *Quod aliquantum*, which condemned these legal changes and thus irreversibly changed the relations in France between political power and religion. The dispute that resulted caused a split in the loyalty of all French Catholics. On the one hand, the Assembly demanded that its citizens follow the laws that it laid down, and on the other hand, the pope insisted that Catholics follow the voice of Rome. The situation became even more acute when, after the downfall of the monarchy in August 1792, the Legislative Assembly proceeded to unpick the religious fabric of French society and began a process of separating religion from the normal functioning of society: that is to say, began what we today call the modern process of secularisation.

The first move in this direction was the institution of a civil registry. This replaced the cataloguing of social life that had previously been carried out by the clergy. Birth, marriage, and death were no longer to be recorded in an ecclesiastical framework but, rather, in a purely civil one. Thus, birth would no longer be recorded by the certificate of baptism but, rather, by entering one's name and birthplace on the civil registry, which was kept at the town hall. This changed a tradition that had been in place for centuries and removed the ecclesiastical control of the recognition of individual and social identity. Marriage would now also become a civil affair, recorded in a civil registry that paid no attention to the religious denomination of the couple.[12]

A further form of secularisation occurred through the measures taken by the Assembly against the religious orders. The whole conception of what it meant to be part of a religious order—the collective sharing of goods and the lifelong commitment to a life of poverty, chastity, and obedience—was anathema to the spirit of the Revolution, which had stressed individual liberty. In February 1790, the Constituent Assembly declared that the vows of religion were invalid and banned them from being taken in the future. Monastic orders were ordered to disperse, and priestly celibacy was abolished. In this direct interference in the life of the religious orders, the State showed that it had power to determine the forms that religion could take in its territory. This was an assertion of the supremacy of secular jurisdiction over ecclesiastical jurisdiction and thus further underlined the elimination of the religious dimension from the fabric of social life. The thinking which gave rise to such attitudes had to some extent been formed by the criticisms of religious life by eighteenth-century thinkers such as Voltaire, Hume, and Rousseau. One needs only to think of the satirical portrayal of Pangloss in Voltaire's *Candide* to gain some idea of the literary and philosophical background that shaped such a rejection of the basic Christian values of religious life.

However, this new spirit of secular liberty undermined not only religious life but also the Christian conception of marriage, which had played a central role in the structuring of social life. The Legislative Assembly decreed that divorce was allowed and argued that the liberty of the individuals involved required that the consent which constituted the marriage contract could be withdrawn. Again, this was an argument based on the new secular notion of liberty and the right of individuals to choose and decide their own destiny. The instituting of divorce after the Revolution was especially significant, since it was the first time that a teaching contrary to that of the Catholic Church had been legalised by the French State. Whilst this may be commonplace today in all member countries of the European Union, at the time of revolutionary France it was epochal. It instigated a major secularisation of society by separating religion and religious ideas from the institutional fabric of society. The Catholic doctrine of the indissolubility of marriage, which had guided French society from time immemorial, was thus replaced by the secular doctrine of the freedom of the individual to withdraw consent. Indeed, the question of divorce in French society would act as a barometer for the relations between religion and society, moderate governments tending to repeal it and radical governments tending to reinstitute it.[13]

The change in relations between religion and society in France during and after the Revolution was exported to other European countries through military conflict under Napoleon.[14] In conquered territories, such as Belgium and the left bank of the Rhine, the State seized church property and forced the religious orders to leave. Furthermore, the states in these areas instituted civil registry and separated citizenship from creed, as it had done in France. French influence in the Germanic areas was no less significant. In 1803 Napoleon imposed the "Secularisation," which dissolved all ecclesiastical states and confiscated all church property. Moreover, he also declared the dissolution of the Germanic Holy Roman Empire, the empire that had united political and religious interests in continental Europe for more than a thousand years. It was, as Rémond suggests, the end of the Middle Ages in Europe and a turning point in the history of secularisation in the modern era.[15]

The Secularisation of German Thought in the Nineteenth Century

The Middle Ages in Europe ended not only at a social level but also at an intellectual level. The Augustinian understanding of the "two cities" and the separation of the heavenly from the earthly realm were conceptually eliminated in nineteenth-century theories of world history.[16] The conception of the world or universal history that became prominent instead can be understood as a secularisation of time, since it sought to consider time purely from within—that is to say, without recourse to the eschatological perspective that theories of history, as developed by St. Augustine, had considered would fulfil and make ultimate sense of secular time. This removal of the transcendental nature of time and the substitution of an understanding of it as a purely immanent historical reality is a characteristic of nineteenth-century theories of secularisation. It became the framework in which the events of the French Revolution and its aftermath would be interpreted and understood.[17]

German thinkers of this time used the word *Verweltlichung* (the "making worldly" of someone or something), to express the concept of secularisation. Thus the two meanings of secularisation, the juridical sense of making someone or something the property of the State and not of the Church, and the sense of the transformation of the conception of history are both present. This can be seen in the work of Hegel and in his understanding of history. In fact, in Hegel the concept of *Verweltlichung* is used in both a positive and in a negative sense.

In his *Vorlesungen über die Geschichte der Philosophie (Lectures on the History of Philosophy)*, Hegel considers the negative aspect in the sense of the decadence of the Church in the Middle Ages and its compromise with the world to the extent of becoming worldly. This is a loss of the meaning of Christianity for Hegel and, thus, a *Verweltlichung* in a negative sense. It is a consequence, for Hegel, of the inability of Scholastic theology to find a true reconciliation between transcendence and immanence, which resulted in a form of worldliness that caused the crisis of the medieval Church. In his *Vorlesungen über die Philosophie der Geschichte (Lectures on the Philosophy of History)*, by contrast, Hegel considers the positive aspect of *Verweltlichung*. In this context, he considers the opening out of the Christian principle to the world and, as such, a movement of the absolute spirit into the world and, thus, a transformation of the private interiority of spirit into the public exteriority of history. Here, secularisation is understood as the way in which the interior message of Christianity, originally outside of history, the Christian principle, becomes the immanent principle of world history. The incarnation of Christ is, for Hegel, the decisive moment in which the absolute spirit enters history and turns from a transhistorical interiority into an immanent exteriority of absolute spirit in history. The incapacity of the Church to mediate this spirit to history causes the spirit to turn to the State as the place in which the realisation of spirit can occur. This realisation of the spirit in the State is the basis for Hegel's understanding of secularisation and makes him, in the words of Löwith, the last of the Christian philosophers.[18]

Hegel so marked the nineteenth century that the relationship between religion, philosophy, and world history would become the standard point of departure for the generations that followed him.[19] Indeed, the debate about the understanding of secularisation is considered by one contemporary philosopher to be the heart of the conflict between the so-called left and right Hegelians.[20] However, as Owen Chadwick has argued, it is in the work of Karl Marx that the most significant development of the Hegelian notion of secularisation occurs in the nineteenth century.[21]

Marx is the one who took the controversies of David Friedrich Strauss and Ludwig Andreas Feuerbach against Hegel's Christian philosophy and the debate on the crisis of Christianity of Bruno Bauer and Søren Kierkegaard and developed the most radical consequences of the critique of Hegel's *Grundlinien der Philosophie des Rechts* (*Elements of the Philosophy of Right*), which had been begun by Arnold Ruge. The debate about the end of philosophy and its transformation into a practical reality that ensued in the debates after the death of Hegel, is really just another way of speaking about his secularisation theory. Thus in *Zur Judenfrage (On the Jewish Question)*, Marx speaks about the need for the Christian State to become the secular or worldly State in order for the realisation of the human spirit to take place.[22] Indeed, for Marx, in his *Zur Kritik der Hegelschen Rechtsphilosophie (On the Critique of Hegel's Philosophy of Right)*, the critique of religion is the precondition for any critique whatsoever in Germany.[23] Secularisation does not mean the disappearance of religion for Marx, but rather that religious consciousness will be determined by the plurality of religions and their mutual conflicts.[24]

Marx considers the question of the realisation of philosophy in his introduction to *Zur Kritik der Hegelschen Rechtsphilosophie*. Here he follows and further develops Feuerbach's critique of Hegel and argues that the disappearance of the transcendental conception of truth has left the task of reconceptualising truth purely from the immanent perspective of praxis in history.[25] This is Marx's understanding of the secularisation (*Verweltlichung*) of philosophy, and he sees it as the entry of philosophy into the conflicts with the present ruling powers in order to build and manage a future. Marx expressed this understanding in a letter he wrote to Arnold Ruge in 1843:

> Philosophy has secularised itself and the clearest proof of this is that philosophical consciousness has itself been pulled into the agony of the struggle not only externally but also internally. If the building of the future and its managing for all times concerns us, then even more so does the completion of the present, that is to say, *the care free critique of all existing powers*. It is care free in the sense that the critique is not afraid of its results and even less so of the conflict with the present powers.[26]

The critique of the heavenly realm has thus now transformed itself into the critique of the earthly realm.[27] Marx argues that just as we have been alienated by believing in the heavenly realm and using our energies to attain a false goal, so too have we been alienated by the false vision of the capitalist society. In order to truly realise this, philosophy needs to turn from being a critique of theology, as it had been for Feuerbach, and become an engaged critique of politics.[28]

In his critique of Hegel's *Grundlinien der Philosophie des Rechts*, Marx also uses the notion of secularisation in its juridical sense to mean the expropriation of church property and personnel.[29] Thus Luther's reforms, which led to this expropriation, are the first steps toward secularisation. The transformation of religion from a priestly to a lay organisation, and thinkers from monks to philosophers, are both aspects of the revolutionary background of Germany. However, Marx held that if this process, which had begun in Germany, is to catch up with that of England and France, philosophy must free itself of this theoretical obsession and become practical. For Marx, social revolution is necessary if this secularisation is not simply to remain the confiscation of church property.

It was not only the philosophers of the nineteenth century who considered the question of secularisation; theologians also reflected on the changing nature of the relationship between religion and society. Richard Rothe, for example, in the first volume of his *Theological Ethics* (1845), argued that Christianity had first embodied itself in the form of the Church, and now this inner Christian principle had been incarnated in the State. Moreover, like Marx, he saw the Reformation as the crucial turning point in this secularisation. He argued that as the Church had begun to secularise itself during the Reformation, the State had begun to desecularise itself and become the institution through which the message of the gospel could finally be mediated to the whole of society.

Perhaps the most interesting theologian of secularisation during the nineteenth century was Johann Friedrich Overbeck. Greatly influenced by his lifelong friend Friedrich Nietzsche, Overbeck asserted that theology itself was the death of Christianity.[30] Initially, in primitive Christianity, he argued, the separation of Christianity from pagan philosophy was absolute. Christianity was not meant to be yet another philosophy to compete with the multitude already on offer in the ancient world. Christianity was thus to be separated from worldly thinking. This view illustrates Overbeck's fundamental thesis that the whole of Christianity is a process of decay, from an initial position of the rejection of the world and its philosophy to one of steady compromises with the world and its philosophies until the final death of Christianity in the historical theology of the nineteenth-century Protestant theologians. For Overbeck, the key to real Christianity is to understand that the original intention at the time of Jesus and the writing of the Gospels was to accept its powerlessness in this world, making Christianity a real alternative to the ways of the world.[31]

The nineteenth century was not only a time in which ideologies between left and right were fought out theoretically; it was also a time of great social conflict in Europe. New ideas influenced these events and fuelled social conflict. The three phases of historical development outlined by the French sociologist Auguste Comte in his *Cours de philosophie* (1830–1842)—the theological, the metaphysical, and the scientific—fitted well an age of rapid industrialisation and growing urbanisation.[32] Such social changes could hardly fail to alter the relations between Church and State.

The Secularisation of European Society in the Nineteenth Century

In the period between the defeat of Napoleon in 1815 and the revolutions of 1848, most parts of Europe saw a return to more conservative forms of Christianity. This was because governments felt that liberal religion and scepticism had been major factors in causing the instabilities of the previous years. Thus in France, Charles X (1824–1830) vigorously promoted the alliance of the throne, altar, and chateau; and in Germany, especially in Prussia, Friedrich Wilhelm IV (1840–1861) sought to bring about a "Christian State."[33]

In England too, as in most other Protestant countries, the early nineteenth century was a period of religious awakening involving large-scale conversions to Christianity and the rapid growth of evangelical religion. However, resistance to Christianity was strong amongst the working class and lower middle class. Socialists such as Robert Owen had a large influence on the working class, and works by Thomas Paine, such as *The Rights of Man* (1791) and *The Age of Reason* (1794), were widely read at the beginning of the nineteenth century. These encouraged a critical attitude towards Christianity.[34]

The revolutions of 1848–1849 marked a dramatic change in the relations between the Church and the State and had a significant effect on the process of the secularisation of European society for generations. At first, they were welcomed by the Churches as they saw opportunities for relaxing controls implemented during the eighteenth and early nineteenth centuries. Religious minorities, such as the French Protestants and the German Jews, especially hoped for increased freedom and frequently were the most enthusiastic supporters of the revolutions.

Roman Catholic reaction to the revolutions varied. On the one hand, many priests believed that the changes would bring about new freedom for the Church, and indeed Catholic priests stood as candidates for the Frankfurt parliament and many state parliaments in the hope that they could influence the political situation for the betterment of the Church. However, in Prussia, priests tended to concentrate more on internal church matters, not hoping for much from the revolutions and tending to favour a constitutional monarchy.[35]

In 1848, both the Protestant clergy in Germany and the Catholic clergy in France moved to the right. In Germany, Friedrich Wilhelm IV sought to improve relations with the Catholic hierarchy, and the Constitution of 1850 achieved major breakthroughs for the Catholic Church in Prussia. The increased freedom granted to Catholics allowed for the re-establishment of religious orders that had been repressed, and orders began to hold large missions, which were a significant feature of religious life in the 1850s. The "Christian State" championed by Friedrich Wilhelm IV aimed to combine a strict form of government with a religious curriculum in the schools in order to give a strong religious basis for society.

In France, where the revolution in Rome of November 1848 had horrified the clergy, Louis Napoleon rewarded Catholics for their support. Under his patronage, laws were passed that gave them much greater freedom. The Falloux Law of 1850, for example, lifted restrictions on religious schools, leading very rapidly to the founding of both primary and secondary schools run by religious orders in many parts of France. The issue of taking Sunday as a day of rest assumed political importance, dividing the liberals, who saw this as a matter of personal choice, from the conservatives who thought that it should be legally enforced in order to ensure a sense of solidarity and collective submission to the law of God as a basis for society.[36]

A significant development in the mid-nineteenth century was the tendency for the left in both Germany and France to become secular. This went hand in hand with an anticlerical tendency in left secular parties in continental Europe. Under the Third Republic in France (1870–1940), religion became the key to dividing the left from the right. This was due not only to the difference of religious policies between the parties, but also to the political language that they employed. The secular left tended to use antireligious language and drew on the anti-Christian ideologies of the time to discredit the policies of the right. The right, in contrast, tended to use religious rhetoric to justify their policies and often backed up their statements with references to teachings of the Catholic Church. In Germany, whilst strong secularising tendencies influenced German socialism, religious language and arguments continued to play a significant part in the political debate. This was mainly due to the fact that German Catholicism was a significant political force at the time, and conservatism was heavily influenced by Protestantism.

As is often the case, the situation in Britain was different. Britain had already gone through huge social upheavals in the 1830s and 1840s, such as the reform of Parliament, the reform of the Church of England, the reform of town government, and also the enactment of the Poor Law, which had met with great resistance from the aristocracy. Consequently, there was little energy left for revolution. Moreover, the 1840s saw a rise in the prosperity of Britain, and this also dampened any revolutionary tendencies in the country. In terms of the religious influence in politics during the nineteenth century, England clearly differed from France and Germany. Whilst on the continent the secular parties tended to be on the left and the religious parties on the right, religion in England crossed the political divide and influenced both sides of the ideological debate. Thus in England, moderate liberalism, radicalism, and even socialism continued to be influenced by religious convictions and language.

The 1860s and the 1870s saw many Nonconformists enter into the British parliament, and the very fervent high Anglican William Gladstone,[37] who had been deeply influenced by Anglican clergymen such as John Henry Newman, John Keble, and Edward Bouverie Pusey (the leaders of the Oxford Movement), assumed the leadership of the Whigs on the death of Lord Palmerston in 1865. Gladstone often used biblical rhetoric in his political speeches, and many social and political movements, such as the rural labourers' movement, began their meetings with hymns and readings from the Bible. Thus, whilst in France and Germany the conservatives tended to monopolise the political use of the Bible, in Britain all sides claimed biblical legitimation for their points of view. This split in Germany would lead to a major confrontation between the State and the increasingly strong Catholic Church.[38] The resulting clash, known as the *Kulturkampf*, would further polarise both political and religious factions.

In other European countries, such as Italy, Spain, France, Belgium, Switzerland, and Austria, anticlericalism had already become politically significant at this time. The Catholic Church posed a threat to the major force of nineteenth-century politics, namely, nationalism. In 1864, Pope Pius IX published the *Syllabus of Errors*, which condemned liberalism, secularism, and rationalism and made it clear that the Catholic Church would not be an easy partner in the forging of the new national identities in Europe. The distance between secular society and the Church was widened when in 1870 the doctrine of papal infallibility was declared. In fact, this doctrine sought to limit the power of the pope to the traditional areas of faith and morals, but liberals perceived the doctrine as one more sign of papal political interests.

In the same year, Italian troops entered Rome and stripped the papacy of the last vestiges of its temporal power. The pope argued that without temporal power his spiritual independence would be threatened, and he sought support from other European countries to regain his temporal base. Bismarck, seeing political advantage for the formation of the new German nation-state, offered the pope asylum, believing that this could help the stability of the empire. At this point, Bismarck, himself an orthodox Lutheran, was relatively unconcerned about the influence of the Church in political matters. However, events would quickly cause him to change this neutral position. After the declaration of the dogma of papal infallibility, internal divisions developed in the German Catholic Church. Two lay theologians—Ignaz Döllinger, who had been a good friend of Gladstone in England, and Johann

Friedrich—led the group known as the "Alt Katholiken," the "Old Catholics," who refused to accept the dogma and broke with the Roman Catholic Church. In 1871, the Bishops of Breslau and Ermland, together with the Archbishop of Cologne, pressed the Prussian authorities to expel the "Old Catholics" from teaching posts in schools and universities. The government refused to do so on the grounds of religious toleration and, when the bishops pressed further, retaliated by suspending state subsidies to them. This dispute in itself would not have led to the so-called *Kulturkampf*, as Bismarck was more concerned with political issues than matters of theology, but it led to confrontation between Bismarck and the newly founded Catholic Centre Party, the *Zentrum*, of 1870.[39]

The *Zentrum* had been formed in the face of mounting liberal hostility to the Catholic Church and as a reaction to the growth of Protestant Prussia. By 1871 it had become the second largest party in the *Reichstag* and had a very capable leader in Ludwig Windthost. The party was pledged to defend the Church against the liberals and Protestant Prussian state hostility, to support the cause of confessional schools, and to campaign against the introduction of civil marriage. The *Zentrum* also made a significant positive contribution to social reform: Catholic social thinkers such as Bishop Wilhelm von Ketteler and Father Kolping, Christian trade unions were formed, workers' cooperatives were encouraged, and social help for the unemployed was initiated.[40] These measures ensured that social Catholicism in the nineteenth century would make a significant impact on the new German socio-political scene.

A number of measures led to the events that came to be described as the *Kulturkampf* between the new Bismarckian Empire and the Catholic Church.[41] The annexation of Italy and the confiscation of the papal lands in 1870 provoked the *Zentrum* to put pressure on Bismarck to intervene militarily in Italy. Bismarck resisted, as he wanted to maintain stable relations with Italy and was not prepared to risk a military operation at the start of the formation of the German nation-state. The *Zentrum* further pressured him to incorporate the religious guarantees of the 1850 Prussian Constitution in the new Imperial Constitution. Bismarck tried repeatedly to loosen the support of the Vatican and the German bishops for the *Zentrum*, but to no avail. Catholic Church support for the Polish language in the east of the Prussian empire further anguished Bismarck, as this fuelled Polish nationalist sentiment and threatened to destabilise the empire. Consequently, in 1872 he appointed Adalbert Falk to be Prussian Minister of Religious Affairs. Falk was a fervent anticlericalist and was determined to put the Church under the legislative control of the State. His first step was to remove Prussian schools from all church control, both Catholic and Protestant, and introduce legislation forbidding the Jesuit order to set up works in Germany.[42] The so-called "May Laws" of May 1873, passed by the Prussian *Landtag* gave the State power over the education of priests by forcing each candidate to spend three years at university before entering the seminary, and removed many of the disciplinary powers of the bishops. Furthermore, all church appointments of bishops and priests had to be subjected to the veto of the state authorities.

In the following year, 1874, the freedom of movement of the clergy was restricted. Also Prussia introduced civil marriage and required all births, deaths, and marriages to be recorded with the registrar, not, as previously, with the church authorities. As in France, this was a significant social form of secularisation that carried with it a deep symbolism. Social life was to be regulated in accordance with a civil, not ecclesiastical, pattern, which significantly changed the framework of relations between the Church and the State. It further promoted what Kaspar von Greyerz has called, for a slightly earlier period, the "privatisation of devotion."[43] The interaction of life and religious ritual was marginalised to the private realm of devotion and excluded from the public marking of rites of passage such as birth, marriage, and death.

Hostilities reached a climax in 1875, with laws empowering Prussia to suspend subsidies to all church members who resisted the new legislation and the suppression of all religious orders except for those engaged in nursing. Papal condemnation of this legislation further intensified tensions between the Church and the State. These anti-Catholic measures galvanised support for the *Zentrum*, and lay people rallied to support their bishops and priests in their struggle against the State.[44] Bismarck came to see that force was not the way to control the Catholic Church, and on the death of Pope Pius IX in 1878 he took the opportunity to negotiate with the Vatican to put an end to the *Kulturkampf*. The negotiations were not easy, however, and it would take until 1887 to reach a final solution. The solution dismantled the May Laws, allowed exiled clergy to return to Germany, and resumed state payments to the Church. However, Bismarck ensured that civil marriage remained compulsory, that the Jesuits were still banned in Germany, and that church appointments would continue to be monitored by the State.[45]

The results of the *Kulturkampf* were significant for German Catholics. In effect, Catholics remained a marginalized group well into the twentieth century, and poverty was significantly higher among Catholics than among Protestants.[46] Educationally too, the differences between Catholics and Protestants remained significant. In the 1880s, for example, a Catholic boy was half as likely as a Protestant boy to go to university and as late as 1924, only 12 per cent of the highest-ranking civil servants were Catholics.[47]

The Secularisation Debates of the Twentieth and Twenty-First Centuries

For much of the twentieth century, the theory of secularisation was a cultural *a priori* that informed all thought about the modern world and its emergence from the medieval past. However, towards the end of the twentieth century this consensus broke down. José Casanova, in *Public Religions in the Modern World*, explains how this changed in the 1980s and notes that sociologists of religion seem now to be as dismissive of the theory as they were initially faithful to it.[48] There are several reasons for this shift, and here I will simply outline two.[49]

The first can be attributed to what we might call the "end of modernity" thesis. The argument runs as follows. The project of modernity aimed, amongst other things, to shake off the domination of the Church and religious authorities. Kant's call, "to have the courage to think for oneself," was formulated specifically in this context. Thus, one of the main aspects of the liberation sought in this project equates precisely with what the theory of secularisation proclaims: namely, the autonomy of the subject to use his or her reason according to general principles to which any reasonable person of whatever religious persuasion or none could admit. This, in short, was the basic reading of the Enlightenment in Kant's celebrated essay of 1784, *Was ist Aufklärung?* Thus, when the normative basis of this initial project of modernity is called into question,[50] so too are the claims of the theory of secularisation.

The second reason for this change can be understood by what has been called the return of spirituality or the sacred in contemporary societies.[51] The idea here is that there seems to be a return of various forms of non church-based spirituality in modern European societies. Interest in Eastern religions, New Age movements, ecological movements, and new forms of paganism is considered to be an indicator of this. Because it had been assumed that one consequence of secularisation would be the decline of spiritual beliefs and practices, the return of such beliefs and practices has called the theory of secularisation into question.[52] This has led to a second debate on the nature and limits of the theory of secularisation at an interdisciplinary level.[53]

The issue of secularisation is further complicated by the fact that the phenomena of religious belief and practice are specific to the cultural context in which they occur.[54] As Theodore Caplow argues, religious belief and practice has declined in many European countries since World War II, but no significant decline in religious belief or practice has occurred in the United States in the same period.[55] If that were not complicated enough, there is also the question of just what qualifies as religious belief and practice and how one measures this.[56] As Grace Davie puts it, many people in Great Britain, for instance, "believe but they do not belong" to a particular church.[57] Moreover, other countries follow their own patterns of secularisation in the context of their own particular histories and forms of religious belief and practice that are more or less appropriately described by the theory of secularisation.[58] There are also societies in which the separation of religion and politics is not the chosen path. We might think here of countries like Israel and Iran. Clearly, the formulation of an adequate theory of secularisation is very much an ongoing project in the changing circumstances of the contemporary world.

Callum Brown has recently proposed an interesting thesis for the case of modern Britain.[59] He suggests that only since the mid-1960s has secularisation really begun as a form of basic change in the language and the identity of people in British society. He criticises the view that secularisation should be equated with the long process of modernity, beginning in the eighteenth century and going on into the twentieth century. Using statistical data, he shows how the 1940s and 1950s exhibited the largest growth in church attendance in Britain since the mid-nineteenth century. The key to the change in the 1960s, for Brown, was the end of Christianity as a dominant narrative for social and individual life. This, he suggests, was brought about through the end of moral censorship after the trial over *Lady Chatterley's Lover* in 1960, through the legalisation of abortion and homosexuality in 1967, the easing of the divorce laws in 1968, the flourishing of the youth culture of the 1960s, and the student rebellions of 1968 and 1970. Callum Brown is not alone in arguing that the 1960s were the start of secularisation. Peter van Rooden also suggests that this was the key time at which society in Holland underwent secularisation.[60]

At the same time, there are also mounting signs that those who defend the theory of secularisation may be concentrating overly on Western European trends. Peter Berger, a sociologist of religion who had significantly contributed to formulating the modern theory of secularisation, is now convinced that the assumption that we live in a secularised world is false.[61] He considers the world to be "furiously religious," perhaps even "more than it ever was." Danièle Hervieu-Léger, one of the leading French sociologists of religion today, is also convinced that the theory of secularisation is of limited value. She comments:

> Can one still speak of secularisation? For the notion to preserve some semblance of heuristic relevance its validity requires a dual qualification. In terms of extent first, in line with Peter Berger's view

> of Europe as its only valid field of application; then of density, remarking that even in this arena it fails to reach down into the deeper layers of culture. One may as well admit that in the final analysis it cannot be taken very far.[62]

What has been treated as the norm, that is, Western Europe, seems in the end to finish as being the exception when one looks at the question of secularisation on a global level. Berger suggests that there are two exceptions to his desecularisation thesis. The first is Europe, and even here it is perhaps more accurate to hold that the institutional focus of religion has shifted than to conclude that people themselves are more secularised.[63] The second is an international subculture of a Western-educated elite who act as carriers for the Enlightenment version of the secularisation thesis.[64] These people are a highly articulate minority and consequently have a disproportionate influence on the legal system, on the media, and on the educational system. In the face of these two exceptions, according to Berger, we are experiencing a resurgence of religion and its influence on world politics.[65] He mentions a number of examples.

The first is the influence of Roman Catholicism on political issues across the globe since the Second Vatican Council.[66] Examples would include the role of John Paul II in influencing the downfall of Communism, the international influence of Roman Catholic communities such as Sant'Egidio and their role in peace mediation, such as the negotiation of peace in Mozambique and Uganda, and the presence of Vatican representation at international organisations such as the U.N. and the European Parliament. The second form of resurgence identified by Berger is that of evangelical Protestantism. The last three or four decades has seen a steady increase in conservative Protestant Christianity, especially in Latin America, sub-saharan Africa, and Southeast Asia.[67] The influence of conservative Protestantism on American politics is also a significant factor that adds weight to the desecularisation thesis.[68] The third form of resurgence Berger mentions is that of fundamentalist Islam. Here perhaps the effects on global politics are most dramatic, as whole countries define their political systems in terms of the Shariah, the

Islamic law that defines the comprehensive ethical and legal system of many Islamic nations.[69] Indeed, the presence of more than 12 million Muslims in France, Germany, and Great Britain has raised the question of how modern Western countries relate to Islam within their own societies, not only as an external international phenomenon.[70]

Abdullahi An-Na'im suggests that the major question confronting Islam is how its own understanding of religion and politics relates to its own conception of secularism.[71] This same question is considered by a number of authors in a study published by the London-based Institute of Islamic Political Thought.[72] They look at the origins of the movements that have recently abolished the secularisation of the past century by creating political orders guided by Shariah law. As John Esposito suggests:

> The post-Enlightenment tendency to define religion as a system of belief restricted to personal or private life, rather than as a way of life, has seriously hampered our ability to understand the nature of Islam and many other world religions.[73]

This is another way of saying that the theory of secularisation, as it has been used in the Western world, will have considerable difficulty in coming to terms with Islam. The question of religion and politics, of the forms religion takes in the public sphere, is becoming more and more of a central question.[74] Whilst we are uncertain of exactly how these forms will turn out, we can, with Peter Berger, be certain of one thing. "Those who neglect religion in their analyses of contemporary affairs do so at their peril."[75]

In the light of the return of religion to public significance, Klaus Eder, the German sociologist, has developed an influential theory of Europe as a "postsecular society."[76] By the notion of a "postsecular society" Eder simply means that just as a secular society was one in which religion was confined to the private sphere, the return of religion to the public sphere in recent times inaugurates a postsecular society.[77]

Whatever the final outcome of these debates, they have without doubt enriched our understanding of the main questions involved in the use of secularisation as a category for understanding modernity, and also highlighted some of the possible strengths and weaknesses of such a use. The question we are faced with today is how to use the concept of secularisation with sufficient critical awareness of its limitations as a framework for understanding the origin and progress of the contemporary world, without losing the ability to draw on its heuristic usefulness as a category that continues to stimulate our hermeneutical imagination.[78] Whilst this breakdown in consensus over the interpretation of the theory of secularisation has complicated matters, greater analytical clarity over exactly what is meant by the theory has also been gained.

Karel Dobbelaere, for example, makes some helpful distinctions by describing three key dimensions of secularisation.[79] The first is the tendency for individual belief and piety to decrease in both qualitative and quantitative terms. The second is the decreasing role of churches and religion in public life. The third is the internal change that occurs in religion itself, causing it to become more worldly and weakening its claim to possess exclusive truth. All these aspects, according to Dobbelaere, contribute to making the theory of secularisation a multidimensional concept that functions at a variety of different explanatory levels.

Hartmut Lehmann considers that it is necessary to use a combination of mutually complementary concepts in order to describe and analyse the relation of Christianity and modernity. He suggests that the concepts of secularisation, de-Christianisation, and re-Christianisation are required in order to be able to grasp the phenomena of religion today.[80]

Hugh McLeod suggests that contemporary theories of secularisation can be grouped into four major types.[81] The first type he describes as "the march of science view." This focusses on the intellectual origins of secularisation.[82] It considers the period from Copernicus to Newton to be the start of the process in which modern secular thinking emerged. This was developed further in the biological discoveries of Charles Darwin and the biblical and theological critiques of the Tübingen School and Friedrich Strauss and Ernest Renan. Social scientific accounts of the origin and functions of society developed by people such as Auguste Comte and Herbert Spencer also fostered the growth of modern secular thinking.

The gradual replacement of a theological vision by a scientific vision of the world is, in this model, the main cause of secularisation. McLeod describes the second type as the "modernisation account," which highlights the idea of social rather than intellectual change. The main transition here is from rural agrarian societies, which, in being hierarchical and traditional, tended to favour religion to societies that are predominantly urban, industrial, and democratic, and tend to favour a secular society.[83] McLeod's third type is the "postmodernist," which is based on the idea that secularisation did not really occur until around the 1960s, the time of the significant changes in Western society that have been grouped under the heading of postmodernism.[84] And he describes his fourth type as the "selling God" interpretation. This is propounded by people such as Jeffrey Cox and suggests that whilst secularisation has occurred, it is by no means an inevitable consequence of modernisation, as the differences between the United States and Europe illustrate. The issue of the capacity of a religion to present itself (hence the phrase "selling God") in an acceptable and interesting way to people is the decisive question as to whether or not it survives.[85]

In addition to these four general types of theories, debates about secularisation seem themselves to have occurred in particular phases and context-providing constellations. Thus, for example, in the so-called first secularisation debate, three major positions competed for dominance. The first position, held by Bryan Wilson and Peter Berger, argued that a decline in religion was an inevitable consequence of the process of modernisation.[86] Wilson suggested that this decline was due to the shift from agricultural to industrial life styles in modern times. Berger argued that, due to the structural differentiation of society, the various spheres of modern life that emerge create their own logics and their own truth claims. This has a tendency to undermine the monopoly that religion formerly held on truth claims, and the resulting competing pluralism tends to undermine the identity of the various religious worldviews and leads to their decline. The second position, held by Andrew Greeley, suggested that the theory of secularisation was a myth.[87] He based his argument on the persistance of religious practice in America since the Second World

War. He accounted for this phenomenon by suggesting that the clear separation of religion from political institutions allows religion to thrive in its own sphere.[88] The third position, held by Thomas Luckmann[89] and Robert Bellah,[90] developed Durkheim's functional understanding of religion as a form of social solidarity. Luckmann suggested that religion does not disappear; rather, it is transformed into the private codes of "self-expression" and "self-realisation" in an invisible or private form of religion that maintains the symbolic production and reproduction of modern societies. Bellah argued that religion transforms into both a private system of meanings that help individuals find meaning in life, and also a public form of civil religion that supports the production and reproduction of the myths of social solidarity.

All of these theories and debates indicate that it would be wrong to consider the theory of secularisation as a uniform theory of social change. Rather, in order to fully grasp its significance, it is necessary to place it in the context of the various interpretations given to it by those who associate themselves, either positively or negatively, with this theory.

In theological debates about secularisation, the work of Friedrich Gogarten has most significantly shaped subsequent interpretations. Gogarten was a disciple of Harnack in Berlin and of Troeltsch in Heidelberg, and together with Barth, Thurneysen, Merz, Bultmann, and Brunner, launched the *dialektische Theologie* (dialectical theology) that played such a significant role in theological thinking during the twentieth century.

In 1952 Gogarten published his *Der Mensch zwischen Gott und Welt (Man between God and World)* followed in 1953 by his *Verhängnis und Hoffnung der Neuzeit. Die Säkularisierung als theologisches Problem (Fate and Hope of the Modern World. Secularisation as a Theological Problem).* In both books, he set out his basic understanding of the relationship between the modern world and Christianity. His intention in these works was to rethink the biblical and Protestant theological faith in the light of the modern phenomenon of secularisation. He understood secularisation to be the transformation of ideas, knowledge, and experience that had formally been Christian into the realm of autonomous human reason, which no longer depends on the Christian framework of action and understanding for its expression.[91] He also described secularisation as the capacity to complete processes thought previously to be spiritual by purely human means.[92] Gogarten suggests that there are three possible responses to this situation. The first, which he suggests is characterised by Kierkegaard, is to refuse the process of secularisation, since it ultimately leads to a destruction of the Christian faith.[93] In the second response, which he associates with Nietzsche, secularisation is embraced precisely because it rids the world of Christianity by destroying it.[94] The third response, Gogarten's own, is to propose another way of considering the interaction of the Christian faith and secularisation.[95] He suggests that secularisation is a legitimate consequence of Christianity. This he does by outlining three areas in which secularisation can be considered to arise out of Christianity itself.

First, he uses the Pauline formula of justification (Rom 3:28), frequently employed by Luther, to divide the sphere of faith from the sphere of worldly action. Worldly action, he holds, should be considered as an autonomous human activity that ought to be valued in its own right and not to be linked to the religious question of salvation. He believes that activity can flow naturally out of one's faith but not that this should be understood as a soteriologically significant sphere. The second area of secularisation arises out of the Christian belief in the world as the creation of God. Since God has made the world, this effectively demythologises the world from the ancient conception of gods and spirits who inhabit and control the destiny of the cosmos. Humans have thus been given autonomy to act in the world. This makes the world simply the world and removes from it an ancient sense of sacredness. The third area of secularisation arising out of Christianity is related to the filial relation between God and humans. Since humans are considered sons and daughters of God, this confers sovereignty on individuals that makes us responsible partners of God and autonomous agents in the world.

Gogarten makes a key distinction, one that has been much used by other theologians, between secularisation and secularism.[96] He understands secularisation to be the legitimate and indeed inevitable consequence of the Christian faith leading to the liberation of the world from mythical understandings. However, he understands secularism to be the degeneration of the secularisation process into an attack on its very own source. This distinction allows him to develop a normative conception of secularisation that is compatible with a form of Christianity lived out in the modern world.

Gogarten's work on the concept of secularisation has been enormously influential in theology concerned with the relationship between Christianity and the modern world. Harvey Cox's *The Secular City* (1965), for example, uses Gogarten's framework to develop the conception of secularisation as urbanisation. Karl Rahner,[97] who does not explicitly mention Gogarten, nonetheless uses many themes that Gogarten raised. And J. B. Metz develops his own conception of a "theology of the world" as a critique of Gogarten's understanding of secularisation.[98]

The Blumenberg-Löwith Debate

The relationship of Christianity to the modern world was also the question that the so-called Blumenberg-Löwith debate addressed, although this time the question focused more on the origins of the modern world than on the future prospects of Christianity in it.[99] In 1949 Löwith published his *Meaning in History*, in which he set out to show that the modern idea of progress is a secular transformation of the Christian conception of eschatology. Crucial to Löwith's argument is Hegel's understanding of the relationship between Christianity and history. For Hegel, the modern spiritual and political world arises out of the *Aufhebung*[100] of world history that occured during the Christian Reformation. The concept of *Aufhebung*, or its English equivalent "sublation," carries with it a number of meanings. It is simultaneously a raising, a destroying, and a preserving of a concept or thing. A simple way to understand this notion is to think of what happens in the seasoning of food. For example, when salt is added to a tomato, the taste is drawn out in the sense of being raised to a new level; it is changed or destroyed in this alteration, and it is also preserved in some sense.[101] In an analogous way to Hegel, Löwith considers the process of secularisation to be an *Aufhebung* of Christian categories such as eschatology into the notion of progress in the modern philosophy of history. For Löwith, the origins of this notion are to be found in the Jewish and Christian faith in an ultimate fulfilment of history in the coming of the Messiah. This inheritance, suggests Löwith, reaches a conclusion in the modern philosophy of history.

In order to trace this genealogy of modern secularisation, Löwith begins by looking at the major authors who have contributed to the modern philosophy of history, and attempts to show how the basic idea guiding their philosophies is the understanding of history as moving towards a final point of unification and fulfilment of the human condition.[102]

For Löwith, a Jew who was forced to flee Germany during the Hitler era, this notion of progress in history is not convincing. The core of his thesis is that the modern era has a basically false self-knowledge. It considers itself to be based on autonomous human rationality, but is actually based on an inherited theological conception of progress.[103] He argues that the unique contribution of Christianity was the transformation of the ancient world's cyclical conception of time into a linear conception of time as progress.[104] He uses this guiding metathesis to organise the various modern philosophies of history around the idea of the secularisation of eschatology in the notion of progress. Modern thought, in his view, is stuck in indecision about whether to be pagan or Christian, and, unlike the ancient and biblical world, it does not know what it wants to be.[105]

Blumenberg's *Die Legitimität der Neuzeit (The Legitimacy of the Modern Age)* is significantly influenced by Löwith's thesis, although he also enters into debate with other defenders of the secularisation thesis, most notably Carl Schmitt.[106] Blumenberg begins his response by asking what it means for concepts and structures to be secularisations. He suggests that Löwith's thesis depends on a number of premises. First, that the secularisation thesis proposes the view of a common substance that undergoes a change of form but not of content during the process. Second, that the contents of this substance are essentially Christian. Third, that the transformation of this substance is one-sided (from a Christian to a secularised form, and does not consider how the Christian form came about as itself the result of an ancient form).[107] Blumenberg points out that there is a formal difference between the notion of eschatology and that of secularisation: namely, that eschatology is based on a transcendent factor entering history from outside, such as God or the Messiah, whilst secularisation is based on a principle immanent in the logic of history.[108] Blumenberg also pursues another line of criticism by questioning the genealogical process that is meant to have brought this secularisation about. He proposes an alternative genealogy to the notion of progress, which he suggests has been brought about by two major factors.

First, the scientific advances made in the sixteenth and seventeenth centuries produced a new method, the scientific method, based on the work of many generations of thinkers and resulting in a better explanation of the motions of the planets. Second, the quarrel between the "ancients and the moderns" resulted in overcoming the Renaissance idea of the perfection of classical art, which all later generations had to try and recover, and the belief that each generation expresses its creative spirit in ways appropriate to its time. In freeing the modern era from the belief that the summit of high art had been already reached in the Classical era, the way was cleared for modern art to consider itself better than the art of previous eras.

This genealogy of scientific method and aesthetic understanding, Blumenberg suggests, united in the eighteenth century to produce the notion of progress, which portrays humans making their own history and represents the emergence of the notion of progress as a general historical category for understanding social change. This modern notion of progress differs from eschatology in two basic ways: substantially, in that it is an immanent and not a transcendent consummation of history; and genealogically, in that it arises out of self-assertion.

In his reply to Blumenberg in the review article in the *Philosophische Rundschau* of 1968, Löwith points out the differences between the ancient and the modern notions of progress and the fact that Christianity occurred between these periods. He then suggests that it would be highly improbable for the modern age to be original and autonomous. This would account for the overambitious claims of the philosophy of history in wanting to fill the space previously occupied by Christian eschatology.

Blumenberg frames his response to Löwith in the context of another explanation as to why the philosophies of history in the eighteenth and nineteenth centuries tended to be over-ambitious. He suggests that they overextended the more modest notions of progress presented in the sixteenth and seventeenth centuries because they tried to answer questions left over from the Christian Middle Ages. As a result, they attempted to use the modest idea of regional progress to account for the universal drive of history in terms of a general movement of progress. In fact, he argued, the origin of the idea of progress and its application to the question of the universal meaning of history as inherited from the Christian tradition are two distinct events. Blumenberg suggests that whilst modern thought was able to discredit Christian answers to the meaning and pattern of history, it was unable to critically eliminate the questions of Christianity, which continued to drive them to provide answers. In a similar fashion to thinkers like Ludwig Wittgenstein and later Richard Rorty, Blumenberg proposes that we need to realise that certain questions are no longer relevant for an age and so no longer need to be answered. Thus for Blumenberg, progress is the implementation of self-assertion, and it is this which constitutes the legitimate core of the modern age. This he derives from his consideration of the problems that had been left over by the late medieval Nominalism of thinkers such as Ockham.[109]

Nominalism, suggests Blumenberg, solved the problems of world-denial, sin, and evil by focussing on the divine will as omnipotent and the human will as free and responsible. This allowed for a positive valuation of the world as the creation of God and, at the same time, for an account of the presence of sin and evil in the world as the consequence of human free will.[110] The consequence of this dependence on will is that salvation and creation are taken out of the sphere of human meaning and reliability and are considered simply as part of God's will. This contingency can either focus on the next world, as was the official medieval solution, though this was made more difficult by the notion of grace and predestination, or it can consider this world *etsi deus non daretur* (as though there were no God), which was the official modern solution to this problem.

Thus, human self-assertion was the only available conceptual space left over for humans in a world of pure causal contingency ruled by the absolute will of God. In this way, the modern idea of progress is codetermined by the Christian legacy without it being the transformation of a Christian substance. Another way of saying this is that the notion of progress is truly modern in its content, but affected by the heritage it has received from Christianity in the function that this concept has played in the philosophy of history. Thus, the concept's legitimacy is understood by Blumenberg in a two-fold way: as not being a borrowed category from a previous era and also as drawing a justified conclusion given the logical possibilities available.

Löwith's reply in the *Philosophische Rundschau* seems to indicate that he did not really engage with the seriousness of Blumenberg's critique, as he does not consider the possibility that historical change can occur as a result of ideas coming in from outside the dominant tradition. The result of the debate between Blumenberg and Löwith over the understanding of secularisation and the use of the concept of progress reveals an interesting basic difference between the two thinkers. Löwith has a conception of history essentially similar to that of Polybius and the Roman conception of repetitive cycles of fate which leave humans relatively helpless to cause any real change in their history. Blumenberg, by contrast, considers history to be open, dependent on the capacity of humans to realise their projects and goals through self-assertion and cause real change in the patterns and dynamics of human history.

The debate between Blumenberg and Löwith leaves many questions still to be answered in understanding the meaning of secularisation and its use as an interpretative category to better understand the origin of the modern world. In his review of Blumenberg's work, Hans Georg Gadamer considers the category of secularisation to be a legitimate hermeneutical concept for understanding the relation between the modern and medieval worlds.[111] Ulrich Ruh concludes that Blumenberg gave a one-sided and rather selective reading of the origin and essence of the Christian faith. He suggests that in eliminating the category of secularisation as a legitimate hermeneutical concept, Blumenberg also eliminates the possibility for serious confrontation and exchange between the modern world and Christianity.[112]

Religion and Society in the Twentieth and Twenty-First Centuries

René Rémond suggests that a consideration of the relations between religion and society over past centuries leads to the conclusion that religion can only be understood in the context of political events and intellectual trends.[113] This is perhaps especially true for the twentieth century, where the rise of ideologies in Europe and the two World Wars significantly coloured relations between religion and society.

In 1914, at the start of the First World War, religious differences in Europe were enormous. At one extreme was Holy Russia, a nation united by its Orthodox faith, and at the other extreme was the thoroughly secular republican France. These differences would gradually narrow, in Western Europe at least, through the experience of the mixing and movement of peoples that occurred during the wars. Moreover, as the Catholic Church became increasingly aware of the dangers of both communism and fascism, it aligned itself with democracy as the best political system for preserving freedom and justice.

In 1944, for example, Pope Pius XII gave a number of radio broadcasts at Christmas in which he praised democracy as the way to preserve freedom. Inside the Catholic Church as well, the recognition of the doctrine of religious freedom after 1945 was a significant step towards the recognition of religious pluralism and the freedom to choose one's own religion. The documents produced in the Second Vatican Council of

1962–1965 reinforced this tendency in the Catholic Church and placed it in a much less confrontational position with modern Western democracies. This can be seen in the concordats that were drawn up between the Vatican and the various nations.

In Italy, for example, the Concordat of 1984, which was the result of more than twenty years of negotiation between the Vatican and the Italian State, did a great deal to harmonise the principles of Italian democracy with the demands of the Vatican. State subsidy of the Church would from then on be a choice for the individual citizen, who could choose if she or he wanted to pay up to 0.8 per cent of their income tax to the Church.

Secularisation also brought increased freedom for the Church. The separation of religion and politics meant that the political authorities had less and less justification for interfering in the internal workings of the Church. Furthermore, the increasing regional autonomy in the Catholic Church meant that local churches were increasingly free to decide on particular issues concerning their dioceses.

This all made possible the increased emphasis on collegiality that was evident in the Second Vatican Council. National Protestant churches were also underway to separate Church and State. Thus, since 1997 in Sweden, newborns are no longer automatically enrolled in the Church, and legal separation between the Protestant Church and the State was reached in 2000. Also in Finland, since 1997 the government has not intervened in the administration of the eight chapters of the national Lutheran Church. Even in England there has been serious debate about disestablishing the Anglican Church. Paradoxically, in conjunction with this movement to separate Church and State, there also has been a renewed legal recognition of religious groups in France since 1970. This is particularly significant in the French context, as it means that the state acknowledges that citizens may belong to intermediate communities, something that does not come naturally to the national republican model of solidarity in France. Moreover, since 1987 French taxpayers have been able to obtain tax reductions for their church contributions. The recognition of intermediate communities, of which religious communities form a significant part, has also been a major development in Holland's "pillarisation" system. Holland was originally organised on confessional lines, and the pillarisation system develops a tradition that crystallised Dutch national consciousness. Schools and even radio stations are organised on denominational lines and, due to the dramatic increase of people claiming no religious affiliation in Holland, Humanists are considered one of these intermediate communities. A similar situation exists in Belgium, where universities are based on confession; the Free University of Brussels (ULB) was set up precisely to educate those who profess neither Protestant nor Catholic allegiance.

As has already been noted, in speaking of the Western world as a secular world one needs to be careful to distinguish between Europe and the United States. In the United States, church/state relations have been central to public debates in recent years. Whether they are over constitutional amendments such as reciting "under God" in the Pledge of Allegiance, or prayer in public schools, or the political significance of religious lobbying, the United States has been awash with debates about religion and the public sphere.[114] In theory, the United States accepts a strict church/state separation as enshrined in the First Amendment to the U.S. Constitution (which stipulates that there shall be no establishment, and free exercise of religion). This is meant to guard the neutrality of the State in matters religious, and to prevent one religious group from having unfair state advantages or, indeed, unfair state influence.

In his study of American national identity, Samuel P. Huntington asks the question, "Is America also a Christian nation?"[115] The answer he gives is a resounding "yes," based on the fact that between 80–85 percent of Americans regularly identify themselves as Christians.[116] Thus, the many judicial cases concerned with maintaining the strict separation of Church and State should not be interpreted as a sign of growing irreligiousness. The case of the United States seems to suggest that secularisation, understood as the separation of the church and state, is the basis for a strong religiosity in society.[117] Americans rank as some of the most religious people in the world according to World Values Survey figures.[118] In fact, Huntington suggests that at the start of the twenty-first century, Christian identity in the United States is stronger than ever.[119]

Notes

1. Cf. Martin (2003): 30.

2. The question of causality is obviously central to this account. The disputes over which factors are more fundamental in social change and the relationship between cause and effect in theories of social change has a long history. In fact, one motivation for Weber's Protestant ethic thesis was to provide an alternative account to that of Karl Marx's theory of social change in his theory of historical materialism. See Fischoff "Die protestantische Ethik und der Geist des Kapitalismus." In Winckelmann (ed) (1972): especially 353, 355. This is not surprising since Weber is known to have perceived that thinkers of his times were characterised by their relationship to the thought of Marx and Nietzsche. See Hennis (1987): 167. The question of causality has been one of the most disputed aspects in the history of the reception of Weber's work and will be considered in looking at his Protestant Ethic thesis.

3. For an excellent survey of the various aspects of this transformation, see Baechler, Hall, and Mann (eds) (1988).

4. See, for example, Luhmann (1998): 259–357. Dobbelaere (1999) follows a similar approach to Luhmann.

5. Martin notes how some models of secularisation have adopted the Enlightenment master narrative of the supercession of religion (2005b: 171).

6. The reasons here are generally of two kinds. The first type tends to consider that religious convictions will colonise the public opinion and thus, in some form or another, hijack the neutrality of debate. The second type tends to fear that with substantive religious views in the foreground, consensus will not be possible.

7. For an excellent overview of the history of modern secularisation from the time of the French Revolution to the First World War, see Burleigh (2005).

8. On the clash of early modernity with monarchy and the established Church in England, see Martin (2005b): 66.

9. For the importance of Protestantism in forging the British national identity, see Colley (1996): 10–58.

10. See Burleigh (2005): 311–364.

11. See Rémond (1999): 41.

12. This separation of society from its religious framework would continue to such an extent in the century ahead that in 1872 no

mention of religion occurred on the census forms. See Rémond (1999): 45.

13. Thus, for example, the second Restoration, which had wanted to re-establish something of the earlier moderate views, abolished it in 1816, and the republicans, who followed the more radical views of the Revolution, re-established it in 1884.

14. The impact of secularisation in France should not be overestimated, since there was a significant religious revival in the late 1790s. The result of this revival was that Napoleon was persuaded to come to an agreement with the Church over the "religious question." A Concordat with Pope Pius VII was issued in 1802 and Napoleon modified the so-called "Organic Articles" unilaterally, making Catholicism the religion of the majority of the French people, although not the official religion of France as the pope had desired. From henceforth, the State would pay the salaries of the clergy, but no new parishes could be established without State authorisation, and bishops would be nominated by the State and ratified by the pope. The fact that the majority of French citizens remained Catholic meant that the significance of the recognition of other denominations and even faiths was watered down at a practical day-to-day level.

15. Rémond considers the secularisation of Europe under two major aspects. The first, which he calls the "liberal era of secularisation," is the gradual separation of the State from the influence of the Church. The State itself was confessional in the first phase but gradually shed its religious affiliation and started to separate the political and the religious domains of jurisdiction. Rémond's second phase is the removal of religious influence on the basic institutions of society such as marriage, education, and moral values. His account of the secularisation of Europe is, however, somewhat overly dependent on the French experience and French influence in other European countries. For his account of these two phases of secularisation, see Rémond (1999): 127–218.

16. See Brunner et al (eds) (1984): 809–829, and Marramao (1999): 29.

17. One example of such a conception is Hegel's understanding of Napoleon as a "world historical individual." By this Hegel means a person who in a particularly incisive way understands the spirit of the age and can move society to its next stage of development. See Hegel (1994): 17, 100.

18. See Löwith (1949): 52–59, and (1995): 59–64.

19. For a full account of the controversies between Hegel's successors, see Löwith (1995).

20. See Marramao (1999): 37.

21. See Chadwick (1975): 48–87.

22. See Marx and Engels (1927): 590.

23. Ibid.: 607.

24. Ibid.: 591.

25. Ibid.: 608.

26. "Die Philosophie hat sich verweltlicht, und der schlagende Beweis dafür ist, daß die Qual des Kampfes nicht nur äußerlich, sondern auch innerlich hineingezogen ist. Ist die Konstruktion der Zukunft und das Fertigwerden für alle Zeiten nicht unsere Sache, so ist desto gewisser, was wir gegenwärtig zu vollbringen haben, ich meine *die rücksichtlose Kritik alles Bestehenden*, rücksichtlos sowohl in dem Sinne, daß die Kritik sich nicht vor ihren Resultaten fürchtet und ebensoweniger vor dem Konflikte mit den vorhandenen Mächten." Ibid.: 573.

27. On this point, see Van Leeuwen (1972).

28. Marx and Engels (1927): 608.

29. Ibid.: 615.

30. It is interesting to note that for Nietzsche, German philosophy is simply a continuation of the philosophical atheism of Protestantism. Thus, for Nietzsche, German philosophy is at heart the development of the theology of the "Tübingen School." "Definition des Protestantismus: die halbseitige Lähmung des Christentums—und der Vernunft. Man hat nur das Wort 'Tübinger Stift' auszusprechen, um zu begreifen, was die deutsche Philosophie im Grunde ist—eine hinterlistige Theologie." Antichrist n. 10 quoted from Nietzsche (1969) (Definition of Protestantism: the one-sided paralysis of Christianity and reason. One has only to pronounce the word "Tubingen Foundation" in order to realise that basically German philosophy is an insidious theology). For a discussion of the relation between theology and German philosophy in the nineteenth century, see Löwith (1995): 350–415.

31. Overbeck was also an influence on the theology of Karl Barth and his rejection of philosophy as a mediator for the message of Christianity. See Barth (1947): 457.

32. For an interesting study of Comte's sociology and the post-theistic program of French social history, see Wernick (2001).

33. See Siemann (1995): 278–291.

34. See Mcleod (2000): 23–24.

35. See Sperber (1984): 99–102.

36. See McLeod (2000): 41.

37. Gladstone himself actually wrote on biblical and theological issues, publishing in 1838 his *Church and the Relations with the State*, which outlined his religious convictions that motivated his political engagement and outlined how Church and State were both necessary for the well-being of society.

38. The growth of strength in German Catholicism in the nineteenth century is often seen as a contrary movement to the advance of secularisation. For a discussion of this point, see Anderson (1997) and Schieder (1997).

39. For an interesting discussion of the role and importance of confessional parties in nineteenth and twentieth century European history, see Nipperdey (1986): 126–139.

40. See Mann (1958): 421–426.

41. For an excellent overview of the formation and history of the *Deutsche Reich* (German Empire), see Haffner (1989).

42. See Pulzer (1997): 25–32.

43. See Greyerz (2000): 285–324.

44. Indeed, the *Zentrum* would continue to play a significant role in German politics for the next sixty years until its disbanding in July 1933, shortly before the Concordat signed between the Hitler government and the Vatican, which gave back to the Church significant parochial and educational independence.

45. See Carr (1991): 119–135.

46. The inability of Catholicism to act as a motive force for capitalism was perhaps too uncritically analysed by Max Weber in his Protestant Ethic thesis. Thus, these structural disadvantages against Catholics were not seen as possible causes of the inability of Catholicism to act as such a motivating force for capitalism. See *GARS* I: 17–30.

47. Pulzer, Peter (1997): 27.

48. Casanova (1994): 11–39. See also Casanova (2003): 18. In this later article Casanova notes that American sociologists of religion in particular have discarded the secularisation paradigm.

49. Although, as Casanova argues, the traditional theory of secularisation has come under attack, some (often Europeans) still defend it, among whom the foremost is probably Steve Bruce. See Bruce (2000, 2002). Other thinkers, such as Rodney Stark, have presented alternative reasons for finding the secularisation thesis inadequate. Together with William Sims Bainbridge, Stark argued that the prediction of the end of religion in some versions of the secularisation thesis is wrong because religion can provide what secular rewards cannot: immortality (i.e., our desires outstrip what secular rewards can provide). See Stark and Bainbridge (1987). Stark has also argued that theorists had overestimated the religiosity of the past and so started from too high a baseline in their predictions of decreasing religious belief and practice. Moreover, in his "market model" of religiousness, the increased "competition" since the Reformation increased "supply" and tends to generate an increased "demand." See Stark (1998, 1999).

50. A typical and well-known example here is the essay by Jean-François Lyotard (1979). The normative critique of modernity is even more forcefully put in Lyotard (1988).

51. The quantity of literature here is vast; examples include Hammond (1985) and Berger (1999).

52. Employing a Durkheimian position, Paul Heelas and Linda Woodhead attempt to account for both the fall in traditional forms of

religion and the emergence of holistic spiritualities by their theory of the "subjective turn." They suggest that the turn to the subject in modernity has led to a shift from transcendent sources of meaning to inner-worldly sources that are to be found in the self. Based on their empirical research carried out in Kendal, they use the categories of "life-as" (life lived according to external expectations) to stand for religion and "subjective-life" (life lived in deep connection with the unique experiences of my self-in-relation) to represent spirituality. See Heelas and Woodhead (2005).

53. The first secularisation debate included such voices as David Martin and Andrew Greeley and began to suggest that empirical findings contradicted the claims of the decline of religion in the theory of secularisation. A good summary of the first debate on the theory of secularisation can be found in Casanova (1984). The second secularisation debate is ongoing and has become truly interdisciplinary. Examples include in philosophy: Vattimo (ed) (1986); Vattimo (1996); Berry and Wernick (eds) (1992); Janicaud (1991); and Chrétien, Henry, Marion, and Ricoeur (eds) (1992). In sociology: Kaufmann (1989); Luhmann (2000); Hervieu-Léger and Willaime (2001); Casanova (1994). In theology: Milbank (1990); Blond (ed) (1998); Pickstock (1998). In history: McLeod (2000); Lehmann (ed) (1997a); Langlois (1992).

54. Much of the current literature on the issue of secularisation makes the distinction between institutionalised forms of religion and types of noninstitutionally bound spirituality. Whilst this distinction has some sociological use, it is theologically inadequate because it ignores the fact that religious belief and practice are components of spirituality. See McGrath (1999): 1–5.

55. Caplow (1985). See also Casanova (2003).

56. On this question, see Henkel (2001): 22–37.

57. Grace Davie has developed her view on the weakness of institutional religion in Europe and introduced the notion of "vicarious religion" to suggest that although people may not attend churches, they often consider churches to act for them in a variety of ways. See Davie (1994) and (2001).

58. Cf. Davie and Hervieu-Léger (1996), and Casanova (1994).

59. See Brown (2001).

60. See Rooden (1997).

61. See Peter Berger (ed) (1999): 2.

62. Hervieu-Léger (2001): 125.

63. This point has been well made by the British sociologist of religion Grace Davie. In her phrase of "believing but not belonging," she suggests that the crisis in the West for religion is with institutional attachment of beliefs rather than lack of belief. She has later modified this thesis by introducing the notion of "vicarious religion," by which

she means that people may not attend church themselves but they will give their tacit support to many of the voluntary services that the churches carry out. For her understanding of modern religious experience as "believing and not belonging," see Davie (1994): 93–116, and for her understanding of "vicarious religion," see Davie (2001).

64. See Peter Berger (ed) (1999): 10.

65. The thesis of Samuel Huntington is obviously significant in this debate. Berger is somewhat cautious that the end of the Cold War signifies the end of ideological conflict. When one considers nationalism, for example, as a form of ideology, then this is by no means at an end. Yet the fact that the cultural dimension of politics is reconfiguring global politics is a thesis that seems to overlap with that proposed by Berger in his desecularisation thesis. For Huntington's argument, see Huntington (1997).

66. For a discussion of this, see Weigel (1999): 19–35.

67. This point is well brought out in Jenkins (2002).

68. For a discussion of the influence of conservative Protestant Christianity on world politics, see Martin (1999).

69. See An-Na'im, Abdullahi A. (1999).

70. The classical conflict here occurred in France in the so-called "querelle des foulards" (quarrel of the headscarfs). In 1989, three young girls who wore the Islamic headscarf were forbidden to attend their school, Gabriel–Havez in Creil, because wearing the headscarf was said to contravene the French principle of *laïcité*, the separation of religion from the public institutions of France. For a full consideration of this conflict, see Coq (1995): 265–330. On the wider implications of this issue for modern societies, see Carroll (2004).

71. By secularism he means the tendency for Western politics to place religion in the private sphere and to consider it as politically insignificant. See An-Na'im (1999): 120.

72. In the Middle East, for example, the Western version of secularisation, as implememted by Atatürk, Bourguiba, and others, has increasingly come under attack by Islamist intellectuals who consider it to be the main cause of the region's social problems and political instability. See Esposito and Tamini (eds) (2000).

73. See Esposito (2000).

74. See, for example, Taylor (2002).

75. Peter Berger (1999).

76. See Eder (2002).

77. Klaus Eder's notion of a "postsecular society" has been influential on the debate, which took place between Jürgen Habermas and the then Cardinal Joseph Ratzinger in Munich 2004. Both Habermas and Ratzinger accepted the term "postsecular society" in their exchange on the normative foundations of modern democratic states. See Habermas and Ratzinger (2005).

78. This is Inglehart's and Norris' approach to their reformulation of the classical secularisation theory. See Norris and Inglehart (2004).

79. See Dobbelaere (1981).

80. Lehmann considers the concepts of de-Christianisation and re-christianisation to complement the concept of secularisation in that they allow for a better description of the varying influence of Christianity on society. Secularisation alone tends to see this process as a one–way decline that does not correspond to the reality of modern European history. See Hartmut Lehmann (1997b).

81. See McLeod (2000): 5–12.

82. For an example of this model, see Chadwick (1975).

83. See, for example, Gilbert (1976).

84. See, for example, Brown (2001).

85. Against such "supply" explanations of secularisation, Pippa Norris and Ronald Inglehart suggest rather that it is "demand" for religion that varies. They suggest that in countries of greater existential insecurity, the demand for religion is higher. They also suggest that religious beliefs, values, and practices are rooted in long-standing cultural traditions and histories that affect societies even when individuals are not themselves practicing believers. In their account of the secularisation thesis, they suggest that although advanced industrialised societies are becoming more secular, the world as a whole is becoming more religious due to demographic differences between modern industrialised societies and less developed societies. They explain the apparently anomalous position of the United States as caused by the lack of a welfare system to shield its citizens from socio–economic risks and also by the large numbers of immigrants from less developed countries. See Norris and Inglehart (2004).

86. Wilson (1966) and (1976). Peter Berger (1967).

87. Greeley (1972).

88. On the notion of the paradigm of secularisation being considered as a myth, see Martin (2005b): 22.

89. Luckmann (1967).

90. Bellah (1970).

91. See Gogarten (1953): 7–11.

92. See Gogarten (1952): 149–152.

93. Ibid.: 10.

94. Ibid.

95. Ibid.: 11.

96. Ibid.: 129–143.

97. See Rahner (1967).

98. See Metz (1992): 38–41. For Metz's earlier position on the subject, see Metz (1968). A good general overview of the role of Gogarten in the theology of secularisation debate can be found in Ruh (1980): 31–46.

99. In reconstructing this debate, I have drawn on the excellent article by Robert Wallace (1981).

100. In the sense of a suspension and a carrying forward that is meant by the Hegelian concept of *Aufhebung*.

101. For a discussion of the concept of *Aufhebung* in Hegel's thought, see Inwood (1992): 283–285.

102. He treats, among others, Marx, Hegel, Proudhon, Comte, Voltaire, Vico, Orosius, and Augustine.

103. John Milbank has recently used this basic idea to argue that the modern social sciences are illegitimate because they are simply secularisations of medieval ecclesiology. See Milbank (1990).

104. For a critique of Löwith's conception of the Christian transformation of the ancient understanding of time, which argues that neither the ancient nor the Christian conception of time can be characterised as simply cyclical and linear respectively, see Marramao (1999): 98–110.

105. See Löwith (1949): 202. Löwith clearly is influenced by Nietzsche on this point. See Löwith (1949): 214–222.

106. See Blumenberg (1996). Although it is fair to say that Löwith is Blumenberg's main opponent, Löwith was not the only one to propose such a secularisation thesis. The most significant other person to have also proposed such a secularisation thesis is Carl Schmitt. In a famous sentence from his 1922 *Politische Theologie*, Schmitt states, "Alle prägnanten Begriffe der modernen Staatslehre sind säkularisierte theologische Begriffe" (All significant concepts of the modern doctrine of the state are secularised theological concepts); see Schmitt (1934): 49. For Blumenberg, this sentence is the strongest expression of the secularisation theory in both its assertion and in the deductions it inaugurates. See Blumenberg (1996): 102.

Secularisation is the key idea for Schmitt's political theology in the transformation from the theological conception of absolute sovereignty to the democratic modern understanding of sovereignty. The structural analogy between the absolute right of God to decide in a state of emergency is reproduced by the secular ruler who has the right to decide when a ruling is in accord with the sovereign legitimacy of the State. Both God and the secular sovereign are in retreat, resulting for Schmitt from the tension between Deism and Theism that removes God from the rule of law and, in the liberal bourgeois State, which increasingly seeks to minimise the power of the sovereign even in the form of being exempt from the law. This is a form of profanation or secularisation of the power of the State as the authority of the sovereign is tamed. For Schmitt, modern notions of sovereignty embody the dualism between friend and enemy that is constitutive of the secular dynamics of modern politics. For a discussion of the concept of secularisation and its relation to political theology in Carl Schmitt, see Ruh (1980): 279–299 and Marramao (1999): 67–81. For Blumenberg's own criticism of Schmitt, which takes into account the rethinking Schmitt had done in his 1970 edition of *Politische Theologie II*, see Blumenberg (1996): 99–113.

Essentially, Blumenberg argues that whilst the relationship between theology and politics is one of structural analogy, this does not imply a transfer of the contents of the theological conception of sovereignty to the modern notion by a process of secularisation. Furthermore, Blumenberg suggests that Schmitt's critique of his legitimacy thesis operates at a diachronic level, whilst Blumenberg is arguing at a synchronic level: that is to say, legitimacy is itself a normative conception produced in history, not something already implicit in it, traversing it for all time, remaining unchanged. Thus Blumenberg rejects Schmitt's critique that Blumenberg is speaking of historically contingent normatively regulated legality and not of the inherent legitimacy of an age.

107. This is a point of contrast with John Milbank, who suggests that late Nominalist theology secularised itself from within: that is to say, invented the notion of a secular space in which a secular society could be possibly conceived. For Milbank, this was then later taken up in the form of secular social sciences that described the new object of the secular space, power. See Milbank (1990): 13–17.

108. Löwith seems to have been conscious of this possible counterargument to his thesis when he suggests that both conceptions function as a form of horizon to aim for. See Löwith (1949): 84, 111, 196, 204. He further brings this defence forward in his review of Blumenberg's book in the *Philosophische Rundschau*. See Löwith (1968).

109. For Blumenberg, the modern age originated in the human opposition to the nominalistic view of an omnipotent and arbitrary God. This opposition gave rise to a view of human subjectivity and autonomy that founds the modern age. For a critique of Blumenberg's reading of Ockham and his view of the origin of the modern era, see Goldstein (1998). Goldstein suggests, in contrast to Blumenberg, that the modern era starts with the conception of subjectivity originating in Medieval Nominalism and not in opposition to it.

110. Blumenberg discusses how this Augustinian solution to warding off the problem of Gnosticism and to uniting the conception of God as both saviour and creator substantially set the agenda for medieval theology in its consideration of the relations of the creator and saviour God to both humanity and the entire creation. See Blumenberg (1996): 143–149.

111. See Gadamer (1968): 201–202.

112. See Ruh (1980): 122.

113. See Rémond (1999): 156.

114. See, for example, Casanova (1994): 167–207, and Monsma and Soper (1997): 15–50.

115. Huntington (2004): 82.

116. Ibid.

117. See Casanova (2003).

118. Cf. Huntington (2004): 91.

119. Ibid.: 103.

CHAPTER 2

Setting the Scene

In this chapter, I consider some preliminary issues concerning Max Weber and a reading of his work as a theory of secularisation. First, I will justify my decision to choose Max Weber as a major source of the contemporary understandings of the theory of secularisation. Then I will go on to place Weber's social theory within its political, philosophical, religious, and theological context. Finally, I will review the torturous history of the interpretation of the work of Max Weber in order to clarify my own intentions in this regard.

Weber and Social Theory

> Max Weber is without doubt the greatest German sociologist. Jurist, economist, historian, philosopher, he has finally become the master of "comprehensive" sociology. Through the extent of his erudition, by the variety of the questions he posed, by the rigour of his method, by the depth of the philosophy which inspired him, his work imposes itself as the model of both historical and systematic sociology.[1]

When Raymond Aron wrote this in 1935, it was not at all apparent that Weber was one of the giants of sociology. Indeed, it was only after his reimportation, through the work of people such as Talcott Parsons,[2] that Weber came to be seriously studied in Germany during the mid-1960s.[3] Today his work and place in the history of social and political reflection is being reassessed once more. It is not an exaggeration to say that today social theory is not in good standing.[4] Recent critiques of the Enlightenment and of modern reason have left it, as a product of the Enlightenment, in bad shape. Some critics suggest that under the conditions of postmodernity it is no longer possible to provide a general theory of society and its processes.[5] The question of the importance of the so-called "founding fathers," namely, Marx, Durkheim, and Weber, has become controversial.[6] What counts as foundational material has been subjected to feminist, Nietzschean, and deconstructive analysis; the use of the classical thinkers of social theory as a means of exploring the question of secularisation therefore needs some justification.

In defence of the classics in social theory, Jeffrey Alexander and Gianfranco Poggi provide grounds for considering the texts of the classical thinkers of social theory as being still relevant to social questions today. Alexander suggests that these early texts provide a form of agreed language that acts as a medium for debate in the social sciences. They condense the theoretical language domain into a manageable area and can thus constitute a common field for both agreement and disagreement.[7] Without such canonical texts, it would be impossible to come to any agreement about what the field of study is or indeed should be. Poggi suggests that classical thinkers should be read because of their intrinsic quality, even if they may be of little direct practical use for today's social theory. He entitles his argument *Lego quia inutile* (I read them because they are useless).[8] That is not to suggest that he thinks the classical authors of social theory to be of no use, but rather that he wants to broaden the concept of usefulness from a purely pragmatic conception to one that includes the importance of a broad intellectual formation and is aware of the tradition of reflection in social theory.

The arguments of Alexander and Poggi provide grounds for considering the classical thinkers of social theory to be of value and still worthy of study. A number of other reasons also speak for their contemporary significance. First, it is clear that for the modern leaders in social theory, for example, Habermas, Luhmann, and Giddens, the work of Max Weber has been a major source of inspiration in their reflections on the place of religion in society. Jürgen Habermas's conception of rationalisation and disenchantment, for example, is clearly worked out in dialogue with Max Weber's own theory of modernity. If one is to engage critically with such contemporary theory, it is important to be able to access the sources from which it has been formed. The reception of classical authors in the formation of contemporary social theory is thus very important for analysing the key decisions and judgements made by contemporary social theorists in the production of their own theories of society and the place of religion therein.

Second, I consider the work of Max Weber to be of more than historical interest. The basic concepts and ideas that he used are still of actual interest precisely because they speak to our present situation. His use of metaphors such as an "iron cage"[9] and the "battle between the gods and demons" still captures something of our imagination and experience of life in contemporary Western society. The question when thus considering the terminology of Weber is: To what extent do these terms still speak to our present reality? The ability of Weber's concepts intellectually to stretch the distance between the early twentieth century and the early twenty-first century is a matter for serious consideration in contemporary social theory.

Third, analysing Weber's social theory from the perspective of the theory of secularisation is an interesting and fruitful way to reconstruct his work. It is a labour of hermeneutics; Weber never wrote a particular treatise on the theory of secularisation, but his understanding of the issue of secularisation permeates his work. The reconstruction that follows will thus make explicit his theory of secularisation.

Finally, part of the present challenge to the standard theory of secularisation is a challenge to the theory of modernity itself. As Bryan Turner has argued, Weber is, above all, a theorist of modernisation.[10] His confrontation with the notions of rationalisation, secularisation, disenchantment, and the growing pluralism of values and beliefs has shaped the basic categories used in theorising modernity and postmodernity.[11] Thus, in investigating the theory of secularisation in the work of Weber, one also enters into the debates about modernity and postmodernity.[12] It is therefore not by chance that

Habermas at the start of his lectures on *Der philosophische Diskurs der Moderne (The Philosophical Discourse of Modernity)*, refers to the intimate connections between Weber's accounts of rationalisation and secularisation.[13]

The Political Context of Weber's Social Theory[14]

> Max Weber did not produce a philosophical system. It would not be possible to outline his philosophical teaching. He refused to be called a philosopher. However, he is for us the true philosopher of his time. Since philosophy is not a progressing science which comes to know a timeless truth it must become an historical reality out of its unconditional transcendental life. Max Weber did not teach a philosophy; he was a philosophy.[15]

The connection between life and work is very obvious for Max Weber.[16] He was engaged in the vital questions of his day and, in his own research, searched for answers to them. Indeed, Gregor Schöllgen, in his introduction to the life and work of Max Weber, goes so far as to suggest that the key to understanding his theoretical enterprise lies in his biography.[17] Schöllgen thinks that the greatest challenge to Weber research today is to find a more balanced account of his life to replace that by his wife Marianne, written in 1926.[18] I hope to show how Weber's own understanding of secularisation is in many ways shaped by the historical context in which he lived. As Wolfgang Mommsen puts it in his Cambridge lectures: "Politics, social theory and history cannot be separated in his [Weber's] thought; rather they must be seen as aspects of one and the same reality, and none of these aspects can be analysed in isolation."[19]

Karl Emil Maximilian Weber was born in Erfurt on April 21, 1864 and died in Munich on June 14, 1920. His life thus roughly covers the period of the Second German Empire (1871–1918). One major feature of this period was the rapid change in the economic situation of Germany, which had hitherto been principally an agricultural economy and was far less developed than other western European countries such as France and Britain. Germany's rapid industrialisation, was, however, confined to regions like the Ruhr, Saar, and Upper Silesia. Many other areas, such as East Prussia, were still very much based on a feudal economy and continued to be characterised by an agrarian society.[20] Moreover, this rapid economic development did not go hand in hand with a concomitant political development. The politically important class of the German Empire continued to be dominated by the agrarian nobility, who strongly defended their own political and economic privileges.[21] This clash between the political and economic levels of development is the major tension highlighted in Weber's political writings. The Junkers, the old ruling agrarian class who had dominated the political culture of the empire, were now in economic decline, yet the rising industrial classes, whilst increasingly economically significant, lacked the political maturity to take on the role of leadership. Thus, as Anthony Giddens has noted, the key to Weber's political writings is understanding that he sought to stimulate a liberal political consciousness that was capable of leading the German Empire.[22]

This aporia between economic success and political leadership is a key theme in Weber's political thinking. It became most acute for him after 1890, when Bismarck resigned as chancellor. After Bismarck's authoritarian style of leadership, no political class could replace him, and Weber feared that Germany would fall behind in the imperial race with Britain and America. He was sure that this problem could not be solved by returning to the ethical foundation of natural law[23] as the basis for democracy, since, under the conditions of secularisation, such forms of law lacked the legitimacy required in a modern State.[24]

How to conceive authority and legitimation in a postmetaphysical era is one of the pressing issues of the day to which Weber's intellectual activity is oriented, and the bureaucratic domination of German politics after the accession of Emperor Wilhelm II and the resignation of Bismarck is key to understanding his political and social thought.[25] Bismarck had successfully led the German polity, without politically mobilising the social classes in Germany, towards a rapidly expanding and highly successful state-controlled capitalism.[26] The social vacuum created by his departure was bureaucratically managed rather than politically filled. A main feature of the development of German capitalism during this period was that it developed not, as in Britain for example, through the internal competition of a laissez-faire capitalist stage, but rather as a clear form of organised monopoly capitalism that was tightly managed by the State. Such strong bureaucratic control played a major role in determining the general direction of the German political economy. It also contributed further to the lack of political experience, which meant that none of the emerging classes could take the reins in the newly emerging capitalist Germany.[27] As a result, from 1890 until the fall of the monarchy in November 1918, Germany was in a constant crisis of government and polycracy.[28] Parliamentary institutions had low status, and members of the government saw themselves as the emperor's servants rather than as active politicians striving for real political goals. Consequently, the real question on the fall of the monarchy was how to prevent the same vacuum occurring in the Republic.[29]

The Philosophical Context of Weber's Social Theory[30]

If the political context provides a framework in which to understand the theory of secularisation in Weber's work, then the philosophical context illustrates the major influences that shaped the very content of his social theory. In this section, I will consider the three major influences on Weber's work, that is to say, Neo-Kantianism,[31] Nietzsche, and Marx.[32]

Nineteenth-century Neo-Kantianism was a reaction to the dominance of the speculative metaphysics of Hegel. For the Neo-Kantians, the central issue was scientific methodology. The rise of the natural sciences had posed serious philosophical questions, and Neo-Kantians sought to bring together two diverse aspects of knowledge in one theory. On the one hand, the Kantian view was that reality could not be known in itself, that is, without the mediation of humanly constructed concepts. On the other hand, they wanted to preserve the objectivity of science as a discipline based on universally accepted facts.

The Neo-Kantians were divided into six separate schools of thought, but for Weber the most important was the so-called Baden or Southwestern School, whose main representatives were Wilhelm Windelband and Heinrich Rickert. For Windelband, the way to understand the differences between the various types of science was to see how their different methods worked. He drew a distinction between ideographic and nomothetic sciences,[33] describing nomothetic sciences as those which try to formulate general laws and ideographic sciences as those which try to describe and explain single events. Natural sciences are nomothetic because, rather than being concerned with the particularities of an object, they are concerned with the law-like generalities that operate for all such objects. In contrast, a subject such as history is an ideographic science, because the historian is concerned not with seeking the general laws that govern history, but rather with describing and explaining individual events.[34] Windelband did not follow the division made by Dilthey between the *Naturwissenschaften* (Natural Sciences) and the *Geisteswissenschaften* (Spiritual/Mental Sciences). He thought that this distinction made an inappropriate ontological distinction between nature and mind in the objects studied. For Windelband, the real difference is at the formal or methodological level rather than at the substantive or ontological level.[35] He used the example of psychology to demonstrate that its classification as either a nomothetic or an ideographic science depended on the point of view taken.

The influence on Weber of Windelband's disciple, Heinrich Rickert, has been the subject of much scholarly discussion.[36] We know from Marianne Weber's biography that Weber was impressed by Rickert but had some reservations about his terminology.[37] Weber shared Rickert's view of reality as an infinite multiplicity.[38] This conception meant that one could not fully represent reality by science, and hence scientific concepts were a means of highlighting aspects of the world that are in a continual state of flux. Following on from Windelband's distinction between the nomothetic and ideographic sciences, Rickert held that there are two types of knowledge. The first attempts to understand reality as a totality by developing general laws, whilst the second attempts to understand individual phenomena. Both fail to attain complete knowledge. For Rickert, this concept formation in the humanities is also related to values: because in the humanities we have to choose the individual phenomena to be studied, our concept formation is necessarily related to the value-relevance (*Wertbeziehung*) of phenomena. Thus, to choose a certain phenomenon is to say that it is worth studying according to a certain value. Since reality is infinite and the objects of research are constituted by their value-relevance, Rickert thought that the objectivity of the ideographic sciences cannot be based on the degree of correspondence between the scientific concepts and reality. Rather, objectivity in the ideographic sciences is constituted by the relation of the values that constitute the value-relevance to objective, transcendent values.[39] The cultural values that establish value-relevancies can be aesthetic or theoretical as well as ethical. These epistemological views influenced Weber's writings and helped to shape his understanding of the ideal types and the value spheres.[40] Moreover, such methodological approaches informed his analysis of religion and the ways in which religions relate to the world and to the value spheres.[41]

The Southwestern School of Neo-Kantians also developed a philosophy of religion that shares some affinities with Weber's thought.[42] Windelband based his philosophy of religion on the assumption that human consciousness is organised into four spheres of experience: the logical, the ethical, the aesthetic, and the religious. For Windelband, the human mind has three psychological functions: cognition, volition, and feeling.[43] Since none of these functions can cover the religious aspect of reality, Windelband proposed a fourth sphere, the religious, which is concerned with the holy (*das Heilige*).[44] The religious sphere becomes apparent to us through the imperfection that we feel on being unable to unite the real and the ideal in our knowledge. This sense of imperfection makes us realise that our consciousness is built on the "metaphysical reality of the norm consciousness,"[45] which is grounded in the transcendent and can be called "the holy." The holy is the normative consciousness of the logical, the ethical, and the aesthetic life, and it cannot be reduced to the empirically real.[46] Thus, for Windelband, to be religious is to feel oneself bound by norms that have a transcendent source. Whilst the dogmatic content of religion is a product of the historical context, religion has its ground in the experience of the holy. In this conception, religion is not so much a cognitive sphere as a way of life related to the conscience, and not to the cognitive faculties of the human mind.[47]

Weber shared Rickert's conception of reality as an infinite multiplicity that can only be known by selecting certain phenomena for study. Furthermore, Weber accepted the importance of values in scientific work. However, he disagreed with Rickert in his conception of the importance of value-relevance as a way of justifying claims to objectivity. For Weber, objectivity is a formal attribute of the scientific analysis of reality, implying that no value premise may be part of the argument. Weber illustrated this point by saying that the scientific analysis of reality should be acceptable even for the Chinese, who do not accept our values as a starting point.[48]

Weber's views on the role of values and religion also differ from Windelband in at least one important respect. For Windelband, the consciousness of norms has an objective quality, while for Weber, values are essentially contested, making the world value pluralistic and the modern consciousness fragmented. Yet, Weber shares Windelband's view that religion cannot be reduced simply to social and economic causes, but rather is a basic human response to life, grounded in autonomous human experience of the personality.[49]

Windelband's notion of the autonomous human personality had a significant influence on Weber's own conception of the self.[50] This is particularly evident in Windelband's *Lehrbuch der Geschichte der Philosophie (Textbook of the History of Philosophy)*, first published in 1891. Windelband had played a key role amongst the Neo-Kantians in recovering the Kantian notions about duty and the self, which through the influences of Goethe and Wilhelm von Humboldt had come to be understood as the ethical conception of "personality." In his textbook, Windelband analysed the origins of the concept of "personality" in the classical thought of the Stoics and in Christian thought. He followed Kant in holding the origins of the conception of "personality" to lie in the Stoic notions of unity and independence of the self. However, it is really with Christianity, for Windelband, that the inward dimension of the spiritual self becomes significant for the West. St. Augustine provides the foundation for the reflections on the soul of medieval philosophy and the Protestant Reformation. The soul is seen as the fullness of "personality," a united centre in a multi-layered self, which draws its own purpose from the divine self that gives it life. Weber draws on Windelband's reflections on the conception of "personality" in his own analysis of the Puritan personality[51] and uses the Kantian-inspired understanding of the self as a critique of Karl Knies's view of the unpredictability of events in the social world due to human free will:

> In the sense which is being employed here 'free action,' namely action which does not bear the marks of 'natural events,' is precisely that which brings the concept of 'personality' into play, which finds its essence in the constancy of its inner relations to certain ultimate 'values' and 'meanings in life.' The more these are realised as purposes and converted into teleological-rational action, the more the romantic-naturalistic idea of the 'personality,' which seeks the sacredness of the personal in what the 'person' shares with the animal, disappears.[52]

In *Max Weber's Methodologies*, Sven Eliaeson makes the interesting point that in moving away from essentialist forms of concept formation and downgrading the importance of the metaphysical approach to social science, Weber followed the "Back-to-Kant" movement and thus promoted the secularisation of German social science.[53] The conflict between historical and theoretical modes of reasoning, a conflict known as the "*Methodenstreit*," which began in 1883 with the debate between Gustav Schmoller of the historicist school and Carl Menger of the Austrian marginalist economic school, clearly provided the context for Weber's own reflections on methodological matters.[54] Indeed, the debate found its urgency in the need to find a new way of understanding action in a secularised world.[55] Eliaeson connects these methodological debates with the process of secularisation by suggesting that, in developing the method of rational interpretation, Weber played a significant part in replacing the religious explanations of human action with purely secular methods and concepts.[56]

Stephen Kalberg, in his study of Weber's comparative historical sociology, also focuses on the concept of action as the key to Weber's sociology and the defining feature of his methodology.[57] Weber's sociology starts from the idea that people give subjective meaning to their actions. In other words, they are cultural beings, providing their own meaning for the world.[58] It is this "turn to subjectivity" which is one of the significant ways in which the secularisation of social science is promoted by Weber. Action is no longer seen within the metaphysical schema of the natural law providing objective criteria that transcend the subject.[59] The subject has come of age in a secular world that the subject makes. In this context it is essential that the way in which action is understood—that is to say, the methodology—is itself governed by the "secular laws."

Yet an important difference emerged in this new methodology of the social sciences. Whilst Émile Durkheim considers the social to be almost a new organism and uses concepts such as the *conscience collective* to grasp what is going on in human action, Weber is committed to methodological individualism in focussing on the intentionality of the actor as the source of action.[60] It is thus the interpretative understanding of social action (*Verstehen*) which defines the task of the sociologist for Weber. He outlines four such types of meaningful social action: means-ends rational, value-rational, affectual, and traditional action. Each of these four types refers to a basic ideal-typical motivational orientation of the actor in a specific act or set of acts.

Social action, like all action, may be oriented in four ways:

1. *instrumental-rational (zweckrational)*, that is, determined by expectations as to the behaviour of objects in the environment and of other human beings; these expectations are used as "conditions" or "means" for the attainment of the actor's own rationally pursued and calculated ends.
2. *value-rational (wertrational)*, that is, determined by a conscious belief in the value for its own sake of some ethical,

aesthetic, religious, or other form of behaviour, independently of its prospects of success.

3. *affectual* (especially emotional), that is, determined by the actor's specific affects and feeling states.
4. *traditional*, that is, determined by ingrained habituation.[61]

Weber is clearly committed to a pluralism of motives for action and seeks to understand the various forms of social action according to their various motives and orientations. It is within this philosophical context, concerned with the new secular view of human action, that his methodological reflections are carried out. Therefore, it is not surprising that one should find an implicit theory of secularisation within his methodological writings.

The Influence of Marx and Nietzsche

Neo-Kantianism was not the only major philosophical influence on Weber. Weber is reported by Eduard Baumgarten, in a discussion with Oswald Spengler in January 1920, to have said that the influence of Marx and Nietzsche was definitive for all modern scholarship.[62] Commentators on Weber have varied greatly in their assessment of this influence.[63] Bryan Turner believes that Nietzsche influenced Weber in a number of important ways.[64] He suggests that Weber's pessimistic view of history resulted from his encounter with the philosophy of Nietzsche.[65] He also believes that Nietzsche's philosophy influenced Weber's formulation of a sociology of action. Thus, Turner sees Weber's *PE* as a way to describe the victory of Apollo, the god of form and reason, over Dionysius, the god of emotion and sexuality. As a result, the formation of vocations in the economic sphere can be seen as a way in which the Apollonian principle dominated over the Dionysian principle in Western societies.[66] This is displayed, according to Turner, in Weber's analysis of the civilising function of religious values.[67]

Robert Eden has noted the relation between Weber's concept of charisma and Nietzsche's concept of the superman.[68] Here, charismatic power represents the principal challenge to the traditional pattern of authority and leadership. Like Troeltsch, Weber viewed Protestant sects as an illustration of collective charisma in their challenge to organised Christianity. People such as J. P. Mayer and Wolfgang Mommsen have also seen the influence of Nietzsche's views on the "will to power" in Weber's concern with power and politics.[69] But Bryan Turner suggests that these commentators have missed the central influence of Nietzsche on Weber: the growth of a group of rational state specialists who were motivated by Calvinist ideas and sought to dominate the world by a commitment to an ethic of mastery.[70] For Nietzsche, these specialists were associated with the domination of Calvinist theology and the expansion of the new Prussian State. Wolfgang Schluchter is more sceptical about Weber's dependence on Nietzsche. He suggests that whilst Weber found Nietzsche's work to be a significant moment in intellectual history, he did not consider Nietzsche's work to be a basis for social science.[71]

Whatever the influence of Nietzsche on Weber, it seems that the "death of God" thesis proposed by Nietzsche provided a background to Weber's working out of an immanent science of life.[72] The struggle between the gods resulting from the death of God is a consequence of secularisation for Weber. As Wolfgang Schluchter has pointed out, Weber spoke not of a godless time, but, rather of a time in which God is foreign.[73]

No less important an influence on Weber was Marx. Weber has often been seen as opposed to Marx's ideas; just as Marx proposed a materialist conception of history, so Weber proposed an idealist conception.[74] However, as we know from Weber's *PE*,[75] Weber considered Marx's views on the importance of economic factors in the formation of ideas, especially religious ideas, to be vital. What he criticised, as Anthony Giddens has noted,[76] is Marx's notion that ideas are simply a passive reflection of material reality. This would eliminate the role of actors creating their own social reality.[77]

Weber's real opposition to the ideas of Marx is to a certain form of dogmatic materialism that tends to deduce all social phenomena from economic factors. This is unscientific for Weber, because it presupposes what it sets out to prove: that is, the causes of a social phenomenon.[78] For Weber, the causes of each single phenomenon have to be investigated, not presupposed, and history is the product of multicausality, not of monocausality.[79] Indeed, Weber makes fun of the monocausal position of economic dogmatism by ironically illustrating how limited such a one-sidedness would be if only spiritual factors were admitted as causally significant.[80]

Karl Löwith has pointed out that Weber's critique of the materialist conception of history only really touches on the "vulgar economic Marxism" of the later Marx and Engels.[81] In fact, Weber's critique of monocausal explanation in history is critical of both materialist and idealist conceptions of history, since both fail to view reality as an infinite manifold that can only be studied through our concept formation.[82] This means that the search for ultimate principles that guide the course of history is futile. For Weber, the assumptions of such theories of history make the scientist blind to what may be the actual causes of social and historical phenomena.

Weber is also critical of the notion of "scientific socialism." He charged that it mixes up the status of values and facts, presenting the values of scientific socialism as if they were objective facts. In reality, for Weber, these are subjective values, which, whilst necessary for concept formation and the motivation of scientific study, cannot be premises in scientific explanation.[83] And he is also critical of the Marxist notion of determinism, charging that it is unrealistic to consider history to be guided by scientifically discoverable laws and heading towards a utopian future.[84] Instead, Weber holds that we are condemned to the problem of growing bureaucratisation as a result of increasing socialisation.[85]

Yet, there is also a basic similarity between Marx and Weber. Fundamentally, their interest in social theory lies in the question of the possibility of human emancipation.[86] Both theorists are concerned with the question of the fate of humanity in a world that poses new dangers and challenges to human freedom. They share the view that capitalism, whilst bringing many advantages, is also a chief source of enslavement. However, whilst Marx proposed a form of therapy in the formation of a communist society, Weber only proposed a diagnosis of the ills of society. In this sense, one can consider Weber to be a more pessimistic social theorist than Marx. As we know from his *Wissenschaft (Science as a Vocation)*, he held out little hope for the emergence of modern people from the iron cage of bureaucratic rationalism that was growing in capitalist societies.

The Religious and Theological Context of Weber's Social Theory

It is important to remember, as Martin Albrow has noted, that Weber wrote within a Christian tradition.[87] This is not to say that Weber was a practising Christian, which he was not, but rather to suggest that without some understanding of the influence of Protestantism on Weber's work, it is impossible to fully understand his social theory. Weber's own relationship to the Protestant faith of his family was complex and fraught with many tensions. His mother Helene and her sister Ida Baumgarten, both of whom were devout Protestants, exercised a considerable influence on him. Weber spent a year with the Baumgartens in Strasbourg as a student and later, through much correspondence on religious matters, was significantly influenced by the values of Protestantism. It is not an exaggeration to suggest that religion held a deep emotional significance for him and shaped the direction of much of his life's work.[88] Some of this complicated relationship to religion is brought out in his famous letter to Ferdinand Tönnies of February 19, 1909:

> It is true in respect of religion I am absolutely unmusical and have neither the need nor the ability to erect some spiritual "edifice" of a religious character in myself—that's not on, or I reject it. But on closer inspection I am neither antireligious nor irreligious. In this respect I feel myself to be a cripple, an amputee, whose inner fate it is to have to admit this honestly and to come to terms with it so as not to lapse into romantic swindle.[89]

Weber's own understanding of secularisation is shaped by his Protestant tradition. Indeed, the conception of modernity of which his understanding of secularisation forms a part is strongly influenced by the Protestant Reformation.[90] This is not surprising since, as Friedrich Wilhelm Graf notes, Max Weber was the most theologically literate sociologist of his century, and without some understanding of the theological sources that informed his religious sociology, it is difficult to understand his intellectual programme.[91] Weber himself wrote to his mother on May 16, 1882, during the first semester of his law studies at Heidelberg, "Moreover, I am quite engaged in theology; I read Strauß, Schleiermacher and Pfleiderer (Pauline studies) and besides that only Plato."[92] Indeed, even a cursory glance at his *PE* shows how acquainted Weber was with theological and biblical literature.[93] Graf suggests that there are three main dimensions to the relation of Weber to the theology of his time.[94]

First, in Weber's youth and most especially through his cousin Otto Baumgarten, who later became professor of practical theology in Kiel, he became acquainted with the liberal theology of the time and with the concern to relate religion to the ethical dimension of life; also to conceive religion as occupying an autonomous sphere of human consciousness. Second, he cooperated with a number of theologians in various ways. He wrote articles for the journal *Die Christliche Welt (The Christian World)*, which was edited by the brother-in-law of Friedrich Naumann, Martin Rade.[95] Weber also collaborated with both his cousin Otto Baumgarten, who edited the journal *Evangelisch-soziale Zeitfragen (Protestant Social Questions of the Times)*,[96] and also Ernst Troeltsch[97] in developing a theory of religious sects.[98] The extent to which Weber and Troeltsch shared ideas has been the subject of much discussion amongst scholars.[99] At the very least, it seems highly likely that Troeltsch helped Weber to become aware of the theological literature that he required to write *PE*.[100] Third, Graf suggests that Weber shared with the liberal theologians of the time an interest in the fate of the individual personality in modern capitalistic society.[101] This is not surprising since, with the advent of industrial society, the question of the freedom of the individual in the face of the large anonymous structures of the capitalistic society was central to most reflections about the future of humanity.[102]

A very important early theological influence on Weber was his contact with the History of Religion School (*religionsgeschichtliche Schule*).[103] They used ordinary historical methods to investigate religion as a historical phenomenon, and Weber often quoted members of the school in the footnotes to his own work on the sociology of religion. This group of theologians was particularly interested in investigating the ways in which religion and culture interact in the shaping of individual and social life. Religion was for them a form of *a priori* in human cognition, and mediated between the Christian faith and reason.[104]

Another point of contact with theological influences for Weber was the Evangelical-Social Congress. He regularly attended its annual conferences, which consisted of Protestant ministers and scholars, and between 1892 and 1897 was a member of the Council that directed the movement.[105] The Congress aimed to promote an active engagement of the Church in matters of social policy and to bring the concerns of the workers closer to the Church. Weber considered the Congress to be a place in which he could promote his own political ideas of developing a social-liberal imperialistic German Reich.[106] It would certainly have been a forum in which the main liberal and conservative theological ideas of the time, developed by theologians such as Adolf Harnack, Albert Ritschl, and Adolf Stöker, would have become accessible to him.

In Thomas Ekstrand's study of Max Weber, he points out three areas of affinity between Weber's thought and the theological ideas of the time.[107] The first is a common understanding of the origins of religion. Weber rejects reductionist tendencies to explain religion away as the product of a more fundamental phenomenon. He holds that whilst the influence of the social and cultural context in which the religious experience occurs is important, religion cannot be reduced to any of these factors. Religious experiences are autonomous (*endogen*) for Weber and can never be explained by reference to any monocausal explanations.[108] He is particularly interested in the charismatic origins of religion and deals with the Old Testament prophets and their charismatic origins in considerable length in *Das antike Judentum (AJ)*. In his analysis of the prophets and the origins of Old Testament religion, Weber is very close to one of the central figures of the History of Religion School, namely, Hermann Gunkel.

For Weber, the origins of the Old Testament prophecy are found in the magicians and seers who played a significant role in the Israelite community before the establishment of the Davidic kingdom. He sees these prescriptural prophets as charismatic figures who deliberately brought on their ecstatic states through dance and music.[109] After the Davidic kingdom had been established, these prophets, who had mainly prophesied good fortune, were replaced by the prophets of doom, who criticised the rulers of the kingdom for adopting the ways of the pagans.[110] However, even though Weber repeatedly stresses the importance of the social and political influences on these prophets and their prophecies, he spells out clearly that their prophetic origin lies in their own inner experience as prophets, and is not simply the product of emotional mass influence.[111]

The effectiveness of the post-Davidic prophets is, for Weber, based on their capacity to interpret their ecstatic experiences in a way that made sense to the Israelites and thus indicated that they had received a mission (*Sendung*) from God to speak.[112] Two characteristics separate these prophets from other prophets: they are solitary figures, and they do not seek to generate their own ecstatic experiences, but rather, come to them spontaneously.[113] The point here is that Weber accepts that there is a religious experience that cannot be reduced to other causal factors. This is not to say that such religious experiences are unmediated by the social and historical circumstances in which they occur. Indeed, he considers them to be mediated by the religious-symbolic world in which they occur.[114] Nevertheless, it is clear that, as an example of his account of religious experience and, hence, religion, Weber's analysis of the charismatic prophets reveals that he is not a reductionist and that he holds to the autonomous (*endogen*) nature of religion.

Much of Weber's analysis of ancient Judaism is dependent on the History of Religion School and, most especially, on the work of the founder of the method of Form Criticism, Hermann Gunkel.[115] Indeed, he quotes from a number of published articles that were later assembled into Gunkel's book on the prophets and remarks that they are "glänzend wie immer" (brilliant as ever).[116] What separates Weber from theologians like Gunkel is that he had no explicitly theological pretensions in his explanation, but rather, confined himself to the social role played by such religious experiences.[117]

A second area of affinity between Weber and the theologians of his time was the rejection of the metaphysical claims of religion and the concentration on ethical perspectives. This locates him within the limits of the modern scientific world epistemologically defined by Kant and accepted by liberal Protestant theologians such as Albert Ritschl (1822–1889). Thus, the truth claims of religion about the origin of the world and the existence of spirits and angels are rejected in favour of the ethical impulse that religion can give to living life in this world.

Weber is clear that, historically, religions have played two major roles, providing both a basic value orientation and a rational explanation for a reality that seems to present itself as irrational.[118] That is to say, for Weber, the question of theodicy is the motive force behind the development of the world religions.[119] The various religions, he explains, have developed different strategies to cope with the problem of human suffering. For instance, Indian religions, such as Hinduism, have developed the concept of karma, and Christianity has developed the concept of the *deus absconditus* and also the Calvinistic notion of predestination.[120]

Weber illustrates his understanding of religion as providing a basic value orientation through his analysis in *PE* of the ascetic Calvinist way of life. This is a clear example for Weber of how human behaviour can be guided by a religious worldview. It is also a clear point of contact with the antimetaphysical liberal Protestant theology of Ritschl. Ritschl, following Kantian epistemology, rejects the notion that we can know anything about God in himself, or even of the nature of Jesus. What we can know is only what God and Jesus mean for us in our concrete lives.[121] This antimetaphysical and ethically oriented approach to theology was typical of the liberal Protestant theological thinking of Weber's time.[122] The best-known example can be seen in Adolf Harnack, a disciple of Ritschl, who taught that since the heart of the Gospel message was love, religion finds its embodiment in morality.[123]

A final affinity between Weber and the theologians of his time, noted by Ekstrand, is interest in the fate of the individual in modern capitalist societies. Nineteenth-century liberal Protestant theologians were significantly influenced by the Kantian conception of the individual as a "personality." Their search for an ethical understanding of the individual who could be a coherent social actor took place in the context of the growing importance of the social question. Troeltsch was the most significant of Weber's theological contemporaries for whom the notion of "personality" played a crucial role. He had argued in his *Die Soziallehren der Christlichen Kirchen und Gruppen (Social Teaching of the Christian Churches and Groups)* (1912) that the way forward for the Church was to follow Calvinism's lead in demonstrating that the notion of ethical personality was intimately bound up with the modern economic, political, and legal systems of the West.[124]

Both Weber and Troeltsch seem, however, to be rather pessimistic when it comes to the future of the individual in modern society.[125] For Weber, religion holds out hope for the individual but not for the public sphere. He sees no possibility of constructing a religious worldview that is able to dominate a whole society. What remains is the possibility of retreating from the modern world into the privacy of a religious worldview, but this is only at the price of the "*Opfer des Intellekts*" (sacrifice of the intellect).[126] While Troeltsch holds out the possibility that religion can still act in an integrating capacity to bridge the conflicts that occur in modern society,[127] Weber holds that the only form of resistance to the onslaught on the individual is through the outburst of a new form of prophetic charisma.[128] This idea is also found in the work of Hermann Gunkel and is probably a concept that Weber borrowed from his encounter with the theologians of his time.[129]

Modern political life was a further threat to individuality for Weber. He saw the great challenge of modern politics as being the competition between an ethics of conviction (*Gesinnungsethik*) and an ethics of responsibility (*Verantwortungsethik*).[130] The *Gesinnungsethiker* is chiefly concerned with holding to his or her principles of politics and leaves the consequences of his or her actions to God. The *Verantwortungsethiker* is concerned with the practical situation as it exists and thus seeks to achieve his or her goals by whatever means seem most appropriate. It is clear for Weber that the ethics of responsibility are more appropriate for modern politics, since they do not presume the goodness and perfection of people, but take the average nature of most people as their starting point.[131] This for Weber is a departure from the basic principles of Christianity, and he suggests that politics and religion will be in permanent conflict on this point. Whilst religious persons can content themselves that they did what is right in the face of the consequences, the politician has to bear the brunt of the consequences and is thus often forced to fight violence with violence. Weber puts it rather lyrically when he says:

> The genius, or demon of politics lives in a state of inner tension with the god of love, and even with the Christian God as manifested in the institution of the church, a tension that may erupt at any moment into irresolvable conflict.[132]

Ekstrand notes that Weber's position is very similar to that of his cousin, the liberal theologian Otto Baumgarten.[133] Both hold that modern politics is guided by the means-ends ethics of the *Verantwortungsethiker* and that this clashes with the ethics of love of Christianity. Yet, it should be noted that liberal theologians such as Baumgarten often accepted the necessity of a split between private and public morality in modern society. Baumgarten understood politics to be the struggle for power, and thus to lose power would be equivalent to sinning in a political sense. This is not quite Machiavellianism, since for both Baumgarten and Weber the purpose of obtaining and maintaining power is not an end in itself, but they did see political power as a means of implementing one's own vision of society.[134]

Both the rationalisation of modern society and the plurality of value-systems make the place of religion in modern society problematic for Weber. The need to compete in the marketplace with the rest of the gods and demons makes Christianity's claim to universal truth an essentially contested one. That means that the dominance of the public sphere by religion is no longer an option for Weber. The question is, what if any role remains for religion?

Interpreting the Work of Weber

In Hermann Lübbe's study of the history of the concept of secularisation, he states: "The way in which Weber occasionally uses the concept of secularisation would justify placing his whole research in the sociology of religion under this title."[135] Whilst Lübbe's position is very clear on this matter, the history of the interpretation of Weber's work reveals that one must proceed with caution when advancing a possible hermeneutic of Weber's corpus. In order to consider the question of interpreting the work of Max Weber as a theory of secularisation, I would like to review the debates that have occurred over the last decades concerning how one should correctly understand his basic intention in his various works.[136]

The question of the correct interpretation of Weber's work is chiefly a product of the fact that much of his work has been published posthumously. Until now, a great deal of attention has focused on his famous *PE*, which was first published in 1904 and 1905 in the *Archiv für Sozialwissenschaft und Sozialpolitik*. In some ways, this focus has prevented Weber's other works from being sufficiently read, and consequently, has led to a rather uneven reception of his work.

Frederich Tenbruck posed the question of correct interpretation. In 1975, he published an article entitled "*Das Werk Max Webers*" (Max Weber's Work) in which he sought to propose a hermeneutical key to understanding the Weber corpus, which would supply it with an inner unity.[137] Until Tenbruck proposed his own criteria of interpretation, a number of competing models had been used to organise the work of Weber. One organising principle had been to concentrate on his *PE* thesis as his main work. This led to much debate about the question of causality in the economic evolution of modern societies. A second organising principle had been to propose *Wirtschaft und Gesellschaft (WuG)* as his main work, since it was much more systematic and dealt with methodological questions, while it also covered a number of different areas of sociology.[138] A third organising principle had been to consider the work of Weber as an anticipation of the proposals of the Neo-Positivists. Weber's repeated criticism of monocausality was thus considered a way to combat the claims of positivists, and his work was primarily viewed as a contribution to methodological analysis in the social sciences. Yet other ways of organising the work of Weber had been accomplished by those theorists who had wanted to use it in their own systematic theories of society. This group includes people such as Talcott Parsons and his development of structural-functionalism, which was heavily dependent on Weber's theory of action;[139] Raymond Aron's reception of German sociology in France and his use of Weber's concept of political domination;[140] and Critical Theory, which also used the work of Weber in its reflections on social action and rationality.[141]

Reinhard Bendix sought to overcome these limited receptions of Weber's work by trying to locate both his life and work in a historical context. In his *Max Weber: An Intellectual Portrait*, he concluded that two major themes were present throughout Weber's work: the investigation into the nature of civilisation through his religious and ethical sociology; and his political sociology centred on the questions of legitimation and domination.[142] For Bendix, the central clue to understanding Weber's work was to see that the concept of ethical rationality was the key idea that guided his study of modern rationality.[143] This interpretation dominated Weber scholarship until the intervention of Tenbruck. Tenbruck challenged Bendix's contention, which drew on Marianne Weber's biography of Max Weber, that *WuG* was Weber's principal work. He criticised Bendix's chronology of composition, which had identified the concept of rationalisation as the key defining term of Weber's work. Tenbruck argued that this did not respect the real order of composition and revision that Weber had followed with respect to *WuG* and his *Die Wirtschaftsethik der Weltreligionen (The Economic Ethics of the World Religions) (WEWR)*. Moreover, Tenbruck maintained, Bendix's focus ignored the importance of a considerable number of Weber's other works. The key issue for Tenbruck lay in the fact that Bendix had not seen that the main idea of

Weber was that of disenchantment (*Entzauberung*), a concept which had already appeared in *PE*, but had been considered to be a later addition. Whilst Bendix had considered disenchantment to be a particular moment within the general process of rationalisation, Tenbruck considered disenchantment to be the key idea that allows us to understand the entire logic of rationalisation in the work of Weber. He based this interpretation on his investigation of *WEWR* and also of *WuG*, in the course of which he concluded that the importance of *WuG* had been overemphasised to the detriment of Weber's more historical work, *WEWR*. This had led to a falsification of, or at least an inattention to, the real chronology of their production and revision. Tenbruck thus concluded that *WEWR*, not *WuG*, was Weber's most important work. Furthermore, Tenbruck argued that the guiding idea that gave a thematic unity to Weber's work could be found in *WEWR*, most especially in the two introductions to his religious sociology, the *Vorbemerkung* (Preliminary Remark) and the *Einleitung* (Introduction), and in the excursus *Zwischenbetrachtung* (Intermediate Reflection), which for Tenbruck represent Weber's most elaborate reflections on the nature of disenchantment and its relation to rationalisation.[144] Thus, Tenbruck proposes that in order to properly understand the systematic intention of Weber, we have to realise that:

> For Weber, on the other hand, the decisive discovery lay in the knowledge that rationalisation, in all its historical fragility, was drawn forward by the compulsion of an inner logic which was tied to the unstoppable impulse of the rationalisation of religious ideas. Consequently, the rationalisation process is in its core a religious history of disenchantment from which it draws its moments and stations of unity. Not the identification of partial processes but rather the inner necessity of its succession determined Weber's solution.
>
> The key, however, to this interpretation of Weber's work lies in the work which despite all the interpretative progress still resists interpretation in its central part, that is to say, the *Wirtschaftsethik der Weltreligionen*.[145]

WEWR is thus, for Tenbruck, the place to find the guiding idea of Weber's complete work. It is also in many ways a counter-example to the thesis proposed in *PE* and illustrates that the process of disenchantment is a way to investigate the interaction between ideas and interests, which produces the process of rationalisation.

The difficulty with interpreting just what Weber means by the concept of rationalisation lies in the ambiguity of the term, which he applies to a multitude of processes and social spheres. In general, he seems to mean by rational orientation a formal method of matching means to ends without making a value judgement. He outlines the importance of religion in this evolution of value neutrality in science as the response to the theodicy question: the need to give meaning to the history of suffering and to understand how this is compatible with a loving and just God. Without this internal evolution in the religious ideas of rationalisation, which has reached its goal in disenchantment, it would have been impossible for rationality to have progressed in its cognitive-technical modality. For Tenbruck, what Weber decides in his discussion of *WEWR* is the priority of ideas as the motive force of history. As Weber puts it in the *Einleitung*, it is both ideas and interests (material and ideal) that determine the direction that action progresses.[146]

These ideas thus cause societies to move in particular directions for Weber and determine the future direction of social action.[147] Tenbruck goes on in his article to find connections between Weber's later works and essays and his disenchantment thesis, and he concludes on a rather pessimistic note when considering the practical consequences of the disenchantment thesis for society.

Despite the provocative intervention of Tenbruck in the debate about the correct interpretation of Weber's work, it was not until 1980 that two publications addressed his claims to have uncovered the real Weber.[148] In his 1980 article Johannes Winckelmann contradicted the chronology proposed by Tenbruck, who had found the concept of disenchantment (*Entzauberung*) to be a late summation of Weber's whole understanding of the process of rationalisation. Winckelmann found the term already employed by Weber in his essay *Ueber einige Kategorien der verstehenden Soziologie*, published in 1913,[149] and indeed in the introductory note to it Weber explains that he had already written the part of this essay, in which he uses the concept of disenchantment, a considerable time before.[150] Winckelmann also found the concept in the first edition of *WuG* in the chapter dedicated to the sociology of religion, which he deduced had been ready for publication in 1913.[151] In this context, the term *Entzauberung* plays the role of an ideal-typical category[152] used to illustrate the process of the decline in the magical explanation of the world. Moreover, Winckelmann found that the very concept on which Tenbruck had hung his thesis did not occur in *WEWR*, which, according to Tenbruck, was Weber's principal research work. Winckelmann went on to show that the use of the category of *Entzauberung* in Weber's essay *Wissenschaft* was only used in the same sense as employed in *WuG*, that is to say, as a way to explain the fall from grace of magic as an intellectually respectful mode of explanation.

However, Tenbruck's thesis was undermined not only by Winckelmann's critique of his chronology but also by inconsistencies in his systematic claims. Winckelmann argued that Weber had never accepted the notion of a single idea guiding the inner logic of history. In order to justify his claims, Winckelmann drew on *PE* and also on Weber's own reply to Karl Fischer regarding the correct interpretation of his own theory.[153] Winckelmann emphasised that Weber was most of all concerned to stress the interdependence of factors in the dynamics of history and was clearly against any notion of monocausality in history.[154] Winckelmann also rejected Tenbruck's hypothesis that Weber had discovered the importance of religious factors after 1915. Instead, Winckelmann saw a continuity in Weber's writings that portrayed religious and economic factors in a relationship of mutual interdependence. Winckelmann went on to criticise the notion of worldview (*Weltbild*) that Weber had used as a legitimation for various accounts of social action and Tenbruck had used in his evolutionist reading of Weber, and he proposed an alternative conception of worldviews to account for the various stages of human evolution.[155]

In his response to Tenbruck's claims, Martin Riesebrodt agreed with Winckelmann's criticisms both of Tenbruck's chronology and of his systematic claims. Riesebrodt showed that both the introductory and systematic parts of *Gesammelte Aufsätze zur Religionssoziologie (GARS)* were already composed by 1913, which contradicted Tenbruck's claim that later editions of these works had added the disenchantment concept. He also showed that this supposed new orientation was not incorporated into *WEWR*, such as in the parts concerning Hinduism and Judaism, which had later been revised, and could thus have included this new conception, as had occurred in the 1920 version of *PE*. Riesebrodt also suggested that rather than the chapters on the sociology of religion in *WuG* and *GARS* being superimposed upon one another, there was a relation of complementarity and inner unity between these works.[156] On the level of systematic critique, Riesebrodt argued that the importance of particular social classes had been ignored by Tenbruck. These are important because it is only in particular social classes that religious ideas and interests can be brought together in order to impose a particular vision on society. Religious ideas alone could never act independently as motive forces for the evolution of history.[157] As Weber had argued, the evolution of religion itself was conditioned by external factors, as had been shown by the case of the overcoming of magic.[158] Thus, the notion of finding an ultimate cause or a dominant factor in history in the work of Weber is, for Riesebrodt, not consistent with Weber's overall systematic claims.

In 1979, Wolfgang Schluchter had already criticised the chronology proposed by Tenbruck,[159] but only in an article published in 1984 did he situate the problem of the organisation of Weber's work in a systematic context.[160] Schluchter attempted to define the interests that oriented Weber's work. He disagreed with perspectives such as that proposed by Wilhelm Hennis, who seemed to think that Weber's intentions were camouflaged in his work and needed to be uncovered.[161] Schluchter held that Weber had no hidden intentions in his work and that the work was clear enough in its intentions. He also considered it futile to seek the one notion that would give a thematic unity to the variety of his output. Rather, Schluchter proposed that it would be more fruitful to identify the main questions raised by Weber and consider how, in his works, he proceeded to give different solutions to them. He proposed three countertheses to that proposed by Tenbruck.

First, he argued that *WEWR* and *WuG* should be read in the light of each other and should thus be seen as complementary studies. Second, he suggested that *Einleitung* and *Zwischenbetrachtung* of *WEWR* provide a form of *summa* for Weber's religious sociology. However, they are neither hurriedly written in 1915 nor belated reflections, but rather, are resources used by Weber to remodel his religious sociology and develop his reflections in this area. Third, Weber did not conceive *WEWR* as a simple elaboration of *PE*, nor did he abandon his project of studying Islam and Christianity. Rather, from the basis of these studies he intended to reintegrate *PE* into the context and significance of *WEWR*.[162] Schluchter concludes that the change in perspective that Weber underwent around 1910 is important in understanding the direction of his later work. After this time, Weber abandoned his initial project of investigating the various elements that had contributed to the process of modernisation in the West and instead enlarged his investigations by means of the concept of rationalisation that is so clearly expressed in the *Vorbemerkung*.[163] Marianne Weber expresses this in her biography: "For Weber, this knowledge of the particularity of Western rationalism and its most important role for Western culture was one of his most important discoveries."[164]

In this context, for Schluchther, it is thus important to value the *WEWR* and *WuG* equally, as different ways of working on the same question. In *WuG*, Weber's intention is to elaborate categories, ideal types, and concepts derived from his empirical and historical studies, useful for practical application and the understanding of reality. In *WEWR*, Weber considers these historical and empirical investigations in the form in which they have combined to shape modern rationality. For Schlutchter, both works need to be read in the light of each other in order to gain a clear idea of Weber's later intention of investigating the specificity of Western rationality. *Einleitung*, *Zwischenbetrachtung*, and the eleventh part of the sociology of religion in *WuG* are, for Schluchter, theoretical and methodological works that were necessary if he was to pass from his earlier empirical work to his later works and, indeed, set out to define their field of research.[165] Thus, rather than seeing disenchantment as the unifying key to Weber's work, Schluchter proposed the idea of rationality. Its incompleteness, he suggests, is the reason why *PE* and *WEWR* are not totally integrated with one another.

Tenbruck returned to the debate nine years later with an article providing a new interpretation of Weber's work.[166] Instead of a category to provide a thematic unity to its content, he proposed to view the work of Weber from the point of view of the specificity of his methodology. The key concept for Tenbruck was now *Wirklichkeitswissenschaft* (the science of reality) that opposed *the Gesetzwissenschaft* (nomological science), which sought to provide laws for understanding reality. Instead, the *Wirklichkeitswissenschaft* attempted to understand the meaning of social reality without reducing this to general laws that negated the liberty of social processes. Now Tenbruck saw Weber's *Gesammelte Aufsätze zur Wissenschaftslehre* (*GAW*) as his main work, which testified to his commitment to the freedom of research from all forms of theoretical constraint. This intervention by Tenbruck elicited a quick response by Wagner and Ziprian,[167] and the discussion moved away from the hermeneutical issue concerning the work of Weber to focus on the work of Tenbruck and his ideas about current sociology.[168]

This review of the debates surrounding the work of Weber makes it clear that all of these recent attempts have, in their own way, sought some logic or coherence, some basic preoccupations, which can act as a guide for understanding the systematic intentions that Weber had in his writings. However, its unfinished nature has made it clear that no absolute hermeneutic can be applied to Weber's work. This review has also clarified some of the basic issues involved in considering Weber's work according to the line of enquiry of secularisation theory. Therefore, I would like to make it clear that there is no intention here to find *the* hermeneutical key to the totality of Weber's work.[169] Rather, in considering Weber's work as a secularisation theory, this work highlights one aspect that a textual analysis of his work supports. As Günther Roth suggests, the very enterprise of the sociology of religion is itself part of the historical process of secularisation.[170]

Notes

1. "Max Weber est sans aucun doute le plus grand sociologue allemand. Juriste, économiste, historien, philosophe, il est devenu finalement le maître de la sociologie 'compréhensive.' Par l'ampleur de l'érudition, par la variété des questions posées, par la riguer de la méthode, son œuvre s'impose comme le modèle d'une sociologie historique et systematique à la fois."Aron (1981): 81.

2. Most especially through his *The Structure of Social Action* initially published in 1937.

3. See Schöllgen, Gregor (1998): 159–160.

4. Cf. Woodhead, Heelas, and Davie (2003): 1.

5. In their analysis of Weber's sociology of law, Stephen P. Turner and Regis A. Factor suggest that Weber purported to give not a social explanation of society, but rather, an individual explanation, which could account for social processes. This tension between the individual and the collective is a constituent tension in social theory and seems to me not to disqualify Weber from being a "social theorist," but rather, to disqualify him from being a certain kind of social theorist. See Turner and Factor (1994).

6. For a review of the debates surrounding social theory and its relation to its "founding fathers," see Stephen Turner (ed.) (1996).

7. See Alexander (1996) for his defence of the classics.

8. See Poggi (1996): 39–47. Poggi here adapts the argument for belief used by St. Augustine, "Credo quia absurdum" (I believe because it is absurd).

9. I will discuss in Chapter 3 alternative translations to "Iron Cage" and will myself opt for "casing as hard as steel."

10. See Bryan S. Turner (1992).

11. For a review of the debates surrounding the modernity/postmodernity question, see Bryan S. Turner (ed.) (1990).

12. For a critique of the concepts of modernity and postmodernity and of the tendency to see these as representing integrated and coherent periods of history, see Yack (1997). In arguing that Weber narrates a Protestant account of modernity I am also highlighting a particularity of his reading of modernity.

13. See Habermas (1988): 9.

14. On the Protestant nature of Weber's theory of politics, see Walzer (1976).

15. "Max Weber hat kein philosophisches System entworfen. Es wäre unmöglich, seine Philosophie als Lehre darzustellen. Er hat es abgelehnt, ein Philosoph zu heißen. Doch ist er uns für die Zeit, in der er lebte, der wahre Philosoph. Weil Philosophie nicht eine fortschreitende Wissenschaft ist, die eine zeitlose Wahrheit erkennt, muß sie als ein geschichtliches aus der Unbedingtheit im Blick auf Transzendenz sich

vollziehendes Leben jeweils zur Wirklichkeit werden. Max Weber hat keine Philosophie gelehrt; er war eine Philosophie." Jaspers (1946): 42.

16. A good overall view of the life of Max Weber is still the biography written by his wife Marianne Weber. See Weber, Marianne (1950).

17. See Schöllgen (1998): 169.

18. The recent biography of Weber by Joachim Radkau (2005) is a monumental work of scholarship of over a thousand pages. Radkau's organising thesis for the biography is that Weber is a man in conflict with nature and that this interpretation provides the missing link between Weber's life and work. Radkau understands nature as all the given limits within which Weber had to operate. These limits include the inner ones of his tormented personality and the outer ones of the cultural conventions of the day. Written in "three acts," each act discusses a significant phase of Weber's confrontation with nature. The First Act introduces Weber's childhood and early life up until his mental breakdown after a confrontation with his father. The Second Act charts Weber's period of depression and various travels in the United States, which surround his publication of *PE* in 1904–1905. He also considers Weber's romantic encounters with Edgar Jaffe's wife Else and the pianist Mina Tobler. These incidents manifest the struggles that Weber had with his own sexual nature. Finally, Act Three discusses Weber's return to health after 1910 and his intense intellectual activity that again brought him to his own limits and final death in 1920. For a critique of this biography, which argues that Radkau has neglected the importance of politics in Weber's life in favour of a narrative constructed around the conflict with nature, see Thomas (2006).

19. Mommsen (1989): vii.

20. For a good description of the economic and political transitions of this period, see Wehler (1985).

21. See ibid.: 37–46.

22. See Giddens (1995): 25.

23. See *WuG*: 502.

24. See Bryan S. Turner (1992): 221.

25. The best overall account of Weber's work in this context is Mommsen (1974).

26. German economic expansion under Bismarck was dramatic and very rapid. The population increased from forty-nine million in 1890 to sixty-six million in 1913, and by 1914 Germany's steel production was greater than that of Russia, France, and Britain combined. Giant German electrical firms such as Siemens and AEG came to dominate the European electrical market at this time, and German dominance of the chemical industry was no less successful. See Bryan, S. Turner (1992): 218.

27. Weber is thus sceptical of Marx's confidence that the German working class could effect a socialist revolution, believing that the German

working class lacked an ideology and the political experience necessary for such a revolution. He is further sceptical of the notion that a socialist working-class party could bring about such a utopia, since, for Weber, such socialist planning of the economy would bring about a rationalisation of society similar to capitalism's. As a consequence, a small elite would end up ruling, and the same type of political alienation about which Marx had spoken would exist in a socialist state. See Weber's "Socialism" (Der Sozialismus) in Lassman and Speirs (eds.) (1994): 272–303.

28. See Wehler (1985): 62.

29. This is the background to Weber's arguments for a strong charismatic leadership and a powerful President of the Reich in his "*Politik als Beruf*" *(Politik)* and "*Der Reichspräsident.*" For a discussion of this issue and the influence of Weber's thought on Carl Schmitt's theory of "legality and legitimacy," see Mommsen (1974): 356–415.

30. For Eric Vogelin's and Leo Strauss's early philosophical critiques of Weber's work, see Voegelin (1995) and Strauss (1965): 36–78. A short summary of these critiques can be found in Midgley (1983): 1–16.

31. See McCarthy (2001): 1–212.

32. In confining myself to these three major influences, I do not mean to suggest that other figures were not important in the shaping of Weber's work. Indeed, one figure whom I will not mention, Goethe, seems to have been important for Weber in helping him to resolve the tensions present in the Protestant Kantian ideal framework. Rather, I mean only to suggest that these influences were the most important in the shaping of Weber's overall vision of his work. For a discussion of the influence of Goethe on Weber, see Albrow (1990): 62–77.

33. See Windelband (1924): 136–160.

34. See ibid.: 150. It will become clearer below, when I deal with Weber's relation to Marx, that this Neo-Kantian background was important for criticising Marx's materialist conception of history.

35. Ibid.: 142–143. See also Ringer (1997): 32.

36. For a survey of this discussion, see Ringer (1997): 36–62, and Oakes (1988).

37. See Marianne Weber (1950): 296.

38. See *GAW*: 171 and Rickert (1902): 33.

39. See Rickert (1902): 640, 701–704.

40. For a good survey of the influence of Windelband and Rickert on Weber, see Ringer (1997).

41. See Schluchter (1998): 78–79.

42. For a good survey of the philosophy of religion of the Southwestern School, see Ollig (1987).

43. See Windelband (1924): 299.

44. Ibid.: 297.

45. Ibid.: 304.

46. Ibid.: 305.

47. Ibid.: 342.
48. See *GAW*: 115.
49. See *AJ*: 322, 326–327.
50. For a discussion of this point, see Goldman (1988): 132–134.
51. See *GARS* I: 117 n. 5.
52. *GAW*: 132. "Sondern je 'freier' in dem hier in Rede stehenden Sinn das 'Handeln' ist, d.h. je weniger es den Charakter des 'naturlichen Geschehens' an sich trägt, desto mehr tritt damit endlich auch derjenige Begriff der 'Persönlichkeit' in Kraft, welcher ihr 'Wesen' in der Konstanz ihres inneren Verhältnisses zu bestimmen letzten 'Werten' und Lebens 'Bedeutungen' findet, die sich in ihrem Tun zu Zwecken ausmünzen und so in teleologisch-rationales Handeln umsetzen, und desto mehr schwindet also jene romantisch-naturalistische Wendung des 'Persönlichkeits' Gedankens." For a discussion of the importance of the Weberian understanding of "personality" and its relevance to his social theory, see Albrow (1990): 42–45.
53. See Eliaeson (2002): 14.
54. Ibid.: 5–10.
55. On the Protestant nature of Weber's methodology, see Wolin (1981).
56. Ibid.: 44.
57. See Kalberg (1994): 24.
58. See *WuG*: 1. Cf. *Objektivität*: 180.
59. On this point, see Ringer (1997): 101.
60. See *WuG*: 6.
61. *WuG*: 12. "Wie jedes Handeln kann auch das soziale Handeln bestimmt sein 1. *zweckrational*: durch Erwartungendes Verhaltens von Gegenständen der Außenwelt und von anderen Menschen und unter Benutzung dieser Erwartungen als 'Bedingungen' oder als 'Mittel' für rational, als Erfolg, erstrebte und abgewogene eigene Zwecke,—2. *wertrational*: durch bewußten Glauben an den—ethischen, ästhetischen, religiösen oder wie immer sonst zu deutenden—unbedingten Eigenwert eines bestimmten Sichverhaltens rein als solchen und unabhängig vom Erfolg,—3. *affektuell*: insbesondere emotional: durch aktuelle Affekte und Gefühlslagen,—4. *traditional*: durch eingelebte Gewohnheit."
62. See Eduard Baumgarten (1964): 554–555.
63. Wilhelm Hennis is convinced that Weber's sociology is the first working out of the consequences of Nietzsche's *Zeitgeist* analysis of the scientific analysis of society. He considers Nietzsche's "God is dead" thesis the occasion for Weber to rethink our human situation in a "gottfremden" and "prophetlosen" epoch. See Hennis (1987): 167–191.
64. See Bryan S. Turner (1996): ix–xl.
65. Ibid.: xi.
66. For an interesting argument, which suggests that Weber's sociology was heavily influenced by his reading of classical sources, see

McCarthy (2003): 64–110. McCarthy also makes the same argument for the sociology of both Marx (15–63), and Durkheim (111–156).

67. See Bryan S. Turner (1991).

68. See Eden (1983).

69. See, for example, Mommsen (1989): 27.

70. See Bryan S. Turner (1996): xii.

71. See Schluchter (1995): 107–126.

72. See *GAW*: 608–609.

73. Schluchter speaks of the difference as between a "gottfremden" and a "gottlosen" Zeit. See Schluchter (1995): n. 60. The idea is not that God is simply absent from the times, but rather, that the very notion of God is strange or foreign to the times.

74. See, for example, Schroeder (1992).

75. See *GARS* 1: 192 n. 1.

76. Giddens (1971): 211.

77. For Weber's critique of the materialist conception of history, see his "R. Stammlers Überwindung der materialistischen Geschichtsauffassung," in *GAW*: 291–359.

78. See "Objektivität," in *GAW*: 169–170.

79. For a discussion of this point, see Ringer (1997): 150–167.

80. See Weber, Max "R. Stammlers Überwindung der materialistischen Geschichtsauffassung," in *GAW*: 294–296.

81. See Löwith (ed.) (1982): 100.

82. Here one can clearly see the influence of the Neo–Kantian epistemology of considering reality to be made up of an infinite variety of phenomena which can only be studied through concepts.

83. See Löwith (ed.) (1982): 31.

84. Max Weber, "Objektivität" in *GAW*: 205.

85. Max Weber, "Parlament und Regierung" in *GPS*: 322.

86. See Löwith (1982): 22.

87. See Albrow (1990): 13. I shall consider in some considerable depth below the extent to which Weber's own social theory, and most particularly his theory of secularisation, was influenced by his own Protestant heritage.

88. See Albrow (1990): 14.

89. *MWG* II, 6 (1994): 65. "Denn ich bin zwar religiös absolut unmusikalisch und habe weder Bedürfnis noch Fähigkeit, irgendwelche seelischen 'Bauwerkerke' religiösen Charakters in mir zu errichten—das geht einfach nicht, resp. Ich lehne es ab. Aber ich bin nach genauer Prüfung weder antireligiös noch irreligiös. Ich empfinde mich auch in dieser Hinsicht als einen Krüppel, als einen verstummelten Menschen, dessen inneres Schicksal es ist, sich dies ehrlich eingestehen zu müssen, sich damit—um nicht in romantischen Schwindel zu verfallen." Weber uses this metaphor of religious musicality and unmusicality also in his *Einleitung* to

WEWR. He uses it in this context to differentiate between what he calls "religious virtuosos" and the "religion of the masses." See *GARS* I: 260.

90. For a less enthusiastic reading of the connection between the Protestant Reformation and modernity, see Troeltsch, E. (1906).

91. See Graf (1995).

92. *Jugendbriefe*: 48: "Im übrigen bin ich ziemlich tief in die Theologie geraten; meine Lektüre besteht aus Strauß, Schleiermacher und Pfleiderer (Paulinismus) und außerdem nur Platon."

93. One example is the analysis of the biblical origins of the word '*Beruf*' (calling/occupation) in the 1920 version of his *PE*, *GARS* I: n. 1, 63–65. In this footnote, which extends over three pages, he analyses the various meanings of the Hebrew word *Malakā* in the Old Testament, its related uses in the Greek Septuagint, and the Latin versions used by Luther in his translation of the Bible.

94. See Graf (1987).

95. See Aldenhoff (1987): 196–197. Some of the articles Weber published here include his "*Kirchen und Sekten in Nordamerika—Eine kirchen- und sozialpolitische Skizze*" (Churches and Sects in North America—An ecclesial and socio-political sketch).

96. Otto Baumgarten (1929): 215.

97. See Graf (1987a). Weber seldom referred to people publicly as his friends. It is thus worth noting that in his reply to Felix Rachfahl regarding the critical discussion surrounding *PE*, he refers to Troeltsch as both his friend and colleague. See Max Weber, "Antikritisches zum 'Geist' des Kapitalismus," in Winckelmann (ed.) 1972: 149.

98. Weber uses the distinction between a "sect" and "church" in his essay "Die Protestantischen Sekten und der Geist des Kapitalismus." See *GARS* I: 211.

99. For a very interesting comparison of the ethical ideas of Troeltsch and Weber that sets their relationship in the context of the liberal Protestant theological and philosophical ideas of the time, see Chapman (2001): 161–186. Chapman argues that towards the ends of their lives, both Troeltsch and Weber saw their intellectual work as a contribution to the reconstruction of German culture during the ethical and political crisis of the beginnings of the Weimar Republic (1918–1933). This period in German history was accompanied by a fervent anti-intellectualism and "anti-historicist" trend as a reaction to the breakdown of Wilhelmine culture.

100. Graf (1987): 136.

101. Karl Löwith describes Weber's interest in the fate of the individual personality in modern capitalist society as the project of the "rescuing of an ultimate human dignity." See Löwith (ed.) (1982): 22.

102. Thus the debates occurring in German liberal theology during the early years of the twentieth century tended to look for ways in

which questions of the human spirit and freedom could be safeguarded against the deterministic ideas of materialism and naturalism. This period coincides with a return to the work of Kant in both theology and philosophy as a means to protect the individual against such intellectual onslaughts as materialism and naturalism. It is in this context that the debates about a religious *a priori* took place. See Chapman (2001): 75–137.

103. For a full discussion of this school and its influence in German liberal theology at the start of the twentieth century, see Chapman (2001): 13–74.

104. For a discussion of this point, see Troeltsch (1913): 756–757.

105. See Aldenhoff (1987).

106. Ibid.: 198–199.

107. See Ekstrand (2000): 36–54.

108. See *AJ*, *GARS* III: 308.

109. See *AJ*, *GARS* III: 105–106.

110. See *AJ*, *GARS* III: 119–120.

111. See *AJ*, *GARS* III: 308.

112. See *AJ*, *GARS* III: 303.

113. See *AJ*, *GARS* III: 306.

114. See *AJ*, *GARS* III: 303.

115. See Gunkel (1917).

116. See *AJ*, *GARS* III: 281 n. 1.

117. For an analysis of the relationship between Weber and Gunkel and the History of Religion School, see Ekstrand (2000): 41–44.

118. See Max Weber, "Politik als Beruf," in *GPS*: 554.

119. See *WuG*: 275. In this, Weber's ideas overlap with those of his friend Ernst Troeltsch, though Troeltsch did not seem so pessimistic as Weber as to the possibility of some form of theodicy that could still provide a basis for ethics and politics in modern scientific societies. See Chapman. (2001): 167–172.

120. See *WuG*: 317–318.

121. For Ritschl's theological doctrine, see Ritschl (1888).

122. Disputes between the History of Religion School and the Ritschlian way of doing theology centred not on the anti-metaphysical and pro-ethical bias, but rather, on the historical picture of Jesus, which was central to the History of Religion School. However, it should be mentioned that among the liberal Protestant theologians there were also groups who wanted to integrate the truth claims of Christianity with those of the natural sciences. Thus, whilst Wilhelm Herrmann, a follower of Ritschl, located the Christian faith in the noncognitive realm of pure faith, Ernst Troeltsch defended the more cognitive view that Christianity had to continually revise its claims in light of new scientific findings. For a review of these differences within the tradition of liberal Protestantism, see Sockness (1998).

123. See Harnack, Adolf (1902): 45–47.

124. See Troeltsch (1992), 1: 89. For a discussion of the importance of these debates about "personality," on Weber's own conception of "personality," see Goldman (1988): 134–142.

125. See Graf (1987): 138–139.

126. See Max Weber, "Wissenschaft als Beruf," in *GAW*: 612.

127. See Troeltsch (1925): 335–336.

128. See Max Weber "Politik als Beruf," in *GPS*: 507–508.

129. See Gunkel (1916): 31.

130. Max Weber, "Politik als Beruf," in *GAW*: 551ff.

131. Ibid.: 549.

132. Ibid., 557. "Der Genius, oder Dämon der Politik lebt mit dem Gott der Liebe, auch mit dem Christengott in seiner kirchlichen Ausprägung, in einer inneren Spannung, die jederzeit in unaustragbaren Konflikt ausbrechen kann."

133. See Ekstrand (2000): 53.

134. For Baumgarten's view of politics and ethics, see Otto Baumgarten (1916).

135. Lübbe (1965): 69. "Die Art, in der Weber gelegentlich den Begriff der Säkularisierung verwendet, würde es rechtfertigen, seine religionssoziologischen Untersuchungen insgesamt unter diesen Titel zu stellen."

136. In this reconstruction of the debates surrounding the interpretation of the work of Weber, I have drawn on the work of Torró (1990): 12–24.

137. See Tenbruck (1975).

138. The basis of this interpretation lay in the fact that in Marianne's biography of her husband, she stated several times that *WuG* was his major work. See for example Marianne Weber (1950): 463, 727.

139. See Parsons, Talcott (1949): 500–694.

140. See Aron (1981): 81–126.

141. See, for example, Habermas (1968): 48–103.

142. See Bendix, Reinhard (1977): 96–97.

143. Ibid.: 9.

144. The *Vorbemerkung* is to be found at the start of *PE* in *GARS* I: 1–16; the *Einleitung* is to be found at the start of *WEWR* in *GARS* I: 237–275; the *Zwischenbetrachtung* is to be found in *WEWR* in *GARS* I: 536–573.

145. Tenbruck (1975): 675. "Für *Weber* hingegen lag seine entscheidende Entdeckung in der Erkenntnis, daß die Rationalisierung, bei aller historischen Fragilität, von dem Zwang einer inneren Logik getragen wurde, welche in dem unaufhaltsamen Drang zur Rationalisierung religiöser Ideen angelegt war. Deshalb ist der Rationalisierungsprozeß im Kern ein religionsgeschichtlicher Entzauberungsprozeß, und seine Momente und Stationen erhalten von dort ihre Einheit. Nicht die

historische Identifizierung der Teilvorgänge, sondern die innere Zwangsläufigkeit ihrer Abfolge bestimme die Lösung *Webers*.

Der schlüssel aber zu dieser Auffassung *Webers* liegt in jener Arbeit, die trotz aller Fortschritte der Auslegung in ihrem zentralen Teil der Interpretation widerstanden hat, nämlich in der WEWR."

146. See Max Weber, *Einleitung*, *GARS* I: 252.

147. Tenbruck seeks to ground his interpretation by providing two "empirical" tests that confirm his argument. The first seeks to reconstruct Weber's anthropology and the second to trace the multilinear typology of the religious. See Tenbruck (1975): 685.

148. See Winckelmann (1980), and Riesebrodt (1980).

149. See *GAW*: 433.

150. See *GAW*: 426, n. 1.

151. See *WuG*: 308. Winckelmann deduced from his study of the composition of *WuG* that this part was ready for publication in 1913. See Winckelmann (1980): 45 n. 32.

152. Weber used the notion of an "ideal-type" as a methodological procedure to reduce some of the limitations of social scientific research. Since the "objects" of social science are often not visible, as are the objects of natural scientific research, Weber uses the methodology of "ideal-typical" construction to make common features of social phenomena accessible to investigation. Thus, in the concept formation of the social sciences, certain aspects of empirical reality are selected out for analysis. This is performed by analytically accentuating general phenomena that occur in a range of social phenomena and then by forming a hypothetical model or type based on these analytically accentuated general phenomena. This hypothetical construct, or "ideal-type," can then be compared with actual cultural and social phenomena to analyse differences from the ideal, causal connections between phenomena, and possible motives for such differences based on the notion of "right rationality," which Weber attributed to the ideal agent. Thus, historical developmental dynamics can be analysed according to deviations from ideal social trajectories, based on "right rationality" to "measure" deviations from such ideal rational action. For Weber's understanding of ideal types, see *GAW*: 146–214. For a good short study of ideal-types and their use in Weber's methodology, see Ringer (1997): 110–121. A similar notion is used by Habermas in his reconstruction of historical materialism when he talks about differences between the logic and the dynamics of development. See Habermas (1976).

153. See Max Weber, "Bermerkungen zu der vorstehenden 'Replik'," in Winckelmann (ed.) (1972): 46. Quoted by Winckelmann, J. (1980): 26, 49 n. 90.

154. Winckelmann (1980): 26–27.

155. Ibid.: 31–41.

156. See Riesebrodt (1980): 115–116.

157. Ibid.: 121, 128 n. 36.

158. See *GARS* I: 213, 263.

159. See Schluchter (1998): 40.

160. This article, originally published in the *Kölner Zeitschrift für Soziologie und Sozialpsychologie* was later published in Schluchter (1988a), 2: 557–596.

161. See Schluchter (1988a), 2: 560 n. 2. Schluchter is here referring to Hennis' article "Max Webers Fragestellung," later published in Hennis (1987): 3–58.

162. See Schluchter (1988a), 2: 561–562.

163. See Max Weber, *Vorbemerkung*, in *GARS* I: 1.

164. Marianne Weber (1950): 381. "Für Weber bedeutet diese Erkenntnis der Besonderheit des okzidentalen Rationalismus und der ihm zugefallenen Rolle für die abendländische Kultur eine siener wichtigsten Entdeckungen."

165. See Schluchter (1988a), 2: 564–589.

166. See Tenbruck (1986).

167. See Wagner and Ziprian (1987).

168. It should be stated that not all of the points raised by Tenbruck in his interventions have been rejected by researchers. Indeed, one major contribution that he has made to Weber research is to emphasise the importance of religious sociology as a major part of Weber's systematic concerns. This has been admirably developed in the work of his then assistant Gottfried Küenzlen. See Küenzlen (1980).

169. Günther Roth suggests that Weber's account of the course of revolutionary beliefs in Protestantism, the rise of substantive natural law based on ethical socialism after the French Revolution, and the revolutionary critique of ethical socialism by Marxism predicting the necessary demise of capitalism is a secular theory that attempts to give a specifically historical explanation of modernity and not a total theory of historical society. It is specific and not total in the sense that it analyses the actions of one or more generations without using a global theory of evolutionary stages as in Marxism. See Roth and Schluchter (1979): 147–154.

170. See ibid.: 144. This same idea of locating the sociology of religion within the historical process of secularisation is interpreted in different ways by Milbank (1990): 51–143 and Hervieu-Léger (1987). Milbank considers the theory of secularisation to be an outdated mode of scientific reasoning. Hervieu-Léger considers the historical origin of the sociology of religion to be located in the rise of an alternative scientific description and explanation of social reality that essentially competes with that proposed by theology.

CHAPTER 3

Secularisation in Weber's Sociology of Religion

In this chapter, I will analyse the major texts of Max Weber's sociology of religion[1] that are relevant for elucidating his understanding of secularisation.[2] Furthermore, I will draw out the Protestant metanarrative that informs Weber's theory of secularisation and will assess the importance of this Protestant heritage for his theoretical work.

The *Protestant Ethic* and the Spirit of Capitalism (*PE*)

Max Weber's essay *PE*[3] was first published in the *Archiv für Sozialwissenschaft und Sozialpolitik* Volumes 20 and 21 in 1904–1905. It was reprinted in 1920 as the first study in his *Gesammelte Aufsätze zur Religionssoziologie (GARS)*, which was unfinished due to his death in the same year.[4] The second edition of *PE* incorporated a large number of additions and changes to the original text, which Weber made in the light of the many varied criticisms he had received after the publication of the first edition.[5] The various forms of the word *Säkularisierung* (secularisation) occur in both the 1904/1905 and 1920 texts only four times,[6] the word *Entzauberung* (disenchantment), which plays an important part in Weber's understanding of secularisation, also appears.[7] Yet it is a mistake to think that the only time Weber is talking about the process of secularisation is when he uses this specific word. That would be to fall into a kind of exegetical fundamentalism. My task in analysing Weber's works according to the heuristic category of a theory of secularisation will be to organise his work in this light and to demonstrate how, by looking at Weber according to this category, fruitful insight can be gained into his understanding of the role played by religion in modern society.

It is important to begin by considering the general narrative of *PE* in order to see just how the theory of secularisation can organise the framework of Weber's general argument. Put at its simplest, one might sum up the general argument of *PE* as an investigation into the relationship between the ethic of Protestantism and the spirit of Western capitalism. By ethic of Protestantism, Weber means the main principles of the Protestant way of life, which govern the actions of individual followers. He outlines two main principles that govern individual conduct.

The first is derived from Martin Luther's conception of calling, and the second from Jean Calvin's conception of predestination.[8] For Weber, the radical newness of Luther's conception of calling was that it applied to all people and concerned the daily activities of people in the world.[9] It provided a moral justification for activity in the world, which was now seen as the place in which one fulfilled one's duty towards God. All activities, if they were truly willed by God, were seen as being of equal worth in the eyes of God.[10]

The second principle, Calvin's conception of predestination, meant that God had already chosen those who were to be saved and those who were to be damned, even before their earthly existence. Thus, individual good works did not contribute to one's salvation, and priests could not reassure Calvinists that their sins could be forgiven and that they could go to heaven. Weber believes that this led to a form of inner loneliness, since Calvinists could not be sure or, even worse, be reassured, that they would go to heaven.[11] The only way to gain some reassurance was to live a form of systematic self-control in all one's actions, a notion Weber calls asceticism, since this could be considered as a sign that such a person had been saved by God.[12]

Weber analyses four forms of Protestant asceticism: Calvinism, Pietism, Methodism, and the Baptist sects.[13] He is not particularly concerned with their theoretical basis, but focuses rather on the psychological sanctions that issued from the beliefs and practices of each form of Protestantism and directed the practical actions of individuals.[14] Since in Calvinism the inner loneliness resulting from the doctrine of predestination is the strongest, it leads to the most ascetic form of Protestantism. Weber refers to this Protestant asceticism as "inner-worldly" asceticism (*innerweltliche Askese*), since the rational or systematic control of one's activity is no longer lived outside of the world in monastic communities but in the world, in one's daily activities. He sums up his definition of the ethic of Protestantism by saying:

> But, as we have seen, this ascetic conduct meant a rational organisation of the whole of one's life in accordance with God's will. And this asceticism was no longer an opus supererogationis, but something which could be required of everyone who would be certain of salvation. The religious life of the saints, as distinguished from the natural life, was—the most important point—no longer lived outside the world in monastic communities, but within the world and its institutions. The rationalisation of conduct within this world, but for the sake of the world beyond, was the consequence of the concept of calling of ascetic Protestantism.[15]

Weber turns, in the next section of Part II of *PE*, to a demonstration of how this ascetic Protestantism relates to everyday economic conduct.

Prior to this, in Chapter 2 of Part I of *PE*, he outlines the meaning of the term "spirit of capitalism,"[16] drawing on the writings of Benjamin Franklin, the eighteenth century American politician and author who wrote popular books on how to get rich. Weber draws particularly on two of Franklin's works: *Necessary Hints to Those That Would be Rich* and *Advice to a Young Tradesman* written in 1736 and 1748 respectively.[17] Both works contain popular sayings that have become part and parcel of our modern language: "Time is money," and "The good paymaster is lord of another man's purse," to mention but two. For Weber, the peculiar aspect of this spirit of capitalism is that the pursuit of wealth is combined with the strict avoidance of taking any pleasure in it. To make money becomes a religious duty, a moral precept that must be followed. In contrast, traditional economies had been content to preserve the *status quo*, to earn enough to live on, without aspiring to ever-increased production and wages.[18] Weber quotes the example of the piece-rate policy (that is, pay by amount of work) of the agricultural workers of the time as an example of how they functioned. The terms "ethic of Protestantism" and "spirit of capitalism" provide the basic elements of his main argument. However, the question still remains: What is the relationship between capitalism and Protestantism?

Weber speaks in a number of passages about investigating the "interior relationship" (*innere Verwandschaft*)[19] or "elective affinities" (*Wahlverwandschaften*)[20] between the ethic of Protestantism and the spirit of capitalism. After developing his argument step by step, it is the concept of asceticism[21] that eventually allows him to crystallise this relationship. In the final section of *PE*, entitled "Asceticism and the Spirit of Capitalism" (*Askese und kapitalistischer Geist*), he outlines succinctly his understanding of the relationship, using the concept of asceticism as the link or common term shared by both:

> One of the fundamental elements of the spirit of modern capitalism, and not only of that but of modern culture: rational conduct on the basis of the idea of calling, was born—that is what this discussion has sought to demonstrate—from the spirit of Christian asceticism. One has only to re-read the passage from Franklin, quoted at the beginning of this essay, in order to see that the essential elements of the attitude, which was there called the spirit of capitalism are the same as what we have just shown to be the content of the Puritan worldly asceticism, only without the religious basis, which by Franklin had died away.[22]

Thus, the secularisation of asceticism, that is, the transformation of the religious understanding of following a vocation in a monastery into the Protestant understanding of following a calling in the secular or worldly realm of modern labour, is the basic narrative of *PE*. So, even though Weber only uses various forms of the word *secularisation* four times in *PE*, the general framework in which the narrative unfolds can be understood as a general theory of secularisation.[23] Weber understood this secularisation of asceticism to be a rationalisation of conduct in the world that promoted the spirit of modern capitalism.[24] This is brought out clearly in the introduction to *PE*, which he added in 1920 for the whole series on the Sociology of Religion. Here, the key question is to uncover the particularity of Western rationality as the source of the singularity of Western capitalism. Thus, transposing the area for the application of the principles of Western rationality from the monastery (considered to be outside the world) to the world, and transforming daily life in the world (not in the solitary soul of the cloistered monk) was the result of the secularisation of monastic asceticism.[25] Weber puts this point almost poetically in one of his most famous passages in *PE*:

> Christian asceticism, at first fleeing from the world into solitude, had already ruled the world, which it had renounced from the monastery, through the Church. But it had, on the whole, left the naturally free character of daily life in the world untouched. Now it strode into the market place of life, slammed the door of the monastery behind it, and undertook to penetrate just that daily routine of life with its methodology, to fashion it into a life in the world, but neither of nor for this world.[26]

The Disenchantment of the World

Weber speaks of the disenchantment of the world[27] in a number of ways.[28] The first is in terms of the rejection of the sacramental mediation of salvation.[29] For Weber, the process of the disenchantment of the world, which began in the prophetic tradition of ancient Judaism, had reached its historical fulfilment in Calvinism, which, in his view, presented the most consistent religious form of rejection of the sacramental mediation of salvation.[30]

Weber sees the disenchantment of the world as a process of the elimination of magic, and here he makes little distinction between ancient Egyptian, Babylonian magic, and modern

Catholic sacramental practice. All are considered to be enchanted forms of action.[31] The result of this process of disenchantment was the gradual removal and isolation of the individual from the institutional supports of organised religion. Priests, sacraments, and even the Church itself were seen to be incapable of mediating the grace of salvation to the believer. The Calvinist was alone before the God who had either saved him from or condemned him to eternal damnation.[32] The human mediation of salvation is magic for Weber, following Calvin's own logic, since it would suggest that humans could influence the will of God, just as ancient magicians claimed to coerce the gods by sacrificial practices.[33] Such a sacramental capacity to influence the will of God could lessen the anxiety of the individual believer, who could, for instance, have his or her sins forgiven and thus attain a state of grace through the sacramental mediation of the forgiveness of God. Without this sacramental route to salvation, the believer could be aware of being in a state of grace only through one of two means. Weber explains:

> The religious virtuoso can make himself sure of his state of grace either in that he feels himself to be the vessel of the Holy Spirit or the tool of the divine will. In the former case his religious life tends to mysticism and emotionalism, in the latter to ascetic action; Luther stood close to the former type, Calvinism belonged definitely to the latter. The Calvinist also wanted to be saved "sola fide." But since Calvin viewed all pure feelings and emotions, no matter how exalted they might seem to be, with suspicion, faith had to be proved by its objective results in order to provide a firm foundation for the certitudo salutis. It must be a "fides efficax," the call to salvation an "effectual calling" (expression used in the Savoy Declaration).[34]

Weber's ideal typical description of asceticism and mysticism in the world religions trades on the separation of contemplation and action that results chiefly from Platonic and Neo-Platonic influences on Western thinking.[35] Thus, the disenchantment of the world is also a form of secularisation of human action: the separation of the sacred realm of the grace of salvation from the profane realm of human action.[36] Thus, although human action could now be seen as "the tool of the divine will," it is, so to speak, emptied of its soteriological significance. It now functions simply to indicate the result of being elected by God for salvation; it plays no constitutive role in that election. Moreover, the disenchantment of the world leads to a two-fold separation of grace from nature.[37] Human nature no longer actively cooperates with the saving power of grace, but moreover, nature is no longer, in the words of Gerard Manley Hopkins, "charged with the grandeur of God."[38] The sacred clearly lies in the transcendental realm of God and God's chosen ones; the profane in the world, in nature.[39] We might even talk about a certain disenchantment of salvation itself, because God's saving action cannot be influenced by anything in nature.[40]

As we have seen, Weber identifies two possible post-Reformation routes to salvation: the mysticism of Lutheranism and the asceticism of Calvinism. Lutheranism, in his view, often falls back into a Catholic vision of salvation by works and tends towards an unengaged mysticism;[41] it does not form a systematic and rational control of daily conduct, but rather, promotes a succession of individual acts that are thought to make a limited contribution to one's own salvation.[42] According to Weber, mysticism, with its tendency to seek rest rather than action, cannot promote the spirit of capitalism, which feeds off a religious justification of inner-worldly action. It is in Calvinism, therefore, that he considers the elective affinity between the Protestant ethic and the spirit of capitalism to be strongest, since this particular vision of salvation leads to the inner-worldly asceticism, which promotes the spirit of capitalism.

The second sense in which Weber speaks of the disenchantment of the world as a process of secularisation is in speaking about the consequences of the accumulation of property and wealth for the religious roots that gave rise to the spirit of capitalism. He notes that the tendency of religious orders to become rich is, paradoxically, a consequence of their desire to live poorly. One who lives poorly and with ascetic discipline does not waste, and through hard work one tends to accumulate property. This combination of a poor and ascetic life style with hard work thus has the paradoxical tendency of producing wealth, which can corrupt the initial desire of leading a poor and ascetic lifestyle. Weber calls this the "secularising effect of property."[43]

Weber links the tendency of religious orders to lose their spiritual roots with the tendency of capitalistic societies to lose touch with their own religious roots:

> Calvin himself had made the much-quoted statement that only when the people, i.e., the mass of labourers and craftsmen, were poor did they remain obedient to God. In the Netherlands (Pieter de la Court and others): that had been secularised to the effect that the mass of men only labour when necessity forces them to do so. This formulation of a leading idea of capitalistic economy later entered into the current theories of the productivity of low wages. Here also, with the dying out of the religious root, the utilitarian interpretation crept in unnoticed, in the line of development, which we have again and again observed.[44]

This "line of development" is one effect of the process of disenchantment on religious orders, Protestantism,[45] and capitalist society alike.

This understanding of secularisation can also be seen in *Die protestantischen Sekten und der Geist des Kapitalismus (PS)*, the essay published by Weber in 1906 shortly after *PE*. Here he speaks of the tendency of Protestant sects in America to become secular institutions that maintain the moral rigour of the Protestant sect but lose their original religious roots.[46] The transposition of religious values from the spiritual to the secular realm and the transformation of the notion of calling to religious life into a calling to secular activity can be understood as a process of disenchantment in the sense that these changes also have the tendency to lead to the uprooting or decaying of their religious foundations.[47]

Weber became increasingly aware of secularisation as the disappearance of the religious dimension from social life as his research into the sociology of religion developed. One can see this in his addition to a footnote, made for the 1920 edition of *PE*:

> Furthermore, one may well doubt to what extent the "joy" of the mediaeval craftsman "in his creation," which is so commonly appealed to, was effective as a psychological motive force.

> Nevertheless, there is undoubtedly something in that thesis. But in any case asceticism certainly *deprived* all labour of this worldly attractiveness, which is today destroyed forever by capitalism, and oriented it to the beyond. Labour in a calling *as such* is willed by God. The *impersonality* of present-day labour, what, from the standpoint of the individual, is its joyless lack of meaning, still has a religious justification here. Capitalism at the time of its development *needed* labourers who were available for economic exploitation for *conscience's* sake. [Today it is in the saddle, and hence able to force people to labour without transcendental rewards].[48]

Clearly, Weber saw capitalism's diminishing need to use transcendental rewards as an incentive as a sign of the loss of the significance of religion in modern societies. Disenchantment of the world is thus also a privatisation of religion, in that social processes become gradually less influenced by a religious logic and progressively operate according to the secular scientific principles of a disenchanted world.[49]

A third sense in which Weber speaks of the disenchantment of the world as a process of secularisation is in terms of the pessimistic conclusions with which he ends *PE*. Having worked through, with scientific rigour, the relationship between the ethic of Protestantism and the spirit of capitalism, he then stands back and allows his literary imagination to survey the landscape that he has painted. It turns out to be rather bleak and barren. He returns to Goethe's *Wilhelm Meisters Wanderjahre* and *Faust* and uses them as types to outline the dilemmas of modern man under the conditions of capitalism.[50]

Weber notes that valuable labour is conditioned by the force field created between the modern division of labour, which demands specialisation, and the renunciation of the Faustian dream of the universality of man: in Weber's words, "Deed (*Tat*) and renunciation (*Entsagung*) inevitably condition each other today."[51] Thus, Faustian dreams of a full and beautiful humanity, an age of unhindered creativity in which the soul of humanity reaches its climax in autonomy and productivity, have been transformed into the dialectic of the Enlightenment.

As Jürgen Habermas has noted,[52] the basic idea of the dialectic of Enlightenment was already present in Weber's

PE well before the celebrated publication of Adorno's and Horkheimer's book of the same title in 1944.[53] The impulse of the Enlightenment—described by Kant as "*Sapere aude!*"[54]—had turned into an enslavement. Weber describes this disenchantment in terms of both a loss of freedom and a loss of meaning in modern capitalist society. The loss of freedom is a consequence of the transposition of the religious conception of vocation from the monastic cell into the modern world of economic production:

> The Puritan *wanted* to be a vocational person; we are *forced* to be. For when the asceticism was carried out of monastic cells into everyday life, and began to dominate worldly morality, it did its part in building the tremendous cosmos of the modern economic order. This order is now bound to the technical and economic conditions of machine production which today determine the lives of all the individuals who are born into this mechanism, *not* only those directly concerned with economic acquisition, with irresistible force. Perhaps it will so determine them until the last ton of fossilised coal is burnt. In Baxter's view the care for external goods should only lie on the shoulders of the "saint like a light cloak, which can be thrown aside at any moment." But fate decreed that the cloak should become a casing as hard as steel.[55]

The loss of meaning in human work follows a similar line of development. Prior to the secularisation of religious asceticism, monks and nuns believed that they were disciplining the body through self-sacrifice and labour in order to be united with God. This spirit was initially transposed into worldly affairs, and individuals understood their actions to be a "tool of the divine will." However, as "the secularising influence of property" took root, it in turn uprooted the very religious roots that gave rise to it, and thereby also took with it the reason for acting at all. Thus, as capitalism was entrenched in modern society, human action became subject to the logic of the machine and few if any knew any longer why the machine was running in the first place. Whilst people remained faithful to their duty to work, beyond the reason of basic material survival there seemed to be little justification for taking part in the capitalist production process. The meaning of human labour no longer seemed clear, as human labour had lost its transcendental purpose:

> Today the spirit of religious asceticism—whether finally, who knows?—has escaped from the casing. But victorious capitalism, since it rests on mechanical foundations, needs its support no longer. The rosy blush of its laughing heir, the Enlightenment, seems also to be irretrievably fading, and the idea of duty in one's calling prowls about in our lives like the ghost of dead religious beliefs. Where the fulfilment of the calling cannot directly be related to the highest spiritual and cultural values, or when, on the other hand, it need not be felt simply as economic compulsion, the individual generally abandons the attempt to interpret it at all.[56]

If this were not pessimistic enough, Weber intensifies the tragedy by suggesting that the real drama of this situation is that the agents in the most developed civilisation in the world, who are themselves the products of this civilisation, do not realise the consequences of having a secular vocation forced upon them, of being a *Berufsmensch* (vocational person).[57] In one of the most enigmatic passages of *PE*, Weber announces what he considers to be the real drama of modernity:

> No one knows who will live in this casing in the future, or whether at the end of this tremendous development entirely new prophets will arise, or there will be a great rebirth of old ideas and ideals, or, if neither, mechanised petrification, embellished with a sort of convulsive self-importance. For of the "last people" of this cultural development, it might well be truly said: "Specialists without spirit, sensualists without heart; this nullity imagines that it has attained a level of civilisation never before achieved."[58]

"Specialists," for Weber, were products of the German university system who were subsumed into a bureaucracy that was both necessary and spiritless; "sensualists" were businessmen lacking the ascetic spirit of the early capitalists. For Weber, the problem is that of principles of action without transcendental resources. The secularisation of the religious calling into a worldly activity meant that the new vocational humanity (*Berufsmenschentum*) had to give modern life meaning out of its own resources.[59] Thus, Weber hoped for a new form of person of culture (*Kulturmensch*), a "personality" who could supply his or her own meaning. Such people would be, in his own words, "entirely new prophets," who could carry on the process of disenchantment that had been begun by the ethical prophets of ancient Judaism but now was being carried forward under the modern conditions of secularisation. Just as Marx had identified the proletariat as the agent of social change in bringing about the communist society, so for Weber, the notion of "personality" (referring to those people with the inner conviction of having a secular calling based on the bourgeois conception of doing one's duty) identifies the possible agents of social change. Unlike the specialists of the bureaucratic institutions of the German State, who, like the priests in ancient Judaism, gained their legitimacy from being appointed by the institution, these new prophets of personality would gain legitimacy from their own inner conviction of being vocational people, of having the new secular charisma of creating their own meaning and choosing their own values.[60]

The *Einleitung* to *Die Wirtschaftsethik der Weltreligionen (WEWR)*[61]

WEWR's Einleitung (Introduction) together with its *Zwischenbetrachtung* (Intermediate Reflection),[62] has often been considered a kind of manifesto setting out Weber's general programme in the sociology of religion.[63] Against some criticisms, for example, that he reduces religion to functionalist explanations,[64] it is interesting to note that at the beginning of the *Einleitung* he defends religion against both Marx's ideological account and Nietzsche's psychological vision of religion as a product of resentment.[65] Instead, Weber analyses the economic ethics of the five world religions: that is to say, the "practical impulses for action which are founded in the psychological and pragmatic contexts of religions,"[66] in terms of their capacities to respond to the real "religious needs" of their followers.[67] Weber chooses to focus on the particular religious need to know the meaning of suffering and death and the distribution of good fortune, that is, on the theodicy question.[68]

Weber explains that the need to find an ethical interpretation of the meaning of suffering, death, and the distribution of good fortune increased with the development of rational conceptions of the world. This, in turn, led to a particular metaphysical conception of God and the world. These developments had rational consequences for dealing with the theodicy question:

> The metaphysical conception of God and of the world, which the ineradicable demand for a theodicy called forth, could produce only a few systems of ideas on the whole—as we shall see, only three. These three gave rationally satisfactory answers to the questioning for the basis of the incongruity between destiny and merit: the Indian doctrine of Karma, Zoroastrian dualism, and the predestination decree of the *Deus absconditus*. However, these rationally closed solutions are only exceptionally found in pure form.[69]

Clearly, in mentioning "the predestination decree of the *Deus absconditus*," Weber builds on his reflections in *PE*. However, not so obvious is the fact that he also builds on his critique of Marx's theory of historical materialism, which he made explicit at the end of *PE*, by combining this with a critique of Nietzsche's conception of Christian morality.[70]

Weber's critique of both Marx and Nietzsche has a bearing on his theory of secularisation. It reveals his understanding of the sources of metaphysical conceptions of the world and God, and the role played by the intellectual classes in the rational transformation of these conceptions. He carries out this critique on two levels: at the level of a critique of Marx's and Nietzsche's theory of the relation between class and religion; and as a critique of what he considers to be an insufficiently nuanced conception of the dynamics of history presented by Marx.

Unlike some interpretations of Marx and Nietzsche, Weber does not think that religious ideas are the result of a distorted view of reality; rather, they arise precisely because of the tragic nature of reality. Because the lower classes tend to have a more tragic existence than the upper classes, it is natural that a rational religious ethic should be rooted in the experience of the lower classes.[71] However, this is not to say that this results from the manipulation of class interests, either in terms of the resentment of slave ethics, à la Nietzsche, or from the obfuscation of social reality in order to protect the interests of the bourgeoisie, à la Marx. Weber makes this point clear:

> There can be no doubt that prophets and priests through intentional or unintentional propaganda have taken the resentment of the masses into their service. But this is by no means universally the case. This essentially negative force of resentment, so far as is known, has never been the source of those essentially metaphysical conceptions, which have lent uniqueness to salvation religion. Moreover, in general, the nature of a religious promise has by no means necessarily or even predominantly been the mere mouthpiece of a class interest, either of an external or internal nature.... For the rest, the specific nature of the great religious and ethical systems has been determined by social conditions of a far more particular nature than by the mere contrast of ruling and ruled strata.[72]

Weber's first critique of both Nietzsche and Marx leads quite naturally into his second critique of Marx, by outlining how he sees the intellectual classes as the ones who have systematised the religious ethic of the lower classes into a soteriologically rational image of the world. Interestingly, his understanding of the role of intellectuals in this process reveals a number of features that he sees as characteristic of the Western process of rationalisation. He explains that the basic human need to have some meaningful answer to the theodicy question has led various social groups to play different roles in answering this question.[73] The characteristic of the intellectual groups in this process has been that they have set the answers to this basic question of theodicy in the context of a theory of salvation.[74] The way that they have done this makes them particularly significant carriers of Western rationality and, for Weber, of the dynamics of history.

Originally, Weber explains, punctual magical and religious acts conferred on individuals a temporary psychological sense that they possessed sacred or religious goods, or that they were saved. The problem was how to move from a temporary sense of being saved to a permanent sense. For Weber, this transition from transience to permanence, a process he calls sublimation,[75] was achieved in its most developed forms in two ways: through the development of the religious doctrines of "rebirth" and "redemption."[76] The specific contribution of the intellectual strata to this process has been, "to sublimate the possession of religious goods into a belief in 'redemption'."[77] This belief in redemption played a particularly important role in the evolution of Western societies because it expressed a systematic and rational image of the world and a stance towards it. As ideas create our images of the world and our images of the world determine the direction of our actions, then contrary to Marx, Weber argues, ideas have significantly determined the dynamics of history:

> Yet redemption attained a specific significance only where it expressed a systematic and rationalised "image of the world" and represented a stand in the face of the world. For the meaning as well as the intended and actual psychological quality of redemption has depended upon such a world image and such a stand. Not ideas, but (material and ideal) interests, directly govern men's conduct. Yet very frequently the "world images" that have been created by "ideas" have, like switchmen, determined the tracks along which action has been pushed by the dynamic of interest. "From what" and "for what" one wished to be redeemed and, let us not forget, "could be" redeemed. It depended upon one's image of the world.[78]

Thus, against Marx, Weber argues that the inner rationalisation of religious ideas about the world has significantly determined the course of Western history and the Western way of life. This need to find a metaphysical meaning for the world has been the chief task of intellectuals, and it characterises the core of genuine religious rationalism for Weber. However, and here the disenchantment and secularisation themes occur once again, the further this inner rationalisation has proceeded, the more religion itself been transferred into the irrational realm.[79]

Weber suggests that this paradoxical situation arises because in rationalising the conception of the world and the modern way of life, the religious core of this rationality, as indeed the core of practical and theoretical life, has been found to be based on given presuppositions that are not themselves rational, but products of the interest situation of the intellectual strata who have carried forward this process of Western rationalisation.[80] Intellectuals, understood as those with special knowledge, had a vested interest in defending themselves as possessors of this specialist knowledge. But as this knowledge of the world and of the modern way of life became democratised, through the process of rationalisation according to purposive rationality based on principles open to general understanding, the only area left for this specialist knowledge to retreat to became the area of the supernatural: that is, to the irrational realm beyond the world.[81] Weber expresses this idea in terms of its consequences for the fragmentation of our image of the world:

> The unity of the primitive image of the world in which everything was concrete magic, has tended to split into rational cognition and mastery of nature, on the one hand, and into "mystic" experiences on the other. The inexpressible contents of such experiences remain the only possible "beyond," added to the mechanism of a world robbed of gods. . . . Where this conclusion has been fully drawn, the individual can pursue his quest for salvation only as an individual. This phenomenon appears in some form, with the progressive intellectualist rationalism, wherever men have ventured to rationalise the image of the world as being a cosmos governed by impersonal rules.[82]

The fragmentation of the primitive image of the world through the development of rationality is a form of the disenchantment of the world. This provides a sound basis for understanding the theory of secularisation in Weber as a privatisation of religion, since the public impersonal rules of purposive rationality shift religious experience into the private realm of the individual, which is outside the limits of modern purposive rationality.

Weber is using here two conceptions of purposive rationality that he differentiates clearly only later in *Einleitung.*[83]

The first conception is that of the type of rationality associated with the theoretical mastery of the world, through ever more precise and abstract concepts resulting in a rationalisation of the magical image of the world. The second conception is that of the type of rationality associated with the practical mastery of the world as an object through a means-ends methodological rationality.[84] Together these constitute the two forms of modern purposive rationality. The theoretical mastery of the image of the world, through the work of the intellectuals, and the practical mastery of the world through such means-ends rationality, both are responsible for the disenchantment of the world and the secularisation of religion. This occurs through the internal rationalisation of the answers given to the theodicy question.

First, the rationalisation of the metaphysical image of God and the world answered the need for a meaningful conception of the cosmos. This was initially expressed in a magical form and later was transformed into an image of the world determined by purposive rationality, which left only the private irrational sphere open for the presence of religion.

Second, means-ends rationality made possible the practical mastery of the world. This is responsible for the disenchantment of the world and the secularisation of religion in two ways: through facilitating the transference of religious values from the irrational mystical realm into the rational secular realm; and through the transformation of the notion of vocation from referring to the other-worldly spiritual life of the religious orders to secular work in the world. Weber speaks specifically of this disenchantment when he describes the change that occurs when religious virtuosos combine into an ascetic sect. This occurrence requires two religious conditions: the contemplative or mystical path to salvation must not be seen to be of greater religious worth than the active ascetical path;[85] and the particular religion must abandon the sacramental or magical mediation of grace. Weber concludes that these conditions have been fully met only in Western ascetical Protestantism. This has allowed the necessary focus of religion to shift from nonrational action oriented away from the present world to rational action oriented towards the transformation of everyday life in this present world:

> It was totally different when the religiously qualified virtuosos combined together into an active ascetical sect to strive to shape life in the world according to the will of God. . . . Two aims were completely attained: the disenchantment of the world and the blockage of the path to salvation by a flight from the world. The path to salvation is turned away from a contemplative "flight from the world" and towards an active ascetic "work in the world." If one disregards the small rationalist sects, such as are found all over the world, this has been attained only in the great church and sect organisation of Occidental and ascetical Protestantism.[86]

Consequently, Weber understands Protestantism to have played both a theoretical and practical role in the rationalisation of the world.

At the theoretical level, ascetic Protestantism developed an answer to the question of theodicy based on Luther's notion of the *Deus absconditus* (the hidden God), which rejected metaphysical speculation about God as being the work of the Devil and which was further elaborated in Calvin's doctrine of predestination. This led to a rejection of the Catholic conception of the soteriological significance of human action, which derived from the Scholastic metaphysical view of the grace of God in Creation and issued in a new nonmetaphysical theology (*sola scriptura*) (Scripture alone) based on a *theologia crucis* (theology of the cross),[87] which saw salvation as totally out of the hands of humanity.

At the practical level, due to the changed understanding of works, the Catholic conception of the positive contribution to salvation by human action was further undermined and was eventually seen as no longer having any active contribution to make to salvation. Thus, since human thought could no longer penetrate the hidden mysteries of God, and human action could no longer actively contribute to salvation, the way was opened for both action and thought to be governed by purposive rationality and not according to metaphysical speculation, mystical contemplation, and the religious asceticism of the Catholic tradition. The gradual emergence of the age of Western secular modernity is thus also the emergence of a new theory of action.

Weber's *Einleitung* thus deepens the reflections of *PE* in terms of clarifying the dynamics of the rationalisation processes that lead to the new answers given to the theodicy question by the world religions. Weber outlines how ascetic Protestantism represented the most rationally developed form of these and thus, against both Marx and Nietzsche, illustrates the decisive and positive role played by religion in the evolution of modern Western society.

Confucianism and Taoism

For the purposes of studying the theory of secularisation in the works of Weber, the final chapter in his study of Confucianism and Taoism in *GARS* I is of importance.[88] In it, he compares Puritanism and the religions of China as two extreme forms of ethical rationality.[89] The concepts of rationality and rationalism now clearly become the key terms for Weber in his analysis of the dynamics of history. In his critical confrontation with the work of the ancient historian Eduard Meyer, he states that the purpose of comparing other forms of rationalism with the Western form, exemplified in Protestantism, is to bring out more clearly the specificity of European cultural development.[90] Weber now considers religions according to their stages of rationalisation:

> In assessing the stage of rationalisation embodied by any religion there are two particular criteria, which are, in addition, in many respects internally related to each other. There is first of all the extent to which a religion has freed itself from magic. Then secondly, the extent of the systematic uniformity brought forth by the religion to the relationship between God and world, and accordingly to the religion's own ethical relation towards the world.[91]

Thus, the level to which a religion can be considered to be rationally developed, for Weber, depends on its degree of disenchantment and its capacity for generating an inner-worldly ethic. Both of these criteria constitute central tenets of Weber's theory of secularisation. One might even say that the stage of rationalisation embodied by any religion, for Weber, is the degree to which it is secularised.[92] By evaluating Puritanism and Confucianism according to these two criteria, Weber illustrates how the secularisation of Christianity in the Western world allowed development of a rationality far more advanced than what developed in China. That is why, he asserts, China did not develop capitalism and the West did.[93]

In his study of the religions of China, Weber demonstrates that Protestantism clearly represents the most developed form of religion. In Protestantism, "magical means of salvation" are most systematically eliminated, and the ascetic spirit of Protestantism most effectively leads to an inner-worldly oriented ethic.[94] Let us consider the details of this argument, so we can see more clearly just how Weber understands the level of rationality of a religion to be bound up with the degree of its secularisation.

He first considers the degree of disenchantment that Confucianism and Protestantism have encouraged.[95] For him it is clear that Protestantism represents the highest level of such disenchantment. He even charges that Confucianism's "enchanted garden" vision of ethics was used as a magical means to attain salvation, but also to maintain Confucianism's ruling classes in power.[96] To illustrate this valuation, he observes that even on the death of a loved one, the strict Puritan refuses any form of religious ceremony to be associated with the corpse, so as not to fall back into the "superstition" of the "magical practices" of the sacraments.[97]

Weber then turns to the ethical relations that Confucianism and Protestantism encourage towards the world and to their respective views of the relation of God to the world. Here he also depends upon his assessment of how far they meet the criteria of disenchantment, because, as he states in the formulation of his two criteria, they are internally related to each other. This internal connection is clearly seen when Weber notes that the Confucian considered the world and the things of the world to be good, and that the role of each person was to adapt themselves to this state of affairs. Speaking of the basic conditions of the Confucian ethic, he describes these as an unconditional affirmation of and adaptation to the world, together with the assumption of a purely magical religiosity.[98] Such a vision of the world reduced to a minimum any tension that an individual felt about appropriate being and acting in this world. If all was basically fine, the individual felt no pressure to change the world for the better and could concentrate on perfecting his or her self by education and learning the way (*Tao*) of the world. In this system, wrongdoing was considered not to be a sin against God, but rather, a result of a lack of self-control, which could be corrected by education.[99] The life goals in such a system were health, wealth, a long life, and a good name after death. Crucially, these were this-worldly oriented goals, which further reduced the tension felt within the religious believer, since there was no developed sense of otherworldly goals towards which the believer should strive and no sense of impending judgement. This Confucian vision of the world, based on a form of pantheism and religious anthropology, contrasts sharply with the Protestant vision. For the Protestant, the world was essentially a *massa perditionis*, and the individual a sinner who was called to obey God's commandments and to avoid its evil ways. The believer was saved by faith in the transcendent God alone (*sola fide*).

Already, we learn something of great importance for understanding Weber's theory of secularisation. Without the contrast between the transcendent and the immanent realms, one crucial factor in the tension required to generate ascetical inner-worldly transformative action and an ethically oriented response to the theodicy question is absent.[100] It is clear that Weber uses this aspect to differentiate the various capacities of Protestantism and Confucianism to generate the psychological intensity required to propel forward the purposive rationality of both the theoretical and practical kind.[101]

He sees this conception of the relation to the world as significantly influenced by the presence or absence of a prophetic tradition:

> Genuine prophecy creates from within a way of life systematically oriented towards a single scale of values and in the light of such an orientation the world is regarded as raw material to be shaped

> in ethical terms according to the given norm. Confucianism was the reverse of this, being adaptation to things outside. The most well-adapted man, however, if he has rationalised his way of life only as far as is necessary for such adaptation, is not a systematic, homogeneous entity, but a combination of useful individual qualities.... However, the style which was imparted to the way of life by these factors had to remain characterised by essentially negative elements and was unable to produce the striving towards unity from within which we connect with the concept of "personality." Life remained a series of events, not a whole seen methodically in the light of a transcendent purpose.[102]

The ethical demands of the prophets recalled the Judeo-Christian tradition back to the covenantal agreement between God and humanity and reinforced the religious commitment to act ethically in the world. This clearly increased the psychological tension in the believer, because it exhorted him or her to play an active role in the transformation of the world as a religious duty. The lack of prophecy in Confucianism lessened this tension, since no ethical exhortation made demands on the behaviour of believers; moreover, encouraging the adaptation of the individual believer to the world meant that potentially positive aspects of change were replaced by negative elements of adaptation.

We have also gained insight into the relation between prophecy and the type of individual Weber characterises through the concept of "personality." The prophet is here described as a form of prototype for the modern agent of social change and as possessing the following characteristics: a way of life systematically oriented towards a single scale of values; an inner striving towards unity in one's action; and a whole life vision ordered methodically in the light of a transcendental purpose. These originally religious characteristics are those which need to be transposed into the secular domain and transformed into the basic characteristics of the secular *Berufsmensch* in order for Western purposive rationality to move beyond the aporias associated with the process of the disenchantment of the world. Only such secular prophets hold out hope, for Weber, of being able to transcend the limits of the "specialists without spirit" and "sensualists without heart" in a disenchanted world. The inability of

Confucianism to produce such individuals meant that Confucian life was not methodologically ordered according to transcendental values. The equivalent prototype in Confucianism, that is, the "gentleman," was concerned to save face with his contemporaries in this life and to devote himself to cultural development rather than to the "Philistine" tasks of business professionals:

> For Confucius. . . . all real economic vocational work was the philistine task of professionals. The specialist, however, could for the Confucian, never be elevated to a position of really positive honour, whatever his value in terms of social utility. The reason for this—and this was crucial—was that "the superior man" (the gentleman) was not a "tool," i.e., he was in the self-perfection of his adaptation to the world an ultimate goal in himself; he was not, however, a means to impersonal goals of any kind whatsoever. This central statement of the Confucian ethic was a rejection of specialisation of profession, of a modern professional bureaucracy and of vocational education; above all, however, it constituted a rejection of economic training in the pursuit of profit. In direct contrast to a maxim which was "idolatrous" in this way the question posed by Puritanism was the providing of proof [of salvation] in the special, impersonal purposes of the world and of vocational life.[103]

A further contribution, indeed for Weber "the great contribution," of the prophetic tradition of the ethical religions was to foster the spirit of a universal ethic of love by breaking down the kinship bond as a basis for solidarity. Thus, rather than one caring only for one's immediate family, living or dead, as in Confucianism, and being indebted to them as one's exclusive duty,[104] the prophetic tradition spoke of responsibility to care for all people, especially the poor and those marginalised in society. This spirit of universal solidarity was a key factor in the development of Western business practices because it provided a basis for trust that was no longer tied to the kinship group.[105]

This universal basis of trust gave a rational basis for business transactions. Now the secular transformation of vocation as "objective work at his calling" meant that traditional feudal and familial ties could be broken open to encompass a possible universal market based on the normative grounds of trust. Yet, it would be wrong to see only Western capitalism as able to generate wealth. Indeed, both Western and Chinese systems generated wealth; the difference lay in the attitude with which the religious systems regarded it. Protestantism saw wealth as an unintended by-product of a virtuous life.[106] Indeed, as Weber notes, John Wesley spoke of this as the "paradox of the rejection of the world and the virtuosity in earning,"[107] which is characteristic of the Protestant way of life. Confucianism, in contrast, saw the accumulation of wealth as a basis for maintaining one's cultural status and dignity and as a means towards self-perfection and education. However, both Protestantism and Confucianism saw the excessive accumulation of wealth for selfish interests as improper. It was the orientation towards supramundane things which provided the real difference between the wealth-generating capacities of the West and China. Speaking of the contrast between Puritanism and Confucianism, Weber notes:

> The contrast can teach that mere temperance and frugality in conjunction with an impulse for profit and a high consideration given to wealth did not by a long way constitute the "capitalist spirit" in the sense of the specifically modern, economic vocational spirit; nor could these circumstances give birth to such a capitalist spirit.... The second lesson, which we have to learn is that "rationalism" was contained in the spirit of both ethics. It was only the rational ethic of Puritanism, however, with its orientation toward supramundane things, which carried economic rationalism in this world through to its logical conclusion.... precisely because for the Puritan ethic, work in this world was no more than an expression of striving after a transcendental purpose.[108]

Thus, not only the relation of rationality to the world, but also the relation of rationality to the transcendent world (*Hinterwelt*) was central in determining the stage of rationalisation embodied in a religion.[109] The separation of the world from the transcendental world in the rational schema of the ethic of Protestantism—that is, the degree of secularisation—is a key factor in the development of the economic rationalism that Weber sees in Western capitalism. Such a separation allows for an intensification of ethical rationality that is not possible when one is dealing with a form of pantheism as in the religions of China. Furthermore, the Christian conception of a personal God, who spoke through the prophets, significantly influenced the development of the notion of "personality" in the West and provided an image of a lawgiver and judge who could hold individuals to account. All this provided Protestantism with a basis for a more highly developed ethical rationality and consequently, according to Weber's criteria, characterises Protestantism as a more rationally developed form of religion.

The *Zwischenbetrachtung* (Intermediate Reflection)

The text of the *Zwischenbetrachtung* that concludes volume one of *GARS* is the third edition of a text that Weber first included in the sociology of religion chapter of *WuG*.[110] The second edition of this text was published in the November 1915 edition of *Archive für Sozialwissenschaft und Sozialpolitik*.[111] Its position in the *GARS* is of interest to the content of the essay because it is placed just after the study on the religions of China and just before the study on the religions of India. As the religions of China represent ideal types of world accommodation for Weber, so the religions of India represent ideal types of world rejection. Thus the *Zwischenbetrachtung* represents a type of bridge between two basic attitudes of religions to the world: world accepting or accommodating; and world rejecting. As Wolfgang Schluchter notes, together with the *Einleitung*, the *Zwischenbetrachtung* represents an internal link and a complementary relationship between *GARS* and *WuG*.[112]

Weber begins the essay by explaining his purpose in interposing these reflections within his study of the world religions. He states that his reflections are based on ideal typical constructions of the basic features of the world religions, which should illustrate why certain conflicts between these religious ways of life and the ways of the world are possible. In this way, he hopes to clarify the motives of the ethics of the religious rejection of the world and, hence, in this sense, to understand their meaning better.[113] No less important is Weber's quest for a deeper understanding of the dynamics of Western rationalism, which is a continuing motif in his study of the world religions.[114]

Weber specifically deals with the internal rationalisation of religions, resulting from the need to answer the theodicy question, by considering the ethical response provided by Protestantism. He constructs an ideal typology of two basic life directions (*Lebensführungen*) that are possible for those religions, which reject the world in their quest for a sense of the certainty of salvation. As we have seen,[115] he considers asceticism to involve activity, and mysticism or contemplation to involve passivity.[116] Whilst Weber admits that, in being ideal constructs, these types may in reality combine, he nevertheless considers the internal logic of these types to be distinguishable according to the categories of activity and passivity:[117]

> In both cases [asceticism and mysticism] the contrast can actually disappear in practice and some combination of both forms of the quest for salvation may occur. But the contrast may continue to exist even under the veil of external similarity. For the true mystic the principle continues to hold: the creature must be silent that God may speak. He 'is' in the world and externally 'accommodates' to its orders, but only in order to gain a certainty of his state of grace in opposition to the world by resisting the temptation to take the ways of the world seriously.[118]

Weber's understanding of these basic categories of asceticism and mysticism[119] plays a major role in his categorisation of the world religions and, consequently, in his sociology of rationalism.[120] Consideration of these categories reveals a clear Protestant influence on Weber's argument about the dynamics of Western rationalism. It also reveals a model of action, reason, and society that is based on his reading of Protestant theological and philosophical sources.[121]

F. W. Graf illustrates the importance of this Protestant influence in his exploration of the professional relationship between Troeltsch and Weber. He notes how Weber took most of his understanding of the specialist theological literature from Troeltsch and even quotes many of the same passages from theological works as does Troeltsch. This is particularly evident in Weber's treatment of Albrecht Ritschl's writings in *PE*.[122] Given the closeness of this professional relationship, one can agree with Hubert Treiber's suggestion that both Troeltsch and Weber, in contradistinction to most other late nineteenth-century Protestant theologians, shared a common understanding of the typology of asceticism.[123] The key to understanding Weber's intention in formulating this typology of asceticism and mysticism is to recognise that he constructs various models of rational action through it.[124] His particular interest is to show that ascetic Protestantism helped to bring forth the inner-worldly ascetical action that is governed by purposive rational action and consequently is an important causal factor in the development of Western rationality.

Catholicism has tended to create a form of spiritual aristocracy in the Church by selecting out religious virtuosos who could aspire to the serious business of contemplation, leaving the affairs of the world to the masses. In this sense, inner-worldly activity was not to be seen as an important place for the encounter with God; such encounters occurred in the silence of the soul, far away from the cares and worries of daily life. At least this is the story Weber follows in his ideal-typical construction of asceticism and mysticism. Thus, in two important places, when speaking of the Western understanding of contemplation and action,[125] he refers to the story of Lk 10: 38–43 in which Jesus comes to visit his two friends Martha and Mary. Describing the basic differences between Western and Eastern types of salvation religion, he notes:

> Neither the mystical contemplativeness of St. Bernhard and his followers, nor Franciscan spirituality, nor the contemplative trends among the Baptists and the Jesuits, nor even the emotional suffusions of Zinzendorf were able to prevent either the community or the individual mystic from attributing superior importance to conduct and to the demonstration of grace through conduct, though this was conceptualised very differently in each case, ranging from pure asceticism to attenuated contemplation. It will be recalled that Meister Eckhart finally placed Martha above Mary, notwithstanding the pronouncements of Jesus.[126]

This Martha-Mary motif crystallises in many ways the objective of the *Zwischenbetrachtung*, which aims to form a bridge between the reflections on the inner-worldly asceticism of Protestantism and the works on the different types of mysticism on the one hand, and the inner-worldly mysticism of the religions of China and the other-worldly mysticism of the religions of India on the other hand. In interpreting the Martha-Mary motif through the mysticism of Meister Eckhart, Weber is trying to illustrate the point that the basic tendency of the West is towards ascetical action in the world, and the basic tendency of the East is towards retreat from the world in contemplation.[127] In thus quoting the example of Meister Eckhart, he supports his claim that inner-worldly mysticism tends to become asceticism and removes the possibility of seriously considering the evolution of reflection on the nature of contemplation in the so-called Counter or Catholic Reformation of the sixteenth century.[128] In this point, one might consider Weber in the line of thinking that stretches from St. Anselm of Canterbury to Luther, to Descartes and Kant and through Fichte, Feuerbach, and Nietzsche, and that posits that the metaphysical tradition of the possibility of thinking about God is at an end.[129] That is to say, the "object" of contemplation in the West, namely "God," cannot be encountered as an "object" of knowledge in the emerging philosophy of consciousness tradition. As one greatly influenced by this tradition, Weber quite naturally follows the displacement of this "object" into the sphere of action and not of contemplation.[130] Yet, as with his investigation into the relation between religion and the five cultural value spheres of economics, politics, aesthetics, the erotic, and the intellectual in the *Zwischenbetrachtung*, it is not clear at all where the place to encounter the "object" of Western religion, namely, "God," might be. Western religion, like its God, seems to have no place to call its own.[131]

The displacement of God from the interiority of the human soul to the exteriority of action is a form of critique of the metaphysical theological tradition, which removed religion from the cognitive sphere of truth and replaced it into the practical sphere of ethics. This was a central theme of the liberal Protestant tradition, to which Troeltsch belonged and off of which Weber fed, and it represented a natural progression of the Reformation's critique of the metaphysical tradition of Catholicism. However, on giving up the cognitive claim to truth, religion—particularly from Kant onwards, would be forced to try and occupy the place of the normative grounding of practical reason,[132] which, as Weber seeks to illustrate in *Zwischenbetrachtung*, no longer has any place in the internal logic of the cultural value spheres of economics and politics for either ethics or religion. As with ethics, religion is confined to the private sphere of personal choice.

Weber sees the professional vocational ethic of Calvinism as able to cope with the ethical meaninglessness of the world in a way that is not possible for the contemplative mystic who seeks a meaning in the world. He expresses the practical implications of the renunciation of the metaphysical tradition of mystical contemplation:

> The contrast between both the ascetic and mystical modes of behaviour is clearest when the full implications of world-rejection and world-flight are not drawn. The ascetic, when he wishes to act within the world, that is, to practice inner-worldly asceticism, must become afflicted with a sort of happy closure of mind regarding any question about the meaning of the world, for he must not worry about such questions. Hence, it is no accident that inner-worldly asceticism reached its most consistent development on the foundation of the Calvinist God's absolute inexplicability, utter remoteness from every human criterion, and unsearchableness as to his motives. Thus, the inner-worldly ascetic is the recognised "man of vocation," who neither inquires about nor finds it necessary to inquire about the meaning of his actual practice of a vocation within the world, the total framework of which is not his responsibility but his God's. For him it suffices that through his rational actions in this world he is personally executing the will of God, which is unsearchable in its ultimate significance.[133]

Weber sees the Calvinist inner-worldly asceticism as able to cope with the ethical meaninglessness of the world because, for the Calvinist, the world is ethically meaningless; only God can know its meaning, and human action itself does not constitute any part of one's salvation, but rather, displays only a visible sign of it. For the Calvinist, meaning is bracketed out in the form of an existential *epoché*. The secularisation of the notion of religious calling in the concept of "personality" is the end result of the process of the disenchantment of the Western world, which has emptied out the religious significance of asceticism and converted it into the nineteenth-century bourgeois preoccupation with both work and education.[134] The paradox of this Protestant theory of modernity is that religion ends up having nothing to say to either work or education. The world has come of age, and so has its "personality."

After considering the typologies of asceticism and mysticism, Weber moves on to investigate the tensions that exist between religion and the world in terms of a class of rationalities based on the religious rejections of the world. He analyses objectively possible value conflicts given the religious rationalisation of rejecting the world as a *massa perditionis*.[135]

Religion and the Rationalisation of the Cultural Value Spheres

Weber chooses to focus on one aspect of world-rejecting cultural religions or religions of salvation as a cause of tension with the cultural values spheres of the world: namely, the ethic of universal brotherhood. He notes that in religions of salvation, the communities expand the parameters of solidarity beyond that of the family. In this sense, there is an initial depersonalisation of ethics in terms of a universal ethic of brotherly love. As the cultural value sphere of economics develops, it rationalises according to its own inner logic as a "functional organisation oriented to money prices which originate in the interest struggles of men in the market."[136] So, with the rationalisation of the economy there has also occurred a form of depersonalisation of social relations. However, whilst the religions of salvation have depersonalised their religious ethic in terms of an expansion of solidarity, something that Weber calls *acosmism*, the economic sphere of capitalism has impersonalised its social relations by a shrinking of solidarity in pursuit of profit. It has replaced the traditional forms of social solidarity associated with the master-slave ethics of feudal societies by the functional regulation of interest struggles mediated through money.[137] In this sense, an initial similarity based on the common depersonalisation of social ethics with increasing rationalisation turns into a significant difference and results in a major tension between the sphere of economics and the religions of salvation. Weber notes the Catholic *Deo placere non potest* as the characteristic *external* attitude of the virtuosos of the salvation religions to the profit economy of capitalism. As a result, both ascetical and mystical traditions of salvation religions have been in tension with the emergence of the economic sphere.

However, Weber notes two rational *internal* ways developed by virtuosos of religion, two directions of the religious rejection of the world that have consistently overcome the tension between religion and the economic world. The first is the ascetical attitude of the Puritan ethic of vocation, and the second is the benevolent attitude of mysticism. In the Puritan ethic of vocation, the rules of the economic sphere are accepted as a necessary evil, and the universal ethic of brotherhood is in effect renounced as, like salvation, being beyond the capacity of man. The mystic, in contrast, develops an attitude of benevolence in terms of an *acosmism* of love.[138] In other words, the mystic accepts that all are to be loved as brothers and sisters regardless of the personal consequences. The end result of the relation between religion and the world in the economic sphere is thus either that religion gives up its claim to impose its rational ethic of brotherly love, as in the case of the Puritan ethic of vocation, or it sacrifices itself on the altar of interest struggles in the market. In both cases, however, the rational religious values of universal brotherly love are no longer welcome in the economic sphere. The differentiation of religious ethics from the cultural value sphere of the economy, as a result of this internal and external religious intensification of the rejection of the world, would thus open the way for money prices to replace the ethical regulation of economic life. Consequently, in Weber's analysis, this would lead to a secularisation of the economic sphere; that is, the elimination of the religious control of economic life.[139]

Weber next considers the relation between religion and the political sphere. Once again he sees the brotherly ethic of salvation as the point of conflict between them.[140] As in his description of the relation between religion and the economic sphere, however, his narrative first recalls an era of pre-differentiation. In this era, the clash of the local gods decided the fate of the neighbouring polities. Only with the development of the universal religions of salvation does Weber see the beginning of the differentiation of politics from religion. In these universal religions, God was the God of the whole world and not simply of an individual polity; moreover, when this God was the God of love, politics and religion emerged as separate domains, the one dealing with particular jurisdiction and the other dealing with universal jurisdiction. The clash of these jurisdictions, for Weber, is a consequence of the mutually exclusive nature of their internal logics. In the case of the political sphere, the rationalisation of the polity into a bureaucratic state governing a body of people meant that the traditional substantive morality of the patriarchal past was both depersonalised and formalised according to purposive rationality.[141] The objective of this rationality was to maintain power, and the State consequently claimed for itself a monopoly on the legitimate use of force or violence (*Gewaltsamkeit*) for that same objective. Thus the means-ends rationality of the bureaucratic state calculated the amount of force or violence required to maintain itself in power. This clearly clashed with the ethic of the Sermon on the Mount, which proclaimed the rationality of brotherly love. Weber sees the consequence of the rationalisation of religion and the political sphere as the exclusion of substantive religious ethics from the formal domain of politics. However, for Weber, politics excludes religion from its sphere and can even, unlike the economic sphere, come into competition with religious ethics in two central areas. This happens because the state monopoly on violence inevitably leads to war between polities.

The first area of competition is over community. As a polity engages in war, feelings of community generated by such bellicose activities emerge between those fighting and all those who are in support. Those fighting tend to gather in a sacrificial community and become heroes for the rest of the people. This generates a sense of community in a society, which is analogous to the sacrificial communities of religious virtuosos. The ethic of brotherhood now has two sources: one religious and the other political.

The second area of competition is over the meaning of death. In war, a combatant gains a sacred meaning in death because he or she may die for his or her country. This gives a rational meaning to death in strong competition to the theodicy of death provided by the religions of salvation. It even overlaps with the religious meaning associated with martyrdom. Dying for the cause can thus be either religiously or politically motivated. In this sense, the inner logic of the rationalisation of the political sphere actually competes with the inner rationalisation of religions to give an answer to the theodicy question.[142] From a religious point of view, this political source of community seems to be simply a product of the brutality of the struggle and the consecration of the meaning of death in the glorification of fratricide; but the brotherliness generated in war and in death is in strong competition with the religious ethics of brotherhood.[143]

As in the economic sphere, Weber sees only two rationally consistent solutions to these tensions: the inner-worldly asceticism of Puritanism and mysticism.[144] For Weber, Puritanism holds that the commandments of God should be imposed on the ways of the world, that is to say, through violence. The obligation of brotherliness can be renounced in the interests of implementing the cause of God. In this sense, Puritanism resolves the tension by accepting the conditions of secularisation as a means of implementing the laws of God. The other rationally consistent way to resolve the tension between an ethic of brotherliness and the strategic logic of the political sphere is mysticism. Here the institutionally mediated notion of the universalism of grace provides grounds for rejecting the conflictual logic of the political sphere. The mystic thus adopts an antipolitical attitude, withdrawing from political action and leaving the political sphere to run itself. These two options represent the ideal types of world rejection: instrumental use of the world for a religious objective, and flight from the world into contemplation. In both forms of religious ethics the world has no intrinsic meaning.

Weber notes that religious institutions in practice, however, make compromises with the world in order to safeguard their own interests. This results in a number of interesting principles and types. The first form of compromise can be found in Calvinism and to some extent in Islam. Here the notion of just and unjust wars mediates the legitimate compromise with the ways of the political sphere. When the just war is understood as a means of implementing the laws of God, then the Calvinist accepts such a conflict as a holy war and the political strategy as ethically justified.[145] The second form of compromise can be found in Luther's understanding of the separation of the spiritual and secular jurisdiction in his Two Kingdoms doctrine.[146] Even though Lutheranism rejected violence from a religious perspective as a worldly form of pragmatism, it accepted the legitimacy of the State in matters of secular jurisdiction and also allowed its members to be conscripted into war on the basis of the ethical autonomy of the secular authority.

To these two Protestant routes of compromise with the secular political sphere, Weber adds the route of organic social ethics. This, in contrast to the two Protestant routes, considers the world, at least partially, as religiously meaningful.[147] The point of departure for organic social ethics is the inequality of religious charisma. Unhappy with the notion of virtuosos, this ethic attempts to synthesise religious and secular inequalities through a functional differentiation of services that individuals and groups are to perform in a meaningful world. This answer to the theodicy question is similar to that provided by the Indian doctrine of karma.

Weber concludes his reflections on the political sphere by noting the dilemmas that arise from this separation of political action from the ethic of brotherliness. Here he essentially pre-empts his reflections in *Politik*, when he describes the dilemmas politics encounters in attempting to provide its own justification for political action. Either the intention of the act, that is, the ethics of conviction, or the consequences of the act, that is, the ethics of responsibility, define success in political terms. The problem arises, of course, when the ethics of the salvation religions are eliminated. Then the moral resources to decide which course to take are attenuated. After the secularisation of the political sphere, politics can only be a vocation.[148]

Next Weber turns to the aesthetic sphere.[149] He considers this to be a nonrational or even an irrational domain. Once again he follows the same argumentative structure that he employed in his analysis of the other cultural value spheres. That is, he begins by noticing the original similarity of religion and art, then explains how, through the process of rationalisation, art, and the ethic of brotherliness of religion have separated and come into competition and conflict. He concludes by outlining possible and actual strategies to overcome these conflicts and reduce the tension between religion and art.

Magical religions have always used some form of art, whether it be music, dance, or decoration. The rationalisation of both the aesthetic sphere and religion has led to tensions, because the aesthetic sphere tends to focus on form and religion tends to focus on meaning. Salvation religions have tended to devalue form as something merely contingent on, and even distracting from, the true meaning, which lies deeper. However, as intellectualism has developed, art has become a form of inner-worldly salvation, a shelter and refuge from the theoretical and practical rationalism of everyday life. This redemptive function of the aesthetic sphere begins to compete with the redemptive function of the salvation religions. Moreover, the retreat of the ethic of responsibility, as a result of the rationalisation of the cultural value spheres that has led to the attenuation of moral sources of practical justification, has facilitated the transformation of the moral judgements of the ethic of conviction into aesthetic judgements of taste. The social consequence of this is, of course, individualism, which replaces the universal validity of ethical norms with the subjective norm of taste. Ethical norms transcend the individual by providing a moral framework for common life. Even when individuals reject one another's motivations for action, they can still participate together in social life because the rules of engagement, the ethical norms, provide a basis for universal validity. However, when aesthetic judgements replace moral judgements, conversation about matters of taste replaces discussion about universal moral validity. This undermines the normative basis of common life. The social ethic of brotherliness conflicts with the individualistic ethic of the aesthetic sphere. To one, the individualistic ethic of the aesthetic sphere seems like a form of un-brotherliness; to the other, the social ethic of brotherliness seems like coercion against creativity.

Whilst the virtuoso ethics of both mystical and ascetical salvation religions have rejected the logic of the aesthetic sphere in principle, the historical reality of religions has entered into varied alliances with the aesthetic sphere in order to attract the masses. Thus, the pretension to universality of the salvation religions, itself a consequence of their internal rationalisation, has required frequent compromise with the aesthetic sphere in order to provide emotional incentives to the masses to follow their creed. Weber sees this as of great significance for the intellectual groups. Because art seems able to elicit quasi-religious feelings without requiring a sacrifice of the intellect, intellectual groups can find one coherent route into the salvation religions through art.[150]

In his reflections on the erotic sphere, Weber notes that religion comes into profound tension with the greatest irrational force of life.[151] The use of orgiastic rituals in magical religions represents an initial intimacy between religion and the erotic. Separation of religion from the erotic sphere occurs, for Weber, as a consequence of the rationalisation of these two domains. As human society emerged from the agricultural way of life, in which the human was in close contact with nature and followed its cycles, culture took on a much more important role. This enrichment of culture through the increase of intellectual knowledge and social experience rationalises areas of life and carries forward the process of the disenchantment of the world. In this context, eroticism becomes culturally important as the consciousness of the irrational core of life. In a certain sense, eroticism begins to play the role of the sacred, as the "other" of reason, which now takes the secular form of erotic sexuality. Weber charts the evolution of this replacement in medieval vassals and in salon culture, and he notes how it eventually clashes with the religious ethic embodied in the vocational specialists.

These specialists, who lead a disciplined professional life, have lost all contact with nature, and their sexual life has become rationalised in the form of monogamous marriage. Weber suggests that, subject to the tension between a rationalised everyday life and the erotic sphere, an extramarital sexual life is the only place in which the vocational specialist could reconnect with the natural rhythms of life and find the irrational source of the rational world. The erotic sphere here acts as the secular vestige of the original brutality of relationships, and clearly conflicts with the religious ethic of brotherliness, with its universal love and consensual marriage.[152] The erotic sphere also preserves a moment of inner-worldly transcendence through the "boundless giving of oneself" to the other in an irrational logic that breaks out of the cycle of *do ut des*.[153]

The erotic sphere has grounds to compete with the religions of salvation as routes to salvation. Moreover, psychological similarities between religious experience and erotic experience signal the possibility of the erotic substituting for the religious in a rationalised world. Weber notes that only the linkage of marriage with ethical responsibility for one another, that is extra-erotic sources, confers an inner-worldly dignity to marriage. Both ascetical and mystical paths of salvation tend to reject the erotic and can at best resolve the tension with the erotic sphere in terms of rationally regulated marriage.

In Weber's analysis of the relationship between the erotic sphere and the rational ethic of the salvation religions, eroticism plays a role similar to aestheticism. Both act as an emotional release from the rational tendencies of modern society. As religion becomes more methodically controlled through its own internal rationalisation, its own erotic dimension becomes equally rationalised in marriage. This displaces the erotic from the domain of the religious ethic, while preserving its own irrational life force in the promiscuous realm of extramarital sexuality. Secularisation of the erotic sphere is thus the transformation of the sober sexual naturalism of the peasant into the sublimated conscious cultural enjoyment of erotic irrationalism in the otherwise rationalised life of the vocational professional.[154]

The final cultural sphere that Weber considers is the intellectual sphere.[155] He considers the tension between religion and this sphere to be the greatest and the most principled, because the characteristic view of religion, namely, that the world is a meaningful cosmos, is systematically eroded in the process of the disenchantment of the world.

> The tension between religion and intellectual knowledge definitely comes to the fore wherever rational, empirical knowledge has consistently worked through to the disenchantment of the world and its transformation into a causal mechanism. For then science encounters claims of the ethical postulate that the world is a God-ordained, and hence somehow *meaningfully* and ethically oriented, cosmos. In principle, the empirical as well as the mathematically oriented view of the world develops refutations of every intellectual approach, which in any case asks for a "meaning" of inner-worldly occurrences. Every increase of rationalism in empirical science increasingly pushes religion from the rational into the irrational realm; but only today does religion become *the* irrational or anti-rational supra-human power.[156]

The meaningful and ethical unity of the world found in the traditional preindustrial era of Western civilisation is clearly the casualty of this process of the disenchantment of the world. Religion, for Weber, is the carrier of the meaningful and ethically oriented nature of the cosmos, so it is clear that during the process of the disenchantment of the world, religion will be shifted into the irrational realm as the questions of meaning and ethics become bracketed out by the intellectual sphere. Yet, internal rationalisation in the religious domain results in the dogmatic codification of religion and, as a result, rational apologetics of these dogmas become institutionalised through the priestly and prophetic social carriers. Weber sees this as a religious equivalent of bureaucratisation in the political sphere. Nevertheless, the fundamental difference between the intellectual sphere and religion remains: religion is forced at some point to sacrifice its own intellect in order to believe, "*credo non quod, sed quia absurdum.*"[157]

This differentiation between religion and the intellectual sphere results in religion's claim to occupy a separate sphere, distinct from the other cultural spheres.[158] Moreover, this claim is quasi-epistemological, for Weber, because religion claims that its way of looking at the world finds the meaning of the world and the meaning of human existence. This religious knowledge is neither descriptive nor normative, but illuminative; it thus constitutes a principled difference between the domain of religion and the cultural value spheres:

> Redemptory religion defends itself against the attack of self-sufficient intellect. It does so, of course, in the most principled fashion, by raising the claim that religious knowledge moves in a different sphere and that the nature and meaning of religious knowledge is entirely different from the accomplishments of the intellect. Religion claims to offer an ultimate stand towards the world by virtue of a direct grasp of the world's "meaning." It does not claim to offer intellectual knowledge of what is or should be.[159]

Thus for Weber, the irrationality of the world, which makes the question of meaning so important, finds its intellectual formulation in the theodicy question. Religions provide differing answers to this question, depending on their own principles. So the human need for life to make sense corresponds to the religious need for salvation. However, whilst these needs may correspond, their coexistence results in a dialectical logic that tends to oppose the autonomous claims of each sphere. Increasing rationalisation of the religious sphere, in its most developed form of Protestantism, tends to devalue the world as in itself meaningless. Increasing rationalisation of the intellectual sphere, that is, human culture in its widest sense, tends to devalue the possibility of an other-worldly solution to the world as in itself irrational, as beyond the empirically verifiable truth claims of science.

The history of this mutual suspicion between religion and human culture is a long one.[160] It is interesting to note that Weber follows the biblical and Augustinian teaching that the irrational basis of human culture is located in sin. Thus, some aspects of the Christian tradition invest culture as a product of this sinful temporal realm, with a sense of shame and guilt. The maintenance of the cultural spheres by the brutal force of the economic basis, which excludes *a priori* the notion of brotherly love, further intensifies the shame and guilt. The reasons for the separation of the ethical and natural visions of the cosmos become clear. But this separation, as Weber notes, increasingly exposes cultural knowledge of the intellectual sphere to its own meaninglessness. In the face of death, the search for inner-worldly perfection seems futile. Moreover, the specialisation of intellectual knowledge results in a fragmentation of human culture, as intellectuals become vocational specialists about less and less. The guilt of Cain becomes the lot of the earthly city, the punishment for this guilt: condemnation to meaninglessness. Both the theoretical reason of purposive rationality and the practical reason of religious ethics drive this process of the disenchantment of the world:

> The need for "salvation" responds to this devaluation by becoming more otherworldly, more alienated from all structural forms of life, and, in exact parallel, by confining itself to the specific religious essence. This reaction is the stronger the more systematic the thinking about the "meaning" of the universe becomes, the more the external organisation of the world is rationalised, and the more the conscious experience of the world's irrational content is sublimated. And not only theoretical thought, disenchanting the world, led to this course, but also the very attempt of religious ethics practically and ethically to rationalise the world.[161]

The *Zwischenbetrachtung* describes the effects of this process of rationalisation on the cultural value spheres as a journey towards disenchantment. This occurs through the elimination of the religious ethic of brotherliness from the cultural value spheres, and thus describes the emergence of cultural autonomy as a theory of secularisation. As Dirk Kaesler suggests, Weber's theory of Protestantism, and thus his theory of secularisation, is inseparable from a theory of rationalisation, a theory of bureaucratisation, and a theory of capitalism.[162] We can understand how interwoven these three dimensions are in Weber's work when we are conscious of his multicausal framework of social analysis. Otherwise, we risk becoming stuck on the question of the chicken and the egg.

According to Weber, when the original magical-religious traces of knowledge were divorced from the developed rationalised spheres of culture, the question of meaning emerged as the most pressing issue for human culture. The three most rational responses to this question—the metaphysical route of the Indian religions, the ontological route of dualism in Zoroastrianism, and the ethical route of Protestantism—represent the three types of theodicy that tried to answer this question.

The Religion of India

Weber organises his study of the religions of India similar to the way he organised his study of the religions of China. He first looks at the nature of Hindu social structure, focussing particularly on the caste system as the key to understanding Indian society.[163] The caste system of India played a role equivalent to that played by the kinship group and bureaucracy in China. It structured Indian society according to its own principles and controlled all aspects of social life. Weber next turns to the role of intellectuals in the religions of India, considering the orthodox teachings of Hinduism and the heterodox teachings of Jainism and ancient Buddhism. After considering the influence of popular religiosity on the major religions of India, he concludes by assessing the impact of Buddhism and Hinduism on the secular ethic of Indian society.[164]

For the purpose of considering Weber's sociology of religion as a secularisation theory, his final chapter on the religions of India will suffice. Here he attempts to pull together his conclusions by comparing India to the West. Weber's main intentions are to analyse why Western-style capitalism did not develop in India, and to explore the role that the religions of India played in this.[165]

In his final chapter on the religions of India, Weber outlines the general characteristics of the Asiatic religions that are relevant for his study of *WEWR*.[166] His study of the world religions is organised around different types of response to the theodicy question; the Indian response represents the metaphysical solution:

> The third form of theodicy, which we are going to consider, was peculiar to the religiosity of *Indian* intellectuals. It stands out by

> virtue of its consistency as well as by its extraordinary metaphysical achievement: It unites virtuoso-like self-redemption by man's own effort with universal accessibility of salvation, the strictest rejection of the world with organic social ethics, and contemplation as the paramount path to salvation with an inner-worldly ethic.[167]

Described thus, the religious worldview of the Indian intellectuals could promote the spirit of capitalism. An outline of Weber's judgement to the contrary will clarify his understanding of the link between economic ethics and world religions, and, thus, of the connection between religion and social change in his own theory of secularisation.

Weber begins by remarking that Asian models of soteriology are characterised by exemplary promises that are typically embodied in the monastic life, rather than by ethical promises embodied in the dutiful action of the laity.[168] The path to salvation required the follower to seek a special form of knowledge, philosophical or mystical knowledge, which reveals the significance of the world and of life. And this has had consequences for the type of rationality and the preferred mode of action in India.

First, mystical knowledge, because of its special nature, has tended to promote a form of *redemption aristocracy*, since not everyone has the charisma of knowing the secrets of life and the world. Second, such knowledge assumes an asocial and apolitical character, since the energy required to obtain such knowledge goes into the intensive training of the body and the mind, not into social and political action. Third, because such knowledge lies hidden to the reasoning of the world, it cannot ultimately be rationally communicated in the language of this world. Last, since such knowledge is not bound by the limits of space and time, it leads the possessor into a realm beyond this world and beyond earthly rationality.

However, this experience of mystical enlightenment led to partially rational doctrines about the world as expressed in the teachings of *samsara* and *karma*.[169] Because these teachings gave a causal explanation for suffering, they salvaged a degree of rationality for the world. Yet, the doctrine of *karma* made nonsense of the notion of eternal damnation, thereby eliminating the effects of a Western-style soteriology on inner-worldly action that Weber had outlined in *PE*. The relativisation of inner-worldly action facilitated flight from the world, and such a knowledge-based soteriology served the needs of the literary intellectual strata that were the main carriers of Indian religion.[170] The Indian middle classes played a much less important role than their Western counterparts, since Asian soteriology offered no basis for a rational methodology of inner-worldly life conduct that supported the role of the bourgeoisie. Moreover, the mystical soteriology of the Indian religions led to a form of worship of the holy man or guru, who possessed and could lead others into the specialised knowledge of Nirvana. Weber considers their magical power to be a form of charismatic power that, together with the power of the family and magical practices, determined the course of the Asiatic social order. He describes the difference between the Western notion of a miracle and the Asian notion of a spell as paradigmatic for the differences in their modes of religious rationality:

> The meaning of the "miracle" is always seen as an act of some rational world-guidance, of a divine conferring of grace, and tends to be more interiorly motivated than the "spell" whose meaning is that the whole world is filled with irrationally effective magical powers. These magical powers are stored up in charismatically qualified, but according to their freely arbitrary acting essence, men or supermen, through their ascetical or contemplative achievements.[171]

Thus, the meaning of the miracle is connected to some rational event, guiding the world through an inner motivation, typified by Weber's notion of the "personality." It is not simply a magical act based on the cultivation of the magic garden in which the guru grows to maturity. The spell of the Asiatic religions, however, became the way to master this magic garden of daily life. The consequences of these alternative modes of religious rationality would have significant influence on the development of a practical ethics that could engage in rational conduct in the world:

> A rational practical ethic and life methodology did not emerge from this magical garden to transform all life within the "world." Certainly

> the opposition of the sacred and the secular appeared—that opposition, which in the West historically conditioned the systematic unification of life conduct, describable in the usual manner as "ethical personality." But the opposition in Asia was by no means between an ethical God and the power of "sin," the radical evil, which may be overcome through active life conduct. Rather, the aim was to achieve a state of ecstatic Godly possession through orgiastic means, in contrast to everyday life, in which God was not felt as a living power. Also, it involved an accentuation of the power of irrationality, which the rationalisation of inner-worldly life conduct precisely restricted. Or the aim was the achievement of apathetic-ecstatic Godly possession of gnosis in opposition to everyday life as the abode of transient and meaningless drives. This, too, represents an orientation that is both extra-worldly and passive, and thereby from the standpoint of inner-worldly ethics it is irrational and mystical, leading away from rational conduct in the world.[172]

Moreover, even where an inner-worldly ethic occurred, as in the Hindu inner-worldly caste ethic, the psychological conditions required to translate this into a systematic control of practical behaviour were missing:

> And a consistent and psychologically workable systematisation was lacking. . . . It was lacking in precisely that which was decisive for the economics of the Occident: the refraction and rational immersion of the drive character of economic striving and its accompaniments in a system of rational, inner-worldly ethic of behaviour, as in the "inner-worldly asceticism" of Protestantism in the West.[173]

In his analysis of the religion of India, Weber uses the basic categories that he developed in his investigation of the West. Indian religions represent the ideal type of religions of contemplation, the polar opposite of the ideal type of Protestantism as the religion of inner-worldly asceticism. Weber's clear understanding of the significance of contemplation or mysticism is of particular interest. The opposition between contemplation and action, between mysticism and asceticism, structures his whole analysis of rationality, social action, and the progress of modernity. Weber sets the ideal type of contemplation within a general methodological narrative of causal historical sociology.[174] It functions as a component in his sociology, which attempts to account for patterns of historical development across cultures. He identifies two sociologically significant historical explanations for the closing off of the Asian cultures to the development of capitalism.

In the case of the Chinese society, he maintains this closing off is rooted in the multilayered causal influences of both the kinship structure and the centrally controlled bureaucratic Chinese administration. In the case of Indian society it is rooted in the multilayered causal influences of the caste system. Within the caste system, contemplation functions as a measure of and legitimation for a redemption aristocracy. Traditional societies are characteristically constituted by various forms of aristocracy, which often use religious resources for their own legitimation. The Indian model, which placed such a high premium on contemplation, closed off Indian society to capitalist development because the inner-worldly rationality that capitalism requires could not gain a socially significant foothold. Once again, Weber's interpretation of the Martha and Mary passage, in which Martha represents action and Mary contemplation, is significant. Since contemplation is seen as separate from action, as being essentially passive, then clearly the religions of India, in favouring contemplation as the way of salvation, could not support a social rationalisation based on inner-worldly action.

Weber's contemplation and action dichotomy is another expression of his secularisation theory. The translation of religious energies from contemplation into action is in itself a form of secularisation: it shifts the focus from the otherworldly to the inner-worldly. In such a change of emphasis, the corresponding models of rationality equally shift. Purposive rationality of both a theoretical and a practical kind is, for Weber, clearly blocked by the contemplative otherworldly rationality of the religions of India and, for that matter, of Catholicism. His view of contemplation as essentially otherworldly is a fairly one-sided reading of the varied world religious traditions, a certain form of cultural Protestantism. This is not to suggest that Weber was an active religious believer, adhering to the tenets of the Protestant faith; rather, it is to suggest that the general framework, the *Weltanschauung* in which he operated, was guided by the Protestant conception of the separation of grace from nature. This total separation meant that contemplation had to be otherworldly. What was there to contemplate in this world except the fact that all was sin?

In order to appreciate the impact of this Protestant conception of reality, it is important to remember the first of Luther's 95 Theses: "As our Lord and Master Jesus Christ says: 'Do penance' etc. (Mt 4:17). That is to say, the whole of the life of the believer should be one of penance."[175] In other words, life in this world was basically one of sin—the opposite of grace—and hence all of life needed to be a response of penance.[176] Grace no longer permeated nature—nature was cut off from grace; the unbridgeable gap between heaven and earth expressed in Luther's notion of the *Deus absconditus* structured this separation. The absence of grace from nature makes a positive understanding of contemplation impossible. The heart and mind can no longer be raised to God, because God is no longer to be found. This is the Protestant *Weltanschauung* that makes sense of Weber's own understanding of contemplation. It provides grounds for situating Weber's own interpretation of modernity within a Protestant framework, and thus makes problematic the assumption of confessional neutrality or, at least, irrelevance in his own social theory.

Weber's study of the religions of India reveals his understanding of contemplation to be rather unmusical. He does not understand that the majority of world religions do not place contemplation and action in opposition but that they rather form an intrinsic unity that is expressed as "contemplation in action" in various religious traditions—Catholicism, some contemporary Protestant traditions, (e.g., Anglicanism), Judaism, Taoism, Buddhism, Hinduism, and Islam. Perhaps Weber sets up his oppositional typology of contemplation versus action because of his own lack of musical ability in religious matters, but perhaps also because of the specific confessional metanarrative that informs his general sociology of religion.[177] His study of the religions of India illustrates the implications of this for his methodological and empirical levels of analysis. This is not to suggest that it invalidates his research. Rather, it merely positions his general sociology within a particular

Protestant architecture, a framework that has its strengths and weaknesses, like all metanarratives.[178]

Ancient Judaism

Max Weber's monumental work on ancient Judaism, *Das antike Judentum (AJ)*, was written and amended during the last period of his life between 1917 and 1920.[179] It was also most probably influenced, like his *PE*, by Werner Sombart's two-volume study of the origin of capitalism, first published in 1902. In this work, Sombart had argued that the Jews living in Western Europe had fostered the capitalist money-making spirit during the High Middle Ages.[180] This made Protestantism more a result than a cause of capitalism, and it probably stimulated Weber to propose his alternative genesis of modern capitalism in *PE*.[181] However, as Schluchter argues, Weber returned to study ancient Judaism in order to show that the origins of Western rationalisation lay in the religious and cultural developments of ancient Israel and of the Near East.[182] He distinguishes between four stages in the development of ancient Judaism: the period of political confederacy, the period of the kingdom, the period of transition from primitive to universal religion, and finally the post-exilic period.[183] He explains that the Jews, especially the pious poor, possessed the character of resentment, based on their exclusion from political society and categorisation as a pariah community.[184]

Weber's version of the origins of Western rationality in *AJ* has recently been criticised by the Egyptologist Jan Assman in his study of political theology in ancient Egypt, Israel, and Europe.[185] Reversing the arguments of Carl Schmitt, Assman argues that the understanding of modern politics as a secularisation of theological concepts was predated by a time in which politics gave birth to theology. He argues that the biblical narration of the Exodus of the Israelites out of slavery in Egypt was quite understandably heavily influenced by an anti-Egyptian ideology. Rather than lacking an ethical and rational basis of life, ancient Egypt shared many of the characteristics which have been transmitted to Western culture in the biblical writings of the Old Testament. Such questions as concern for justice were expressions of a belief in the embodiment of divine justice in the sovereignty of the Pharaohs, the kings of Egypt. The Israelites theologised their original experience of political alienation in Egypt, according to Assmann, and in this sense politics gave birth to Israelite theology, through a process he calls theologisation. Thus, Assmann claims that the process of secularisation is historically opposed by a movement begun in ancient Israel and representing a form of sacralisation of the political. Rather than seeing the disenchantment of the world as the vector of modern rationality, as Weber suggests, Assmann sees both secularisation and sacralisation governing the force field of Western rationality. Nevertheless, Assmann sees ancient Judaism as an Archimedian point in the evolution of Western rationality and religion. He suggests that ancient Judaism is positioned at the origin of what he calls "secondary religion," which consciously distances itself from "primary religion" and, indeed, begins the process of separating the sacred from the profane or secular sphere.[186]

Weber also considers ancient Judaism to be positioned at the origin of the Western process of secularisation and rationalisation. Even though the word "disenchantment" (*Entzauberung*) does not appear even once in the whole of his study, it is clear that this process is central to Weber's understanding of the religion and society of ancient Israel.[187] Bendix summarises Weber's key intuition into the importance of ancient Judaism in the development of Western rationalism:

> Free of magic and esoteric speculation, devoted to the study of law, vigilant in the effort to do "what was right in the eyes of the Lord" in the hope of a better future, the prophets established a religion of faith that subjected man's daily life to the imperatives of a divinely ordained moral law. In this way ancient Judaism helped create the moral rationalism of Western civilization.[188]

Thus in ancient Judaism, Weber sees a process that would eventually reach its fulfilment in Calvinism, the Baptist sects, the Mennonites, and the Quakers: that is to say, in the puritanical groups of Protestantism.[189] Weber, in a way that already hints at the dialectical process of secularisation and sacralisation, sees the origins of this process to lie in a number of key developments which took place in ancient Judaism.

First is the development of a charismatic prophetic elite in the pre-exilic period from Amos to Jeremiah.[190] These were essentially teaching prophets who received a personal vocation from God, rather than an institutional office as in the priesthood, to teach the Israelites the laws and ways of God. This prophetic movement represents a rationalisation of the religious ethic based on the moral principles of Yahweh. Second is the emergence of Levitical Torah teachers in the pre-exilic period. These were a teaching tribe of priests who studied and transmitted the Jewish law, or Torah, to the people.[191] This movement represents the other side of the dialectical movement, a theologisation of the law. Weber asserts that both of these movements were embodied in the Josianic reforms of the Deuteronomic tradition:

> A strict separation of "jus" and "fas" could no longer be maintained with their increasing importance and with increased consideration given to their views by the Yahwistically interested laity. The ancient, never forgotten significance of the "debarim Yahweh" [*debarim* is the Hebrew for *word, name,* or *commandment*] for all important decisions also benefited their influence upon legal views. This cooperation of devout Yahwistic laymen with ethically reflective priests resulted in the theologisation, on the one hand, of law, and the rationalisation of religious ethics on the other. Deuteronomy was the most important product of this cooperation after the fall of the Northern kingdom.[192]

Crucial to both of these movements of rationalisation and theologisation is the development of a nonmagical response to the questions of theodicy:

> In practice, the rejection of magic meant primarily that, unlike the process elsewhere, it was not systematised by priests for the sake of the taming of the masses. . . . One of the fundamental theses even of the first prophet (Amos) was that Yahweh also sent all evil. In Israel, all evil was punishment or decree of the powerful god. Therefore, the development of the magical defence against demons was confronted with that of the purely ethical Torah and with the confession of sins as genuine means of control in the

> hands of the Levitical priests. This exerted an all-pervasive influence upon the religious development of Israel.[193]

In thus rejecting magical practices as ways of dealing with the reality of evil, Weber sees Israel's conscious rejection of the Babylonian dualism leading to an ethical response to the theodicy question, which characterises inner-worldly religions from Judaism to ascetical Protestantism.[194] This represents the origin of the process of disenchantment, which will eventually lead to its logical conclusion in the puritanical groups of Protestantism.[195] It also reinforces the central opposition that Weber suggests exists between mystical contemplation, as practiced in India, and inner-worldly asceticism.[196] It reinforces this binary opposition because for magic, one can read mystical contemplation, whilst for ethics, one can read inner-worldly rational action and knowledge. This opposition between magic and knowledge is embodied in the institutionalisation of the legal reforms of the Torah in the Deuteronomic tradition. It represents the way in which the contractual agreement of Yahweh and Israel in the *Berith*, or Covenant, is made manifest in the social organisation of the community of Israel.[197]

A key aspect of this social organisation, which prefigures that of Protestantism, was the institutional rejection of a spiritual hierarchy. The Catholic distinction between virtuosos and laity did not find an institutional home in either Judaism or Protestantism. All believers were required to follow the self-discipline and ascetical practices of the faith, not only the chosen few.[198] However, it would be wrong to think that Weber uncritically saw Judaism as the precursor of ascetic Protestantism. At the end of *AJ*, when he considers the teachings and ethics of pharisaic Judaism, he remarks:

> Judaism certainly did not represent an ascetic way of life. In one point, however, its way of life resembled the rational ascetic principles: in its commandment of vigilant self-observation and absolute self-control. The necessity of the first unavoidably resulted from constantly measuring one's correct deportment by the law with its innumerable ritual commandments, and, especially, observation of prohibitions.[199]

Framed in this way, Judaism, for Weber, seems to be more a precursor of the notion of "personality." This enables the internal connection between Weber's understanding of "personality" and his ethical/rational rejection of mystical contemplation to be seen more clearly. The "spiritual aristocracy" that represents, for Weber, a type of traditionalism is manifested in such diverse social forms as the Chinese notion of the "gentleman" and the Catholic notion of the "contemplative." This informs Weber's understanding of the action/contemplation motifs, such as in the Mary-Martha typology, and the inner-worldly and the flight-from-the-world typology of his sociology of religion. Moreover, it structures Weber's reflections on the ways in which religious ideas act as carriers of the social impetus to change. The spiritual aristocracy of the various forms of virtuoso in religions such as Confucianism and Catholicism created a certain sense of traditionalism in society. Because only the few could attain to such ideals, the rest, the masses, had to be content with playing an ancillary role, remaining agents of service to the *status quo* rather than active agents of social change. However, in both Judaism and Protestantism the extension of religious duty to the masses represented a type of democratisation of spiritual capital.[200] Now the masses represented the ones who held the power of change; they too possessed the spiritual capital necessary to facilitate and, indeed, to legitimate playing an active role in the process of social change.[201]

The transferring of spiritual capital from the magical garden of the monastery to the rational marketplace of the city, which was prefigured in the disenchantment movement of ancient Judaism, is a crucial development in the process of Western secularisation. Weber's identification of the city as the place that mediated between the spiritual and the political in the origins of Western history has not received a great deal of attention until now.[202] It is clear, however, that prior to Harvey Cox's *The Secular City*, Weber had grasped the importance of the development of the city as the place of the realisation of the disenchantment of the world—the place of the transferral and of the transformation of capital.[203]

The opposition between contemplation and action is further seen in the prophetic belief of ancient Judaism that Yahweh is the God of the political destiny of the nation. For the Israelites, Yahweh was the God of history. Unlike the Asian deities, Yahweh continually intervened in history: he was a war god who fought on the side of the Israelites like a superhuman prizefighter. Weber concludes that this conception of God closes off any Asian or contemplative notion of striving for mystical union with God. The God of the Israelites was a God to be obeyed in fear and trembling, not one who encouraged the quest to discover the meaning of the world as in the Indian religions:

> It was likewise very important that Yahweh remained a God of history, especially of political-military history. This differentiated him from all Asiatic deities and was due to his original relationship to Israel. For his most devout believers he always remained the war god of the confederacy. No matter whether he was also a rainmaker God or whether speculation in north Israel elevated him to heavenly king, for truly Yahwistic and especially prophetic belief, he remained the God of political destinies. Hence he was no God with whom one could seek mystical union by contemplation, but a superhuman yet understandable personal master whom one had to obey. He had given his positive commandments, which one had to follow. One could enquire into his divine purposes, the reasons for his wrath, and the prerequisites of his mercy, just as with a great king. Beyond that, there was nothing. This presupposition, indeed, precluded the development of speculation about the "meaning" of the world in Indian fashion. For different reasons speculation with the Egyptians and Babylonians did not go beyond certain, quite narrow limits either. In Ancient Israel it had no footing whatsoever.[204]

The key theme of Weber's conception of the "personality," that the quest for meaning should not take away the energies for inner-worldly action, is clearly grounded in this Judaic-Protestant conception of the God of the law. Just as law solves disputes based on personal differences, the conception of God upon which Weber's notion of "personality" trades dissolves the question of meaning. With such a God, that question is firmly off the agenda. One's task is to follow God's law and leave the rest to Him.

Weber explains that the pre-exilic prophets could never pursue the mystical paths of the Indian and Chinese prophets because, rather than bringing peace, the God of the pre-exilic prophets disturbed the peace and tranquillity of His chosen ones.[205] He disturbed their peace in order to empower them to speak unsettling words, to awaken the Israelites again to their agreement, to their covenant with Yahweh. Jeremiah is the classical figure here. As Weber notes, rather than feeling the blissful presence of God, he experienced the presence of God as a "duty" and a "command" to hectic action.[206] In such a prophetic experience there was no time to search for the meaning of life or the world; the urgent demand was the call to action:

> Neither the prophets nor (so far as we know) their public ever raised the question of the "meaning" of the world and especially of life in the attempt to justify its fragmentary, woeful, and guilty transience and its contradictions. Such questions gave the decisive motive of all holy knowledge in India. In connection with this neither the prophet nor his public had ever in any way been driven to seek God out of the need for salvation, redemption, and perfection of the soul out of and against this imperfect world. Moreover the prophet never felt himself deified by his experience, united with the godhead, removed from the torment and meaninglessness of existence, as happened to the redeemed in India, and for the Indian represented the true meaning of his religious experience. The prophet never knew himself emancipated from suffering, be it only from the bondage of sin. There was no room for a *unio mystica*, not to mention the inner oceanic tranquillity of the Buddhistic *Arahat*. Nothing of this sort existed. Finally, there was no thought of a metaphysical gnosis and interpretation of the world. The nature of Yahweh contained nothing supernatural in the sense of something extending beyond understanding. His motives were not concealed from human comprehension.[207]

Of central importance here is the indication of the turn to rational principles as the basis of religious experience. Rather than mystical union, the goal of ancient Judaism was right action governed by divine law. This represents a significant transformation in the meaning and nature of religious experience and represents what Robert Bellah has defined as the historic period of religion.[208] Ancient Judaism begins the process of the shift from cult to ethics as the medium of commerce with the transcendent. Rather than the sacrifice of animals or even people to ensure peace with God, the emphasis shifts to the area of the moral life, the following of the moral law inscribed in the heart. The hardening of the heart made this moral law so difficult to see that its inscription on the tablets of stone represented the external and visible form of the interior reality of the covenant between Yahweh and the people of Israel.

This ethical transformation thus manifests manifold dimensions of secularisation: it shifts the emphasis from the cult to action; it redirects energy from mystical practices, oriented to hidden knowledge, towards daily life and its rational principles; it extends the notion of religious observance from the elite magicians and mystics to the whole people of God, in this case, the people of Israel; it transforms the temporal understanding of divine action and the religious observance of the people from the transcendental realm of the heavens to the immanent realm of the political history of the community of Israel; it transforms the spatial understanding of divine action and religious observance from the heavenly realm to the world; and it transforms the notion of religious knowledge from being hidden, that is mystical, or, one might say, sacramental, to being publicly accessible and easily understood.[209] For Weber, these dimensions of secularisation in ancient Israel represent a key moment in the history of Western rationality and, indeed, of the process of disenchantment. Understanding the ways of Yahweh according to rational principles and the preaching of this to the people was the task of the prophet. The transformation of religious teaching into law based on justifiable motives was the task of the Torah teacher. Both tasks were made possible because the religious experience of the people of Israel had gone through these dimensions of secularisation. This ethical response to the theodicy question represented the singularity of the people of Israel and, later, of Protestant Christianity.

It is quite possible that Weber's concern for the ethical and political stability of the German nation significantly motivated his search for the roots of this ethical transformation of the religious impulse. Indeed, this would make perfect sense in the context of liberal Protestant theology in which Weber was so well-versed.[210] Certainly, *AJ* makes clear that the opposition of contemplation/mysticism and action/asceticism plays a key role in Weber's own theory of secularisation.[211] Indeed, one might say it structures the very basis of his Protestant theory of modernity:[212]

> Thus mystic possession of otherworldly godliness was rejected in favour of active service to the supernatural but, in principle, understandable God. Likewise, the speculation concerning the ground of being of the world was rejected in favour of plain devotion to the positive godly commandment. No need was felt for a philosophical theodicy and where the problem, which the Indians elaborated ever anew still arose, it was settled with the simplest means conceivable.[213]

Weber concludes *AJ* by considering the role of the Pharisees in Judaism and contrasting Judaism with early Christianity.[214] Indeed, Weber had planned to write a monograph on early Christianity, but his untimely death prevented this.[215] He holds early Christianity to be a fallback into an enchanted world in comparison with ancient Judaism, although its development of a new type of asceticism represented a step in the direction of a methodologically planned lifestyle.[216] Commenting on Weber's conception of asceticism in early Christian monasticism, Han J. W. Drijvers suggests that his conception of inner-worldly/other-worldly and asceticism/mysticism categories is determined by Neo-Kantian *a prioris*, which, from a historical perspective, require correction, and indeed invite new conceptualisations of their role in the development of Western rationality and modernity.[217]

Furthermore, Gedaliahu G. Stroumsa, in his analysis of Weber's conception of the Gnostics in early Christianity, suggests that, historically speaking, mysticism and asceticism were generally found together rather than as separate phenomena. He sees the notion of flight from the world in the monastic Christian tradition not as escape from the world, which is created good by God, but rather as escape from the perversions of the world.[218]

For Weber, Catholicism stands on the enchanted side of sacramental mediation; it cannot encourage the systematic control of inner-worldly action. Like the Indian religions, though in a less pure form, it stands on the enchanted side of mystical contemplation and not on the side of ascetic inner-worldly action. One might say that, for Weber, Catholicism, like the religions of India, places Mary over Martha, whilst Protestantism (and Meister Eckhart) places Martha over Mary. Whilst Martha does the secular service, Mary basks in the enchanted garden of contemplation. Martha is thus the bringer of secularisation, the embodiment of the attitude of the Protestant ethic; Mary is the guardian of tradition, the embodiment of the passive attitude of contemplation.

The problem with this typology is that it fails to recognise the transformation in Catholicism, which began in the sixteenth century and continues to work itself out in the spirituality of modern Catholicism. The Catholic response to the Reformation, as contemporary historians have shown, was not simply a matter of countering the Protestant Reformation, but also involved internal renewal.[219] This appreciation seems to be absent from Weber's own account of Catholicism and from his understanding of contemplation and ascetic action.

Clearly, Weber makes use of binary oppositions—his conceptual apparatus—in order to narrate a story of Western rationality and the emergence of a secular modernity. Yet the narrative that he tells, rather than being a confessionally neutral rendition of Western history, as is often thought, in both substance and form represents a Protestant conception of modernity and of secularisation.

Notes

1. Weber's texts on the sociology of religion are gathered together in *GARS* I, II, and III.

2. For a theological assessment of the theory of secularisation in Weber, which I have drawn on in my own philosophical consideration here, see Torró, (1990).

3. Note that *PE* is a general abbreviation used for *Die protestantische Ethik und der Geist des Kapitalismus*. When differences between the 1904–1905 and 1920 editions of *PE* are significant for the point being made, I will note this in the endnotes. I will use the abbreviation *LW* for the critical edition of *PE* containing both versions and simply *GARS* I for the 1920 edition. In using *LW* after the *GARS* I edition, I will give (for reference) the equivalent 1904–1905 version of the text quoted and translated. The critical edition of the text containing the original

1904–1905 edition and all 1920 additions and changes is gathered and edited by Lichtblau and Weiß (eds.) (2000).

4. For an excellent introduction to this work of Weber, see Guttandin (1998).

5. For a full documentation of these changes and editions, see the version of *PE* edited in *LW*.

6. See *GARS* I: 24, 87, 196, 199. *LW* 6, 56, 149, 151.

7. Weber used the word *Entzauberung* four times in the 1920 edition but not at all in the 1904–1905 edition. See *GARS* I: 94, 114, 156, 158. *LW* Anhang (1920) n. 163, 242, 331, 337. This played an important part in the debate between Tenbruck and Winckelmann. One can conclude that Weber added the term *Entzauberung* sometime between 1905 and 1913.

8. For a good introduction to the importance of Luther's and Calvin's ideas in shaping the foundations of modern political thought, see Skinner (1978b).

9. For a good short study of Weber's Luther interpretation, see Lehmann (1996): 30–41.

10. See *GARS* I: 69–71. *LW*: 37–41.

11. See *GARS* I: 93–94. *LW*: 60–63.

12. See *GARS* I: 111. *LW*: 74–75.

13. It should be noted that Weber's analysis here rests to a large degree on the work of the liberal Protestant theologian Matthias Schneckenburger, who gave Weber the resources to differentiate between active Calvinism and passive Lutheranism (see *GARS* I: 75 n. 2, 112, n. 1. *LW*: 43 n. 50, 76 n. 115). On this point, see Tyrell (1992): 188. This distinction plays a vital role in Weber's sociology of religion, as we shall see, and represents an important influence of liberal Protestantism on Weber's general sociology of religion.

14. See *GARS* I: 86. *LW*: 55.

15. *GARS* I: 163. "Dieser asketische Lebenstil aber bedeutete eben, wie wir sahen, eine an Gottes Willen orientierte rationale Gestaltung des ganzen Daseins. Und diese Askese war nicht mehr ein opus supererogationis, sondern eine Leistung, die jedem zugemutet wurde, der seiner Seligkeit gewiß sein wollte. Jenes religiös gefordete, vom 'natürlichen' Leben verscheidene Sonderleben der Heiligen spielte sich—das ist Entscheidende—nicht mehr außerhalb der Welt in Mönchgemeinschaften, sondern innerhalb der Welt und ihrer Ordnungen ab. Diese Rationalisierung der Lebensführung innerhalb der Welt im Hinblick auf das Jenseits war die Wirkung der Berufskonzeption des asketischen Protestantismus."

For the 1904–1905 edition, see LW: 120.

16. For a more comprehensive and critical reconstruction of the terms *Protestant ethic* and *spirit of capitalism* in Weber, see Disselkamp (1994): 20–103.

17. See *GARS* I: 31–32. *LW*: 11–13.
18. See *GARS* I: 44–45. *LW*: 19–20.
19. See *GARS* I: 26. *LW*: 7.
20. See *GARS* I: 83. *LW*: 51. This concept is taken over by Weber from Goethe, who was an important influence on Weber and his theoretical work.
21. Hubert Treiber (1999) provides an in-depth study of the concept of asceticism in Weber's work, showing the important influence of the Protestant liberal theologians of the nineteenth century as well that of the third part of Nietzsche's *On The Genealogy of Morality* on Weber's understanding of the concept of asceticism.
22. See *GARS* I: 202–203. "Einer der konstitutiven Bestandteile des modernen kapitalistischen Geistes, und nicht nur dieses, sondern der modernen Kultur: die rationale Lebensführung auf Grundlage der Berufsidee, ist—das sollten diese Darlegungen erweisen—geboren aus dem Geist der christlichen Askese. Man lese jetzt noch einmal den im Eingang dieses Aufsatzes zitierten Traktat Franklins nach, um zu sehen, daß die wesentlichen Elemente der dort als "Geist des Kapitalismus" bezeichneten Gesinnung eben die sind, die wir vorstehend als Inhalt der puritanischen Berufsaskese ermittelten, nur ohne die religiöse Fundamentierung, die eben bei Franklin schon abgestorben war."

LW: 152–153. One textual difference between the 1904–1905 and 1920 versions is that in the *GARS* one reads "abgestorben war" whilst in *LW* we read "abgestorben ist," with no change in the 1920 version endnotes.
23. Weber thus describes both the history of monasticism and the spread of the spirit of capitalism in terms of the secularising influence of possessions. See *GARS* I: 196.

"Ist doch die ganze Geschichte der Ordensregeln in gewissem Sinne ein stets erneutes Ringen mit dem Problem der säkularisierenden Wirkung des Besitzes. Das gleiche gilt in grandiosem Maßstabe auch für die innerweltliche Askese des Puritanismus." *LW*: 196. "In fact the whole history of monasticism is in a certain sense the history of a continual struggle with the problem of the secularising influence of possessions. The same is true on a grand scale of the inner-worldly asceticism of Puritanism."
24. Weber spells out very clearly in *PE* that he is not suggesting that the spirit of capitalism could only have arisen as a consequence of certain effects of the Reformation. Rather, he is interested to investigate if and to what extent religious factors have been influential in the spreading of the spirit of capitalism over the world. See *GARS* I: 83. Many of the initial arguments against Weber's *PE* (collected together in Winckelmann (ed.) [1972]) failed to realise this point even though it was already clearly spelled out in the 1904–1905 version of

the *PE*. For the 1904–1905 version, see *LW*: 50–51. For an excellent review of the history of *PE* and the critical debate surrounding the text, see Chalcraft and Harrington (eds.) (2001): 1–19. Chalcraft and Harrington also present an English translation of these important debates in the history of *PE*.

25. It is interesting to note that the original definition of secularisation: that is, the transfer of a religious person from a monastic state, *regulares*, to the state of the secular clergy, *canonicus*, or to the lay state, and indeed the later definition of the transfer of property from the Catholic to the Protestant Church after the Peace of Westphalia, fits very well with Weber's own understanding of the transposition and transformation of Christian asceticism.

26. *GARS* I: 163. "Die christliche Askese, anfangs aus der Welt in die Einsamkeit flüchtend, hatte bereits aus dem Kloster heraus, indem sie der Welt entsagte, die Welt kirchlich beherrscht. Aber dabei hatte sie im ganzen dem weltlichen Alltagsleben seinen natürlich unbefangenen Charakter gelassen. Jetzt trat sie auf den Markt des Lebens, schlug die Türe des Klosters hinter sich zu und unternahm es, gerade das weltliche Alltagsleben mit ihrer Methodik zu durchtränken, es zu einem rationalen Leben in der Welt und doch nicht von dieser Welt oder für diese Welt umzugestalten." *LW*: 120–121.

27. As I noted above, the phrase, "Entzauberung der Welt" (disenchantment of the world) is added by Weber four times to the 1920 edition of *PE*. It is thus fair to say that it represents a maturation of his thinking about the role of religion in the modern world. Consequently, it may be taken to elaborate his more mature understanding of secularisation.

28. For an exhaustive study of the nature and meaning of disenchantment in the work of Weber, see Bouretz (1996).

29. See *GARS* I: 94 n. 3. "Entzauberung der Welt. Ueber diesen Prozeß s. die Aufsätze über die 'Witschaftsethik der Weltreligionen.' Schon die Sonderstellung der altisraelitischen Ethik gegenüber der ihr inhaltlich nahe verwandten ägyptischen und babylonischen und ihre Entwicklung seit der Prophetenzeit beruhte, wie sich dort zeigen wird, ganz und gar auf diesem Grundsachverhalt: der Ablehnung der sakramentalen Magie als Heilsweg." [Disenchantment of the world. On this process see the other essays in my *Wirtschaftsethik der Weltreligionen*. Already, the peculiar position of the old Israelite ethic, as compared with the closely related ethics of Egypt and Babylon, and its development after the time of the prophets, rested, as is shown there, entirely on this fundamental fact, the rejection of sacramental magic as a road to salvation.] Not in the 1904–1905 edition.

30. See *GARS* I: 94–97. *LW*: 62–64.

31. However, in *WuG* he does differentiate between the concepts of religion and magic, on the basis of supplication and coercion, and

indeed between magicians and priests, on the basis of coercion and worship. Nevertheless, he does see the characteristic elements of divine worship, prayer, and sacrifice as having their origins in magic. See *WuG*: 258–261.

32. See *GARS* I: 94. *LW*: 62.

33. See *WuG*: 258.

34. *GARS* I: 108–109. "Der religiöse Virtuose kann seines Gnadenstandes sich versichern entweder, indem er sich als Gefäß, oder, indem er sich als Werkzeug göttlicher Macht fühlt. Im ersten Fall neigt sein religiöses Leben zu mystischer Gefühlskultur, im letzteren zu asketischem Handeln. Dem ersten Typus stand Luther näher, dem letztern gehörte der Calvinismus an. 'Sola fide' wollte auch der Reformierte selig werden. Aber da schon nach Calvins Ansicht alle bloßen Gefühle und Stimmungen, mögen sie noch so erhaben zu sein scheinen, trügerisch sind, muß der Glaube sich in seinen objektiven Wirkungen bewähren, um der certitdo salutis als sichere Unterlage dienen zu können: er muß eine 'fidex efficax,' die Berufung zum Heil ein 'effectual calling' (Ausdruck der Savoy declaration) sein."

35. For the classical discussions of the influence of Platonic and Neo–Platonic thinking on questions of contemplation and action, see Festugière (1936) and Daniélou (1944). For an in-depth study of the influence of Neo-Platonism on Martin Luther's criticism of Greek philosophy and Scholastic theology, see Beer (1980).

36. Human action no longer has any cooperative role, in St. Thomas Aquinas's sense, in salvation.

37. The Greek *charis*, translated into Latin as *gratia*, and into English as *grace*, is used by St. Thomas Aquinas to mean God's action in humanity leading us to union with him. For St. Thomas Aquinas (the most important representative of this Catholic or, in Weber's terms "enchanted," understanding of human action), grace works in us (*operans*) and with us (*cooperans*). So for St. Thomas, human action and divine action (as indeed St Augustine's theory of sacrifice suggests, *De Civitate Dei*, X, vi.) are not by nature in contradiction, but rather are ordered to cooperate together in living a free virtuous life, which leads to eternal life. Nature is understood as all that is not God, such as humans and the rest of creation. See Aquinas (1991): 307–324. For a fuller consideration of the nature–grace problematic, see Stephen Duffy (1992) and (1993).

38. Hopkins (1970): 66.

39. Thus in Weber's analysis of the role of asceticism and mysticism in the various models of salvation, mysticism and both inner-worldly asceticism (*innerweltliche Askese*) and world-rejecting asceticism (*weltablehnende Askese*) treat the world as a *massa perditionis*. See *WuG*: 329, 332.

40. It is interesting to note that recent study of the work of Nietzsche often sees him as obsessed by the question of salvation even after the

"death of God." This interest in the question of salvation is perhaps another area of Nietzsche's influence on the work of Weber. For a good example of this interpretation of Nietzsche, see Fraser (2002). In his study of Weber, Martin Albrow devotes a whole chapter of his book to the theme of "The Scientist in Search of Salvation." See Albrow (1990): 62–77.

41. See *GARS* I: 111–112. *LW*: 75.

42. See *GARS* I: 113. *LW*: 76–77.

43. See *GARS* I: 196. *LW*: 149.

44. *GARS* I: 199. "Schon Calvin hatte den oft zitierten Ausspruch getan, daß nur wenn das 'Volk,' d.h. die Masse der Arbeiter und Handwerker, arm erhalten werde, es Gott gehorsam bleibe. Die Niederlander (Pieter de la Court und andere) hatte dies dahin 'säkularisiert': daß die Masse der Menschen nur arbeite, wenn die Not sie dazu treibe, und diese Formulierung eines Leitmotivs kapitalistischer Wirtschaft mündete dann weiterhin in den Strom der Theorie von der 'Produktivität' niederer Löhne. Auch hier schob sich die utilitarische Wendung dem Gedanken unvermerkt mit dem Absterben seiner religiösen Wurzel unter, ganz nach dem Entwicklungschema, welches wir immer wieder beobachtet haben." *LW*: 151.

45. Weber notes that a superficial analysis of Protestantism made by Catholics is that materialism arises from the secularising of religious ideals by Protestantism. Although Weber suggests that this is a superficial analysis, the notion that through Protestantism the emphasis is shifted from the spiritual to the material is a motif that recurs in his work. See *GARS* I: 24. *LW*: 6.

46. See *GARS* I: 212.

47. Weber notes this effect of the process of disenchantment in a long footnote on the tendency of American universities to lack the relevant theological material that he required for his study of *PE*. He considers this to be an aspect of the general tendency towards secularisation in American society, observing that many of these same universities had sectarian origins. See *GARS* I: 86–87 n. 2. *LW*: 55–56 n. 66.

48. *GARS* I: 200–201 n. 4. "Und noch eins: Man kann ja zweifeln, wie stark die 'Freude' des mittelalterlichen Handwerkers an dem 'von ihm Geschaffenen,' mit der so viel operiert wird, als psychologisches Agens ins Gewicht gefallen ist. Etwas war immerhin daran. Jedenfalls aber *entkleidete* nun die Askese die Arbeit dieses—heute durch den Kapitalismus für immer vernichteten—diesseitigen weltlichen Reizes und richtete sie auf das Jenseits aus. Die berufliche Arbeit als solche ist gottgewollt. Die *Unpersönlichkeit* der heutigen Arbeit: ihre, vom Standpunkte des Einzelnen aus betrachtet, freudenarme Sinnlosigkeit, ist hier noch religiös verklärt. Der Kapitalismus in der Zeit seiner Entstehung aber *brauchte* Arbeiter, die um des *Gewissens* willen der

ökonomischen Ausnutzung zur Verfügung standen. [Heute sitzt er im Sattel und vermag ihre Arbeitswilligkeit ohne jenseitige Prämien zu erzwingen.]" (The text in square brackets was added for the 1920 edition; see *LW*: 201 n. 434).

LW: 152 n. 310.

49. I shall consider this point in more detail when I discuss Weber's *Zwischenbetratchung*. These intermediate reflections reveal that as scientific logic of the empirical sciences develops, the logic of religious discourse tends to be pushed more and more into the irrational sphere of private experience. I noted above the importance of the epistemological debates of the Neo-Kantians on Weber's own religious epistemology, and it is clear that in his analysis of the world religions, Weber sees the rise of scientific logic as a major cause of the privatisation of religion into the realm of personal value judgements. He considers this to be part of the general process of the disenchantment of the world. See *GARS* I: 564.

50. Goethe was a very important influence for Weber and Nietzsche. Indeed Weber is purported to have secretly read all forty volumes of the Cotta edition of Goethe's works during his *Tertia* classes in the *Gymnasium*. See Marianne Weber (1950): 53. For a study of the importance of Goethe on Weber's thought, see Albrow (1990): 62–77. For Weber, Goethe is really the ideal type of a *Kulturmensch*, a man of culture who was the product of traditional society, a type that Weber uses to oppose the *Fachmensch* or specialist, who was a product of modern bureaucratic capitalist societies. I shall consider below the importance of these opposing categories for Weber's theory of secularisation in terms of his understanding of *Berufsmenschentums* or vocational humanity. Goethe stands in the German tradition (with Kant, the *Sturm und Drang* writings, and Humboldt) as one of the major German thinkers who tried to find a way forward for the German understanding of the self as a "personality." This notion of the self as a "personality," that is, the self as a unified whole acting out of inner conviction to realise itself through disciplined work in a vocation, is very important for Weber's work. It provides him with a model for a new type of prophet to meet the challenges facing German culture and to build a world under the conditions of disenchantment. For an analysis of the concept of "personality" in Weber, see Goldman (1988).

51. *GARS* I: 203. "'Tat' und 'Entsagung' einander heute unabwendbar bedingen."

LW: 153.

52. See Habermas (1981a): 461–474.

53. It is interesting to note that the opening page of their essay speaks of the programme of the Enlightenment as a disenchantment of the world. See Adorno and Horkheimer (2001): 9.

54. See Kant (1999): 20.

55. *GARS* I: 203. "Der Puritaner *wollte* Berufsmenschen sein, wir *müssen* es sein. Denn indem die Askese aus den Mönchszellen heraus in das Berufsleben übertragen wurde und die innerweltliche Sittlichkeit zu beherrschen begann, half sie an ihrem Teile mit daran, jenen mächtigen Kosmos der modernen, an die technischen und ökonomischen Voraussetzungen mechanisch–maschineller Produktion gebundenen, Wirtschaftsordnung erbauen, der heute den Lebenstil aller einzelnen, die in dies Triebwerk hineingeboren werden—*nicht* nur der direkt ökonomisch Erwerbstätigkeiten,—mit überwältigen—dem Zwange bestimmt und vielleicht bestimmen wird, bis der letzte Zentner fossilen Brennstoffs verglüht ist. Nur wie "ein dünner Mantel, den man jeder Zeit abwerfen könnte," sollte nach Baxters Ansicht die Sorge um die äußeren Güter um die Schulter seiner Heiligen liegen. Aber aus dem Mantel ließ das Verhängnis ein stahlhartes Gehäuse werden." *LW*: 153. It should be noted here that the expression "stahlhartes Gehäuse" has been originally translated by Talcott Parsons as "iron cage." For a discussion of this term, see Chalcraft (1994), Baehr (2000), and Swedberg (ed.) (2005): 132–133.

56. *GARS* I: 204. "Heute ist ihr Geist—ob endgültig, wer weiß es?—aus diesem Gehäuse entwichen. Der siegreiche Kapitalismus jedenfalls bedarf, seit er auf mechanischer Grundlage ruht, dieser Stütze nicht mehr. Auch die rosige Stimmung ihrer lachenden Erbin: der Aufklärung, scheint endgültig im Verbleichen und als ein Gespenst ehemals religiöser Glaubensinhalte geht der Gedanke 'Berufspflicht' in unserm Leben um. Wo die 'Berufserfüllung' nicht direkt zu den höchsten geistigen Kulturwerten in Beziehung gesetzt werden kann,—oder wo nicht umgekehrt sie auch subjektiv einfach als ökonomischer Zwang empfunden werden muß,—da verzichtet der einzelne heute meist auf ihre Ausdeutung überhaupt." *LW*: 153–154.

57. For an analysis of this concept of "Berufsmenschentums" in Weber, see Constans Sefarth's article, "Die protestantische Ethik und die Entwicklung des Berufsmenschentums in der modernen Kultur," in Raulet (ed.) (1997): 26–47.

58. *GARS* I: 204. "Niemand weiß noch, wer kunftig in jenem Gehäuse wohnen wird, und ob am Ende dieser ungeheuren Entwicklung ganz neue Propheten oder eine mächtige Wiedergeburt alter Gedanken und Ideale stehen werden, oder aber—wenn keins von beiden—mechanisierte Versteinerung, durch eine Art von krampfhaftem Sich-wichtig-nehmen verbräumt. Dann allerdings könnte für die 'letzten Menschen' dieser Kulturentwicklung das Wort zur Wahrheit werden: 'Fachmenschen ohne Geist, Genußmenschen ohne Herz, dies Nichts bildet sich ein, eine nie vorher erreichte Stufe des Menschentums ersteigen zu haben'." *LW*: 154.

59. In replies to his critics, Weber outlines his concern to find an "ethical style of life" that was "spiritually adequate" for the formation of modern capitalism. See Winckelmann (ed.) (1972): 55, 286.

60. For an account of this project of the new men of culture in Weber, see Scaff (1991): 73–120. Here we see again Nietzsche's influence on Weber. Nietzsche's "last men who invented happiness," in the prologue to his Zarathustra, is surely behind Weber's account of the fate of modern man in these final passages of *PE.*

61. This was written in 1913 and originally published in 1915 in the *Archiv für Sozialforschung*, vol. 41. Weber reviewed it for the 1920 publication in *GARS* I, as *Die Wirtschaftsethik der Weltreligionen. Vergleichende religionssoziologische Versuche. Einleitung*: 237–275. For a useful summary of the main arguments of Weber in *Einleitung*, see Küenzlen (1980): 79–88.

62. *GARS* I: 536–573.

63. See Tenbruck (1975): 676.

64. See, for example, Milbank (1990): 75–100.

65. See *GARS* I: 240–241. For an alternative interpretation of Weber's relation to Marx, see Bryan S. Turner (1977).

66. See *GARS* I: 238. "In den psychologischen und pragmatischen Zusammenhängen der Religionen gegründeten praktischen Antriebe zum Handeln." The five world religions chosen by Weber are Confucianism, Hinduism, Buddhism, Christianity, and Islam. He also notes a sixth, Judaism, which has particular importance for Christianity and Islam and, indeed, for the development of the modern Western economic ethic.

67. See *GARS* I: 240.

68. As Weber notes, this question also includes a religious justification of good fortune. See *GARS* I: 242. For a consideration of the importance of the theodicy question in the work of Weber, see Bryan S. Turner (1996): 142–176.

69. *GARS* I: 246–247. "Die metaphysiche Vorstellung über Gott und Welt, welche das unausrottbare Bedürfnis nach der Theodizee hervorrief, vermochte gleichfalls nur wenige,—im ganzen, wie wir sehen werden, nur drei—Gedankensysteme zu erzeugen, welche rational befriedigende Antworten auf die Frage nach dem Grunde der Inkongruenz zwischen Schicksal und Verdienst gaben: die indische Karmanlehre, den zarathustrischen Dualismus und das Prädestinationsdekret des Deus absconditus. Diese rational geschlossensten Lösungen aber traten nur ganz ausnahmsweise in reiner Form auf."

70. See *GARS* I: 205–206. Note that the substance of this critique was already present in the 1904–1905 version: that is, before the critical discussion on *PE* that forced Weber to make more explicit his basic argument against Marx's theory of historical materialism. For the 1904–1905 version of this text, see *LW*: 155.

71. See *GARS* I: 248. "Und die Entwicklung rationaler religiöser Ethik gerade auf dem Boden der sozial minder gewerteten Schichten hatte ebenfalls zunächst positive Wurzeln in deren innere Lage." [The

development of a rational religious ethic has had positive and primary roots in the inner conditions of those social strata which were less socially valued.]

72. *GARS* I: 248–249. "Daß die Propaganda der Propheten und Priester daneben, absichtlich oder nicht, auch das Resentiment der Massen in ihren Dienst gestellt hat, ist nicht zu bezweifeln, aber keineswegs universell zutreffend. Vor allem war diese wesentlich negative Macht nirgends, so viel bekannt, die Quelle jener dem Wesen nach metaphysischen Konzeptionen, welche einer jeden Erlösungsreligion ihre Eigenart verliehen. Und vor allem war die Art einer religiösen Verheißung, allgemein gesprochen, keineswegs notwendig oder auch nur überwiegend, lediglich Sprachrohr eines Klasseninteresses, sei es äußerlicher oder innerlicher Art. . . . Im übrigen aber war die Eigenart der großen religiös–ethischen Systeme durch weit individuellere gesellschaftliche Bedingungen als durch den bloßen Gegensatz von herrschenden und beherrschten Schichten bestimmt."

73. For a consideration of the importance of religious stratification in Weber, see Bryan S. Turner (1996): 109–141, and Swedberg (ed.) (2005): 37–38.

74. Well before Pierre Bourdieu, Weber broadens the understanding of class to include ideal interests as well as material interests. In this sense he uses Marx and Nietzsche to root the different answers given to the theodicy question in the needs of different social strata. In doing this, Weber broadens the materialist conception of class to include both material and ideal interests, which corresponds to the different internal and external class interests of the social situations of the various social classes. For a discussion of this point, see Sam Whimster, "The Secular Ethic and Modernism," in Lash and Whimster, (eds.) (1987): 261–264.

75. The systematic control of one's actions, which Weber saw united in the vocational personality of the ascetical Protestants, is thus also understood to be part of the process of disenchantment (de-magification although closer to the original, *Entzauberung*, sounds rather strange in English). In moving away from punctual sacramental actions of the individual self to a unified life project of the personality, the transient sense of being in a state of grace is sublimated into a permanent sense of the person being called, and hence saved, by God. Thus, the intellectual strata represent a significant model for Weber's notion of a unified vocational personality.

76. See *GARS* I: 250.

77. See *GARS* I: 252. "Die Sublimierung des religiösen Heilsbesitzes zum 'Erlösungs'– Glauben."

78. *GARS* I: 252. "Aber eine spezifische Bedeutung erlangte die Erlösung doch erst, wo sie Ausdruck eines systematisch–rationalisierten 'Weltbildes' und der Stellungnahme dazu war. Denn was sie ihrem

Sinn und ihrer psychologischen Qualität nach bedeuten wollte und konnte, hing dann eben vom jenem Weltbild und dieser Stellungnahme ab. Interessen (materielle und ideelle), nicht: Ideen, beherrschen unmittelbar das Handeln der Menschen. Aber: die 'Weltbilder,' welche durch 'Ideen' geschaffen wurden, haben sehr oft als Weichensteller die Bahnen bestimmt, in denen die Dynamik der Interessen Handeln fortbewegte. Nach dem Weltbild richtete es sich ja: 'wovon' und 'wozu' man 'erlöst' sein wollte und—nicht zu vergessen:—konnte."

79. See *GARS* I: 253. "Die moderne Form der zugleich theoretischen und praktischen intellektuellen und zweckhaften Durchrationalisierung des Weltbildes und der Lebensführung hat die allgemeine Folge gehabt: daß die Religion, je weiter diese besondere Art von Rationalisierung fortschritt, desto mehr ihrerseits in das—vom Standpunkt einer intellektuellen Formung des Weltbildes ausgesehen:—Irrationale geschoben wurde." [The general result of the modern form of thoroughly rationalising the conception of the world and of the way of life, theoretically and practically, in an intellectual and purposive manner, has been that the more this type of rationality has progressed, from the standpoint of an intellectual articulation of an image of the world, the more religion has been shifted into the realm of the irrational.]

80. See *GARS* I: 253.

81. See *GARS* I: 253–254.

82. See *GARS* I: 254. "Die Einheitlichkeit des primitiven Weltbildes, in welchem alles konkrete Magie war, zeigte dann die Tendenz zur Spaltung in ein rationales Erkennen und eine rationale Beherrschung der Natur einerseits, und andererseits 'mystische' Erlebnisse, deren unaussagbare Inhalte als einziges neben dem entgotteten Mechanismus der Welt noch mögliches Jenseits.... Der Einzelne kann sein Heil, wo diese Konsequenz restlos gezogen ist, nur als Einzelner suchen. Diese mit fortschreitendem intellektualistischem Rationalismus sich in irgend einer Form einstellende Erscheinung trat irgendwie überall da auf, wo Menschen die Rationalisierung des Weltbildes als eines von unpersönlichen Regeln beherschten Kosmos unternahmen."

83. See *GARS* I: 265–266.

84. Habermas and others call this type of rationality "instrumental" rationality. It represents the typical scientific-instrumental attitude of a subject who treats the world as an object or a means simply for his or her own purposes.

85. This argument has been very influential in Charles Taylor's account of the origins of modern identity. See Taylor (1989): 211–247.

86. *GARS* I: 262–263. "Ganz anders da, wo das Virtuosentum der religiös Qualifizierten sich zu einer asketischen, die Formung des Lebens in der Welt nach dem Willen eines Gottes erstrebenden Sekte zusammenschloß.... Voll erreicht wurde beides: Entzauberung der Welt und Verlegung des Weges zum Heil von kontemplativen 'Weltflucht'

hinweg in die aktiv asketische 'Weltbearbeitung,'—wenn man von einigen kleinen rationalistischen Sekten, wie sie sich in aller Welt fanden, absieht,—nur in den großen Kirchen- und Sektenbildungen des asketischen Protestantismus im Okzident."

87. For an excellent discussion of this theological transformation, see Ebeling (1972): 226–241. Key to understanding Luther is his reading of St. Paul's letters concerning the futility of a philosophical conception of God, such as in 1 Cor: 18–19.

88. For a useful critical introduction to this work, see Schluchter (1988a), 2: 15–61. The set of critical essays, edited by Schluchter, on this work of Weber is also of interest. See Schluchter (ed.) (1983). It should be noted that Weber concentrates his comparison between Protestantism and the religions of China on his analysis of Confucianism, since Confucianism rejected the magical beliefs of Taoism as not being traditional. In this sense, Confucianism represents the most developed form of the religion of China for Weber.

89. For an overview of the criticisms of Weber's understanding of the role of Confucianism in economic development in China, see Love (2000): 172–185. These criticisms include his failure to come to terms with Neo-Confucianism, his failure to realise the presence of a this-worldly/other-worldly tension in Confucianism, and the evolution of Chinese science and economic development in the period 1100 to 1500. Whilst these criticisms point to weak spots in Weber's argument, Love suggests that they are not sufficient to overturn Weber's general account.

90. See *GAW*: 258. This is clearly the theme on which the *Vorbemerkung*, later in 1920 and placed at the start of his *GARS*, focuses, as the question of the universal historical significance of European cultural developments. Wolgang Schluchter also interprets this as the key idea behind Weber's study of Confucianism and Taoism, suggesting that Weber sees the religions of China as representing systems of life organisation (*Lebensreglementierung*) completely opposed to the Western organisation. See Schluchter (1988a), 2: 21.

91. *GARS* I: 512. "Für die Stufe der Rationalisierung, welche eine Religion represäntiert, gibt es vor allem zwei, übrigens miteinander in vielfacher innerer Beziehung stehende Maßstabe. Einmal der Grad, in welchem sie die Magie abgestreift hat. Dann der Grad systematischer Einheitlichkeit, in welche das Verhältnis von Gott und Welt und demgemäß die eigene ethische Beziehung zur Welt von ihr gebracht worden ist."

92. This is the key intuition that Marcel Gauchet adopts in his own political history of religion. He suggests that the specificity of Christianity is that it has been able to bring about a form of religion that bears, in its own developmental logic, the seeds of its own dissolution. See Gauchet, M. (1985). Whilst valuing much of Gauchet's analysis,

I think he fails to realise that what he terms "La religion de la sortie de la religion" (The religion of the exit from religion) is more accurately understood as the kenotic dimension of Christianity. The Protestant theologian Eberhard Jüngel expresses this idea in his treatment of Hegel's understanding of the "death of God" when he says, "By designating the feeling that 'God himself is dead' *as* a moment of the supreme Idea, talk about the death of God gains a *twofold* meaning. First of all, in talk about the death of God, the situation of absolutised finitude expresses itself, which corresponds to abstract infinitude as empty negativity. Once that feeling is grasped as a moment of the supreme Idea, then the death of God is understood as an event of the *self-negation* of God, who does not desire to be 'in and for himself' and does not desire to forsake the world in its finitude." [Durch die Bezeichnung des Gefühls 'Gott selbst ist tod' *als* Moment der höchsten Idee gewinnt die Rede vom Tode Gottes nun allerdings eine *zweifache* Bedeutung. Zunächst drückte sich in der Rede vom Tode Gottes die Situation verabsolutierter Endlichkeit aus, der die abstrakte Unendlichkeit als leere Negativität korrespondiert. Ist jenes Gefühl aber erst einmal als Moment der höchsten Idee begriffen, dann ist der Tod Gottes als Ereignis der *Selbstnegation* Gottes verstanden, der selbst nicht nur "an sich" sein will und der Welt nicht ihrer Endlichkeit überlassen will.] Jüngel (1992): 98.

93. For a criticism of Weber's understanding of capitalist development in China, which suggests that Weber did not take into account medieval Chinese history from the fall of the Han (ca. A.D. 200) until the rise of the Ming (1368), see Collins (1990): 58–73.

94. See *GARS* I: 512–513. Here Weber speaks specifically of ascetical Protestantism being the most *consequent* disenchantment of the world.

95. Although Weber considered both Confucianism and Taoism in this work, in the final chapter he concentrates on Confucianism and Protestantism as two possible ways of conceiving the relation between God, man, and world. Cf. Bendix (1977): 135.

96. See *GARS* I: 513.

97. Ibid.

98. See *GARS* I: 515. "Die innere Voraussetzung dieser Ethik der unbedingten Weltbejahung und Weltanpassung war der ungebrochene Fortbestand rein magischer Religiösität." [The inner assumption of this ethic of an unconditional affirmation of and adaptation to the world was the unbroken continuation of purely magical religiosity.]

99. See *GARS* I: 515.

100. Cf., Schluchter (1988a), 2: 26 n. 36.

101. It will become clear in the following section when I consider the *Zwischenbetrachtung* that Weber holds this contrast between a supramundane God and an immanent realm to be important in generating inner-worldly asceticism; but only when present with other

circumstances, such as particular types of religious promises and the paths of salvation determined by these promises, is this sufficient to determine the direction and nature of Occidental asceticism. See *GARS* I: 538.

102. *GARS* I: 521. "Eine echte Prophetie schafft eine systematische Orientierung der Lebensführung an einem Wertmaßstab von innen heraus, der gegenüber die 'Welt' als das nach der Norm ethisch zu formende Material gilt. Der Konfuzianismus war umgekehrt Anpassung nach außen hin, an die Bedingungen der 'Welt.' Ein optimal angepaßter, nur im Maße der Anpassungbedürftigkeit in seiner Lebensführung rationalisierter Mensch ist aber keine systematische Einheit, sondern eine Kombination nützlicher Einzelqualitäten.... Aber der Stil, welchen sie der Lebensführung verliehen, mußste durch wesentlich negative Elements charakterisiert bleiben und konnte jenes Streben zur Einheit von innen heraus, das wir mit dem Begriff 'Persönlichkeit' verbinden, nicht enstehen lassen. Das Leben blieb eine Serie von Vorgängen, kein methodisch unter ein transzendentes Ziel gestelltes Ganzes."

103. *GARS* I: 532. "Konfuzius.... alle eigentliche ökonomische Berufsarbeit war banausisches Fachmenschentum. Der Fachmensch aber war für den Konfuzianer auch durch seinen sozialutilitarischen Wert nicht zu wirklich positiver Würde zu erheben. Denn—dies war das Entscheidende—'der vornehme Mann' (Gentleman) war 'kein Werkzeug,' d.h.: er war in seiner weltangepaßten Selbstvervollkommung ein letzter Selbstzweck, nicht aber Mittel für sachliche Zwecke welcher Art immer. Dieser Kernsatz der konfuzianischen Ethik lehnte die Fachspezialisierung, die moderne Fachbureaukratie und die Fachschulung, vor allem aber die ökonomische Schulung für den Erwerb ab. Einer solchen 'kreaturvergötternden' Maxime setzte der Puritanismus gerade umgekehrt die Bewährung an den speziellen sachlichen Zwecken der Welt und des Berufslebens als Aufgabe entgegen."

104. See *GARS* I: 523.

105. See *GARS* I: 523. "Die große Leistung der ethischen Religionen, vor allem der ethischen und asketischen Sekten des Protestantismus, war die Durchbrechung des Sippenbandes, die Konstituierung der Ueberlegenheit der Glaubens—und ethischen Lebensführungsgemeischaft gegenüber der Blutsgemeinschaft, in starkem Maße selbst gegenüber der Familie. Oekonomisch angesehen: die Begründung des geschäftlichen Vertrauens auf ethische Qualitäten der Einzelindividuen, welche in sachlicher Berufsarbeit bewährt waren." [The great achievement of the ethical religions, and in particular of the ethical, ascetic sects of Protestantism, was to break down kinship bonds and confirm the superiority of community-based faith and an ethical way of life over community based on blood ties to a considerable degree over the family itself. In economic terms this meant confidence in business

matters being founded on the ethical attributes of each individual as proved in his objective work at his calling.]

106. See *GARS* I: 524; 532.

107. *GARS* I: 532.

108. *GARS* I: 534. "Der Gegensatz kann lehren, daß auch bloße Nüchternheit und Sparsamkeit in Verbindung mit 'Erwerbsbetrieb' und Schätzung des Reichtums noch bei weitem nicht 'kapitalistischer Geist' im Sinne des spezifisch modernen ökonomischen Berufsmenschentums waren oder ihn entbinden konnten. . . . 'Rationalismus,' dies ist für uns die zweite Lehre, enthielt der Geist beider Ethiken. Aber nur die überweltlich orientierte puritanische rationale Ethik führte den inner weltlich orientierte Rationalismus in seine Konsequenzen durch, . . . gerade weil ihr die innerweltliche Arbeit nur Ausdruck des Strebens nach einem transzendenten Ziel war."

109. Cf., Schluchter (1988a), II: 37–39.

110. See *WuG*: 321–367.

111. For a full discussion of the history of this text and its relation to other sociology of religion texts, see Schluchter (1980): 208–214 and Schluchter (1988a), 2: 557–596.

112. See Schluchter, W. (1988a), 2: 65. Weber himself makes this clear at the start of *WEWR*. See *GARS* I: 237 n. 1.

113. See *GARS* I: 536–538.

114. *GARS* I: 536–537 "Und Schließlich und vor allem muß und will ein Beitrag zur Typologie und Soziologie des Rationalismus sein. Er geht daher von den rationalsten Formen aus, welche die Realität annehmen *kann*, und sucht zu ermitteln, inwieweit gewisse theoretisch aufstellbare rationale Konsequenzen in der Realität gezogen wurden." [Finally, and above all, such an essay in the sociology of religion necessarily aims at contributing to the typology and sociology of rationalism itself. This essay therefore proceeds from the most rational forms reality *can* assume; it attempts to find out how certain rational conclusions, which can be established theoretically, have been drawn in reality.]

115. See Chapter 2.

116. For Ritschl and Harnack, both of whom were major theological influences on Weber, mysticism and contemplation were typically Catholic. For them the paragon of virtue for Catholicism was the monk, whilst for the Protestant it was the inner-worldly ascetic. Moreover, Ritschl saw Pietism because of its tendency towards Quietism, as an evangelical form of Catholicism. Similarly, Weber considered Lutheranism to be closer to Catholicism than to Reformed Protestantism. See Treiber (2001).

117. The question of the relation of contemplation to action has a long history going back at least to Plato. Indeed, following Plato and the Platonic tradition, most notably in the neo-Platonist, Plotinus, a great

deal of the Patristic and medieval period did indeed separate contemplation (*theoria*) and action (*praxis*) and found in contemplation the summit of mysticism. In the *Enneads* of Plotinus: 242, for example, we read: "The relation of action to contemplation is indicated in the way duller children, inapt to study and speculation, take crafts and manual labour" (*Enneads*, III 8.4). There were, of course, notable exceptions, such as St. Bernard of Clairvaux (1090–1153) and the English mystic Walter Hilton (d. 1396), yet it was not until St. Ignatius of Loyola (1491–1556), the founder of the Jesuits or Society of Jesus, that a mysticism of action in the Catholic tradition was fully developed. The famous phrase of one of the early founding fathers of the Society of Jesus, Jerome Nadal, "*in actione contemplativus*," expressed the key intuition of St. Ignatius, which recurs as a motif throughout his writings of "finding God in all things." This expressed the mysticism of action that characterised St. Ignatius and the Jesuit and, indeed, Ignatian tradition since the times of the Counter or Catholic Reformation. The failure of Weber to follow sufficiently the evolution of this relationship is not without significance for his own Protestant conception of modernity. For relevant literature on the question of contemplation and action from early Greek to modern times, see Villier, Cavallara, and DeGuibert (eds) (1953): 1645–2193; Festugière (1936); Plotinus (1962); Alt (1993); and Coreth (1954).

118. *GARS* I: 539. "Der Gegensatz kann in beiden Fällen tatsächlich in der Praxis schwinden und irgendeine Kombination beider Arten der Heilssuche eintreten. Aber er kann auch unter der äußerlich ähnlichen Hülle weiterbestehen bleiben. Für den echten Mystiker bleibt der Grundsatz bestehen: daß die Kreatur schweigen muß, damit Gott sprechen könne. Er 'ist' in der Welt und 'schickt sich' äußerlich in ihre Ordnungen, aber, um sich: im Gegensatz gegen sie, dadurch seines Gnadenstandes zu versichern, daß er der Versuchung, ihr Treiben wichtig zu nehmen, widersteht."

119. For an excellent overview of Weber's understanding of mysticism, his use of the early nineteenth-century research on mysticism and the ancient mystery religions, together with a systematic reconstruction of his concept of mysticism, see Krech (2001b). Also of interest here is the concept of religiosity that Weber uses together with his concept of religion. Generally, he uses religion to represent the objective institutional dimension, and religiosity to represent the subjective or personal dimension of the phenomenon. See Krech (2001a). For a general discussion of Weber's understanding of the category of the "religious," see Tyrell (1992).

120. A general consideration of these categories in *Zwischenbetrachtung* can be found in Schluchter (1988a), 2: 80–96. For a consideration of these categories in terms of the role of women in medieval religious life and how this relates to both Weber's and Troeltsch's own typology, see

Bynum (1988). Due to the complementary nature of *Zwischenbetrachtung* and the sociology of religion chapter of *WuG*, I shall also draw on the sections therein that consider the question of asceticism and mysticism. See *WuG*: 328–334.

121. In highlighting the importance of the Protestant tradition on the life and work of Weber, I am, as Martin Albrow suggests, noting a point that is often forgotten in studies of Weber: that he wrote within a Christian tradition, although he himself was not a practicing Christian. The strongest statement of this fact comes from the leader of the German feminist movement, Gertrud Bäumer, when she says, "The culture of the Protestant confession is the abiding foundation for the shaping of Max Weber's life's work, fate, ideas, and development. . . . This not in the philistine sense of a restricted moral life, but rather as something much more powerful because it dominates and shapes the demonics of a personality which is both passionate and under nervous strain." Quoted in Albrow (1990): 14. In this sense, the influence of Weber's mother, Helene Fallenstein, a woman of deep Protestant conviction, is very important for understanding Weber's personality. Albrow suggests that Weber's social theory cannot be understood adequately without taking into account the fact that he wrote within the Protestant tradition. See Albrow (1990): 13ff.

122. Graf (1987a): 222. "A comparison between *PE* and these works by Troeltsch reveals at least one instance of Weber's reliance on his friend: he was indebted to him for his knowledge of most of the theological literature he drew upon in his historical account of ascetic Protestantism. This debt is evident from the number of quotations alone: much of the specialist theological literature he used consists of the works that Troeltsch also drew upon (in the same editions!) for his studies on the history of ethics and which he in some cases subjugated to a detailed critique. Both men often quote the same crucial passages. Moreover, the critical commentaries with which Weber introduces certain theological works (despite his self-imposed reserve as a non-expert) offer judgements that are remarkably close to those that the same works elicited from Troeltsch. A particularly significant instance is Weber's treatment of Albrecht Ritschl's writings on the history of dogma."

123. See Treiber (1999): 248. Treiber bases his conclusion on a comparison of both Troeltsch's and Weber's works, and also on the fact that their understanding differs markedly from that of the majority of the liberal Protestant theologians of the time, most especially those of Albrecht Ritschl's school, such as Theodor Kaftan and Adolf von Harnack. For these theologians, the world-rejecting asceticism was a specifically Catholic notion associated with the monastic idea of perfection. Thus, to suggest an internal relation between other-worldly and inner-worldly asceticism (as did Troeltsch and Weber), and consequently

between monastic Catholicism and ascetical Protestantism, would be unthinkable to them. The paradox of this situation is that Troeltsch and Weber developed their own conceptions of inner-worldly and other-worldly asceticism from Ritschl's three-volume study of the "History of Pietism," which had suggested that the mendicant orders, most especially the third order Franciscans, had carried monastic asceticism into a form of inner-worldly ascetical action and, indeed, had been the original source of the Anabaptist movement, which carried over into Calvinism. See Treiber (1999): 260–270. On the importance of these lay-brother communities for the transposition of monastic asceticism into inner-worldly asceticism, see Little (1988). Weber himself considers this in *WuG*: 753–755. For Weber's own opposition to Ritschl and his conception of justification by faith, which Weber suggests is governed by Ritschl's religious-political value judgements against Catholicism, see *GARS* I: 128–131 n. 3. For Weber's own opinion about the importance of the Catholic roots of asceticism for Protestantism, again a critique of Ritschl, see *GARS* I: 151–152 n. 1. This criticism is particularly important for Weber's own understanding of both the affinity between Catholicism and Lutheranism, as both tending towards mysticism and contemplation (*Gefäß*/vessel), and also the distinction between Lutheranism and Calvinism, as the former tending towards mysticism (vessel) and the latter to asceticism (*Werkzeug*/instrument/tool).

124. See *WuG*: 330.

125. The two places are *WuG*: 334 and *GARS* I: 258.

126. *WuG*: 334; *ES*: 552. "Sowohl die bernhardinische wie die franziskanische–spiritualistische, wie die täuferische und die jesuitische Kontemplation wie die Gefühlsschwelgerei Zinzendorfs hinderten nicht, daß bei der Gemeinde und oft beim Mystiker selbst, Handeln und Bewährung der Gnade im Handeln immer wieder, wenn auch freilich in sehr verscheidenem Maße, asketisch rein oder komtemplativ gebrochen, die Oberhand behielten, und Meister Eckhart stellt schließlich Marta über Maria, dem Heiland zum Trotz."

It is interesting to note that both times that Weber speaks of the Martha-Mary issue, he also mentions Meister Eckhart. Clearly, Meister Eckhart represented an ideal type of the Western contemplative life for Weber.

127. This is, of course, against the traditional history of Western exegesis on the Lk 10:38–43 passage. See Solignac and Donnat (1980). The Patristic period followed Origen in its interpretation of this passage seeing Martha as the symbol of praxis and Mary as the symbol of theory, yet the inner unity of theory and praxis is to be found in the *unum necessarium*, which is charity for Origen. In St. Thomas Aquinas, Martha and Mary represent symbols of the active and the contemplative life respectively. Traditionally both figures are seen as necessary in the Christian life.

128. See *WuG*: 324 and *GARS* I: 258. The paradigm example here is the evolution of the Spiritual Exercises of St. Ignatius of Loyola, the founder of the Jesuits. Central to St. Ignatius's notion of contemplation was the idea of "contemplation in action," a spirituality that would spearhead the Catholic Reform and play a major role in Catholic modernity, in many spheres such as art (the Baroque), politics, social theory (the Jesuit Reductions in Latin America), the sciences, and knowledge in general. See Benjamin (1963) and Höpfl (2004).

129. On this point, see Jüngel (1992), Chapter 2. For a critique of the notion of postmetaphysical thinking and thus of the conception of metaphysics in both Habermas and Heidegger, see Lutz-Bachmann (2002). For a series of essays on the question of the possibility of a metaphysical grounding of ethics, see Lutz-Bachmann (Ed.) (1995).

130. It is interesting to note that during his time of recuperation in Nervi around 1903, Weber made an attentive reading of the Fifth Lecture of Fichte's *Die Anwesung zum seligen Leben oder auch die Religionsleben* (1806), making particular notes concerning the difficulty of finding God in action today. Furthermore, in his reception of Carlyle's work on asceticism through Schultze-Gävernitz's dissertation of 1891, Weber most probably took the notion of people being an "instrument of God." See Treiber (1999): 284–286.

131. Niklas Luhmann's reflection on religion in modernity uses Weber's *Zwischenbetrachtung* as a point of departure to reflect on the differentiation of religion from the cultural value spheres. His understanding of Weber is influenced by Parsons's interpretation of the cultural value spheres as individual subsystems of the general social system. See Luhmann (1998): 259–357.

132. On the implications of this for the relation between critical theory and political theology, see McCarthy (1991): 200–215.

133. *WuG*: 332; *ES*: 547–548. "Am deutlichsten wird der Konstrast zwischen beiden Verhaltungsweisen, wenn die Konsequenz voller Weltablehnung oder Weltflucht nicht gezogen wird. Der Asket muß, wenn er innerhalb der Welt handeln will, also bei der innerweltlichen Askese, mit einer Art von glücklicher Bornheit für jede Frage nach einem "Sinn" der Welt geschlagen sein und darum sich nicht kümmern. Es is daher kein Zufall, daß die innerweltliche Askese sich gerade auf der Basis der absoluten Unerforschlichkeit seiner Motive des jedem menschlichen Maßstab entrückten, calvinistischen Gottes am konsequentesten entwickeln konnte. Der innerweltliche Asket ist daher der gegebene "Berufsmensch," der nach dem Sinn seiner sachlichen Berufsausübung innerhalb der Gesamtwelt—für welche ja nicht er, sondern sein Gott die Verantwortung trägt—weder fragt noch zu fragen nötig hat, weil ihm das Bewußtein genügt, in seinem persönlichen rationalen Handeln in dieser Welt den für ihn in seinem letzten Sinn unerforschlichen Willen Gottes zu vollstrecken."

134. See Löwith (1995): 284–329. On the importance of the notion of "personality" in Weber's understanding of asceticism, see Treiber (1999): 282–289.

135. See Schluchter (1988a), 2: 76.

136. *GARS* I: 544. "Rationale Wirtschaft ist sachlicher Betrieb. Orientiert ist sie an Geldpreisen, die im Interessenkampf der Menschen untereinander auf dem Markt enstehen."

137. In this analysis Weber is following the work of Simmel on money. See Simmel (1989).

138. Weber quotes Baudelaire's satirical interpretation of mysticism to describe this acosmic love as a "sacred prostitution of the soul." See *GARS* I: 546.

139. This process of the secularisation of the economic sphere, most particularly through the substitution of the impersonal market regulation of money prices for the previous ethical regulation of the trade of goods and property, can be dated back at least to the work of Oresme (ca. 1320–1382), the bishop of Liseux. At the time of St. Thomas Aquinas (1225–1274), the craft guilds were mainly responsible for the regulation of prices through law and custom. However, clearly by the time of Oresme, who investigated the market regulation of prices in merchant capitalism in his *Traicte de la Première Invention des Monnoies*, the guild form of the regulation of prices was being replaced by market regulation. See Galbraith (1987): 25–30. It should be remembered that Weber wrote his doctorate with Levin Goldschmidt in 1889 on *The History of Trading Companies in the Middle Ages*, studying the medieval trading practices of commercial companies in Italian and Spanish towns, and so was well aware of the issues involved in the transformation of the practices of price regulation in the Middle Ages.

140. See *GARS* I: 546–554.

141. See *GARS* I: 546–547.

142. See *GARS* I: 548–549.

143. This analysis of Weber is quite pertinent in the present-day context of the rise of religious fundamentalism that links religious sentiments with nationalism. The recent debate about the definition of martyrdom in connection with suicide bombings is one contemporary example of the political competition with the religious ethic of brotherhood.

The discussion of the notion of sacrifice by René Girard and the nonsacrificial nature of Christianity is of interest here. Girard contrasts the secular social science, as one in which the violent mechanism of excluding a scapegoat from the group generates the sense of community and in so doing gives a certain sacred nature to this victim, with the Christian understanding of community based on the nonviolent solidarity with the victims of history in the new community of the Church. For Girard, the Bible deciphers this violent mechanism of scapegoating culminating in the Christian God, as in Christ, aligning himself personally with the victims of history by becoming a victim himself. See, for example, Girard (1972), (1978), (1982). For an excellent introduction to the thought of Girard, see Kirwan (2004). The notion of the victim as a sacred source of political sovereignty is also used in the work of the Italian philosopher, Agamben (1998).

144. See *GARS* I: 549.

145. Weber mentions here the example of the refusal of Cromwell's army to accept compulsory military service on the basis of such a just or holy war theory. Cromwell is, of course, a paragon of Puritan compromise with the political sphere during the English civil war. See *GARS* I: 550.

146. For Luther, God rules the world in two ways: through the earthly kingdom by law (force); and through the spiritual kingdom by grace or the gospel. Each Christian is a citizen of both kingdoms, and although these serve each other, they should remain separate to prevent the devil from having his way. For an excellent account of Luther's Two Kingdoms doctrine, see Witte (2002): 87–117.

147. For Weber, the two main historical examples of this type of organic social ethics are medieval Thomism and Hinduism. Cf. Schluchter (1988a), 2: 106.

148. As the Calvinist acted without the need to know the meaning of inner-worldly action, because he or she believed only God knew this, then similarly one must be committed to political action without feeling the need to understand, in short, to know its ethical meaning.

149. See *GARS* I: 554–556.

150. It is thus not surprising that much religious energy is going into cultivating this aesthetic route into religion today, through concerts and recitals in churches and artistic pilgrimages and so forth. For a very good example of this religious renewal of interest in art, see Verdon (2001).

151. See *GARS* I: 556–563.

152. The notion of erotic experience being intimately associated with coercion and brutality is perhaps another area of Nietzsche's influence on Weber. This would correspond to the view that human relationships are basically driven by the will to power. For an analysis of Weber's arguments here in the light of contemporary feminist reflections on erotic love, see Roslyn Wallach Bologh, "Max Weber on Erotic Love: A Feminist Inquiry," in Lash and Whimster (eds.) (1987): 242–258.

153. See *GARS* I: 560.

154. For an interesting study of the erotic in Western literature and visual art, see Paglia (1990).

155. See *GARS* I: 563–571.

156. *GARS* I: 564. "Wo immer aber rational empirisches Erkennen die Entzauberung der Welt und deren Verwandlung in einen kausalen Mechanismus konsequent vollzogen hat, tritt die Spannung gegen

die Ansprüche des ethischen Postulates: daß die Welt ein gottgeordneter, also irgendwie ethisch *sinnvoll* orientierter Kosmos sei, endgültig hervor. Denn die empirische und vollends die mathematisch orientierte Weltbetrachtung entwickelt prinzipiell die Ablehnung jeder Betrachtungsweise, welche überhaupt nach einem 'Sinn' des innerweltlichen Geschehens fragt. Mit jeder Zunahme des Rationalismus der empirischen Wissenschaft wird dadurch die Religion zunehmend aus dem Reich des Rationalen ins Irrationale verdrängt und nun erst: *die* irrationale oder antirational überpersönliche Macht schlechthin."

157. See *GARS* I: 566.

158. In his analysis of Kierkegaard in the shaping of modernity, Calvin O. Schrag notes that both Kant and Kierkegaard have resources to propose religion as a fourth cultural sphere of modernity to complement the usual three of science, morality, and art that are proposed in, for example, Habermas's theory of modernity. To Kant and Kierkegaard one might add Weber, which would allow a somewhat external critique of Habermas's theory of modernity found in Shrag to be more strongly stated as an internal critique given the importance of Weber in Habermas's own theory of modernity. See Schrag (1995).

159. *GARS* I: 566. "Die Erlösungsreligion wehrt sich gegen den Angriff des selbstgenugsamen Intellektes am prinzipiellsten natürlich durch den Anspruch: daß ihr eignes Erkennen in anderen Sphäre sich vollziehe und nach Art und Sinn gänzlich heterogen und disparat sei gegenüber dem, was der Intellekt leiste. Nicht ein letztes intellektuelles Wissen über das Seiende oder normativ Geltende, sondern eine letzte Stellungnahme zur Welt kraft unmittelbaren Erfassens ihres 'Sinnes' sei das, was sie darbiete."

160. It is interesting to note in this regard that in the Book of Genesis, Cain, the fratricidal son of Adam, is the founder of the human city (Gn 4:1–24). This has been interpreted by the Augustinian tradition as the origin of human culture in an act of sin: namely, the murder of Abel by his brother Cain. Thus, the notion of producing a world out of one's own capacities without relying on God lies at the heart of this understanding of the origin of human culture.

161. *GARS* I: 571. "Das Bedurfnis nach 'Erlösung' derart, daß, je systematischer das Denken über den 'Sinn' der Welt, je rationalisierter dieser selbst in ihrer äußeren Organisation, je sublimierter das bewußte Erleben ihrer irrationalen Inhalte wurde, desto unweltlicher, allem geformten Leben fremder, genau parallel damit, das zu werden begann, was den spezifischen Inhalt des Religiösen ausmachte. Und nicht etwa nur das theoretische Denken, welches die Welt entzauberte, sondern gerade der Versuch der religiösen Ethik, sie praktisch ethisch zu rationalisierten, führte in diese Bahn."

162. Kaesler (ed.) (2002), 2: 190–212. I shall consider below this question of interpreting Weber's theory of Protestantism as a theory of

secularisation in terms of the importance of *Kulturprotestantismus* (cultural Protestantism) in the work of Weber.

163. For Weber, both the orthodox and heterodox religions of India, Hinduism and Buddhism, compromised in order to adapt to the religiosity of the masses. In this sense, the Confucian religion of China differs from the religions of India; it did not adapt to the religiosity of the masses, but rather, maintained a form of religious aristocracy. Thus, Weber's social analysis of Hinduism can broadly be applied to that of Buddhism. Cf. Bendix (1977): 189 n. 69.

164. For a general analysis of this work, see Bendix (1977): 142–199; Schluchter (1988a), 2: 106–126; and Love (2000): 185–199.

165. See Schluchter (1988a), 2: 108–109.

166. See *GARS* II: 363–378.

167. *GARS* I: 573. "Die dritte, durch ihre Konsequenz sowohl wie durch die außerordentliche methaphysische Leistung: Vereinigung virtuosenhafter Selbsterlösung aus eigener Kraft mit universeller Zugänglichkeit des Heils, strengster Weltablehnung mit organischer Sozialethik, Kontemplation als höchsten Heilswegs mit innerweltlicher Berufsethik, hervorragende Form der Theodicee war der *indischen* Intellektuellen–Religiosität eigentümlich, welcher wir uns nunmehr zuwenden."

168. *GARS* II: 364.

169. The doctrine of *samsara* describes the cycle of rebirth that results from the effects of good and bad deeds as outlined in the doctrine of *karma*. Knowledge of the origin of this process in *Nirvana* results in the liberation of the person from this cycle of rebirth.

170. Weber notes the only exception to this: the caste soteriology of Vedanta Brahmanism, which cultivated a traditional notion of political, social, and economic calling. See *GARS* II: 367.

171. *GARS* II: 370. "Das 'Wunder' wird seinem Sinn nach stets als Akt einer irgendwie rationalen Weltlenkung, einer göttlichen Gnadenspendung, angesehen werden und pflegt daher innerlich motivierter zu sein als der 'Zauber,' der seinem Sinn nach dadurch ensteht, daß die ganze Welt von magischen Potenzen irrationaler Wirkungsart erfüllt ist und daß diese in charismatisch qualifizierten, aber nach ihrer eigenen freien Willkür handelnden Wesen, Menschen oder Uebermenschen, durch asketische oder kontemplative Leistungen aufgespeichert sind."

172. *GARS* II: 371. "Eine rationale praktische Ethik und Lebensmethodik, welche aus diesem Zaubergarten allen Lebens innerhalb der 'Welt' herausgeführt hätte, gab es nicht. Gewiß gab es den Gegensatz des Göttlichen und der 'Welt,' welcher im Abendlande geschichtlich die Konstituierung derjenigen einheitlichen Systematisierung der Lebensführung bedingte, die üblicherweise als 'ethische Persönlichkeit' bezeiechnet wird. Allein in Asien war der Gegensatz

nirgends ein solcher des ethischen Gottes gegen eine Macht der 'Sünde,' des radikal Bösen, welche durch aktives Handeln im Leben zu überwinden wäre. Sondern entweder die ekstatische Gottbessenheit, durch orgiastische Mittel zu gewinnen, im Gegensatz zum Alltag, in welchem das Göttliche nicht als lebendige Macht gefühlt wird. Also: eine Steigerung der Mächte der Irrationalität, welche die Rationalisierung der innerweltlichen Lebensführung geradezu hemmte. Oder der apathisch-ekstatische Gottbesitz der Gnosis im Gegensatz zum Alltag als der Stätte vergänglichen und sinnlosen Treibens. Also: ebenfalls eine außeralltägliche und zwar passive, dabei vom Standpunkt innerweltlicher Ethik aus irrationale, weil mystische, Zuständlichkeit, die vom rationalen Handeln in der Welt abführte."

173. *GARS* II: 372. "Und eine konsequente und psychologisch wirksame Systematisierung fehlte.... Es fehlte gerade das für die Oekonomik des Occidents Entscheidende: die Brechung und rationale Versachlichung dieses Triebcharakters des Erwerbsstrebens und seine Eingliederung in ein System rationaler innerweltliche Ethik des Handelns, wie es die 'innerweltliche Askese' des Protestantismus im Abendland, wenige innerlich verwandte Vorläufer fortsetzend, vollbracht hat."

174. For an analysis of Weber's method of causal historical sociology in his study of the religions of India, see Kalberg (1994): 177–192. Kalberg focuses on the rise to dominance of the caste order to outline Weber's causal methodology in *GARS* II.

175. Aland (1983): 58. "Da unser Herr und Meister Jesus Christus sagt: 'Tut Buße' usw. (Mt 4:17), wollte er, daß das ganze Leben der Glaübigen Buße sein sollte."

176. Weber's notion of "personality" clearly trades on this Lutheran conception of "believer." The methodical control of one's professional life is a secularisation of the religious categories of asceticism and vocation. Luther's understanding of life as penance correlates here with Weber's understanding of inner-worldly asceticism. It is thus important for Weber's general account of rationalisation and modernisation to separate contemplation and action in order to justify his own Protestant conception of modernity.

177. I shall consider this point in some detail below when I look at Weber's theory of secularisation as a Protestant theory of modernity. For the moment let me note that Weber's confessional metanarrative, which informs his sociology of religion, becomes increasingly apparent in his studies of the religions of Asia. This confessional metanarrative has implications for his general sociology on a number of analytically distinguishable levels. On the methodological level, it is significant because of his understanding of the basic typological categories of contemplation and ascetical action. On the empirical level, it is significant because of his account of modernity in terms of social and cultural rationalisation.

178. For a discussion of the importance of confessional metanarratives in the construction of modern political and social thought, see Skinner (1978b). Skinner later makes this point in reviewing the work of Habermas as "Protestantism by other means," see Skinner (1982). For the importance of confessional metanarratives on the development of natural rights theories, see Tuck (1979) and Haakonssen (1998).

179. See Johannes Winckelmann, "Exkurs zur werkgeschichtlichen Stellung des Antiken Judentums," in Schluchter (ed.) (1981a): 219–223; and Schluchter (1988a), 2: 594.

180. See Hartmut Lehmann, "The Rise of Capitalism: Weber versus Sombart," in Lehmann and Roth (eds.) (1995): 195–208.

181. Ibid.: 198.

182. See Schluchter (1981b).

183. In his analysis of Weber's *AJ*, Ralph Schroeder distinguishes between the period of the covenant, the period of the kingdom, and the post-exilic period. See Schroeder (1992): 72–84. However, as David Owen points out, in working with four periods one can see more easily the shift from primitive religion to universal religion, as represented in the first three periods, and the development of rationalism, which is an important feature of all four periods. See Owen (1994): 102.

184. See *AJ*: 381. Weber discusses the question of characterising the Jewish people as a "pariah people," in which the category of resentment plays a politically important function, in *WuG*: 300–304. He compares the ways in which Judaism differs from Hinduism in these respects, and whilst praising Nietzsche for first noticing this aspect in Judaism, he suggests that he mistakenly applies the category of resentment, understood as repression, to Buddhism. Weber suggests the specific nature of resentment in the Jewish experience was that the notion of suffering, from which it derives, was collectively understood as the political and social oppression of a whole people, whom Yahweh, as the universal God of justice, sought to repay by vengeance and retribution against the enemies of Israel. This social understanding of resentment was lacking in Hinduism and Buddhism, where suffering was considered to be individually merited.

185. See Assmann (2002).

186. Assmann describes "secondary religion" as that which reacts iconoclastically or "theo-klastically," as he puts it, against a "primary religion" that has not gone through this dialectical relationship with another religion. Egyptian religion is a primary religion for Assmann, and ancient Israel is at the origin of the invention of secondary religion. See Assmann (2002): 31–32, 70–71.

187. See Winckelmann (1980): 19–26 and Schluchter (1988a), 2: 133.

188. Bendix (1977): 256.

189. See *GARS* I: 94–95. It is interesting to note that Weber's direct reference to ancient Judaism in the first quote is from the 1920 edition. See *LW*: 178, Anhang 163.

190. See *AJ*: 281–314.

191. See *AJ*: 173–181.

192. *AJ*: 243. "Eine strenge Trennung von 'jus' und 'fas' war mit ihrer zu nehemden Bedeutung und der steigenden Berücksichtigung ihrer Anschauungen durch die jahwistisch interessierten Laien nicht aufrechtzuerhalten. Die alte nie vergessene Bedeutung der 'debarim Jahwe' [Hebrew for *word, name, commandment*] für alle wichtigen Entschließungen kam ihrem Einfluß auch auf die Rechtsanschauungen zugute. Die Theologisierung des Rechts einerseits, die Rationalisierung der religiösen Ethik andererseits waren die Folge dieser Zusammenarbeit jahwistisch frommer Laien mit ethisch reflektierenden Priestern. Das wichtigste Produkt dieser Zusammenarbeit, entstanden unter dem beherrschenden Einfluß der Jerusalemiter Priesterschaft nach dem Zusammenbruch des Nordreichs, war nun: das Deuteronium."

193. *AJ*: 236–237. "Die Verwerfung der Magie bedeutete praktisch vor allem: daß sie nicht, wie anderwärts, von den Priestern zwecks Domestikation der Massen systematisiert wurde.... Daß auch alles Uebel von Jahwe stamme, war eine der Grundthesen schon des ersten Propheten (Amos). Der Entwicklung der magischen Dämonenabwehr stand daher in Israel, wo alles Uebel Strafe oder Verfügung des mächtigen Gottes war, die Entwicklung der rein ethischen Priesterthora und Sündenbeichte als des eigentlichen Machtmittels der levitischen Priester gegenüber. Dies wirkte durch das ganze Gebiet der religiösen Entwicklung Israels hindurch."

194. As in his study on the religions of India, Weber discusses the important difference between miracles and magic in terms of the increase of rationality that the religious understanding of miracles represents. See *AJ*: 236–237.

195. The present-day support of the United States of America for Israel is seldom considered in terms of the religious family resemblance that Weber pointed to in his sociology of religion. Whilst economic and political considerations are obviously paramount, it would perhaps open new perspectives to rethink the significance of these religious similarities for contemporary global partnerships.

196. Cf., Bendix (1977): 200.

197. See *AJ*: 233.

198. Cf. Wax (1960): 453.

199. *AJ*: 421. "Es bedeutete sicherlich nicht eine asketische Lebensführung. In einem Punkt freilich ähnelt es in der Art seiner Lebensführung den rationalen asketischen Prinzipien: in dem Gebot wacher Selbstkontrolle und unbedingter Selbstbeherrschung. Die Notwendigkeit der ersteren war die unvermeidliche Folge der

fortwährenden Messung der Korrektheit der eigenen Lebensführung am Gesetz mit seiner außerordentlichen Vielzahl der rituellen Gebote und, namentlich, Verbote auf die zu achten war."

200. Here, I draw on Pierre Bourdieu's notion of capital as being not only material but also cultural and symbolic, and extend this to include spiritual resources as a form of capital. For a consideration of the role of capital in social change, see for example, Bourdieu (1990): 112–121 and Bourdieu and Wacquant (1992): 108–109.

201. This can be seen as one way in which Weber criticised Marx's notion of capital and its role in social change, and thus paved the way for Bourdieu's own much wider notion of capital and its role in social change and social order. For Weber's own view on this, see *AJ*: 239.

202. For Weber's own reflections on the importance of the rise of the city in the process of democratisation, see *WuG*: 727–814. For the importance of this process in the ancient world and its influence on later European development, see Assmann (2002).

203. See Cox (1965).

204. *AJ*: 239–240. "Das Zweite ebenfalls höchst Wichtige aber war: Jahweh blieb ein Gott der Geschichte, und zwar insbesondere: der politisch-militarischen Geschichte. Das unterscheidet ihn von allen asiatischen Göttern und hatte seinen Grund in dem Ursprung seiner Beziehungen zu Israel. Für seine getreuesten Verehrer blieb er immer der eidgenössische Bundeskriegsgott. Mochte er außerdem der Regengott sein und mochte ihn die Spekulation Nordisraels zum Himmelskönig steigern, für die eigentlich jahwistische, namentlich auch die prophetische Frömmigkeit blieb er der Gott politischer Schicksale. Kein Gott also, mit dem man mystische Vereinigung durch Kontemplation suchen konnte, sondern ein übermenschlicher und doch verständlicher persönlicher Herr, dem man zu gehorchen hatte. Er hatte seine positiven Gebote gegeben, daran hatte man sich zu halten. Man konnte seine Heilsabsichten, die Gründe seines Zorns und die Bedingungen seiner Gnade erforschen, wie bei einem großen König. Aber darüber hinaus gab es nichts. Die Entwicklung einer Spekulation über den 'Sinn' der Welt nach indischer Art war auf dem Boden dieser Voraussetzung vollständig ausgeschlossen. Aus untereinander verschiedenen Gründen ist sie auch bei den Aegypten und Babyloniern nicht über gewisse sehr enge Grenze hinausgegangen. Im alten Israel war für sie schlechthin kein Boden."

205. See *AJ*: 327–328.

206. See *AJ*: 327.

207. *AJ*: 328–329. "Nirgends und niemals wird von den Propheten oder (soviel wir wissen) ihrem Publikum die Frage nach einem "Sinn" der Welt und insbesondere des Lebens, nach einem rechtfertigenden Grunde seiner brüchigen, leid- und schuldbehafteten Vergänglichkeit und seiner Widersprüche auch nur aufgeworfen, wie sie in Indien aller

heiligen Erkenntnis den entscheidenden Antrieb gab. Und was damit zusammenhängt: nie und nirgends ist das Bedürfnis nach Rettung, Erlösung, Vollendung der eigenen Seele aus und gegenüber dieser unvollkommenen Welt, was den Propheten oder sein Publikum zum Gott treibt. Niemals vollends fühlt sich der Prophet durch sein Erlebnis vergottet, mit dem Göttlichen vereinigt, entrückt der Qual und Sinnlosigkeit des Daseins, wie dies dem indischen Erlösten widerfährt und für ihn den eigentlichen Sinn religiösen Erlebens darstellt. Niemals weiß er sich dem Leiden oder auch nur der Knechtschaft unter der Sünde entronnen. Nirgends ist Raum für eine unio mystica oder gar für die innere seelische Meeresstille des buddhistischen Arahat. All dergleichen gab es nicht und vollends eine metaphysische Gnosis und Weltdeutung kam gar nicht in Betracht. Denn das Wesen Jahwehs enthielt nichts Uebersinnliches in der Bedeutung von etwas jenseits von Verstehen und Begreifen Liegendem. Seine Motive waren menschlichem Verständnis nicht entrückt."

208. Bellah describes five evolutionary stages in the development of religion: primitive religion, in which religion and society are fused; archaic religion, in which myths become particularised as gods and celebrated in cults; historic religion, a period of demythologisation in which religious action becomes a necessary means for salvation; early modern religion, such as at the time of the Reformation, when a direct and immediate relation to transcendence develops and one's whole life is considered to be the place for religious action; and finally, modern religion, in which there is a collapse of the dualism between this world and the next. See Bellah (1970): 32–36.

209. It is interesting to note that the original Greek term for sacrament, *mysterion* (or *musterion*), denotes mystery and derives from the expression *muo*, meaning "to shut the mouth." *Mysterion* in biblical terms refers to a hidden thing or a mystery and in the Old Testament stands for the mystical or hidden sense of an Old Testament saying or an image seen in a vision. The Latin word *sacramentum* is used to translate the Greek *mysterion* into the Vulgate. The English word *sacrament* is used to translate this Latin equivalent and was originally used to symbolise something sacred or secret and involved the initiation of someone into a particular form of service. See Paul Haffner (1999): 5–8.

210. For the importance of the influence of Protestant liberal theology for Weber's own understanding of mysticism, see Krech (2001b).

211. Weber's rejection of the Indian, and, in another sense, Catholic notion of the deification of the self as a goal for the pre-exilic prophet clearly fits with his own Protestant conception of the relation between contemplation/mysticism and action/asceticism. See *AJ*: 329. Weber constructs his binary oppositional types according to his systematic sociological interests, and not as historically pure phenomena. See

GARS I: 539. However, whilst he is conscious that in reality these types have overlapped, the practical consequences for his systematic sociology of religion rule out a Catholic modernisation in his exclusive thematisation of the Reformed Protestant lifestyle (*Lebensführung*) as the exclusive way of modernisation in the West.

212. A good overview of Weber's conception of mysticism can be found in Volkhard Krech's article on this topic in Kippenberg and Riesebrodt (eds.) (2001): 241–262. It should be remembered that the Protestant suspicion of mysticism is more clearly expressed in the reformed-influenced branches of Protestantism. Lutheranism, as Weber himself realises (*GARS* I: 108), has a tendency towards mysticism. As I noted in considering *PE*, the work of the Protestant theologian Matthias Schneckenburger is a major source for Weber's understanding of these differences between Lutheranism, which tends toward the *unio mystica*, and Calvinism, which tends towards unemotional ascetic action. On this point, see Tyrell (1992): 188.

213. *AJ*: 330. "Wenn so das mystische Haben eines außerweltlichen Göttlichen abgelehnt wurde zugunsten des aktiven Handelns im Dienst des überweltlichen. Aber prinzipiell verständlichen Gottes, so ebenfalls die Spekulation über den Seinsgrund der Welt zugunsten der schlichten Hingabe an die positiven göttlichen Gebote. Irgend eine philosophische Theodizee wurde gar nicht zum Bedurfnis, und wo sich dies Problem, an welchem in Indien immer erneut gearbeitet wurde, doch meldete, wurde es mit den denkbar einfachsten Mitteln erledigt."

214. See *AJ*: 401–402.

215. See Schluchter (1988a), 2: 197ff. Evidence of his research for this work can be found in sections of the "Sociology of Religion" part of *WuG*, in his study of the religions of India in *GARS* II, and in the conclusion of his work on ancient Judaism. For a series of critical essays on this part of Weber's work, see Schluchter (ed.) (1985).

216. See Schluchter (1988a), 2: 254.

217. See Drijvers (1985): 459–460.

218. See Stroumsa (1985): 502–503 and (1981). In the Jewish and Christian conception of the person, Stroumsa sees a form of disenchantment because from now on God, the world, and humans will be separated and no longer fused together as in the ancient conceptions of the cosmos. See Stroumsa (1985): 504.

219. See, for example, Mullet (1999), O'Malley (1993), and Lindberg (1996).

CHAPTER 4

Secularisation in Weber's *Wirtschaft und Gesellschaft (WuG)* and Munich Speeches

Asceticism and Mysticism in *Wirtschaft und Gesellschaft*

In the development of Weber's concepts of asceticism and mysticism, the "Sociology of Religion" section in *WuG*[1] plays a key role. In it he significantly deepens his understanding of these concepts from his first systematic use of them in the first edition of *PE* in 1904/1905.[2] Weber wrote this material before his study of the types of world-rejection in the *Zwischenbetrachtung*,[3] and by reconstructing the evolution of these concepts one can better understand the decisions and selections that he made in working out his religious typologies.

Weber is not interested in religion for its own sake. Rather, he pursues his studies of religion in order to investigate the effect that types of religious attitudes and stances towards the divinity and the world have on social action:

> A definition of what religion "is," is not possible at the start of a presentation such as this. A definition can be attempted, if at all,

> only at the end of the study. The essence of religion is not even our concern, as we make it our task to study the conditions and effects of a particular type of social action.[4]

In this sense, Weber's sociology of religion is not a theory of rationality, but rather, a typology of the various rational forms that religious traditions have in fact embodied, and also of the forms that could possibly be rationally embodied.[5] In his "Anti-critical reply to Felix Rachfahl," he clarifies what he means by Protestant and Catholic types of asceticism.

> There is not a patented concept of "asceticism." That one can understand this concept in a larger sense than I have, where I have compared an "inner-worldly" ascetical direction of life with an "other-worldly" monastic asceticism is to a certain extent self-evident and is something that I accept. I refer by Catholic asceticism expressly to rationalised asceticism (that in its most potent form is shown in the Jesuit order) in contrast, for example, to "unmethodical flight-from-the-world" (on the Catholic side) and a merely emotional "asceticism" (on the Protestant side).[6]

Clearly, Weber understands the Catholic or Counter Reformation innovation, as typified in the Jesuit order, to be one of asceticism and not one of mysticism. As we read in *WuG*, this is clearly based on Weber's mutual exclusion (perhaps based on his own self-declared religious unmusicality) of the rational harmonisation of mystical contemplation and ascetical action in the Christian tradition.[7]

On this point, even in Weber's final understanding of this conceptual type in the *Zwischenbetrachtung*, mysticism remains insignificant as a type of social action.[8] Even in Wolfgang Schluchter's attempt to reformulate Weber's typology of the means to salvation for religious virtuosi, this point remains undeveloped.[9] However, this should not be a reason to ignore the major developments in Weber's conception of asceticism and mysticism.

A significant moment in this development was Weber's study of the Russian Revolution in 1917, in which his appreciation of the role of Russian Orthodoxy helped him to become more aware of the issues involved in understanding mysticism.[10] Yet, as Schluchter notes, his concept of mysticism at this stage still remains within the framework of the first edition of *PE*, where he contrasts an active ascetic attitude with a mystical and emotional one.[11] Moreover, the differentiation between Lutheranism and Calvinism, upon which this contrast rests, relies heavily on Matthias Schneckenburger's *Vergleichende Darstellung des lutherischen und reformierten Lehrbegriffs* (1855). Weber's typology of asceticism and mysticism thus can clearly be traced to the Protestant theological sources upon which he depended to construct his typology of religious forms.[12]

Another key element in Weber's formulation of the concept of mysticism was his study of the religions of India. This study led him to significantly reformulate his concept of mysticism. In Buddhism, he had encountered a methodical/rational world-flight that did not lead to the acosmic form of love that he considered characteristic of the Christian conception of mysticism.

In *WuG*, Weber organises his reflections on asceticism and mysticism according to the answer given by each religious form to a particular heuristic question: How is it possible for a religious believer to gain a sure sense of salvation (*certitudo salutis*)?[13] A third party, such as another person or an institution, can either dispense this sense of salvation, or the individual can pursue this goal directly. The particular religions that foster individual pursuit of this goal, according to Weber, tend to promote in the individual an awakening of a methodological attitude to life. The three historical paths to obtaining such a certainty of salvation have been ecstasy, asceticism, and contemplation. After certainty is achieved, however, the individual must ensure that the certainty endures. Thus ecstasy, since it only provides a temporary sense of the certainty of one's own salvation, is assimilated into contemplation.[14] In fact, Weber suggests that asceticism and contemplation are the two most important soteriological methods open to religious believers to assure themselves of a lasting certainty of being saved. He understands asceticism as a practical attitude that manifests itself in right action: in short, a religiously guided form of permanent behaviour. He considers contemplation, in contrast, to be theoretical, leading to right knowledge of a mystical kind: in short, contemplation is associated with a permanent type of consciousness in which the certainty of salvation is manifested.[15]

This categorisation clearly shows Weber's analytical strategy. He unites the aspects of means and end in each category. Thus, on the one hand, asceticism is the means and action is the end; and, on the other hand, mysticism is the means and contemplation is the end. Both means and ends get fused into the same analytical category and are often, in Weber's work, used synonymously. This explains why he never considers the possibility of conceiving of mystical action as a significant type of social action. Clearly, if the means to action is asceticism and the means to contemplation is mysticism, then Weber's categorisation logically makes the respective means and ends of these categories mutually exclusive. Schluchter suggests that this classification is influenced by Weber's integration of specific religious traditions into these categories.[16] The theocentric Christian tradition and the cosmocentric Asian religions structure the relation to the divine accordingly. In the Christian tradition, this classification is embodied through either becoming a servant or a child of God whilst, in the Asian traditions, union with the divine is paramount. Weber's typology equates the Christian tradition with the Reformed Protestant tradition and ignores the significance of the Catholic and, indeed, Lutheran traditions for a sociological theory of action. This is true to the extent that these other types are not considered to be sociologically significant in the promotion of the spirit of capitalism and, thus, of Western rationalism.[17]

Weber goes on to refine his typology of asceticism and mysticism by looking at the ways in which these types relate to the world. A person striving to attain salvation can either accept the ways of the world or reject them. Weber calls these two responses "this-worldly" and "other-worldly" respectively in *PE*. In *WuG*, however, he renames the "other-worldly" response as "world-rejecting" asceticism. This change refines the contrast between the ascetic rejection of the world and the world-flight of the contemplative mystic, and allows him to identify two different this-worldly responses: the this-worldly ascetic and the this-worldly mystic. This allows him to contrast the behaviour and attitudes to the world displayed by the Protestant ascetic and the mystical monk.[18] The "this-worldly" ascetic thus can either choose to change the world or to dominate it, whereas the "this-worldly" mystic can only accept the world and God's providence for him in it; he has no inner motivation, no basis in religious attitude to rationally reshape the world:[19]

> On the other hand, the contemplative mystic is concerned with perceiving the essential meaning of the world, but he cannot comprehend it in a rational form, for the very reason that he has already conceived of the essential meaning of the world as a unity beyond all empirical reality. Mystical contemplation has not always resulted in a flight from the world in the sense of an avoidance of every contact with the social milieu. On the contrary, the mystic may also require of himself the maintenance of his state of grace against every pressure of the mundane order, as an index of the enduring character of that very state of grace. In that case, even the mystic's position within the institutional framework of the world becomes a vocation, but one leading in an altogether different direction from any vocation produced by inner-worldly asceticism. Neither asceticism nor contemplation affirms the world as such. The ascetic rejects the world's empirical character of creatureliness and ethical irrationality, and rejects its ethical temptations of sensual indulgence, epicurean satisfaction, and reliance upon natural joys and gifts. But at the same time he affirms individual rational activity within the institutional framework of the world, affirming it to be his responsibility as well as his means of securing certification of his state of grace. On the other hand, the contemplative mystic living within the world regards action, particularly action performed within the world's institutional framework, as in its very nature a temptation against which he must maintain his state of grace. The contemplative mystic minimises his activity by resigning himself to the institutions of the world as it is, and lives in them incognito, so to speak, as those "that are quiet in the land" (Psalm 35:20) have always done, since God has ordained once and for all that man must live in the world. The activity of the contemplative mystic within the world is characterised by a distinctive brokenness, coloured by humility. He is constantly striving to escape from activity in the world, back to the quietness and inwardness of his God. Conversely, the ascetic, whenever he acts in conformity with his type, is certain to become God's instrument. For this the ascetic's humility, which he considers a necessary obligation incumbent on a creature of God, is always of dubious genuineness.

> The success of the ascetic's action is a success of the God Himself, who has contributed to the action's success, or at the very least the success is a special sign of divine blessing upon the ascetic and his activity. But for the genuine mystic, no success that may crown his activity within the world can have any significance with respect to salvation. For him, his maintenance of true humility within the world is his sole warranty for the conclusion that his soul has not fallen prey to the snares of the world. As a rule, the more the genuine mystic remains within the world, the more broken his attitude towards it becomes, in contrast to the proud aristocratic feeling with respect to salvation entertained by the contemplative mystic who lives apart from the world.[20]

This passage demonstrates Weber's intention in constructing his typology of asceticism and mysticism. It also illustrates the selective criteria that he uses to eliminate the sociological significance of the "this-worldly" mysticism as a type of action. Indeed, this intention and these criteria fit well with Weber's general understanding of secularisation. This shift of emphasis from the "other-world" to "this-world," the focus of analysis from contemplation to action, and the institutional prioritisation of the world's structures over the Church's institutions all neatly fit into the Protestant metanarrative in which Weber tells the story of secularisation and of the progress of Western rationalism. The categories of contemplation and action, mysticism and asceticism, are used as analytically constructed historical landmarks that chart the development of Western history from the darkness of magic to the light of reason. The march of reason in this story even pushes the categories of contemplation and mysticism themselves to rationalise. However, in so doing, they become neutralised of any real sociological significance for action in the world.

Although Weber recounts the story from the Western point of view, he does distinguish between the Western Christian tradition and the other salvation religions, most especially those of India. This has the typological effect of causing Weber to insufficiently thematise the contemplative and mystical traditions of Christianity and to project them onto the religions of India. On this basis, he constructs his typology of religious attitudes to the world and their impact on social action:

> The decisive historical difference between the predominantly oriental and Asiatic types of salvation religion and those found primarily in the Occident is that the former usually culminate in contemplation and the latter in asceticism. The great importance of this distinction, for our purely empirical consideration of religions, is in no way diminished by the fact that the distinction is a fluid one. Recurrent combinations of mystical and ascetic characteristics demonstrate that these heterogeneous elements may combine, as in the monastic religiosity of the Occident. For our concern is with the consequences for action.[21]

This passage brings out clearly a vital presupposition that Weber uses to organise his sociology of religion and theory of action. Contemplation and action follow the principle of *ora et labora*, and whilst the West has examples of the contemplative type, it is really in the East, most especially in India, that these techniques of ensuring a permanent sense of one's own salvation have been most rationally developed. However, Weber's typology understands *ora et labora* as *ora aut labora*, that is to say either contemplation or action. He rules out *ora in labora*, which is one of the key intuitions of the Catholic or Counter Reformation. Weber's understanding prevents attributing any sociological significance to mysticism for action, as, whilst the distinction may be "fluid" and combinations may have occurred, Weber understands them within his *ora aut labora* typology, and for him contemplation and action are mutually exclusive. That is to say, whilst means (mysticism and asceticism) may combine, ends (contemplation and action) cannot.[22] Moreover, this passage brings out clearly the confusion of the historical and analytical levels in Weber's sociology of religion, which has had major implications for his theory of action. In tying his analytical separation of asceticism and mysticism to the historical distinctions between the Occidental and the Indian salvation religions, he effectively precludes the possibility that the historical category of mysticism could have sociological significance in the Western world after the medieval Catholic organic ethics of St. Thomas Aquinas. This, of course, makes the narration of the rise of Western rationalism a much neater tale. However, it distorts the picture of the historical development of the Western world in favour of a Protestant metanarrative. In short, Weber's theory of secularisation has to be seen as part of a broader Protestant metanarrative of the rise of Western rationalism.

As Wolfgang Schluchter notes, Weber's *Einleitung* even lags behind *WuG* in regard to precision in separating the analytical and historical levels of analysis.[23] Here Weber drops the distinction of world-rejecting asceticism and considers both mysticism and asceticism as types of salvation that reject the world. Nonetheless, he continues to contrast the various types of world rejection in the *Einleitung* according to the "inner-worldly" and "other-worldly" (flight-from-the-world) schema of *WuG*. This precludes his distinguishing between inner-worldly asceticism and inner-worldly mysticism, since inner-worldly is now equated with asceticism, and "other-worldly" or "flight-from-the-world" is equated with mysticism.[24] Schluchter attempts to rescue Weber's typology from analytical and historical confusion by broadening the concepts of asceticism and mysticism from their equation with activity and passivity respectively. However, he continues to make the Weberian assumption that the direction of the religious effort of the mystic is necessarily other-worldly. Even though he allows for activity in the life of the mystic, this cannot be considered as soteriologically significant action within the world: "If we follow our scheme, it appears, at least on the level of the virtuosi, as if cosmocentrism and inner-worldly asceticism as well as theocentrism and inner-worldly mysticism "exclude" one another."[25] This is a logical consequence of the Protestant understanding of theocentrism, as the *Deus Absconditus* of Luther, and of the *Rechtfertigungs* (Justification) debate, which is implicit in both Weber's and Schluchter's typological construction. This becomes clearer a little later in Schluchter's analysis of the specific contribution of ascetic Protestantism to the process of the disenchantment of the world:

> Only in Calvinism, and especially in the Baptist denominations, in short in ascetic Protestantism, is sacramental grace completely

> devalued in favour of a spiritual attitude and system of personal sanctification. With this spiritual turn ascetic Protestantism carried the "religious disenchantment of the world" to its ultimate conclusion.
>
> In Weber's view, ascetic Protestantism combines five characteristics, which up to the Reformation no other salvation movement had successfully fused in Asia or the West: theocentrism, asceticism, inner-worldliness, personal sanctification, and virtuosity. Only this combination produces the religious motivation for world mastery.[26]

A Reformed Protestant interpretation of the sacramental mediation of grace as a hindrance to world mastery informs Schluchter's analysis here. This leads him to conclude by proposing a typically Protestant conception of modernity:

> We can say, then, that the religious ethic of ascetic Protestantism is a monological ethic of conviction with unbrotherly consequences. Exactly, herein lies its developmental potential. This ethic not only places the relationship of human beings to God above their relations to one another—as does all consistent Christian religion—it also provides a new meaning to this relationship by no longer interpreting it in terms of filial piety. Thus, it creates a motivation for depersonalising first religious and then non-religious human relationships. This reinforces the tendency of the patrimonial order toward the formalisation of law, bureaucratisation, and the extension of the market principle.[27]

It is this Protestant conception of modernity and secularisation, typical of Weber and those in this tradition like Schluchter and Habermas, that provides the dominant metanarrative of the Western world about its own fate and crisis.[28] In Schluchter's words:

> However, even in its mechanised and spiritless manifestations, the autonomous vocational culture of Western modernity reveals the remnants of the religious elements, which helped bring about its birth. They continue to haunt us in the secularised attitude of world mastery and world domination of impersonality and lack of brotherhood.[29]

No less does the Reformed Protestant conception of the divine inform Schluchter's own conception of the divine: "The

Occidental mystic cannot after all engage in a union with God because of the particular nature of his conception of the divine."[30]

That Weber stands within a particular tradition is, of course, self-evident. However, this tradition has not been made thematically explicit at a systematic level. And this has resulted in an insufficient appreciation of the extent to which the Protestant metanarrative informing his work has had analytical and historical consequences for his social theory.[31]

Theocratic and Secular Law: The Dialectics of Formal and Substantive Rationalisation

The importance of Max Weber's sociology of law for his general sociology has until recently been insufficiently noted in the literature.[32] One should not forget that his academic background was in law; he wrote his *Habilitationschrift* and doctorate on Roman law and the law of medieval trading companies respectively. Moreover, his father had been a lawyer, and before Weber began his sociological work, he had passed the examination of a junior barrister (*Referendar*) in May 1886 and served in this function for six years during his studies in Berlin. He also began teaching law at Berlin in 1892, and it was his appointment to the chair of National Economics at the University of Freiburg that shifted his focus from legal matters to the academic social sciences.

In tracing the narrative of secularisation in the work of Weber, it should come as no surprise that the topic of the rationalisation of law provides an index of this process. The secularisation of modern law has often been considered a major indicator of the process of secularisation.[33] Whilst it is clear that the rationalisation of natural law does not have the same function as the question of theodicy in Weber's sociology of religion—that is to say, as a developmental foil wrapping together the various elements into a coherent narrative—it is clear that the dialectic of formal and substantive rationalisation in his sociology of law is a major aspect of his understanding of the disenchantment and systematisation of modern secular rationalism.[34] Weber sees the increase in rationality of the law to be intimately tied to the increase in the rationality of the administrative system in a given society:

> The more the rationality of the organisation of the authority increased, irrational forms of procedure were eliminated and the substantive law was systematised, i.e., the more the law as a whole was rationalised.... However, these rationalising tendencies were not part of an articulate and unambiguous policy on the part of the wielders of power; they were rather driven in this direction by the needs of their own rational administrations, as, for instance, in the case of the administrative machinery of the Papacy, or by powerful interest-groups with whom they were allied and to whom rationality in substantive law and procedure constituted an advantage as for the middle classes in Rome in the late Middle Ages and modern times. Where these interests were absent the secularisation of the law and the growth of a strictly formal mode of juridical thought either remained in an incipient stage or was even positively counteracted. In general terms, this may be attributed to the fact that the rationality of ecclesiastical hierarchies as well as of patrimonial sovereigns is substantive in character, so that their aim is not to achieve the highest degree of formal juridical precision which would maximise the chances for the correct prediction of legal consequences and for the rational systematisation of law and procedure. The aim is rather to find a type of law which is most appropriate to the expediential and ethical goals of the authorities in question. To these carriers of legal development, the self-contained and specialised "juridical" treatment of legal questions is an alien idea, and they are not at all interested in any separation of law from ethics. This is particularly true, generally speaking, of theocratically influenced legal systems, which are characterised by a combination of legal rules and ethical demands.[35]

As Hubert Treiber has noted, the notion of propagating strata, or carriers of important ideas, is common to Weber's sociology of religion and indeed also to his sociology of domination.[36] It is a key notion that Weber employs in these various fields of sociology, seeing the intellectual classes as propagating the ideas that influence the direction of societal and cultural rationalisation. Indeed, these similarities led Treiber to suggest that the way to understand Weber's sociology of law is through his sociology of religion:

> If the elective affinity thesis should prove true, then this would mean, among other things, that access to the sociology of law would have to take place via the sociology of religion.... The result is that the concept of the propagating strata, which also has considerable influence in the sociology of law, is more systematically established, which is illustrated by the fact that approaches to a theory of professionalisation take it as their starting point. From this point of view, "priests" and Western legal experts (*Fachjuristen*) can be considered to be prototypes of "professionals" who have an ambivalent relationship to the process of (increasing) rationalisation: on the one hand it has produced them and on the other they have had an influence on it.[37]

That Weber's understanding of the sociology of law should be closely connected to his sociology of religion can also be supported on the basis of his important debt to the Protestant Church historian and anti-Catholic canon lawyer, Rudolf Sohm.[38] Sohm was a major influence on Weber's conception of charisma and on many of his historical themes in the sociology of religion, such as the importance of asceticism in individual salvation.[39] Sohm, like Weber, was also a member of the Evangelical Social Congress, and both had influenced Friedrich Naumann in his creation of the *Nationalsozialer Verein* (National Social Party)[40] in 1896.[41]

Both Weber and Sohm saw the separation of religion and politics as a way forward for the German national identity in the newly-founded German Empire of 1871.[42] Sohm defended the view that the Church was no longer a useful vehicle for social policy in the new German empire (a view shared by Weber,[43] as shown by his vigorous attack on Friedrich Naumann's proposal for a nationalist motivated political theology) in his Freiburg inaugural address, and in his review of Naumann's essays on this matter in the liberal Protestant journal *Die Christliche Welt* of 1894.[44]

In his analysis of the substantive rationalisation of sacred law, Weber reviews the varied dynamics of Indian, Chinese, Islamic, Persian, Jewish, and canon law.[45] In all but the canon law of Christendom, Weber considers the process of separating sacred and secular law to have been blocked by one or another form of religious control of society.[46] He attributes the peculiarly rational form of sacred law in Christendom to nine factors:[47] the formal nature of canon law; the early development of dualistic thinking in which jurisdictional authority became divided between secular and sacred domains; the adoption of the Stoic conception of natural law and the rational traditions of Roman law as a basis for canon law; the medieval use of Germanic law in the creation of the Penitentials, the code used to guide confessors; the separation in the medieval university of the teaching of theology and secular law from canon law, which hindered the growth of theocratic political structures; the development of a logical and professional legal technique using ancient philosophy and jurisprudence; the employment of jurists with the resolutions of church councils as in the decretals; the fact that, in the post-charismatic era of the Church, church functionaries held rationally defined bureaucratic offices (this was most important in the Gregorian period of the late eleventh century); finally, the inquisitorial procedure that was developed in canon law provided a rational method which aided its substantive rationalisation. The combination of these nine factors made the canon law of Western Christendom the most rational form of sacred law. Whilst being a substantive form of law, it both contains and gives rise to formal aspects of law, illustrating the dialectic of substantive and formal law, which for Weber characterises legal rationalisation in the West.[48] He considers this dialectical understanding of Western legal rationalisation to be a consequence of a specifically Christian understanding of the world and its consummation:

> As a consequence of the New Testament's eschatological withdrawal from the world, the basic writ of Christianity contains only such a minimum of formally binding norms of a ritual or legal character that the way was left entirely free for purely rational enactment.[49]

Weber follows the more Protestant understanding of eschatology defended by Luther and particularly Calvin in rejecting the realised eschatology in ecclesial and sacramental form.

This found new form in the Protestant History of Religion school conception of eschatology. The publication in 1892 of Johannes Weiß's *Die Predigt Jesu vom Reiche Gottes (The Sermon of Jesus on the Kingdom of God)* had marked a crucial moment in nineteenth-century Protestant theology.[50] Weiß rejected the view put forward by his stepfather Albrecht Ritschl, that eschatology found its embodiment in ethical action for the kingdom of God. Rather, like Calvin, he saw the kingdom of God as an eschatologically future-oriented transcendental reality of which no trace could be found in present historical reality.

This clearly fits well with Weber's notion that legal rationalisation was allowed by the eschatological withdrawal from the world, as interpreted by the liberal Protestant eschatology of Johannes Weiß. It left morality and law the eschatological freedom to be grounded in secular reason and, in this way, allowed Weber to interpret Luther's opposition between "the law and the gospel" as being prefigured in the New Testament eschatological rejection of the world. Of course, this opened the door to rationalise the legal procedure of the world, because whilst the gospel concentrates on the world to come, secular rationality serves the needs of this world.[51] The withdrawal of eschatology from the world thus serves the advance of Weber's Protestant conception of modernity and its legal rationalisation.[52]

Günther Roth has already noted the important role played by natural law in Weber's understanding of the process of secularisation.[53] In considering the role played by natural law in the French Civil Code, proclaimed in 1804,[54] Weber charts the formal qualities of revolutionary law as the formal rationalisation of natural law. Weber reproduces the dialectic of formal and substantive rationalisation here as the secularisation of natural law, which, emptied of metaphysical and theological contents, can provide a normative standard for positive law. In this way, Weber sees the process of disenchantment within natural law as not destroying the capacity of natural law to be a legitimate source for positive law. Disenchantment here is understood (mistakenly) not as a loss of legitimation, but rather, as a shifting of the grounds of legitimation from theological to rational sources.

> We encountered the *lex naturae* earlier as an essentially Stoic creation, which was taken over by Christianity for the purpose of constructing a bridge between its own ethics and the norms of the world. It was legitimated by God's will for all men of this world of sin and violence, and thus stood in contrast to those of God's commands, which were revealed to the faithful and are evident only to the elect. But here we look at the *lex naturae* from another angle. Natural law is the sum total of all those norms, which are valid independently of, and superior to, any positive law and which owe their dignity not to arbitrary enactment but, on the contrary, provide the very legitimation for the binding force of positive law. Natural law has thus been the collective term for those norms, which owe their legitimacy not to their origin from a legitimate lawgiver, but to their immanent and teleological qualities. It is the specific and only consistent type of legitimacy of a legal order, which can remain once religious revelation and the authoritarian sacredness of a tradition and its bearers have lost their force.[55]

As Ludger Honnefelder has shown, Weber and, indeed, Troeltsch both fail to recognise that this secularisation of natural law was already present in Thomas Aquinas's understanding of natural law in the thirteenth century and was an invention of neither the modern nor the revolutionary era.[56] Honnefelder suggests that this mistaken reading of Aquinas derives more from a reading of the Neo-Thomism of the nineteenth century, which was strongly represented in the First Vatican Council (1869–1870). This Neo-Thomist position fails to understand that Aquinas, in his reading of the prologue of Aristotle's *Nichomachean Ethics*, acknowledges a plurality of sciences and upholds a separation of theoretical and practical knowledge. Furthermore, Thomas derives ethics not from a metaphysical or a theological source, but rather, from the autonomous nature of practical reason.[57] Weber's reading of this tradition and his application of the dialectical opposition of theocratic and secular law to the Western natural law tradition is thus seriously flawed, when he writes:

> Compared with firm beliefs in the positive religiously revealed character of a legal norm or in the inviolable sacredness of an age-old tradition, even the most convincing norms arrived at by abstraction seem to be too subtle to serve as the basis of a legal

> system. Consequently, legal positivism has, at least for the time being, advanced irresistibly. The disappearance of the old natural law conceptions has destroyed all possibility of providing the law with a metaphysical dignity by virtue of its immanent qualities. In the great majority of its most important provisions, it has been unmasked all too visibly, indeed, as the product or the technical means of a compromise between conflicting interests.[58]

In his study of natural right,[59] Leo Strauss suggested that Weber's commitment to objectivity and his reservation to the rational basis of value judgements clearly reveals Weber to be a product of the tradition and social situation that was the only home of nonevaluating objectivity: namely, the liberal Protestant tradition of the late nineteenth and early twentieth centuries.[60] His analysis of the substantive turn to natural law, in the socialist understanding of the labour theory of value, reveals a fatalism in the face of the advance of legal positivism.[61] Clearly, Weber saw the only way forward as being the championing of the liberal individualism in which he himself was at home. One important resource for this liberalism is the work on charisma of Rudolf Sohm, the Protestant professor of law at Leipzig.

Charisma, Sacred and Secular

Weber's discussion of the concept of charisma in *WuG* plays an important role in his reflections on political sociology, most especially in his theories of power, rule, and the State. His starting point for these reflections is, as is often the case in Weber's work, the elucidation of a differentiated typology. He outlines three types of rule—charismatic, traditional, and legal-rational:[62]

There are three pure types of rule. The validity of the claims of legitimacy may be based on:

1. Rational grounds—resting on a belief in the legality of enacted rules and the right of those elevated to authority under such rules to issue commands (legal authority).
2. Traditional grounds—resting on an established belief in the sanctity of immemorial traditions and the legitimacy

of those exercising authority under them (traditional authority); or finally,

3. Charismatic grounds—resting on devotion to the exceptional sanctity, heroism, or exemplary character of an individual person, and of the normative patterns or order revealed or ordained by him (charismatic authority).[63]

Indeed, as noted by Peter Lassman,[64] rule is the leitmotif that runs through the whole of Weber's political sociology. The importance of rule is also of central importance for an understanding of Weber's theory of social action:

> Rule in the most general sense is one of the most important elements of social action. Of course, not every form of social action reveals a structure of ruler-ship. But in most of the varieties of social action ruler-ship plays a considerable role, even where it is not obvious at first sight.... Without exception every sphere of social action is profoundly influenced by structures of ruler-ship.[65]

It is important to realise that *Herrschaft* (ruler-ship), in Weber's understanding, takes on a different and new meaning.[66] Weber is no longer concerned with the normative dimension of rule, which previous interpreters have read into his concept of *Herrschaft*.[67] The oversimplified way in which "value neutrality" has been understood in Weber's sociology is the central cause of this misunderstanding, according to Peter Lassman.[68] Rather, Weber understands the legitimacy of *Herrschaft* according to the principle of legality, and thus more closely related to political expediency, the *de facto* acceptance of the laws, rather than to the *de jure* normative meaning of legitimacy.[69] This is more than a terminological point. Such a worldview fits with a Protestant metanarrative, and thus one could suggest, following the commentators who have already seen similarities between Weber's and Macchiavelli's political thought, that in Macchiavelli (1469–1527), Renaissance and Reformation were brought much closer together than has until recently been thought.[70]

In "Charisma and Twentieth-Century Politics," Luciano Cavalli neatly summarises the way in which Weber employed charisma in his general political sociology, and also the functions that charisma fulfilled in the relations of ruler-ship:

> In other writings I have developed a paradigm of elements, corresponding in my opinion to the crucial moments in the dialectics of the charismatic process, from its beginning to its end. The paradigm in its shortened form is as follows: (1) extraordinary situation; (2) "calling" of the potential leader and his request for obedience from the potential following; (3) acknowledgement by the following and its request for a confirmation; (4) confirmation shown by the success of the leader and an act of commitment of the following; (5) structuring of the following as a leader-centred community of movement, with a leader-dependent elite ('charismatic aristocracy'); (6) the leader as the principal source of values and norms; (7) change of mind of the leader-centred group, manifest in new feelings and attitudes (feelings of togetherness, self-confidence, activism and pugnacity in the case of a movement); (8) maximum individual and collective effort for the "cause," with positive results; (9) in the case of repeated lack of success, repudiation and possible disintegration of the following; (10) leader's death followed by succession (either the institutionalisation of charisma or the disintegration of the following); (11) a new personal charisma arises in a dialectical relationship with institutionalised charisma as and when an extraordinary situation confronts it.[71]

Cavalli uses this reconstruction of the process of charisma in Weber to analyse the way in which the various totalitarian dictatorships and plebiscitary democracies of the twentieth century have used this charismatic process to legitimise their rule and to propagate their ideas. In his analysis of the rise to power of Hitler, Cavalli shows just how well Weber's schema fits the complex relation of Hitler to the Nazi Party and helps to explain the absolute power he enjoyed as German chancellor after January 1933. Cavalli's reconstruction also helps to make explicit the aspects of the process of charisma that bring to light features of Weber's theory of secularisation already encountered in his other works. Thus, the common aspect of Weber's theory of secularisation that translates or carries over theological categories into a secular framework can be seen not only in the concept of charisma itself, but also in the categories of the social process through which charisma becomes politically significant. The notion of an extraordinary situation (*Außeralltäglichkeit*), originally used by Weber in his description of prophetic experience in Judaism, now finds a secular equivalent in that the transcendent is defined as "that which transcends the everyday economic routines," and their particularly special quality is identified as "that not everybody could have access to them."[72] The ecstatic experience of the Israelite prophets is reproduced as the "transcendental" experiences of politicians conferring them with special gifts in body or mind, and with a resulting form of magnetic attraction.[73] Cavalli outlines Hitler's ecstatic "vision" in Pasewalk, after his hospitalisation following the German defeat of 1918, as just such a secular equivalent of prophetic ecstasies.[74] Clearly the notion of the "calling" of an individual, originally developed by Weber in his study of Luther in *PE* and in Israelite prophecy, functions to provide the political leader with a sense of mission and destiny that he is called to fulfil. Followers, called to accept as a matter of duty this charismatic leader, resemble the hierarchical social structure and authority of religious leaders and followers.[75] Even the institutionalisation of charisma through its various forms of routinisation clearly draws on Weber's knowledge of the early Christian Church and translates or transposes these models from the theological to the political domain. The transformation of charismatic authority from the original charismatic religious founder or political leader to the church or state apparatus of rationally institutionalised bureaucratic apparatus is strikingly similar in Sohm's work on early Christianity and the origin of church law and Weber's account of charisma and its transformation.[76]

Recent research is uncovering the Protestant theological sources behind Weber's own concept of charisma and is thus providing more evidence that Weber's theory of secularisation fits within a general Protestant metanarrative.[77] The most important of these sources for Weber's concept of charisma is without doubt the Protestant Rudolf Sohm.[78] Andreas Bühler, in his study of the relation of Church and State in Sohm's work, has called Rudolf Sohm "the most important church father of the end of the nineteenth century".[79] As is known from his *Jugendbriefe*, Weber was aware of Sohm and his work from his student days in Strasbourg in 1883, when he had attended a lecture of Sohm's.[80] Weber was also aware of Sohm through their joint political engagement with the National Social Party (*nationalsozialen Verein*), which included a mutual friendship with Friedrich Naumann (founder of the National Social Party), and through Sohm's work on the BGB (*Bürgerliches Gesetzbuch*—a series of five books on private law, introduced on January 1, 1900).[81] The important *Evangelisch-sozialer Kongreß* (ESK) (Evangelical Social Congress), founded in May 1890 under the leadership of Adolf Stöcker, also provided a forum in which the major ideas in Protestantism and the social sciences were aired, and both Sohm and Weber, together with Friedrich Naumann and Adolf von Harnack were members and regular contributors to the activities of the ESK.[82] The journal *Die Christliche Welt (The Christian World)* provided an important channel for the ideas of the ESK, and one to which Weber contributed significant ideas. Heinrich Hermelink recorded:

> The years from 1892 to 1896 are the high point of the Christian-social movement and thus of the Evangelical Social Congress: The *Christliche Welt* considered itself the advocate of the Congress. Naumann took control during these years, beginning with his Berlin lecture of 1892 on "Christianity and the family." He and Stöcker are still holding together despite the conflict about leadership. The conference met for the first time outside of Berlin in 1894 in Naumann's and Rades home city of Frankfurt am Main. The competitive exchange between the young national economist Max Weber and the previous General Secretary Paul Goehre on "the situation of the German agricultural workers" was humourlessly objected to by the conservative press.[83]

Beyond this contextual evidence, Weber himself made clear, in his *WuG*, his reception of Sohm's historical research in canon and civil law and its importance for his own understanding of the concept of charisma:

> The concept of "charisma" ("the gift of grace") is taken from the vocabulary of early Christianity. For the Christian hierocracy Rudolf Sohm, in his *Canon Law*, was the first to clarify the substance of the concept, whilst others (for example Karl Holl in *Enthusiasm and the Power of Penance*) have clarified some of its consequences. It is therefore, nothing new.[84]

And again:

> It is to Rudolf Sohm's credit that he worked out the sociological character of this kind of structure of power; however, since he developed this category with regard to one historically important case (the rise of the ecclesiastic authority of the early Church) his treatment was bound to be one-sided from the point of view of historical diversity. In principle, these phenomena are universal, even though they are often most evident in the religious realm.[85]

Sohm distinguished three basic moments in the history of the decline of the Church into a worldly corporation through Catholic legal decadence. In the first period, the original Church was produced by the direct action of God in and through the charismatic gifts given to the early apostles, prophets, and teachers. There was no juridically constituted Church. The *ecclesia*, the people of God, formed a type of visible church, but its visibility was directly made by God in the power of the Holy Spirit, and not by any church law. The second period began at the end of the first century when the juridification of the sacramental celebration of the Eucharist was controlled through the installation of the office of bishop. According to Sohm, this period lasted until the work of the legal scholar Gratian in the twelfth century. The third period, the one in which ecclesial law is transformed into civil law, occurs between 1160 and 1170, with Rufin and Alexander III. Here the notion of the Church as the body of Christ becomes transformed into a legally constituted corporation, making the Church an earthly society and no longer the body of Christ. Sohm's basic argument, which ran through his works *Canon Law*[86] and *Essence and Origin of Catholicism*,[87] was that the charismatic origins of the original Church had been destroyed by the development of canon law in the Catholic Church. This meant that the distinction between "law" and "spirit," original to St. Paul but only systematically developed by Luther, had been lost in the confusion of the invisible church of Christ (the Church in a religious sense) with the visible legally constituted body of the Catholic Church. It was really only after Luther, for Sohm, that this distinction of the two senses of the Church became clear, and with this distinction, the specificity of Protestantism came into being:

> Right down to Luther however, the opposition between the church of Christ and the legally constituted Church was not clear in the Christian life. The ancient period, from the first century until the end of the Middle Ages, did not attempt to make a clear distinction in this regard. The acceptance of this distinction (that today dominates the cultural world) defined Protestantism. This clearly also meant that the lack of this distinction defined Catholicism.
>
> The essence of Catholicism is the lack of distinction between the religious (church of Christ) and the legal sense of the Church.[88]

The crucial point here, for Sohm, is that it is Luther who stresses the invisible nature of the Church that cannot be constituted or ruled by canon law.[89] Thus, the Church is not to be identified with any visible structure, with any man-made institution such as the Catholic Church. Rather, the Church resides in the invisibility of the true church of Christ, which is made present in the hearts of Christians directly by the Spirit. For Sohm, Protestantism represents a recovery of the spirit of the original charismatic Church before the onset of decadence in the legal colonisation of the Christian life-world in Catholic canon law.[90] Peter Haley, in his account of Sohm's conception of charisma, suggests that Sohm's work is best understood when seen in the context of the attempt of nineteenth-century Protestant theology to recover the historically prior as the purer: a general belief of the Protestant historicism of the nineteenth century. Speaking of Sohm's debate with the other major Protestant theologians in the debate on the Church, Haley suggests that the works of the great Protestant thinkers—Harnack, Hatch, and Sohm—demonstrated a close connection between Protestantism and historicism. These thinkers tended to believe that the historically prior was the most correct form of Christianity. This helped nineteenth-century Protestant scholars to discard the immediate past of Roman Catholicism on the grounds that it was a less pure form of Christianity. In fact, for many Protestant thinkers of the time, Roman Catholicism was merely a successful heresy that had become orthodoxy.[91]

Clearly, Sohm's conception of charisma played a particularly important role in Weber's own understanding of the revolutionary nature of charisma as expounded in *WuG*.[92] Both Weber and Sohm understood the opposition of tradition and charisma.[93] Indeed, following Sohm, Weber calls charisma the "specifically creative revolutionary force of history."[94] The archetypal Protestant focus on the individual and his or her liberty (*sola scriptura*), against the "legal imprisonment" of the authoritarian Catholic tradition, clearly colours Weber's conception of the revolutionary and personal nature of charisma in a post-*Kulturkampf* Germany.[95] Even the very definition of charisma and charismatic rule is rooted in Sohm's understanding of the individual nature of charismatic gifts:[96]

> The term *charisma* will be applied to a certain quality of an individual personality (originally in prophets, therapists, wise-men, hunting leaders, war-heroes: magically determined) by virtue of which he is considered extraordinary and treated as endowed with supernatural, superhuman, or at least specifically exceptional powers or qualities. These are such as are not accessible to the ordinary person, but are regarded as of divine origin or as exemplary, and on the basis of them the individual concerned is treated as a "leader."[97]

Sohm described the gifts of the Holy Spirit as mysteriously distributed to individuals in the community, and Weber uses this notion to develop his own conception of the heterogeneous nature of charismatic rulership. In this sense, as Factor and Turner argue, Weber takes over Sohm's mysterious conception of charisma, and in Weber, this simply becomes a secular rather than a theological mystery.[98]

Weber's use of the concept of charisma has also been criticised from a number of other theological-sociological perspectives. Thus Peter Haley, for example, suggests that Weber's value-neutral approach to the concept of charisma drains away the religious meaning of the concept that was clearly present in Rudolf Sohm's use of this category.[99] Alan Berger argues that in separating the concept of charisma from the tradition in which it is embedded, Weber fails to understand that it is the tradition which legitimates a charisma.[100] Peter Berger has criticised Weber for too sharply separating the charisma of the Israelite prophets from the institutional legitimation of the Israelite priesthood. He suggests that the prophets were also closely related to certain cultic offices and thus, in a certain sense, also institutionally legitimated.[101] Leo Strauss even criticised Weber's general typology of *Herrschaft*, suggesting that, rather than the traditional, rational, and charismatic schema representing an objective neutral and universal categorisation of forms of rule, this was a parochial schema rooted in the experience of a few generations of continental Europe of the nineteenth century.[102] Yet Thomas Ekstrand argues that despite these shortcomings, Weber's secular conception of charisma is still of use, even in the theological domain.[103]

It would be wrong to see Weber's analysis of charisma as confined to the Judeo-Christian tradition. He also knew the importance of charisma for the prophet Muhammad and for the rise of Islam. Yet, as Bryan Turner has suggested, due to Weber's exclusive focus on the charismatic prophet Muhammad as a warrior-type and the emphasis he placed on the warrior group in Islam as the main carrier of the religious ideas of Islam, together with his neglect of the Koranic and other Muslim accounts of early Islam, Weber presented a reductionist account of Islam, in which Islam comes out looking like a secular quest for booty and real estate, and in which the religious dimension was considered to be an epiphenomenon.[104] Nevertheless, that Weber embarked at all on a study of Islam makes him, on this issue, more intellectually adventurous than both Marx and Durkheim. In fact, only his untimely death prevented him from embarking on a full-scale study of Islam, which would have broadened and complemented his sociology of religion.[105] These shortcomings should not overshadow the importance of Islam in Weber's existing work.

Islam

> Industrialisation was not hindered by Islam as a religion of individuals . . . but rather by the religiously determined structure of Islamic states [Staatengebilde], their officialdom and their jurisprudence.[106]

By 1914, Weber had collected the basic information he required to include Islam in his *WEWR*.[107] But after the outbreak of the First World War in 1914 until his death in 1920, he did not carry out any more research on the subject. His early research provided him with the data that he included in his various publications and scattered particularly throughout *WuG*. His study of Islam raises interesting questions about the global nature of secularisation. As Bryan S. Turner noted in 1974:

> It goes without saying that, if secularisation is taking place, then the secularisation of Islam is likely to be very different from the secularisation of Christianity. Unfortunately, this somewhat obvious point seems to be lost on those theorists who start with some assumptions that secularisation is a global phenomenon.[108]

Indeed, it would be wrong to consider Islam and even Islamic countries as representing a monolithic system that can be considered as one phenomenon.[109] Clearly, the history of secularisation in Turkey under the leadership of Kemal Ataturk in the 1920s is very different from the experience of Asian and African Islamic countries, to say nothing of the Middle East.[110]

For Weber, a key difference between Islam from Western religion is the influence of Christianity in the development of the city.[111] He suggests that it was only in "Christian Europe" that cities became urban communities, since Christianity helped to break the influence of the clan and the tribe and, thus, fostered creation of an association of individuals based not on familial or tribal loyalties, but rather, on social and legal agreements:

> When Christianity became the religion of these peoples who had been so profoundly shaken in all their traditions, it finally destroyed whatever religious significance these clanties retained; perhaps, indeed, it was precisely the weakness or absence of such magical and taboo barriers which made the conversion possible. The often very significant role played by the parish community in the administrative organisation of medieval cities is only one of many symptoms pointing to this quality of the Christian religion, which, in dissolving clan ties, importantly shaped the medieval city. Islam, by contrast, never really overcame the divisiveness of Arab tribal and clan ties, as is shown by the history of internal

> conflicts of the early caliphate; in its early period it remained the religion of a conquering army of tribes and clans.[112]

Weber suggests five features necessary for a geographically specific association of individuals gathered together in a non-agricultural commercial settlement to constitute a city:[113] a fortification or a means of defending the settlement from the attacks of invaders; a market in which the exchange of goods can occur according to rational principles; a court of law governed by autonomous law, again based on clear rational principles; an associative structure that orders the way in which social relations occur; and finally, at least partial autonomy and autocephaly, which includes administration by authorities in whose appointment, at least in principle, the citizens could actively participate. These five conditions make the ideal type of the Western city for Weber. They mark the evolution from medieval times to modern times, the transition from traditional forms of rule in the feudal period to the modern rational-legal form of rule of the early modern period.

Clearly, for Weber, the traditional patrimonial character of Islamic rule blocks the process of Western rationalisation, which amongst other things helped to give rise to the Western city.[114] In this sense, the city is the social embodiment of the process of secularisation, the form in which the principles of the disenchantment of the world take their social shape. Interestingly, one detects a clearly confessional motive at work here too. The break from the hierarchical structure of the Catholic Church and its social equivalent in the hierarchy of feudal society is one of the social and religious gains of the Reformation. In this sense, the Catholic Church resembles Islam in its traditional form of rule, favouring the hierarchical over the democratic model. Weber notes that most Islamic cities, such as Cairo, Damascus, Aleppo, and Baghdad, were not socially unified communities, but instead, tended to be divided into quarters, because the clan and tribal basis of Islamic societies favoured such forms of social cohesion.[115]

Weber also considers Islamic law to be a significant hindrance to the development of Western capitalism[116] and rationalism in general.[117] Unlike the Western legal tradition, which, as Weber notes, was the only one to develop systematic forms of thought based on rational principles,[118] the Islamic tradition did not develop a dualistic approach to law separating sacred and secular law. Instead he notes Islamic law consisted of the interpretation, by specially trained theological-legal jurists, of all areas of life according to tradition of the interpretations of the prophets of the Holy Law and based on the *Koran* and the *Sunna* (the written sources on the life of the prophet Mohammad):

> The sacred law of Islam is throughout specifically a "jurists law." Its validity rests on *idshmâ (idshmâ -al-ammah = tacitus consensus omnium)*, which is defined in practice as the agreement of the prophets of the law, i.e., the great jurists (*fuqahâ*). Besides the infallible Prophet, only the *idshmâ* are officially infallible. Koran and Sunna are merely the historical sources of the *idshmâ*. The judges do not consult the Koran or the Sunna, but the compilations of the *idshmâ*, and they are not allowed to independently interpret the sacred writings or traditions.[119]

Weber analyses Islamic law with the heuristic intention to discover the particularity of the development of Western rationalism.[120] He concludes that it is obvious that the lack of separation of sacred and profane law results in Islam's inability to develop a formal-rational law. Wolfgang Schluchter puts this point well:

> However, the closing of sacred tradition results in the running dry of the charismatic source of law. This immobilises the evolution of the law. A stereotypical law of jurists results which with every means resists secularisation. Three processes mutually support one another: immobilisation, stereotyping, and the rejection of secularisation. This allows for a systematisation, however, one which is finally not juristically formal but rather theologically material.[121]

Thus, the living tradition has been fossilised, so to speak, by the jurists who systematise the law according to theologically material principles. The crucial formalisation of the law that allows for the all-important separation of the spheres of life is absent. Life is thought of as a substantive whole, described by the sacred tradition and interpreted by the jurists. A bureaucratic class of formal administrators can never develop, because knowledge itself remains subservient to revelation. The process of secularisation that the Western world experienced cannot find a foothold in such circumstances. Typologically, Islamic law is a form of theocratic and patrimonial *kadi* justice,[122] which by its nature blocks the very process of secularisation that acts as one of the defining features of Western rationalism in Weber's account of modernity.[123]

A final area of interest in considering Weber's account of Islam and its relevance for his account of secularisation lies in his own biography. As Bryan S. Turner notes in his study of Weber and Islam, Weber's Protestant background was not insignificant in defining the features of his study of Islam.[124] His moral outlook was strongly influenced by Pietism and the Kantian stress on doing one's duty. Indeed, Turner suggests that this upbringing was responsible to a great extent for Weber's sexual problems.[125]

In today's liberal society, it is relatively easy to underestimate the importance of the moral control of society exerted by religion in Weber's time. Indeed, this was especially significant in the Prussian world of imperial Germany (1871–1918).[126] In such a context, Weber's views on the religious status of marriage and women in Islam reveal the importance of his religious attachments for his general sociology of religion:

> Religion primarily desires to eliminate the sexual orgy (the "whoredom" denounced by the Jewish priests), in keeping with prophetic religion's general attitude toward orgies, which we have described already. But an additional effort is made by religion to eliminate all free sexual relationships in the interest of the religious regulation and legitimation of marriage. Such an effort was even made by Mohammad, although in his personal life and in his religious pronouncements regarding the world beyond he permitted unlimited sexual freedom to the warrior of the faith. It will be recalled that in one of his sutras he ordained a special dispensation regarding the maximum number of wives permitted for himself. The various forms of extramarital love and prostitution, which were legal before the establishment of orthodox Islam, have been proscribed in that religion with a success scarcely duplicated elsewhere.[127]

Clearly, for Weber, Islam embodied the values of male domination and sexual freedom that his own Protestant background considered an anathema.[128] Bryan S. Turner puts the point well:

> Weber's moral perspective is also the key to an understanding of Weber's commentary on Islam. Whereas Christianity contained a hero-ethic, which regulated sexual life, Islam, in Weber's view, was the "average ethic" which accommodated to sexuality rather than challenging it. For Weber, Islam represented values—male domination and sexual freedom, which were inimical to the hero-ethic.[129]

The patrimonialism that in the political and legal spheres had prevented the rise of capitalism functioned no less significantly in the erotic sphere to propagate a sexual ethic of male domination. In Weber's account of Islam, the patrimonial system clearly blocks both the differentiation of the cultural value-spheres, so intrinsic to his account of rationalisation and modernisation, and the process of secularisation, and this prevents the autonomous differentiation and development of the sub-systems of society.

It is testimony to Weber that, even today, the question of the potential modernisation of Islam is a major question. This has become even more significant as a result of the contemporary restructuring of geopolitics around the theme of "the war on terrorism." Whilst significantly limited by the prejudices of his time, it is to Weber's credit that he ventured into a field of research that not only for the other founding fathers of sociology, Marx and Durkheim, but also for many sociologists of religion, philosophers, and theologians nearly one hundred years later, is still a "no-go area."

Science and Politics as a Vocation

Weber delivered his Munich speeches at a crucial moment in the history of Germany and, indeed, in the history of the whole of Europe. *Wissenschaft als Beruf* (hereafter *Wissenschaft*) (November 7, 1917) and *Politik als Beruf* (hereafter *Politik*) (January 28, 1919) were both given in the form of speeches to young students at the University of Munich who faced a very uncertain social and political future.[130] Both speeches were organised by the *Freistudentische Bund* in Bavaria (a left-leaning liberal student group) as a part of a series of responses to the essay published by Alexander Schwab (a pupil of Alfred Weber) called "Vocation and Youth." Schwab took the view that the notion of taking up a profession (*Beruf*) was incompatible with the spirit of objectivity in science. The series of lectures, organised by the students, was meant to discuss the pros and cons of Schwab's views, and included, as well as Weber, such speakers as Kerschensteiner, Hausenstein, Naumann, and the theologian Lippert.[131]

At the end of the First World War in 1918, the foundation of the Inter-party Committee (*Interfraktionelle Ausschuss*) of the Reichstag crystallised the movement towards parliamentary government and the Weimar coalition. However, in the winter of 1918–1919, this political process fell into deep crisis. Despite Woodrow Wilson's "Fourteen Points," issued on January 8, 1918 and stressing the important role of the League of Nations, the armistice conditions threatened plans for peace, and factions in the political left in Germany generated conflict over constitutional issues. In 1917, when Weber delivered *Wissenschaft*, he still expected an acceptable outcome to the war and hoped that Germany would be able to play a role in world politics after it; thus his focus is more on the conditions of knowledge in modernity. By 1919, however, it had become clear that with the alliance between intransigent right-wing chauvinism and left-wing politics of single-minded conviction, there was little hope for a strong and united Germany. It is in this context, from 1917–1919, that Weber spoke to young idealistic students about their future role in German politics and society.[132]

As Erich Wittenberg has argued, because of this context it is important to see *Wissenschaft* and *Politik* as interconnected, as forming an internally cohesive and unified entity.[133] I shall therefore outline their importance for Weber's theory of secularisation together and seek to show, as Friedemann Voigt has argued, the common Protestant heritage informing both speeches.[134]

Weber begins both speeches by outlining basic guidelines for reflecting on questions of science and politics. He opens

Wissenschaft with a consideration of the "material conditions of science as a vocation," that is to say, the prospects a young person has when he or she decides to embark upon an academic career at a university.[135] He opens *Politik* with a definition of the State as "that human community which (successfully) lays claim to the monopoly of legitimate physical violence within a certain territory, this territory being another of the defining characteristics of the state."[136] And thus politics is defined as "striving for a share of power or for influence on the distribution of power, whether it be between states or between groups of people contained within a single state."[137] With these basic considerations in place, Weber moves on to investigate more substantive matters.

Friedrich Tenbruck has observed that, in many ways, *Wissenschaft* and *Politik* are really continuations of the themes Weber took up in his *PE*.[138] Vocation, single-minded commitment to realising an objective, and the modern conditions of the disenchantment of the world were all seen in *PE* and appeared throughout his writings. In fact, in these two speeches, Weber even alludes to the importance of Protestantism in helping to bring about modern science:[139]

> But during the period of the rise of the exact sciences one expected a great deal more. If you recall Swammerdam's statement, "Here I bring you the proof of God's providence in the anatomy of a louse," you will see what the scientific worker, influenced (indirectly) by Protestantism and Puritanism, conceived to be his task: to show the path to God.[140]

If this was the origin of the task of the scientist, the whole tenor of *Wissenschaft* and *Politik* is that these conditions no longer apply. Both speeches raise the question of how one can follow a vocation when one is no longer charged with the task of showing "the path to God." Weber expresses this theme as the impossibility of contemporary science to deal with the question of meaning under the modern conditions of secularisation:

> Under these internal presuppositions, what is the meaning of science as a vocation, now after all these former illusions, "the way

> to true being," the "way to true nature," the "way to true God," the "way to true happiness," have been dispelled? Tolstoy has given the simplest answer with these words: "Science is meaningless because it gives no answer to our question, the only important question for us: What shall we do and how shall we live?" That science does not give an answer to this is indisputable. The only question that remains is the sense in which science gives "no" answer, and whether or not science might yet be of some use to the one who puts the question correctly.[141]

It is interesting also that in *Wissenschaft* Weber defines his concept of disenchantment as mastery of the world through calculation, a consequence of the rationalisation and intellectualisation of the modern world:

> The increasing intellectualisation and rationalisation do not, therefore, indicate an increased and general knowledge of the conditions under which one lives. It means something else, namely, the knowledge or belief that, if one but wishes, one could learn it at any time. Hence, it means that principally there are no mysterious incalculable forces that come into play, but rather that one can, in principle, master all things by calculation. This means that the world is disenchanted. One need no longer have recourse to magical means in order to master or implore the spirits, as did the savage, for whom such mysterious powers existed. Technical means and calculations perform the service. This above all is what intellectualisation means.[142]

Thus, the capacity to calculate provides a nonmagical or disenchanted form of mastery of the world. Again one hears echoes of Weber's notions of asceticism, of personality, and of the nonsacramental understanding of existence. The typically Protestant notion of the removal of all traces of God, the so-called Catholic notion of *vestigium trinitatis*, from the cosmos, is a necessary condition for Weber's understanding of disenchantment, intellectualisation, and rationalisation. The confessional specificity of this view can be and indeed often has been overlooked.[143] This is most likely due to the lack of theological competence of philosophers and social theorists, a consequence itself of the increasing specialisation of science with which Weber deals in *Wissenschaft*. However, as Friedemann Voigt has argued, this has led to a serious lack of awareness of the theological sources upon which Weber drew in *Wissenschaft*, most especially the Protestant theologian Friedrich Schleiermacher (1768–1834),[144] who is, as already mentioned, commonly known as the "church father of the nineteenth century."[145] Schleiermacher distinguished between religion, based on intuition and feeling and thus independent of all dogma, and theology, which Schleiermacher considered to be a positive science. In this way Schleiermacher separated the Catholic understanding of rational theology as a speculative science from the Protestant understanding of theology as based on the individual experience of lived religion, which presumed on this basis a pluralistic conception of religion.[146] Weber clearly draws on Schleiermacher when he interprets St. Augustine to say that in the final analysis one is called to leap the gulf between reason and belief, to make the "sacrifice of the intellect" in order to be a positively religious man:

> Then the question of theology is: How can the presuppositions, which must simply be accepted, be meaningfully interpreted in a view of the universe? For theology, these presuppositions as such lie beyond the limits of "science." They do not represent "knowledge," in the usual sense, but rather a "possession." Whoever does not "possess" faith, or the other holy states, cannot have theology as a substitute for them, least of all any other science. On the contrary, in every "positive" theology, the devout reaches the point where the Augustinian sentence holds: *credo non quod, sed quia absurdum est*. The capacity for the accomplishment of religious virtuosos—the "intellectual sacrifice"—is the decisive characteristic of the positively religious man.[147]

Schleiermacher also strongly defended the importance of the separation of Church and State, arguing that the State required governance by the rule of law, which was uniform and universal, whilst religion was governed by the individual nature of intuition in which free spirits could gather together in the liberty of the true Church.[148] This Protestant conception of religion and theology clearly animated Weber's own reflections on the questions of science and knowledge in a disenchanted world.

Friedemann Voigt has investigated the influence of Julius Wellhausen's research on the prophets of ancient Judaism on Weber's Munich speeches. As Voigt suggests:

> That Weber here uses the images of "true" and "false" prophets at all is worthy of consideration. Herein lies a Protestant heritage, which allows us to see more clearly Weber's intentions in both his Munich speeches. For this reason, a glance at the history of the work is useful, since both Munich speeches and his study of ancient Judaism were written during the same period. The prophets played here a major function, as Weber considers the prophets of destruction (Jeremiah and deutero-Isaiah) to be the high point of the religious development of Judaism. This is his intention in following the work of the Protestant Old Testament scholar Julius Wellhausen.[149]

Julius Wellhausen (1844–1918) was the authority on the history of Israel for late nineteenth- and early twentieth-century scholarship.[150] Weber considered the leadership in the field to be Protestant and German, and he depended on this research in his own study of *AJ*.[151] The key feature that Weber transposes from that study to his Munich speeches is the conception of the prophet as the uncompromising, honest individual who has special knowledge and is charged with communicating this knowledge to the people. This conception essentially becomes Weber's model for the "man of vocation" in both *Wissenschaft* and *Politik*. The prophet represented the individual who stood against the compromises of the institution, the charismatically inspired man of conviction who felt called to speak the truth regardless of the consequences. This intellectual honesty of the Jewish prophets was the sign and the embodiment of reason, of a process of rationalisation in which Judaism clearly represented an advance over the sacrificial practices of the mythological priesthoods of the other ancient Near Eastern peoples. The ethical demands of these prophets, to care for the poor and the weak, for foreigners and widows and orphans, replaced the priestly demands for sacrificial appeasement of the gods through ritually controlled practices. The price paid by the prophet for such uncompromising honesty was separation from the ordinary life of the people in order to ensure the preservation of the integrity of his message. This ascetical picture of the prophets of Israel became for Weber the model for the man of vocation under the conditions of disenchantment: that is, in the modern secular world. This image of the prophet was typical in the Protestant History of Religion school at the end of the nineteenth century, and it clearly provided Weber with a framework for the notions of personality and asceticism that feature so prominently in his works, from *PE* to his Munich speeches.[152] This image of the prophet further provided him with a normative yardstick with which to criticise the practice of modern science by the modern-day dilettantes of the German universities, who lacked the courage to face the fate of the times:[153]

> To the person who cannot bear the fate of the times like a man, one must say: may he rather return silently, without the usual publicity build-up of renegades, but simply and plainly. The arms of the old churches are opened widely and compassionately for him. After all, they do not make it hard for him. One way or another he has to bring his "intellectual sacrifice"—that is inevitable. If he can really do it, we shall not rebuke him. For such an intellectual sacrifice in favour of an unconditional religious devotion is ethically quite a different matter than the evasion of the plain duty of intellectual integrity which sets in if one lacks the courage to clarify one's own ultimate standpoint, and rather facilitates this duty by feeble relative judgements. In my eyes, such religious return stands higher than the academic prophecy which does not clearly realise that in the lecture rooms of the university no other virtue holds but plain intellectual integrity.[154]

Unfortunately, this notion of intellectual integrity and presupposition-free science blinded Weber to his own particular presuppositions, which, as Erik Wolf suggested, were submerged in a Protestant metaphysical historicism typical of nineteenth- and early twentieth-century Germany.[155] Voigt brings out this confessional influence on Weber's position when he says:

> Both Weber's and Wellhausen's picture of the prophet is clearly a Protestant theological construction. Moreover, it was the type of construction that Weber had characterised as "positive" theology. While Weber and Wellhausen differentiated the original purely

> religious character of the prophetic revelation from the priestly, they remained committed to maintaining the difference between religion and theology, which was a basic premise of "positive" theology. As Weber is unconditionally committed to the object of research, which is transposed to the intellectual honesty of science, this cannot be seen as bidding farewell or disposing of religion. It is rather a criticism of the type of science which does not consider the matter of truth in all its seriousness. This illustrates once again a moment of theological critique which he will later follow up.[156]

Thus Weber's notion of value-free science strongly criticised what he considered to be value-bound science as propagated by Catholic intellectuals and those that used their own academic posts to sell their own ideological positions. The *Kulturkampf* background to the German university system is clearly a major Protestant influence on Weber, which sets the framework for his views. It is thus not surprising that we should find a theological critique in Weber's *Wissenschaft*, as theology represented *par excellence* that academic discipline which the history of Germany in the nineteenth and early twentieth centuries had shown was most susceptible to the dangers of indoctrination.

Weber represents Protestantism as the inheritor of the honesty and intellectual rigour of the Jewish prophets against the ideological and institutionally compromised position of the Catholic Church, which only propagated the decadence of intellectual dilettantism.[157] Consequently, the separation of religious convictions from scientific research, the major form in which *Wissenschaft* conceives the disenchantment of the world and the process of secularisation under the modern conditions of intellectualisation, is itself a Protestant position inherited from Schleiermacher and much of nineteenth-century Protestant thought. Weber stresses this line of thought in his address to the students in Munich as his vision of the vocation of an academic in modernity.

The Protestant heritage in his theory of secularisation is no less important in Weber's *Politik*. By 1919 it was clear to Weber that his hoped-for political career would not materialise. He had humiliatingly failed in his attempt to be elected to the German Democratic Party in Frankfurt am Main, and even his appointment as a member of the peace delegation that travelled to Versailles in the spring of 1919 was of little compensation for a man who was so passionately committed to politics. He explained to Karl Petersen at the time of his resignation from the national committee of the German Democratic Party in 1920, "The politician has to make compromises; that is his job. But my calling is that of the scholar. . . . The scholar may not compromise, or allow "nonsense" to remain unexposed."[158]

The opportunity to resume an academic career, which he took up at the University of Munich in mid-June 1919, provided Weber with an exit strategy that both saved his reputation and, probably, helped to maintain his self-esteem. Moreover, this episode reveals another aspect of Weber's identification with Protestantism that helps to explain the definition of disenchantment that we encounter in his Munich speeches. Erich Wittenberg neatly outlines Weber's dual identification with both science and Protestantism when he says:

> It is, we believe, in this context that Weber's dual identification, on the one hand with the structure of the technological age and, on the other, with the spirit of Protestantism, stands revealed; for the spirit of Protestantism seeks equally to eliminate all irrational and affective features from the human being and to attain a state in which human beings, espousing an "inner-worldly asceticism," may employ "rational calculation" as a means of controlling the world. To summarise our argument, we must say then that it is in Max Weber that the decline of the Age of Rationalism finds its embodiment; as Weber descends to his grave, so too does rationalism. For it is he who, for one last grandiose moment, embodies that age in all its splendour and weaknesses.[159]

The vision of both science and Protestantism is embodied in Weber's *Politik* under the category of objectivity. The way in which Weber uses this category of objectivity (*Sachlichkeit*) in *Politik* reveals the specificity of his vision of secularisation and of its Protestant heritage. In *Politik*, Weber indeed criticises the Catholic Centre Party as one reason that Germany could not develop a proper parliamentary system. He argues that because minority parties like the Catholic Centre Party remained bound to particular *Weltanschauungen*, they effectively blocked the parliamentary process, which could not work with competing political convictions.[160] Weber argues that for a politician to be truly effective, he or she needs to have three qualities: "One can say that three qualities are pre-eminently decisive for a politician: passion, a sense of responsibility, judgement. Passion in the sense of *objectivity*, the passionate commitment to a 'cause' to the god or demon who commands that cause."[161] The lack of objectivity, which for Weber was characteristic of Catholicism, clearly found embodiment in the Catholic Centre Party. This confessionalisation of politics, through confessional political parties, and of science, through the confessional appointments of university professors as at Strasbourg, was the context for Weber's criticisms in his Munich speeches and for his outline of potential solutions to such problems in both *Politik* and *Wissenschaft*.

Such criticisms of a form of religious organicism, or religious involvement in political life, become the central subject of *Politik* when Weber turns to the question of the relation of ethics to politics. This discussion leads him to define a new position on religion, clearly different from that which he had defended at the time of his involvement in the Evangelical Social Congress. Weber takes the ethic of love as expressed in the Sermon on the Mount to be the quintessential feature of Christian ethics.[162] On the basis of this uncompromising position, which demands that all people should be regarded as brothers and sisters and, as such, be treated with love and respect, Weber outlines how it is impossible for such an ethic to find a place in the ethical animation of political life, which, by its very nature, requires compromise and the eventual enforcement of its will by violence:

> What has been said about causality in science also applies to this ethic: namely, that it is not a hired cab which one may stop at will and climb into or out of as one sees fit. Rather, the meaning of the sermon (if it is not to be reduced to banality) is precisely this: we must accept it in its entirety or leave it alone. Hence the case of the rich young man: "He went away sorrowful, for he had great possessions." The commandment of the Gospel is unconditional and unambiguous—"give all that thou hast"—*everything*, absolutely. The politician will say that this is an excessive and socially meaningless demand if it is not made to apply to *all*. So, taxation,

> expropriation by taxation, confiscation, in other words, coercion and order applied against *all*. The ethical commandment disregards such questions completely—that is its essence.[163]

Thus, Weber clearly sees the separation of religion from politics as a consequence of the incompatibility of the absolute claim of the gospel with the practical demands of politics. The purity of this conception of religion leads Weber to outline clearly the incompatibility of the goals of religion and politics.

> Anyone seeking to save his own soul and the souls of others does not take the path of politics in order to reach his goal, for politics has quite different tasks: namely, those which can only be achieved by force. The genius—or demon—of politics lives in a state of inner tension with the god of love, and even with the Christian God as manifested in the institution of the church, a tension that may erupt at any moment into irresolvable conflict.[164]

The picture of religion that now emerges is one in which, in order to preserve its own purity (and here Weber draws on the classical Russian author's view of Christianity in Tolstoy and Dostoyevsky[165]), needs to follow its own path, to turn away from the ways of the world and its politics and thus adopt an other-worldly approach to life. This radicalises Weber's theory of secularisation in that it seeks to crystallise religion out of society and its politics. Commentators have too often considered this process of separation and of differentiation of religion from public life a sign of Weber's atheism. But this results from a rather superficial reading of the influence of Nietzsche on Weber, and one that indeed fails to see the importance of the Protestant influences on both Nietzsche and Weber.[166]

Once again, Julius Wellhausen's research on the history of ancient Judaism provides a basis for Weber's thought. Even Nietzsche's own programme of the transformation of all values was strongly influenced by Wellhausen's critique of the decadence of Protestant clericalism.[167] In fact, Weber's own connection of ethical monotheism and polytheism in *Politik* is based on Wellhausen's work on ancient Judaism and the picture he painted of ethical prophecy.[168] Wellhausen himself had engaged in a sharp critique of the Protestant Church and had defended a form of heroic individualism that influenced both Nietzsche and Weber significantly. He had proposed the image of the prophet Jeremiah as a paragon of ethical monotheism, an individual whose communion with God had meant that his distance from the community was a necessary part of the purity of his religious message. This had caused Wellhausen to have a crisis of conscience about his own membership of the church structure of Protestantism. Further, as Voigt suggests, in the prophet Jeremiah he found the archetype of the true religious believer, uncompromising in his convictions and bold in his religious statements.[169]

Thus in *Wissenschaft* and *Politik*, different routes are described to the elimination of religion from these spheres in the process of secularisation. In *Wissenschaft*, on the one hand, religion is eliminated because of the need for intellectual honesty, for freedom from value commitment so as to ensure methodological objectivity. In *Politik*, on the other hand, religion is to remove itself from political engagement because the politics of responsibility, which alone can make the necessary compromises required for parliamentary democracy, are incompatible with the politics of conviction, which are inevitable for the religious believer. Moreover, Weber suggests that for religious convictions to remain pure, the religious believer must remove himself from the political sphere, as Jeremiah did from the community, in order to protect these convictions from contamination by the compromises of the world. Both *Wissenschaft* and *Politik*, then, call for a retreat of the religious sphere into the privacy of the inner convictions of the heroic individual, a retreat mirrored in Weber's own political convictions after the failure of his political career and his withdrawal into the scientifically pure world of academia.

This radicalisation of Weber's position marked ever more clearly the distance emerging between himself and his lifetime colleagues and friends Ernst Troeltsch and Otto Baumgarten with respect to the understanding of religion and its role in the modern world. It is also a clear change for Weber from his earlier engagement with the Evangelical Social Congress, in which he had sought a more positive role for religion within a liberal Protestant framework. Weber no longer shared the optimism of Troeltsch and Baumgarten about the role of Protestantism in building a united and strong Germany. Yet it was in this very same liberal Protestant framework that Weber formed his understanding and arguments about religion in the modern world, a worldview that permeated Weber's thinking, even down to his basic anthropology:

> A man who subscribes to the ethic of responsibility, by contrast, will make allowances for these everyday shortcomings in people. He has no right, as Fichte has correctly observed, to presuppose goodness and perfection in human beings.[170]

Notes

1. See *WuG*: 321–348. The section just before is also of interest since it contains reflections on "This-Worldly" and "Other-Worldly" Salvation, see *WuG*: 319–321.

2. See Schluchter (1988a), 2:557–596.

3. He used the *Zwischenbetrachtung* as a way of linking *GARS* and *WuG*, and in so doing made the reflection on the nature of asceticism and mysticism play a key role in his reflections on the relation between religion and social evolution.

4. *WuG*: 245. "Eine Definition dessen, was Religion 'ist,' kann unmöglich an der Spitze, sondern könnte allenfalls am Schlusse einer Erörterung wie der nachfolgenden stehen. Allein wir haben es überhaupt nicht mit dem 'Wesen' der Religion, sondern mit den Bedingungen und Wirkungen einer bestimmten Art von Gemeinschaftshandeln zu tun."

5. On this point, see the excellent article of Wolfgang Schluchter, "Weber's Sociology of Rationalism and Typology of Religious Rejections of the World", in Lash and Whimster (1987): 92–115. In this section, I draw on Schluchter's article in my own reconstruction of the conceptual history of asceticism and mysticism in Weber's work.

6. Weber, M. "Antikritisches zum "Geist" des Kapitalismus," in Winckelmann (ed.) (1972): 155.

"Einen abgestempelten "Askese"–Begriff gibt es nicht. Daß man den Begriff sehr viel weiter fassen kann, als ich es getan habe, wo ich die von mir als "innerweltliche" Askese bezeichnete Art der Lebensführung mit der "außerweltlichen" Askese des Mönchtums verglich, ist einigermaßen selbstversändlich und von mir selbst zugegeben: ich spreche bei der katholischen Askese audrücklich von der rationalisierten Askese (wie sie in höchster Potenz der Jesuitenorden aufweist) im Gegensatz z.B. zu "planloser Weltflucht" (auf katholische Seite) und bloßer Gefühls-"Askese" (auf protestantische Seite).

7. See *WuG*: 334. Quoted above in Chapter 2.

8. I do not intend to overdo this criticism of Weber's understanding of Catholic spirituality since, even in the Jesuit order, the full implications of the sixteenth-century spirituality of Ignatius of Loyola, the founder of the Jesuits, were not clearly understood until the "rediscovery" of his Spiritual Exercises during the twentieth century. For a clear and concise analysis of the history of the contemplation and action issue, see Coreth (1954).

9. See Schluchter (1987): 109–113. Schluchter attempts to analytically separate out the categories, which he believes Weber failed to do sufficiently. Mysticism is indifferent to the world, resulting in either the acceptance of one's fate in the world or the fleeing-from-the-world. There is no mention of the tradition of mysticism understood as "contemplation in action," which seeks to transform the world for the glory of God. To miss this point is to miss, as indeed Weber himself misses, the importance of the Catholic Reformation and the typology of Catholic social action typified in the Ignatian spiritual tradition. This being the case, it is no wonder that the Protestant (or more correctly Puritan) metanarrative that informs Weber's sociology of religion is inherited, by even the most erudite of his commentators, in a way that overlooks another possibility for conceiving action and, even more importantly, historically and actually significant types of social action.

10. See Schluchter (1987): 100–101. Schluchter draws this conclusion after reading the role Weber had in Ernst Troeltsch's lecture on "Stoic-Christian Natural Law and Modern Secular Natural Law" at the first German sociological conference in 1910. Nevertheless, Weber still seems to have understood mysticism as a form of "acosmism" or, in Baudelaire's words, a form of "holy prostitution" of the soul. In this, Weber seems to have adopted Troeltsch's thesis about the two sides of the gospel: its absolute universalism and its absolute individualism. See Troeltsch (1994), 1: 39–41.

11. See Schluchter (1987): 101.

12. On the importance of Schneckenburger's analysis of the differences between Lutheranism and Calvinism for Weber's construction of *PE*, see Graf (1995): 34–41.

13. See *WuG*: 326

14. See *WuG*: 324–328.

15. This developed categorisation thus helps to better understand why Weber tends to equate asceticism with ethics and contemplation with gnosis. On this point, see Schluchter (1987): 102.

16. See Schluchter (1987): 103.

17. Schluchter raises a key objection to the argumentation of Weber at this point. He suggests that in the argumentation of Weber it is not clear whether this classification is meant to be analytical or is historical in nature. This is important because the developmental history of

Western rationalism that Weber propounds is meant to correspond to the actual types that have occurred in history. If it turns out that Weber has constructed this history around his analytical typology, then it is clear that he has to disfigure the actual religious types in order to fit his own conceptual schema. This would indeed put the neutrality of his scientific approach, which he defended strongly, into question. See Schluchter (1987): 103.

18. See *WuG*: 330–332.

19. Weber notes that this-worldly mysticism had historically occurred in the sixteenth-century Baptists and has had revolutionary consequences (the later seventeenth-century English civil wars constitute a paradigm example here). However, he notes that when an inner-worldly religion is determined by contemplative features, the usual result is one of acceptance and indifference to the world. To illustrate his point he cites the examples of the Chinese mystic Lao Tzu and the fourteenth-century Dominican mystic John Tauler, who apparently could not wait to get home from work to carry on praying! See *WuG*: 333.

20. *WuG*: 332–333. "Dem kontemplativen Mystiker umgekehrt kommt es gerade auf das Erschauen jenes 'Sinnes' der Welt an, den er in rationaler Form zu 'begreifen,' eben um deswillen außerstande ist, weil er ihn als eine Einheit jenseits aller realen Wirklichkeit erfaßt. Nicht immer hat die mystische Kontemplation die Konsequenz von Weltflucht im Sinn einer Meidung jeder Berührung mit der sozialen Umwelt. Auch der Mystiker kann umgekehrt als Bewährung der Sicherheit seines Gnadenstandes dessen Behauptung gerade gegenüber den Ordnungen der Welt von sich fordern: auch für ihn wird dann die Stellung in diesen Ordnungen zum 'Beruf.' Aber mit sehr anderer Wendung als bei der innerweltlichen Askese. Die Welt als solche wird weder von der Askese noch von der Kontemplation bejaht. Aber vom Asketen werden ihr kreatürlicher, ethisch irrationaler empirischer Charakter, ihre ethischen Versuchungen der Weltlust, des Genießens und Ausruhens auf ihren Freunden und Gaben, abgelehnt. Dagegen wird das eigene rationale Handeln innerhalb ihrer Ordnungen als Aufgabe und Mittel der Gnadenbewährung bejaht. Dem innerweltlich lebenden kontemplativen Mystiker dagegen ist Handeln, und vollends Handeln innerhalb der Welt, rein an sich eine Versuchung, gegen die er seinen Gnadenstand zu behaupten hat. Er minimisiert also sein Handeln, indem er sich in die Ordnungen der Welt, rein an sich einer Versuchung, gegen die er seinen Gnadenstand zu behaupten hat. Er minimisiert also sein Handeln, indem er sich in die Ordnungen der Welt, so wie sie sind, 'schickt,' in ihnen sozusagen inkognito lebt, wie die 'Stillen im Lande' es zu aller Zeit getan haben, weil Gott es nun einmal so gefügt hat, daß wir darin leben müssen. Eine spezifische, demutsvoll gefärbte 'Gebrochenheit' zeichnet das innerweltliche Handeln des kontemplativen Mystikers aus, von welchem hinweg er sich immer wieder in die Stille der Gottinnigkeit

flüchten möchte und flüchtet. Der Asket ist, wo er in Einheit mit sich selbst handelt, sich dessen sicher, Gottes Werkzeug zu sein. Seine eigene pflichtgemäße kreaturliche 'Demut' ist daher stets von zweifelhafter Echtheit. Der Erfolg seines Handelns ist ja ein Erfolg Gottes selbst, zu dem er beigetragen hat, mindestens aber ein Zeichen seines Segens ganz speziell für ihn sein Tun. Für den echten Mystiker kann dagegen der Erfolg seines innerweltlichen Handelns keinerlei Heilsbedeutung haben und ist die Erhaltung echter Demut in der Welt in der Tat die einzige Bürgschaft dafür, daß seine Seele ihr nicht anheimgefallen ist. Je mehr er innerhalb der Welt steht, desto 'gebrochener' wird im allgemeinen seine Haltung zu ihr im Gegensatz zu dem stolzen Heilsaristokratsimus der außerweltlichen irdischen Kontemplation."

21. *WuG*: 334. "Es ist nun der historisch entscheidende Unterschied, der vorwiegend morgenländischen und asiatischen, gengenüber den vorwiegend okzidentalen Arten der Erlösungsreligionsität, daß die ersteren wesentlich in Kontemplation, die letzteren in Askese ausmünden. Daß der Unterschied ein flüssiger ist, daß ferner die mannigfachen stets wiederkehrenden Kombinationen von mystischen und asketischen Zügen, z. B. in der Mönchreligiosität des Abendlands, die Vereinbarkeit dieser an sich heterogenen Elemente zeigen, dies alles ändert nichts an der großen Bedeutung des Unterschiedes selbst für unsere rein empirische Betrachtung. Denn der Effekt im Handeln ist es, der uns angeht."

22. Schluchter attempts to correct this assumption of Weber by analytically separating out activity and passivity from a presumed homogeneously constituted passive contemplation and active asceticism. However, he effectively diffuses the sociological potential of contemplation for a theory of action by limiting the attitude to the world held by an active contemplative or a passive ascetic to indifference or accepting one's fate in the world. See Schluchter (1987): 109–115. Thus, the potential for a theory of contemplative action in Schluchter's reconstruction of Weber remains sociologically defused. While he allows for contemplation and action, in the examples of the medieval Catholicism of Thomism and Brahmism, a strategy of organic relativisation following Weber's allusion at the end of the *Zwischenbetrachtung*, he sees this within a framework of dualism. Thus, following Weber, he suggests that the combination of contemplation and an inner-worldly vocational ethic, the third form of theodicy dealt with by Weber in the *Zwischenbetrachtung*, was peculiar to Indian intellectuals. Hence the combination of contemplation and action, by Schluchter, is within a framework of metaphysical dualism (or pluralism) in which this world and the other world remain securely in place and hierocratic and political powers remain separated (*ora et labora* and not *ora in labora*).

23. See Schluchter (1987): 106–107. Schluchter suggests that the key point is not simply terminological here, but rather the need to

broaden the typology of asceticism and mysticism in order to better understand the impact of the religious rejection of the world for elaborating a better typology of attitudes towards the world and hence more sophisticated action theory. In doing this, Schluchter suggests that three aspects need to be analytically separated. First, the relation between the divine, man, and the world. Second, the attitude of the person towards the world: either directed towards the world or away from the world. And third, the content given to these dimensions, that is to say, the end state—active or passive—and the means of getting there—asceticism and contemplation. It is important to note that Schluchter follows Weber in confining this typology to religious virtuosos, since the "masses" tend towards a naïve affirmation of the world. In this sense he remains within Weber's schema of prioritising the aristocratic model of salvation as sociologically significant for a theory of action. Thus, even were one to criticise the innovation of the Catholic Reformation as being confined to the religious virtuosos, this critique would not damage the sociological significance of this innovation for a Weberian typology, which itself is confined to religious virtuosos (cf. Schluchter [1987]: 109). Nevertheless, even in his broadening of the types of asceticism and mysticism to be either active or passive in nature (Weber's "tool" and "vessel" typology) and analytically separating these from the soteriological means of achieving these states (which are in turn reliant on a particular conception of God), that is to say, asceticism and mysticism, Schluchter continues to carry through Weber's assumption of the active contemplative's necessary indifferent attitude to the world into his own revised typology of the religious virtuosos' means to salvation. This effectively restricts the sociologically significant typology of means of salvation to two "historically and psychologically significant" forms. That is to say, to the inner-worldly active mystic who pursues world mastery (type 1 in Schluchter's schema) and the other-worldly passive mystic who flees from the world (type 4 in Schluchter's schema). As Schluchter notes, these are the two main types Weber considered in the *Zwischenbetrachtung*. My critique here is that in so limiting his typological scheme, Schluchter fails (as does Weber) to appreciate the sociological significance of the inner–worldly active mystic who pursues world mastery for a theory of action. This type is one major innovation of the spirituality of the Catholic Reformation that has not been theorised in Weberian-inspired theories of action, which remain, at least implicitly, confined to a Protestant metanarrative of considering the world as a *massa perditionis*, rather than also a place of grace.

24. This is probably due to his analytic interest in the *Einleitung* of contrasting the Christian attitude of action with the Indian attitude of knowledge (and thus not contrasting Lutheranism and Calvinism on the basis of emotionality, as in *PE*).

25. Schluchter (1998): 311–312. "Folgt man den Zuordnungen dieses Rasters, so scheinen sich nämlich, zumindest auf der Ebene der Virtuosenreligiosität, Kosmozentrismus und innerweltliche Askese sowie Theozentrismus und innerweltliche Mystik 'auszuschließen.'

26. Schluchter (1998): 324–325. "Erst im Calvinismus, vor allem aber bei den täufersischen Denominationen, kurz: im asketischen Protestantismus, werden diese als Heilsmittel zugunsten der gottgeheiligten Gesinnung und der zum System gesteigerten Werkheiligkeit total entwertet. Mit dieser 'spiritualistischen' Wendung aber hat er zugleich die religiöse Entzauberung' der Welt in ihren letzten Konsequenzen durchgeführt.

Der asketische Protestantismus kombiniert also in Webers Sicht fünf Merkmale, die bis zur Reformation keine andere erlösungsreligiöse Strömung in Asien oder im Okzident erfolgreich kombiniert hatte: Theozentrismus, Asketismus, Innerweltlichkeit, subjecktive Werkheiligkeit und Virtuosentum. Erst diese Kombination schafft die religiöse Motivation für Weltbeherrschung."

27. Schluchter (1998): 326. "Die religiöse Ethik des asketischen Protestantismus ist also eine *monologische* Gesinnungethik mit *unbrüderlichen* Konsequenzen. Genau darin sehe ich ihr 'Entwicklungspotential' Sie stellt nicht nur, wie letzlich alle Konsequenzen christlichen erlösungsreligiösungs Strömungen, die Beziehung des einzelnen zu Gott über seine Beziehung zu den Menschen, sie gibt dieser Beziehung auch eine neue Bedeutung, indem sie sie nicht mehr in Pietätsbegriffe interpretiert. Sie schafft damit eine Motivation zur Versachlichung zunächst der religiösen, dann der außerreligiösen zwischenmenschlichen Beziehungen. Dies aber kommt einer traditional-patrimonialen Ordnungskonfiguration entgegen, die bereits eine Tendenz zur Formalisierung des Rechts, zur Bürokratisierung der Politik und zur Marktvergesellschaftung zeigt."

28. For this reading of Habermas, see Skinner (1982).

29. Schluchter (1998): 330. "Diese selbständig gewordene moderne okzidentale Berufskultur gibt freilich noch in ihren mechanisierten und versteinerten Gestalten jene religiösen Einschläge zu erkennen, die ihre Geburt begleiteten. Sie wirken fort in dem nun profanisierten Weltverhältnis der Weltbeherrschung und in der nun zur Weltherrschaft gebrachten Unbrüderlichkeit."

30. Schluchter (1987): 111.

31. Here it is important to realise that whilst many people have noted the importance of the Protestant metanarrative on the work of Weber, this has, to my knowledge, not been carried through in any systematic analysis of his work.

32. On the reasons for this, see Turner and Factor (1994): 2–12. Turner and Factor suggest that the historical shift from the social law tradition to legal positivism, which took place in Weber's time, obscured

much of the older legal-philosophical background from which many of Weber's ideas stemmed. Furthermore, they argue that Weber borrowed many of his sociological categories from the legal sciences. They argue that the nineteenth-century work on probabilistic causation in legal causality (used to assess liability) and Rudolf von Ihering's work on legal interests (material and ideal) supplied Weber with the tools and categories that he then applied to sociology. Turner and Factor further argue that Weber has no social theory because he primarily applies these categories to the intention action of individuals, which is satisfied by social means, and consequently rejects Ihering's category of social teleology or social purposes (Ibid.: 52–53). They seem to insufficiently recognise, however, that social theory need not be confined to one model of social teleology, but can, and indeed does, also consist of models that depend on the coordination of the action orientation of individuals. For a general survey of these models in modern social theory, see Craib (1992). Other important legal influences on Weber's work include Rudolf Sohm, who was also a member of Evangelical Social Congress, and Georg Jellinek's work on the practical importance of natural–law doctrines for constitution building. See Bendix and Roth (1971): 308–310. For a comparison of Weber and Habermas on the sociology of law in the context of their importance for constitutional democracy in the European Union, see McCormick (2007): 1–125.

33. The secularisation of modern natural law in the work of Hugo Grotius (1583–1645) is often considered to be the beginnings of a secular rationalism—that is, an alternative method of elucidating the natural law that does not require the scriptures and/or faith in the Christian God as a prerequisite. For Grotius, the natural law can be discovered in the same way as mathematical truths can: through pure secular reason. For a good survey of the evolution of natural law, see D'Entrèves (1994). The secular basis of reason as a ground for natural law was later developed in both Protestant and Catholic European traditions. For a good overview, see Haakonssen (1998).

34. Treiber (1985) argues that Weber uses the same basic explanatory models to reconstruct the religious and rationalisation process. In this sense, he considers these works (both written between 1911 and 1913) to bear "elective affinities."

35. *WuG*: 468. "Je mehr der Herrschaftapparat der Fürsten und Hierarchen ein rationaler.... der Rechtspflege nach Inhalt und Form rationalen—freilich in verschiedenem Sinn rationalen—Charakter zu verliehen, irrationale Prozeßmittel auszuschalten und das materielle Recht zu systematisieren, und das bedeutete zugleich stets irgendwie: zu rationalisieren. In eindeutiger Weise hatten aber jene Gewalten diese rationalen Tendenzen nur da, wo entweder die Interessen ihrer eigenen rationalen Verwaltung sie auf diesen Weg wiesen (wie das päpstliche Kirchenregiment) oder wo sie im Bunde mit mächtigen Gruppen von

Rechtsinteressenten standen, welche an dem rationalen Charakter des Rechts und Prozesses ein starkes Interesse hatten, wie die bürgerlichen Klassen in Rom, im ausgehenden Mittelalter und in der Neuzeit. Wo dies Bundnis fehlte, ist die Säkularisation des Rechts und die Herausdifferenzierung eines streng formal juristischen Denkens entweder in den Anfängen steckengeblieben, oder es ist ihr geradezu entegegengewirkt worden. Dies liegt, allgemein gesprochen daran, daß der 'Rationalismus' der Hierachen sowohl wie der Patrimonialfürsten materialen Charakters ist. Nicht die formal–juristisch präziseste, für die Berechenbarkeit der Chancen und die rationale Systematik des Rechts und der Prozedur optimale, sondern die inhaltlich den praktisch-utilitarischen und ethischen Anforderungen jener Autoritäten entsprechendste Ausprägung wird erstrebt; eine Sonderung von 'Ethik' und 'Recht' liegt, wie wir schon sahen, gar nicht in der Absicht dieser, jeder selbstgenugsam und fachmäßig 'juristischen' Behandlung des Rechts durchaus fremd gegenüberstehenden Faktoren der Rechtsbildung. Speziell gilt dies in aller Regel von der theokratisch beeinflußten Rechtsbildung mit ihrer Kombination ethischer Anforderungen und juristischer Vorschriften."

36. See Treiber (1985): 813. Treiber argues that Weber used three levels of explanation in his sociological studies: 1) the propagating strata; 2) the political conditions; and 3) economic conditions. All three levels interact to produce a constellation of factors that propel forward the process of rationalisation.

37. Treiber (1985): 816.

38. I shall consider in more detail the influence of Sohm on Weber below, when I look at the conception of charisma in *WuG*.

39. On the importance of Sohm as a source for Weber's sociology of religion and sociology of law, see Turner and Factor (1994): 110–118.

40. Indeed, Sohm was one of the founding fathers and leaders of the National Social Movement. The National Social Party was a short-lived left-liberal party that proposed external economic expansion and internal democratisation of Wilhelmine Germany. Naumann was one of the founding fathers of the constitution of the Weimar Republic, and in his most famous work, *Democracy and Empire*, he proposed a broader cooperation between the SPD (Social Democratic Party, especially the revisionist wing under the influence of Eduard Bernstein), founded in 1875 by the union of Ferdinand Lassalle's General Union of German Workers and the Social Democratic Workers' Party of August Bebel, and the various liberal parties. See Thornhill (2000): 22–25.

41. See Ward (1987): 211. On the influence of Weber on Friedrich Naumann and the setting up of the National Social Association, and on Weber's disappointment with this association, see Theiner (1987): 299–310.

42. The founding of the new German empire was the result of a long process of unification between the Prussian and Nationalist movements

jostling for power from 1848 to 1871. The central question in this political history was the nature and scope of German national identity and how to secure this identity in the face of political, cultural, and religious divisions. This need to find and secure a strong German national identity deeply influenced Weber's own political interests.

43. It should be noted here that my attempt to situate Weber's theory of secularisation within a Protestant metanarrative is not contradicted by his clear desire to separate religion from politics. Rather, this is a characteristic feature of the Protestant metanarrative within which Weber's own view of religion and politics (and thus theory of secularisation) is worked out. That is to say, the privatisation of religion is a typically liberal Protestant conception of religion and also indeed of the world as a god-less place.

44. See Ward (1987): 210. Weber attacked Naumann in his Freiburg inaugural address of 1894, which dealt with the nation as the most important value in the politics of national economy, on the grounds that the need for a value-free political sociology ruled out any attempt to create a theological politics, a view which Naumann had been trying to develop. Weber's attack helped Naumann to see that it was necessary to develop a socialism that secured a strong German national identity. See also Mommsen (1974): 35, 37–42. On Weber's evolving views on the question of nationalism and the importance of parliamentary democracy in the nation-state, see Beetham (1974): 119–150, and Mommsen (1974a): 22–46.

45. See *WuG*: 472–482

46. Thus in Indian law, for example, Weber argues that the dominance of the priesthood over the entire legal system, except for particular vocational groups such as merchants and artisans, meant that the secular development of law was confined to the private sphere and could not progress beyond a certain form of fusion of sacred and secular law. According to Weber, this lack of secularisation caused law in India to remain a mixture of magical and rational elements bound up with the religious and theocratic-patriarchal regulation of life. Weber analyses this paradigmatically in his consideration of Islamic law in which he sees the *a priori* rejection of a possible secular sphere to which secular law could even in principle apply.

47. See *WuG*: 480–482.

48. Thus, Weber suggests that canon law actually guided secular law towards its own path of rationality. See *WuG*: 481.

49. *WuG*: 480. "Und das Neue Testament enthielt nur ein solches Minimum formal bindender Normen rituellen oder rechtlichen Charakters—eine Folge der eschatologischen Weltabgewandtheit—daß eben dadurch die Bahn völlig frei war für rein rationale Satzung."

50. See the article "Eschatologie," in *Theologische Realenzyklopädie* (1982), 10: 328.

51. Indeed Weber's argument here also resembles that of Rudolf Sohm's critique of the Catholic understanding of canon law. Sohm argued (following Luther and Calvin) that because any visible church was not the church of Christ but merely a human community, then the true church of Christ was invisible and guided by the Spirit directly through the various charisms, which the Spirit freely gives. This meant that canon law was simply a human creation with no justification in the Gospel since the old law (in the Pauline sense) was in opposition to the new freedom of the children of God. The "Justification by Faith" teaching of Luther provides the framework in which Sohm developed this understanding of canon law. It sees a clear opposition between visible and invisible Church, history and eschatology, and the kingdom of God and the world. This Protestant tradition informs Weber's own categorisation and once again positions his theory of legal rationalisation firmly within the liberal Protestant tradition. For a systematic discussion of Sohm's work and its critique of the Catholic tradition of canon law, see Sebott (1993). For an excellent short article on Sohm's critique of the Catholic tradition of canon law, see Congar (1973).

52. Weber also notes the importance of the strong universalistic Roman law tradition in Italy, which served the Italian bourgeoisie in the Italian city-states in limiting the universalistic pretensions of the papacy and, in this sense, allowed for a secular legal space to be preserved. See *WuG*: 481.

53. See Roth and Schluchter (1979): 147–154.

54. See *WuG*: 496.

55. *WuG*: 497. "Wir lernten die 'lex naturae' früher als eine wesentlich stoische Schöpfung kennen, die das Christentum übernahm, um zwischen seiner eigenen Ethik und den Normen der Welt eine Brücke zu finden. Es war das innerhalb der gegebenen Welt der Sünde und Gewaltsamkeit nach Gottes Willen legitime 'Recht für Alle,' im Gegensatz zu Gottes direkt für seine Bekenner offenbartem und nur dem religiös Auserwählten einleuchtendem Gebot. Jetzt sehen wir die lex naturae von der anderen Seite her. 'Naturecht' ist der Inbegriff der unabhängig von allem positiven Recht und ihm gegenüber präeminent geltenden Normen, welche ihre Dignität nicht von willkürlicher Satzung zu Lehen tragen, sondern umgekehrt deren Verpflichtungsgewalt erst legitimieren. Normen also, welche nicht Kraft ihres Ursprungs von einem legitimen Gesetzgeber, sondern Kraft rein immanenter Qualitäten legitim sind: die spezifische und einzig konsequente Form der Legitimität eines Rechts, welche übrigbleiben kann, wenn religiöse Offenbarungen und autoritäre Heiligkeit der Tradition und ihrer Träger fortfallen."

56. See Honnefelder (1988).

57. See ibid.: 256–258.

58. *WuG*: 502. "Verglichen mit dem handfesten Glauben an die positive religiöse Offenbartheit einer Rechtsnorm oder an die unverbrüderliche

Heiligkeit einer uralten Tradition sind auch die überzeugendsten durch Abstraktion gewonnen Normen für diese Leistung zu subtil geartet. Der Rechtspositivismus ist infolgedessen in vorläufig unaufhaltsamen Vordringen. Das Schwinden der alten Naturrechtsvorstellungen hat die Möglichkeit, das Recht als solches Kraft seiner immanenten Qualitäten mit einer überempirischen Würde auszustatten, prinzipiell vernichtet: es is heute allzu greifbar in der großen Mehrzahl und gerade in vielen prinzipiell besonders wichtigen seiner Bestimmungen als Produkt und technisches Mittel eines Interessenkompromisses enthüllt."

59. In this section I have translated the German *Recht* as the English *law* and not as *right* (following Weber's translators Guenther Roth and Klaus Wittich) because Weber, when quoting the Latin, uses the word *lex* (law) rather than *ius* (right), and this seems more consistent with Weber's own use. The key issue here is of the difference between a conception of nature governed by a law and the right a person has on the strength of that law. Thus, for most writers of the seventeenth century, except for Hobbes (for whom the origin of the law is the will or command of the sovereign, giving grounds for considering Hobbes the first legal positivist), natural law was a necessary presupposition for natural right (cf. John Locke, *Second Treatise*, Bk. I, Ch. VI, 59, 63). Weber agreed that understanding the central meaning of the natural law to be the natural right of the individual provided intellectual support for the American and French Revolutions of 1776 and 1789 respectively. In this sense, one can say that the modern conception of natural law saw itself as a form of radicalism. As the modern period understood itself to be a secularisation of reason and the birth of individualism, the rights of the individual had come to be the perceived transmuted form of the medieval natural law theory. However, as Ludger Honnefelder shows (1988: 268–271), understanding the individual conscience to be the actual subject of moral action can be found in Abelard's (1079–1142) connection of the Stoic conception of the conscience with Christian teaching, and later, in Aquinas's natural law doctrine. For a discussion of the relation of natural right and natural law, see D' Entrèves (1994), Tuck (1979), and Strauss (1965).

60. See Strauss, Leo (1965): 57. Strauss argues that Weber rejects the natural right tradition because of his commitment to the fact/value distinction. This reveals, according to Strauss, Weber's positive commitment to the view of human life being one of inescapable conflict (Ibid.: 65).

61. See *WuG*: 498–503.

62. These three types of domination are developed as ideal-types in Weber's political sociology. Charismatic domination (*Herrschaft*) is the result of a form of leadership that seems extraordinary. People follow this form of leadership because it seems to present a way out of one form of crisis or another. Traditional domination is most clearly represented

in patriarchalism, patrimonalism, and feudalism. Here the leadership is based on what has gone before, on established practices and beliefs that act as a justification for the authority of a leader. Legal-rational domination is the type of leadership characteristic of the modern Western state. Here the form of authority is based on rational rules and laws that crystallise in the bureaucratic operational framework of the modern state. For Weber's descriptions of these three types of domination, see *WuG*: 122–176.

63. *WuG*: 124. "Es gibt drei reine Typen legitimer Herrschaft. Ihre Legitimitätsgeltung kann nämlich primär sein: 1. rationalen Charakters: auf dem Glauben an die Legalität gesatzter Ordnungen und des Anweisungsrechts der durch sie zur Ausübung der Herrschaft Berufenen ruhen (legale Herrschaft), oder 2. traditionalen Charakters: auf dem Alltagsglauben an die Heiligkeit von jeher geltender Traditionen und die Legitimität der durch sie zur Autorität Berufenen ruhen (traditionale Herrschaft), oder endlich 3. charismatische Charakters: auf der außeralltäglichen Hingabe und die Heiligkeit oder die Heldenkraft oder die Vorbildlichkeit einer Person und der durch sie offenbarten oder geschaffenen Ordnungen [ruhen] (charismatische Herrschaft)."

64. See Lassman (2000): 86.

65. *WuG*: 541. "'Herrschaft' in ihrem allgemeinsten, auf keinen konkreten Inhalt bezogenen Begriff ist eines der wichtigsten Elemente des Gemeinschaftshandelns. Zwar zeigt nicht alles Gemeinschaftshandeln herrschaftliche Struktur. Wohl aber spielt Herrschaft bei den meisten seiner Art eine sehr erhebliche Rolle, auch da, wo man nicht sofort daran denkt. . . . Ausnahmslos alle Gebiete des Gemeinschaftshandelns zeigen die tiefste Beeinflussung durch Herrschaftsgebilde."

66. Translators have differed in their translation of Weber's concept of *Herrschaft* into English. Claus Wittich and Guenther Roth alternate between "authority" and "domination" in their English translation of *WuG*. Talcott Parsons, for example, in his translations of Weber used the phrase "imperative coordination," while Reinhard Bendix used the word *domination*, as does Wolfgang Mommsen (1974a). Frank Parkin uses the phrase "legitimate domination" to include a normative sense to the meaning of *Herrschaft*. For a discussion of this point, see Bendix (1977): 292 n. 16; Mommsen (1974a): 72 n. 1; Parkin (2002): 74–75; and Lassman (2000): 86–90. I follow, in my choice of terms, Lassman's suggestion of "rule," and its derivative form "ruler-ship," for the above-stated reasons.

67. See, for example, Parkin (2002): 75.

68. Peter Lassman suggests—drawing on the work of Hintze (1964): 142, Richter (1995): 58–70, and Höffe (2002): 206–209—that viewing Weber's social science as "value free" or "politically neutral" has distorted our understanding of Weber's work. Lassman argues that this has been due to the lack of attention paid to the intellectual and historical

context in which Weber's ideas took shape. Thus, Lassman concludes that it is now clear that Weber was using his political concepts in a highly deliberate manner, contributing to the political debate of his time against positions held by other thinkers of the period. In the context of the meaning of *Herrschaft*, Lassman singles out the "state metaphysics" of Otto von Gierke (1844–1921) and his followers, who stressed the importance of *Genossenchaft* (cooperation, fellowship) over against *Herrschaft*, as Weber's chief opponent. For Lassman, rather than value or political neutrality, Weber's work needs to be understood as defending a "determined realism" influenced by both legal positivism and post-Nietzschian scepticism. Thus, accepting the logical consequences of disenchantment no longer seeks refuge in a secular normativity, but rather, accepts the secular fate of modern society. In this sense, Lassman's comparison between Weber and Machiavelli (98), made also by Antoni Carlo (1959) and Wolfgang Mommsen (1974a) seems fair. See Lassman (2000): 86–98.

69. In this sense, one can understand Weber as already anticipating the Schmitt–Blumenberg debate on secularisation. In effect, following Lassman's interpretation, Weber already defines legitimacy according to legality and thus lies closer to Schmitt than is usually recognised on this point. On Schmitt's understanding of legality and legitimacy in the formation of the Wilhelmian and Weimar German States, see Schmitt (1998).

70. Thus extending Lassman's argument, I suggest that in neglecting the intellectual and historical context of Weber's work, not only has the question of value neutrality been superficially understood in the reception of Weber's work, but also that the Protestant metanarrative that informs Weber's theory of secularisation has neither been sufficiently recognised nor systematically investigated. On the similarities between Macchiavelli (1469–1527) and Luther (1483–1546), see Maddox (2002); and on similarities between Macchiavelli and Protestant political thought, especially that of Locke, see Pangle (1990).

71. See Cavalli (1987): 319.

72. *WuG*: 654. "Die Deckung allen über die Anforderungen des ökonomischen Alltags," "im Sinne von nicht jedermann zugänglich."

73. Cf. *AJ*: 106–108. On the role of Israelite prophecy in Weber's theory of charisma, see Peter Berger (1963).

74. See Cavalli (1987): 326–327.

75. See *WuG*: 655.

76. See *WuG*: 661–681.

77. See Kroll (2001): 47–72. Kroll notes that it is only in the last ten years that serious systematic research into the sources of Weber's typology has begun (48).

78. In Weber's "Die drei reinen Typen der legitimen Herrschaft," published posthumously by Marianne Weber in 1922, Weber notes

that Sohm was the first to develop the concept of charismatic rulership, and this, according to Weber, he did brilliantly. See *GAW*: 482–483.

79. See Bühler (1965): viii. "Sohm ist zweifellos immer noch nicht so bekannt und nimmt nicht den Platz ein, den er seiner Bedeutung nach verdiente. Er gehört aber ohne Frage zu den einflussreichsten Kirchenvätern der Jahrhundertwende—in grösserem Masse sogar als mancher zünftige Theologe."

80. See Weber's *Jugendbriefe*: 85. Although, as Weber notes, it was not at a convenient time of the day for him.

81. See Mommsen (1974): 75, 137, and Hoffman (1966). On this point, see Kroll (2001): 53, from whom I have become aware of this literature.

82. The objective of the ESK was twofold. First, to investigate, in an unprejudicial way, the social situation of the German people; and second, to measure this situation according to the moral and religious principles of the Gospel and thus to seek to make the values of the Gospel more useful to the economic situation of the country. These principles remained constant and provided the motivation for and the objective of the ESK until its eventual demise in 1945. One of Weber's major contributions to the ESK was to have emphasised the importance of a strong German nation-state for German economic and political success at the end of the nineteenth century. Weber met Naumann at one of the earlier ESKs in 1893, and the two remained close personal and professional friends until Weber's death in 1920. Even Weber's mother, Helene Weber, was a member of the ESK, and, as we know from both Theodor Heuß's biography of Friedrich Naumann and Marianne Weber's biography of Max Weber, hearing the arguments of the Protestant pastors was a source of joy and comfort to Helene Weber. See Heuß (1937): 139 and Marianne Weber (1950): 154–155. For a good short introduction to the ESK, see the article on ESK by Klaus Erich Pollman in *Theologische Realenzyklopädie* (1982), 10: 645–650.

83. Hermelink (1953): 387. "Die Jahre von 1892 bis 1896 sind der Höherpunkt der christlich-sozialen Bewegung und damit auch des Evangelisch-sozialen Kongresses; 'Die Christliche Welt fühlt sich ganz als Anwalt des Kongresses.' Naumann setzt sich in diesen Jahren durch, beginnend mit seinem Berliner Vortrag (1892) über 'Christentum und Familie.' Er und Stöcker halten noch zusammen, trotz der Nachwirkungen des Apostolikumstreites. Zum erstenmal tagt man außerhalb Berlins, wohl vorbereitet in der Stadt Naumann's und Rades Frankfurt a.M. (1894). Es wetteifern miteinander die Referate des jungen Nationalökonomen Max Weber und des bisherigen Generalsekretärs Paul Goehre über 'Die Lage der deutschen Landarbeiter,' grimmig beanstandet von der konservativen Presse."

84. *WuG*: 124. "Der Begriff des 'Charisma' ('Gnadengabe') ist altchristlicher Terminologie entnommen. Für die christliche Hierokratie

hat zuerst Rudolf Sohms Kirchenrecht der Sache, wenn auch nicht der Terminologie nach den Begriff, andere (z.B. Karl Holl in 'Enthusiasmus und Bußgewalt' [1898] [haben] gewisse wichtige Konsequenzen davon verdeutlicht. Er ist also nichts Neues."

85. *WuG*: 654–655. "Es ist für einen geschichtlichen wichtigen Spezialfall (die Entwicklungsgeschichte der frühern christlichen Kirchengewalt) Rudolf Sohms Verdienst, die Soziologische Eigenart dieser Kategorie von Gewaltstruktur gedanklich konsequent und daher notwendigerweise, rein historisch betrachtet, einseitig herausgearbeitet zu haben. Aber der prinzipiell gleiche Sachverhalt kehrt, obwohl auf religiösem Gebiet oft am reinsten ausgeprägt, sehr universell wieder."

86. See Sohm (1892) and (1923).

87. See Sohm (1912).

88. Sohm (1912): 13. "Bis auf Luther aber war der Gegensatz zwischen der Kirche Christi und der rechtlich verfaßten Kirche für das Leben der Christenheit nicht vorhanden. Die ganze alte Zeit, vom ersten Jahrhundert bis zum Ausgang des Mittelalters, hat nicht vermocht, zwischen der rechtlich verfaßten Kirche und der Kirche Christi den rücksichtslos scharfen Trennungsstrich zu machen. Die Durchsetzung der Unterscheidung bedeutete das (heute die Kulturwelt beherrschende) protestantische Prinzip. Damit ist von selbst gesagt: der Mangel der Unterscheidung bedeutet das katholische Prinzip.

Das Wesen des Katholizismus besteht darin, daß er zwischen der Kirche im religiösen Sinn (der Kirche Christi) und der Kirche im Rechtssinn nicht unterscheidet."

89. For an excellent study of law and Protestantism, see Witte (2002).

90. For helpful studies on Sohm's work, see Sebott (1993), Bühler (1965), and Congar (1973). As I noted above, Sohm's, and indeed Weber's, position on the importance of the Church keeping out of social policy in the newly-formed German nation makes perfect sense with this model of the Church. The privatisation of religion, the location of revolutionary potential in the charismatic individual rather than in the communal body, so characteristic of Weber's theory of secularisation, clearly finds its roots in such Protestant models of the Church as mediated by legal scholars like Sohm. It should be noted here that there are various Protestant models of the Church. Indeed, Sohm's own model was strongly criticised in his own day by Adolf von Harnack, who suggested that canon law was necessary because the Church was also a human organisation. However, the point is that Weber took his models from these Protestant sources, favouring Sohm's line on charisma over against Harnack's, and thus his own sociological concepts were conditioned by these Protestant sources. On the debate between Harnack and Sohm, see Kroll (2001): 55–64.

91. See Haley (1980): 188–189.

92. See *WuG*: 657–658.

93. On this point, see Kroll (2001): 64.

94. *WuG*: 658. "Die spezifisch 'schöpferische' revolutionäre Macht der Geschichte."

95. Cf. *WuG*: 659.

96. On this point, see Turner and Factor (1994): 113.

97. *WuG*: 140. "Charisma soll eine außeralltäglich (ursprünglich sowohl bei Propheten wie bei therapeutischen wie bei Rechts-Weisen wie bei Jagdführen wie bei Kriegshelden: als magisch bedingt) geltende Qualität einer Persönlichkeit heißen, um derentwillen sie als mit übernatürlichen oder übermenschlichen oder mindestens spezifisch außeralltäglichen, nicht jedem andern zugänglichen Kräften oder Eigenschaften [begabt] oder als gottgesandt oder als vorbildlich und deshalb als 'Führer' gewertet wird."

98. See Turner and Factor (1994): 117. Turner and Factor also suggest that Weber took many more themes from Sohm, such as the individualising effects of the doctrine of predestination and the idea of the importance of Protestantism in the reshaping of practical life. They also suggest that Sohm and Weber share striking historiographical similarities (Ibid.: 187 n. 7). No less important is the notion of hierocratic ruler-ship, which Weber took from the Protestant canon law of the 1870s, which used the notion of hierocracy as a synonym for theocracy. On this point, see Kroll (2001): 65.

99. See Haley (1980).

100. See Alan Berger (1981).

101. See Peter Berger (1963).

102. See Strauss (1965): 57.

103. See Ekstrand (2000): 167–196.

104. See Bryan S. Turner, (1974): 22–38.

105. See Schluchter (1988a), 2: 263, 594.

106. *WuG*: 643. "Nicht der Islam als Konfession der Individuen hinderte die Industrialisierung . . . Sondern die religiös bedingte Struktur der islamischen Staatengebilde, ihres Beamtemtuns und ihrer Rechtsfindung."

107. See Schluchter (1988a), 2: 282.

108. Bryan S. Turner (1974): 160.

109. In his consideration of the secularisation thesis, Rodney Stark suggests that most research on secularisation has been done on Christian nations and so has not adequately considered the issue of secularisation in the context of predominantly other faith societies. He notes that studies in Islamic countries tend to indicate that Muslim commitment increases with modernisation. See Stark (1999): 267.

110. For a good discussion of these issues, see the various articles in Esposito and Tamimi (eds.) (2000).

111. For the importance of the development of the north European Western city in Weber's work, see Domingues (2000).

112. *WuG*: 746. "Und das Christentum, welches nun die Religion dieser in allen ihren Traditionen tief erschütterten Völker wurde und wohl gerade infolge der Schwäche oder des Fehlens der magischen und tabuistischen Schranken bei ihnen dazu werden konnte, entwertete und zerbrach alle solche Sippenbande in ihrer religiösen Bedeutsamkeit endgültig. Die oft recht bedeutende Rolle, welche die kirchliche Gemeinde bei der verwaltungstechnischen Einrichtung der mittelalterlichen Städte gespielt hat, ist nur eines von vielen Symptomen für die Bildung der mittelalterlichen Stadt grundlegend wichtigen Eigenschaften der christlichen Religion. Der Islam hat die Landsmannschaften der arabischen Stämme und die Sippenbande, wie die ganze Geschichte der inneren Konflikte des älteren Kalifats zeigt, nicht wirklich überwunden, weil er zunächst eine Religion eines erobernden, nach Stämmen und Sippen gegliederten Heeres blieb."

113. See *WuG*: 736.

114. For a critical analysis of Weber's claims on the hindrance of the development of Western capitalism and Western rationalism in general by the patrimonial character of Islamic rulership, see Rodinson (1987) and Hardy (1987). For a critical discussion of Weber's analysis and the various criticisms that have been levelled against him, including those of Rodinson and Hardy, see Schluchter (1988a), 2: 341–381.

115. See *WuG*: 739–741.

116. On the question of the role of Islam in Weber's account of the origins of Western capitalism, see Bryan S. Turner (1992): 41–74.

117. For a discussion of the role of Islamic law in preventing the rise of Western capitalism, see Crone (1987).

118. See *Vorbemerkung* in *GARS* I: 3.

119. *WuG*: 475. "Das islamische heilige Recht ist durchweg spezifisches 'juristen.' Seine Geltung beruht auf dem 'idschmâ' (idschmâ–al–ammah = tacitus consensus omnium), der praktisch als Übereinstimmung der Rechtspropheten, der großen Juristen (fuqahâ) also, definiert ist. Offiziell gilt neben der Infallibilität des Propheten selbst nur die Infallibilität des idschmâ. Koran und Sunna sind nur die historischen Quellen des letzteren. Nicht sie, sondern die Kompilationen des idschmâ schlägt der Richter auf; die selbständige Interpretation der heiligen Schriften und Tradition ist ihm untersagt."

120. See Schluchter (1988a), 2: 348.

121. Schluchter (1988a), 2: 351. "Doch mit der Schließung der heiligen Tradition versiegt diese charismatische Rechtsquelle. Die Rechtsentwicklung wird immobilisiert. Ein 'strereotypierte(s) Juristenrecht' ist die Folge, ein Juristenrecht zumal, das sich mit allen Mitteln gegen Säkularisierung stemmt. Diese drei Vorgänge, Immobilisierung, Stereotypierung und Abwehr von Säkularisierung, aber stützen sich wechselseitig. Das erlaubt Systematisierung, aber sie ist letzlich nicht juristisch-formal, sondern theologisch-material."

122. See *WuG*: 657–658. *Kadi* justice consists of informal judgements rendered in terms of concrete ethical or other practical valuations. The term derives from Richard Schmidt, a colleague and contemporary of Weber at Freiburg University. He uses this term in his "Die deutsche Zivilprozessreform und ihr Verhältnis zu den ausländischen Gesetzgebungen," *Zeitschrift für Politik*, I (1908): 266. Weber discusses this point in *WuG*: 563–564. See also Swedberg (ed.) (2005): 136–137.

123. For a discussion of the question of Islam and its relation to modernity and modernisation, see "Islamic Tradition and the Problems of Modernisation" in Bellah (1970): 146–166.

124. See Bryan S. Turner (1974): 181–184.

125. Noting that Weber and his wife Marianne never consummated their marriage, Turner, drawing on the evidence of the letter from Weber to his psychiatrist during the early years of his marriage, suggests that Weber's emotional and moral commitment to Protestantism left him in inner tension with his intellectual convictions. Unable to resolve the conflicts of the head and the heart, Weber was paralysed by a fear of his own sexuality and suffered under severe guilt. This feature is brought out in Weber's letter to a psychiatrist, in which he speaks of his difficulties with sleep from 1898 until his death in 1920 as related to the "terror of uncontrolled nocturnal ejaculations." See Bryan S. Turner (1974): 183.

126. For excellent accounts of this period, see Mommsen and Osterhammel (eds.) (1987), Mommsen (1998), and Wehler (1985).

127. *WuG*: 363. "Zunächst Beseitigung der sexuellen Orgie (der 'Hurerei' der jüdischen Priester)—wie dies der erörteten allgemeinen Stellung speziell der Prophetien zur Orgiastik entspricht,—aber weiterhin auch Beseitigung der freien Sexuallbeziehungen überhaupt zugunsten reglementierter und sakral legitimierter 'Ehe.' Dies gilt selbst für einen Propheten, der persönlich und in der Art seiner Jenseitsverheißungen an die Glaubenskrieger der sexuellen Sinnlichkeit so rücksichtslos Raum gab wie Muhammed (welcher sich für seine Person bekanntlich durch eine eigene Sure von der sonst gültigen Maximalzahl von Weibern dispensieren ließ). Die bis dahin legalen Formen eheloser Liebe und die Prostitution sind im orthodoxen Islam mit einem bis heute sonst kaum zu findenden durchschlagenden Erfolge proskribiert."

128. Clearly, Weber's own lifestyle was in contradiction to this Protestant background. On Weber's struggles with his sexuality, see Radkau (2005): 256–315, and 544–573.

129. Bryan S. Turner (1974): 183.

130. On the question of dating these two speeches and the history of incorrectly dating these two speeches, see Roth and Schluchter (1979): 113–116.

131. Ibid.: 115.

132. This historical context had been lacking in the American reception of Weber's essays translated by Talcott Parsons. In America,

Wissenschaft had been received as a methodological treatise rather than as an essay focussing on the fate of German politics and society. On this point, see Lassman et al. (eds.) (1989): xiv.

133. See Wittenberg (1938): 112.

134. On this point, see Voigt (2002).

135. See *Wissenschaft*: 582.

136. *Politik*: 506. "Staat ist diejenige menschliche Gemeinschaft, welche innerhalb eines bestimmten Gebietes—dies: 'Gebiet' gehört zum Merkmal—das Monopol legitimer physischer Gewaltsamkeit für sich (mit Erfolg) beansprucht."

137. *Politik*: 506. "Streben nach Machtanteil oder nach Beeinflussung der Machtverteilung, sei es zwischen Staaten, sei es innerhalb eines Staates zwischen den Menschengruppen, die er umschließt."

138. See Tenbruck (1999): 246–247.

139. On the importance of Protestantism for the rise of modern science, see Merton (1993). Indeed this was also manifested by the reality that in the German empire of the time, most of the top academic positions were occupied by Protestants. On the question of "Konfessionalismus" at the German university during this period, see Nipperdey (1993): 568–586.

140. *Wissenschaft*: 597. "Aber man erwartete von der Wissenschaft im Zeitalter der Entstehung der exakten Naturwissenschaften noch mehr. Wenn Sie sich an den Ausspruch Swammerdams erinnern: 'Ich bringe Ihnen hier den Nachweis der Vorsehung Gottes in der Anatomie einer Laus,' so sehen Sie, was die (indirekt) protestantisch und puritanisch beeinflußte wissenschaftliche Arbeit damals sich als ihre eigene Aufgabe dachte: den Weg zu Gott."

141. *Wissenschaft*: 598. "Kehren wir zurück. Was ist unter diesen inneren Voraussetzungen der Sinn der Wissenschaft als Beruf, da alle diese früheren Illusionen: 'Weg zum wahren sein,' 'Weg zur wahren Kunst,' 'Weg zur wahren Natur,' 'Weg zum wahren Gott,' 'Weg zum wahren Glück,' versunken sind? Die einfachste Antwort hat Tolstoj gegeben mit den Worten: 'Sie ist sinnlos, weil sie auf die allein für uns wichtige Frage: Was sollen wir tun? Wie sollen wir leben? keine Antwort gibt.' Die Tatsache, daß sie diese Antwort nicht gibt, ist schlechthin unbestreitbar. Die Frage ist nur, in welchem Sinne sie 'keine' Antwort gibt, und ob sie statt dessen nicht doch vielleicht dem, der die Frage richtig stellt, etwas leisten könnte."

142. *Wissenschaft*: 594. "Die zunehmende Intellektualisierung und Rationalisierung bedeutet also nicht eine zunehmende allgemeine Kenntnis der Lebensbedingungen, unter denen man steht. Sondern sie bedeutet etwas anderes: das Wissen davon oder den Glauben daran: daß man, wenn man nur wollte, es jederzeit erfahren könnte, daß es also prinzipiell keine geheimnisvollen unberechenbaren Mächte gebe, die da hineinspielen, daß man vielmehr alle Dinge—im Prinzip—durch

Berechnen beherrschen könne. Das aber bedeutet: die Entzauberung der Welt. Nicht mehr, wie der Wilde, für den es solche Mächte gab, muß man zu magischen Mitteln greifen, um die Geister zu beherrschen oder zu erbitten. Sondern technische Mittel und Berechnung leisten das. Dies vor allem bedeutet die Intellektualisierung als solche."

143. On this point, see Voigt (2002): 245.

144. See Voigt (2002): 251.

145. See Fischer (2001): 137.

146. On this point, Weber understands theology (following Schleiermacher) to be an "intellectual rationalisation of the possession of sacred values," which, because of the individual nature of religious experience, is necessarily manifested in the pluralism of religious traditions (a position Weber would share with William James). See *Wissenschaft*: 610.

147. *Wissenschaft*: 611. "Und ihre Frage ist dann wiederum: Wie lassen sich diese schechthin anzunehmenden Voraussetzungen innerhalb eines Gesamtweltbildes sinnvoll deuten? Jene Voraussetzungen selbst liegen dabei für die Theologie jenseits dessen, was 'Wissenschaft' ist. Sie sind kein 'Wissen' im gewöhnlich verstandenen Sinn, sondern ein 'Haben.' Wer sie—den Glauben oder die sonstigen heiligen Zuständlichkeiten—nicht 'hat,' dem kann sie keine Theologie ersetzen. Erst recht nicht eine andere Wissenschaft. Im Gegenteil: in jeder 'positiven' Theologie gelangt der Gläubige an den Punkt, wo der Augustinische Satz gilt: credo non quod, sed quia absurdum est. Die Fähigkeit zu dieser Virtuosenleistung des 'Opfers des Intellekts' ist das entscheidende Merkmal des positiv religiösen Menschen."

148. On this point, see Pinkard (2002): 152ff.

149. Voigt (2002): 252–253. "Daß Weber hier aber überhaupt mit dem Bild des Propheten argumentierte, und zwar in der Unterscheidung 'echter' und 'falscher' Propheten, verdient Aufmerksamkeit. Hierin ist ein protestantisches Erbe enthalten, das geeignet ist, uns über Weber's Absichten in den beiden Münchner Reden größere Klarheit zu verschaffen. Dazu ist ein werkgeschichtlicher Seitenblick hilfreich: Denn zeitgleich entstanden Webers Studien zum antiken Judentum. Der Prophetie wird hier eine entscheidende Funktion zugeschrieben, denn in der Unheilsprophetie (Jeremia, Deuterojesaja) sieht Weber den Höhepunkt der religiösen Entwicklung des Judentums. Mit dieser Ansicht folgt Weber dem protestantischen Alttestamentler Julius Wellhausen."

150. On this issue, see Liebeschütz (1967): 245–268.

151. See *AJ*: 425–429.

152. See Voigt (2002): 255.

153. Weber had particularly in mind the "Kulturkampfkonstellationen" at the German universities of his time, which argued against Catholic appointments because they were considered to be against the

principle of prejudice-free science. He suggested that the appointment of the Catholic professor Martin Spahn in Strasbourg was contrary to the spirit of true science. See Voigt (2002): 248.

154. *Wissenschaft*: 612–613. "Wer dies Schicksal der Zeit nicht männlich ertragen kann, dem muß man sagen: Er kehre lieber, schweigend, ohne die übliche öffentliche Renegatenreklame, sondern schlicht und einfach, in die weit und erbarmend geöffneten Arme der alten Kirchen zurück. Sie machen es ihm ja nicht schwer. Irgendwie hat er dabei—das ist unvermeidlich—das 'Opfer des Intellekts' zu bringen, so oder so. Wir werden ihn darum nicht schelten, wenn er es wirklich vermag. Denn ein solches Opfer des Intellekts zugunsten einer bedingungslosen Hingabe ist sittlich immerhin doch etwas anderes als jene Umgehung der schlichten intellektuellen Rechtschaffenheitspflicht, die eintritt, wenn man sich selbst nicht klar zu werden den Mut hat über die eigene letzte Stellungnahme, sondern diese Pflicht durch schwächliche Relativierung sich erleichtert."

155. See Wolf (1930): 128.

156. Voigt (2002): 256. "Webers und Wellhausens Prophetenbild ist freilich selbst ein protestantisch-theologisches Konstrukt. Und zwar ein solches, das sich genau der theologischen Auffassung verdankt, die Weber mit der 'positiven' Theologie gekennzeichnet hatte. Indem Weber mit Wellhausen den ursprünglichen, rein religiösen Charakter der prophetischen Offenbarungen und die institutionelle, priesterlichen Folgen unterschied, blieb er jener Differenz von Religion und Theologie verpflichtet, die der 'positiven' Theologie als Grundthema galt. Wenn Weber die unbedingte Verpflichtung auf die Sache, die intellektuelle Redlichkeit in den Bereich der Wissenschaft transponierte, läßt sich dies durchaus nicht als Verabschiedung oder gar Verwerfung der Religion ansehen. Es ist vielmehr als Kritik an einem Wissenschaftstil zu verstehen, der sich den Wahrheitsfragen nicht mehr in voller Ernsthaftigkeit aussetzt. Darin ist dann aber wiederum ein Moment der Theologiekritik zu erkennen, dem noch nachzugehen sein wird."

157. I shall consider the importance of the history of the *Kulturkampf* and *Kulturprotestantismus* on Weber's position in detail below.

158. Quoted in Beetham (1974): 13.

159. Wittenberg (1938): 120.

160. See *Politik*: 542.

161. *Politik*: 545. "Mann kann sagen, daß drei Qualitäten vornehmlich entscheidend sind für den Politiker: Leidenschaft—Verantwortungsgefühl—Augenmaß. Leidenschaft im Sinn von Sachlichkeit: leidenschaftliche Hingabe an eine 'Sache,' an den Gott oder Dämon, der ihr Gebieter ist."

162. See *Politik*: 550.

163. *Politik*: 550. "Von ihr gilt, was man von der Kausalität in der Wissenschaft gesagt hat: sie is kein Fiaker, den man beliebig halten

lassen kann, um nach Befinden ein- und auszusteigen. Sondern: ganz *oder* gar nicht, *das* gerade ist ihr Sinn, wenn etwas anderes als Trivialitäten herauskommen soll. Also z. B. der reiche Jüngling: 'Er aber ging traurig davon, denn er hatte viele Güter.' Das evangelische Gebot ist unbedingt und eindeutig: gib her, was du hast—*alles*, schlechthin. Der Politiker wird sagen: eine sozial sinnlose Zumutung, solang es nicht für *alle* durchgesetzt wird. Also: Besteurung, Wegsteuerung, Konfiskation,—mit einem Wort: Zwang und Ordnung gegen *alle*. Das ethische Gebot aber fragt danach *gar nicht*, das ist sein Wesen."

164. *Politik*: 557. "Wer das Heil seiner Seele und die Rettung anderer Seelen sucht, der sucht das nicht auf dem Wege der Politik, die ganz andere Aufgaben hat: solche, die nur mit dem Gott der Liebe, auch mit dem Christengott in seiner kirchlichen Ausprägung, in einer inneren Spannung, die jederzeit in unaustragbaren Konflikt ausbrechen kann."

165. See *Politik*: 557.

166. An example of this type of reading of Weber can be found in Krech and Wagner (1994): 755–779.

167. This is well brought out in the study of Nietzsche's use of Wellhausen by Hartwick (1996).

168. On this point, see Voigt (2002): 262.

169. See Voigt (2002): 263.

170. *Politik:* 552. "Der Verantwortungsethiker dagegen rechnet mit eben jenen durchschnittlichen Defekten der Menschen—er hat, wie Fichte richtig gesagt hat, gar kein recht, ihre Güte und Vollkommenheit vorauszusetzen."

CHAPTER 5

The Protestant Heritage of Weber's Theory of Secularisation

It would be oversimplistic to reduce Weber's theory of secularisation to the one causal factor of its Protestant heritage. Yet, the a-confessional reading of the history of sociology, philosophy, legal theory,[1] and historiography that has been dominant until recently is also an inadequate position from which to assess it.[2] In this chapter, I intend to clarify the positioning of Weber's theory of secularisation by outlining certain major aspects of this Protestant heritage that informed it.[3] I begin by pointing out the foundational aspects of Protestantism that are significant in Weber's theory.

What is Protestantism?

In his study of the relations between Protestantism and philosophy, Pierre-André Stucki suggests that three fundamental principles of Protestantism can be considered to be defininitive: *Sola Scriptura*, *Sola Fide*, and *Sola Gratia*.[4] In the principle of scripture alone (*Sola Scriptura*), the key issue is that of the origin of ultimate authority in matters of faith. For Luther, the Bible was the only source of authority in the

Church. When the Church diverged from this, the individual was responsible to follow his or her own conscience and part company with the institutional Church. The Bible was thus the normative basis of critique in the Church, and hence the principle of *Sola Scriptura* was essentially the adoption of a clear position with regard to the question of authority and Revelation. God made himself known to each individual through the medium of the Word of God as authoritatively revealed in the Bible, and not through the humanly created institutional hierarchy of the Church. Thus, the declaration of Luther before Emperor Charles V at the Diet of Worms on April 18, 1521 is the birth of the Protestant principle of the freedom of conscience based on the capacity of the individual Christian in faith to decide, *Sola Scriptura*, right and wrong:

> Since then your serene majesty and your lordships seek a simple answer, I will give it in this manner, neither horned nor toothed: Unless I am convinced by the testimony of the Scriptures or by clear reason (for I do not trust either in the pope or in councils alone, since it is well known that they have often erred and contradicted themselves), I am bound by the Scriptures I have quoted and my conscience is captive to the Word of God. I cannot and I will not retract anything, since it is neither safe nor right to go against conscience.
>
> I cannot do otherwise, here I stand, may God help me, Amen.[5]

The principle of faith alone (*Sola Fide*) has had enormous implications for a Protestant understanding of action developed throughout Weber's works. The idea here is that one is saved, or in the words of St. Paul, made righteous, through faith and not through one's own efforts or works. This has been the origin of the so-called justification through faith or works debate between the Catholic and Lutheran Churches right up until our present day.[6] Luther outlined this idea in his speech on *The Freedom of a Christian*, given in early November 1520.

> Our faith in Christ does not free us from works but from false opinions concerning works, that is, from the foolish presumption that justification is acquired by works. Faith redeems, corrects, and preserves our consciences so that we know that righteousness does not consist in works, although works neither can nor ought to be wanting; yet our righteousness is not in them, but in

faith; and yet those works of the body are not to be despised or neglected on that account.[7]

The main point to stress here is that human action is emptied of any positive contribution to salvation; it no longer holds any positive soteriological significance in theological terms.

Closely related to this second principle is the third principle of Protestantism: that is to say, grace alone (*Sola Gratia*). The point to note here is that the mediation of salvation cannot come through the institution of the Church; it can come only through the free action of God, known as grace. Grace alone allows the individual to receive the gift of faith through which the believer can confess Jesus to be Lord and so be saved. No human action or institution can confer this gift. The mystery of the election of the saved and the doctrine of predestination most dramatically bring out the significance of this principle. This principle also expresses clearly the Protestant mistrust of hierarchy. If grace is freely given directly by God's Holy Spirit, then there is no need for priests to administer the sacrament of confession, which restores the individual believer to a state of grace, as in the Catholic tradition. The role of the minister in the Protestant tradition is thus not to administer grace, but rather, to preach the Word of God.

In addition to these three basic principles, another characteristic should be stressed in outlining the basic nature of Protestantism. Crucial to the self-definition of Protestantism is that it itself is essentially an ethical religion, based on the law, and not a metaphysical religion like Catholicism. Pierre-André Stucki makes this point well:

> We can perhaps formulate the thesis of the law in the following way: "God exists as the Creator who has given his law to man." This thesis consists of two parts: The first is the assertion of the existence of God and the second is the qualification of God as the Creator and giver of the law. It is necessary to the Protestant doctrine to pose this thesis. In Luther's conception, we have seen that the law is the first Word of God with which man is confronted. Thus in Protestantism it is not first of all a question of admitting the thesis of the creation and then following on to say that God has given His law to man, rather it is a question firstly of listening to the law, which itself implies that the giver of the law should be understood

> as the Creator. In other words, Protestantism is firstly an ethical and not a metaphysical doctrine.[8]

This feature of Protestantism is clearly present in Weber's notion of the ethical transformation of religion in his work both on Judaism and on Protestantism. Indeed, echoes of all these basic principles of Protestantism have been identified in the textual analysis of previous chapters. The task now is to turn more specifically to the particular aspects of Weber's Protestant heritage that informed his theory of secularisation.

The *Kulturkampf*,[9] Cultural Protestantism and Nationalism

In Friedrich Wilhelm Graf's seminal article on cultural Protestantism, (*Kulturprotestantismus*), *Kulturprotestantismus Begriffsgeschichte einer theologiepolitischen Chiffre*, he outlines four different ways in which this concept has been used in the theological-historical literature:[10] 1. As a concept for the period of Protestant theology between Schleiermacher and Troeltsch; 2. As a concept for the theological school of Albrecht Ritschl, which crystallised around the journal *Die Christliche Welt*; 3. As a category used to describe the religious and social values associated with the Wilhelmine bourgeoisie; 4. Most centrally, as the category used to describe the transformation of Christian values into the values of middle-class capitalism.

These four different uses all consider Protestant Christianity in light of its relevance for modernity.[11] This notion is clearly brought out in one of the most important institutions of cultural Protestantism, the *Deutscher Protestantenverein* (The German Protestant Association), founded in 1863. Richard Rothe, the leading Heidelberg theologian of the time, spoke of the Protestant Association as an attempt to reconcile religion and culture and, thus, to make Christianity a force in modern culture.[12] The Protestant Association criticised Catholicism for being against modernisation and for blocking the development of the national cultural ideal. Catholicism was seen as a form of cultural dominance based on clerical power that threatened the autonomy of culture.

In 1864, Richard Rothe noted that modern culture and morality were essentially Protestant. He projected this descriptive genealogy into a normative futurology as he argued that the development of civilisation and culture could occur only through Protestantism. The Protestant Association saw the future of the German nation in the hands of the popular Protestant majority. Gangolf Hübinger, in his study of cultural Protestantism and the politics of Wilhelmine Germany, considers Heidelberg to have been a sort of "command and control" centre for cultural Protestantism, a type of think tank from which the guiding ideas of the movement:—to renew the Protestant church and to bring Protestantism into harmony with the cultural developments of the day—had flowed.[13] Weber's close friend and associate Friedrich Naumann was an engaged fighter in the cultural Protestant movement, and Weber supported him in his campaign against the clerical regime of the Catholic political parties of the time.[14] Indeed, Weber's contact with the movement included acting as an editor for the major liberal Protestant Lexicon *Religion in Geschichte und Gegenwart*, being responsible for the twelfth part of the Lexicon on the social sciences.

Johannes Weiß points out that Weber's close friend and colleague, Ernst Troeltsch, was the most important theoretician of cultural Protestantism,[15] and there is no doubt that Weber was significantly influenced by the movement. His own commitment to the Evangelical Social Congress is clear evidence of his sympathy for the tenets of the movement. Rita Aldenhoff summarises the extent of Weber's involvement in this important organ of cultural Protestantism, which sought a reorientation of social policy in the 1890s and a Protestant engagement with the social questions of the day:

> Weber was a regular participant in the annual conferences, up to and including that of 1897; from 1892 on, he was a member of the Council that directed the movement. After his move to Baden in 1894, he also became a member of the Council of the local

> Evangelical-Social Union, one of the provincial unions affiliated to the Evangelical Social Congress. He made contributions to a series of courses in political economy for the clergy, of which his October 1893 lectures in Berlin are perhaps the best known. Weber spoke there in company with such widely reputed economists as Adolph Wagner, Karl Oldenberg, and Wilhelm Stieda on a number of basic economic problems, in particular on agriculture and agrarian politics. Further courses, in which Weber lectured on questions pertaining to the Stock Exchange and, again, on agrarian politics, followed in 1896 and 1897. To these must be added—with four individual papers delivered to the Evangelical-Social learned societies and the Upper Hessen Society for Home Missions—his collaboration on Martin Rade's *Die Christliche Welt* [*The Christian World*] and the *Mitteilungen des Evangelisch-sozialen Kongresses* [*Communications of the Evangelical-Social Congress*]. Lastly, his work as director of the inquiry into rural workers, with which the ESC carried out in 1892–1903 in the manner of the earlier survey undertaken by the *Verein für Sozialpolitik*, is of fundamental significance.[16]

A most significant indicator of the Protestant heritage of Weber's ideas can be seen in the overlapping of Protestantism and nationalism in the nation-building project of early modern Germany. As Chris Thornhill has remarked, late nineteenth-century German politics were deeply marked by a commitment to historicism derived from a Lutheran view of history.[17] Cultural Protestantism considered national history and culture to be an expression of the divine will, and the State came to be seen as the highest embodiment of the national culture.

This link between Protestantism and historicism can be clearly seen in the founding fathers of the Weimar Constitution, especially Friedrich Naumann. Thornhill makes the point that Naumann expressly connected the process of constitutional foundation with the first principles of Lutheranism.[18] Both historicism and Protestantism saw national history as a fluid set of customs and beliefs that had become embodied in their highest form in the State.[19] The view of sovereignty as based on a set of coordinated historical reflexes reflected the Lutheran conception of political sovereignty and historicism clearly derived from the Lutheran theology of political history.

It is around the question of nationalism that one can see most acutely the significance of the confessional question for Weber. As the historian Paul Münch suggests, the confessional question permeated nineteenth-century German politics at its most crucial point, that is to say, on the question of nationalism. Speaking about the historical background to Weber's Protestant Ethic thesis, Münch notes:

> The national question became the pivot of confessional dissent. Ever since the three-hundredth anniversary of Luther's theses in 1817, Martin Luther has been celebrated as a German patriot. During the *Kulturkampf*, Protestants claimed the word *deutsch* (German) for Luther, the "most German of Germans," and for his Reformation. The Protestant usurpation of the positive characteristics of diligence and sense of duty associated with the German national character excluded Catholics from the German stereotyped self image and placed them on the national sidelines: Catholic became synonymous with un-German, ultramontane, uncivilised, and lazy. The *Kulturkampf* thus latched on to the typology that originated in the eighteenth century, but beyond that reactivated in almost all areas the excessive interconfessional polemics of the Reformation, and thus also the political and economic dynamite that had lain dormant.[20]

Indeed, Münch goes on specifically to locate Weber within this Protestant tradition of the *Kulturkampf*:[21]

> Only during the *Kulturkampf* was the confessional dispute, forgotten since the Enlightenment, fully resumed. Now it became the most important argument, nationalistically charged at that, for ascribing positions in Wilhelmine society. The essentially materialistic approach of the late eighteenth century was gradually replaced by an idealistic standpoint that could find a satisfactory explanation in the "working of the spirit." Without a doubt, Max Weber stands in this tradition as a German, a Protestant, and a representative of the educated middle classes — at best as "a giant on the shoulders of dwarfs."[22]

This is no surprise, given that Weber was a vehement nationalist all his life. From the days of his Freiburg Inaugural Address and early writings of the 1890s right up until his political speeches of the First World War, he energetically defended the need for Germany to develop a strong sense of national identity.[23] Weber's deep commitment to German nationalism is one important source of the Protestant heritage of his theory of secularisation. However, it would be too hasty to jump to the conclusion that Weber saw Lutheranism as the chief motor of German national identity. On the contrary, it is precisely in his great disappointment with the capacity of Lutheranism to galvanise a strong sense of German national identity that one can see his deep Protestant convictions.[24] His letter of February 5, 1906 to the liberal Protestant theologian Adolf von Harnack makes this point clearly:

> Luther towers above all others, but Lutheranism is—I don't deny it—in its historical articulation the most frightening of terrors for me. Even in the ideal form in which it appears in your hopes for the future, it lacks, I fear, in its impact on us Germans, sufficient transformative power to shape life. It is a difficult and tragic situation: None of us could be a sectarian, a Quaker, a Baptist, etc. Everybody must recognise the superiority of the institutional Church in nonethical and nonreligious [i.e., cultural] respects. The time of the sects, or of something equivalent to them, is definitely over. But the fact that our nation never went through the school of hard asceticism, in no form whatsoever, is the source of everything that I hate about it (and about myself). I can't help it, but in religious terms the average American sect member surpasses our institutional Christians as much as Luther excels, as a religious personality, Calvin, Fox *et tutti quanti.*[25]

Weber's worldview is Protestant.[26] Even when he expresses his bitter disappointment with the institutional form of Lutheranism, it is clear that his terms of reference are Protestant. It is in reformed Protestantism, and especially in Calvinism, that he finds the necessary ascetical spirit that has the transformative power to shape life. His hatred of the German nation and of himself in this letter to Harnack is the hate of the bitter disappointment of one who regrets what might have been—a nostalgia for a Protestantism that might have been so different. This nostalgia is important because it reveals something of the emotional allegiance that confessional division and conflict had burned into the soul of

Germany. Adolf von Harnack put this poignantly in his article in the *Preußische Jahrbücher* of 1907:

> In numerous and important questions of life and of the common weal, our nation is at the outset divided into two camps, and this state of affairs, starting from the centre, works its way into the periphery of our existence, deep into the smallest and most everyday aspects of our lives. Everywhere one confronts confessional prejudice; everywhere one encounters the fence, indeed the wall of confession.[27]

In making thematic this confessional architecture of Weber's theory of secularisation, my aim is to locate his ideas within their historical context. The Protestant heritage of Weber's theory of secularisation constitutes an important dimension of this historical background that has, until now, largely been neglected by scholars. It is not the only historical dimension, but it is a major one, which sheds light on both the substantive and methodological work of Weber.

Moreover, the historical heritage of the *Kulturkampf* was not confined to Germany alone. Between 1860 and 1890, *Kulturkampf* legislation was also passed in Austria, Spain, Switzerland, Belgium, the Netherlands, and France. In each country, particular historical circumstances had encouraged the passing of such anti-Catholic legislation. In the case of Germany, conflict between the State and the Catholic Church focussed on the question of nation building. National values in Germany, largely derived from enlightened Protestantism, formed a core around which the state, conceived in Prussian terms after the victory of the *Kleindeutschland* model of the Northern German League, began the process of nation-building in the newly founded German Empire of 1870–1871.[28]

Norbert Elias remarks that *Kultur*, the German notion of national high culture, had a three-fold association for the German bourgeoisie: with national identity, with specific class values, and with the history of the middle-class struggle for German unity.[29] *Kultur* also became associated with the values of Protestantism. The founding member of the liberal *Protestantenverein* (Protestant Association), Daniel Schenkel, echoed a wide consensus in 1862 when he wrote, "We say with the deepest conviction: the entire cultural progress of peoples in our century is based upon the foundation of religious, moral, and intellectual freedom, and for that reason, upon Protestantism."[30]

Although, as Peter Uwe Hohendahl has shown, the classical German authors provided a literary consensus for civilised people (*Kulturvolk*), religious disunity tended to fragment German cultural life. The literati believed that national literature and culture must be built on the foundations of Protestantism. The German historian Wilhelm Scherer declared in 1874:

> Luther's Bible was the decisive act toward the establishment of a unified German culture and language. It was the act of creation of that which we now call our nation. We attribute to Luther our national unity as Italy attributes its unity to Dante. Luther's Bible is our *Divina Commedia*. It is the foundation stone of the temple which surrounds us.[31]

So much for *Kultur*; but what is the meaning of the military language of *Kampf*? The core of this was a perception that the Catholic Church, with its international structure, was essentially opposed to the consolidation of German nation-building. Thus Bismarck saw the Catholic nineteenth-century Ultramontanist centralism, spearheaded by the restoration of the Jesuits in 1814, as intrinsically hostile to nationalism. It was therefore necessary to fight this Ultramontanist centralism in order to protect the nation.

Hartmann Tyrell notes that in his youth, Weber was greatly influenced by Bismarck's battle against the Catholic Church. Even as late as 1917, Weber described Bismarck's compromise with it as a defeat for the authority of the German State.[32] Tyrell suggests that the heritage of the *Kulturkampf* can be seen in three major areas of Weber's work:[33] in the analysis of political and religious bases of ruler-ship; in Weber's analysis of the Church as an institution of ruler-ship; and, following Georg Jellinik, in Weber's thoughts on the theme of tolerance and freedom of conscience that he considered to have been inhibited by the Catholic Church, as his study of the Maryland Baptist Sects attempts to illustrate. Tyrell is cautious not to overestimate this influence, but clearly considers it to be an important factor in understanding the background and context of much of Weber's work. He draws parallels between Durkheim's sociology of morality and religion, which Tyrell considers to be part of the French *Kulturkampf* during the establishment of sociology in the secular university system during the Third Republic, and Weber's political and religious sociology, with its traces of the *Kulturkampf*.[34]

I have shown through a textual analysis of Weber just how these Protestant themes situate Weber's own theory of secularisation within a Protestant worldview. One way of reading this is to suggest, like Tyrell, that Weber sought the backing of the Protestant establishment for his social science, and so drew on his Protestant heritage in order to make his case. In this sense, one could read Weber's own sociology, like Durkheim's, as a type of ideological legitimation of the German establishment.[35]

When read against this Protestant background, one can detect, even in its methodological dimension of value freedom, traces of the legitimation of the German establishment as opposed to the value-bound scholarship of the Catholic Church, especially after the declaration of papal infallibility in 1870. Weber's commitment to value freedom can be read within the Protestant tradition of Luther's freedom of conscience. Without reducing this theme in Weber to its confessional heritage, his calls for neutrality and objectivity in scientific research clearly fit within this Protestant tradition and carry the traces of a confessional influence; for Weber, to be neutral and objective was simply to be Protestant in one's approach.

Weber and the Question of Religious Confession

It is important to recognise, however, that a form of secularised Protestantism persisted even when regular observance and

> dictates of spirituality had disappeared. What historians call "cultural Protestantism" was an extraordinarily powerful force among the middle classes. It was eminently compatible with the culture of progress—indeed progress was largely equated with Protestantism—and a sublimated Protestant pathos left its traces on bourgeois enthusiasm for everything from German unification to the German literary canon. Most middle-class Protestants would have applauded Schiller's comment about Berlin's destiny as the capital of Protestantism, even though few of them went to church in Berlin by the 1880s, that was not the point: German culture *was* Protestant.[36]

David Blackbourn's incisive comments highlight the importance of uncovering the Protestant heritage of much of German thought in the so-called "long nineteenth century" (1780–1918).

If philosophy, sociology, history, and theology are anything, they are cultural products: artefacts of the thought and the experience of people who are situated within specific cultural and social frameworks.[37] That these particularities can be transcended in universal criteria of reason is not in question.[38] Nevertheless, the absence of sensitivity to the particular frameworks within which theories take shape can lead to the hermeneutical judgements inscribed into the very architecture of theories being overlooked. Many accounts of Weber have forgotten this.[39] As Sven Eliaeson has noted, part of the problem with the interpretation of Weber's work has been the lack of attention to the historical context in which he wrote.[40]

Speaking of the study of religious groups in modern German history, Helmut Walser Smith and Chris Clark suggest that a normative prejudice based on a particular view of the modernisation process tended to treat religion as having a somewhat subsidiary role in the historical process.[41] It was the great German historian Thomas Nipperdey whose groundbreaking study *Religion im Umbruck* signalled a significant change in this state of affairs.[42]

Despite Nipperdey's work, however, a certain prejudice between the perspectives of church historians and secular historians has persisted. It is interesting to note that Smith and Clark describe this prejudice as a "Neo-Weberian modernisation paradigm."[43] By that they mean the form of secularisation theory that ignores the importance of confessional allegiances and conflicts in social history.[44]

It is Thanks to the work of scholars such as Wolfgang Schieder, Johnathan Sperber, Thomas Nipperdey, and Urs Attermatt, this intellectual myopia gradually is disappearing. Nipperdey describes his intention in this regard as making explicit the influence of religion on social and political structures, and so uncovering the importance of religion for the interpretation of culture.[45]

Yet, Smith and Clark note that the internal divisions separating the studies of Protestants, Catholics, and Jews still exist in German establishments.[46] This "confessionalisation" of scholarship in Germany goes back to the late nineteenth-century religious conflicts. Around this time, both the Protestant *Archiv für Reformationsgeschichte* (1883) and the Catholic *Historisches Jahrbuch* (1880) were established. Both of these important journals took shape against the backdrop of the *Kulturkampf*. Indeed, as Lucian Hölscher suggests, Germany's religious divides provided a much greater ideological element in the political and social conflicts of the nineteenth century than was the case in any of its European neighbours.[47] Wolfgang Altgeld proposes a reason why this confessional dimension has been denied in German scholarship, and considers this to fit with the particular model of secularisation associated with German nation-building. He argues that in order to remove the troublesome confessional divisions in Germany and to present a homogeneous picture of the nation, the religious element was denied altogether. This allowed German nationalists to paint a picture of the national religion as the religion of the individual, which bound the individual and the State together in a relation of reciprocal harmony.[48]

It is not difficult to see the parallels between Altgeld's view and the theory of secularisation and its Protestant heritage in Weber's works. The importance of the individual, the strong sense of nationalism, the apparent confessional invisibility that tries to eliminate confessional difference by adopting a sense of cultural superiority, and the general sense that Protestantism was most suited to such nation-building, all find echos in Weber's work.[49]

The common presumption that Weber operated in a confessionally neutral way, a way not significantly drawing on this Protestant heritage, is descriptively false and theoretically lacking. It presumes philosophy and sociology to operate in an historical, cultural, and social vacuum in which factors like religion do not influence the way people think and feel. This may well be due more to the prejudices of the secular academy than to the real historical context in which authors such as Weber actually operated.[50]

Weber's Religious Heritage

> Today it occurs, that what we group together under the name of "our culture" touches in the first place on Christianity. This is the case in the institutions and structures of the whole of society and in their ways of thinking and acting. Indeed, the extent to which this dependence exists is such that we do not always notice this and even are no longer aware of the fact that in all things, what we think and what we do, we remain under the influence of the Christian religion.[51]

Weber wrote this letter to his brother Alfred, on the occasion of his confirmation, from Strasbourg on March 25, 1884, at the age of twenty. Weber's own family had been divided religiously between the fervent Protestant religiosity of his mother and the religious apathy of his father. He had also discussed religious problems with his cousin Otto Baumgarten and his uncle Adolf Hausrath, who was a professor of church history at the University of Heidelberg. Both Baumgarten and Hausrath were pronounced critical liberal Protestants. It is thus not surprising that we find Weber, as a young student in Strasbourg, stressing the important influence of Christianity on all areas of social and cultural life.

Paul Honigsheim, a German sociologist who emigrated to the United States and taught in the Department of Sociology at Michigan State University from 1938 until his death in 1963, has contributed reflections on the religious heritage of Max Weber that are particularly interesting for a number of reasons. First, Honigsheim belonged to the select circle that participated in Weber's discussion group at Heidelberg in the 1910s and, as Marianne Weber notes in her biography of her husband, he was a frequent visitor to their mansion in Heidelberg.[52] Second, Weber respected Honigsheim's own scholarly work, quoting his dissertation on Jansenism in his *PE*,[53] and trusted his scholarly judgement. Finally, Honigsheim published a series of essays, *On Max Weber*, in which he attempted to uncover the unknown Weber from his own personal experience of the man. In his article in *Church History* of 1950, he suggests that the understanding of Weber's work has suffered from too many false assumptions. He writes:

> He is sometimes regarded as emphasizing almost exclusively the importance of the spiritual factor with regard to changes in the socio-economic sphere. More frequently, he is regarded as one who deals with religious phenomena only in a rationalistic way. Both concepts of the man are equally wrong. Thus, it is my purpose to outline his basic religious, philosophical, and ethical convictions as well as the possible interrelationship between such ideas and his investigations.[54]

Drawing on remarks in letters and correspondence, Weber's two main Munich speeches, Marianne Weber's biography, and his own personal reminiscences of Weber, Honigsheim sets out to give a more accurate and balanced account of Weber's religious and ethical background. He divides Weber's life into two major periods: the pre—Neo-Kantian Protestant phase; and the Neo-Kantian Protestant phase. In the pre—Neo-Kantian Protestant phase, Honigsheim draws particularly on Weber's *Jugendbriefe* in order to reconstruct an overall picture of his religious and ethical convictions. He notes that Weber's early interest in ritual showed an overlapping concern for the independence of the individual. This is typically a Protestant theme and indicates that these Protestant principles provided significant motivation and influence in Weber's own thought. Weber had the opportunity to discuss preaching methods with his cousin Otto Baumgarten, whom he often heard preach, and discussed at length with him his concerns about the interference of some authorities in the freedom of the individual preacher to preach and to organise the liturgy in their own way. His own preference was for rituals to be minimally bound by precepts ordained from the central church authorities.[55] This question had troubled Weber since the time of his confirmation, as he felt that the official German Protestant Church was moving in the wrong direction on this matter.[56] He particularly blamed this deviation from the principles of Protestant freedom on the interference of Wilhelm II, viewing him as a religious hypocrite who used the church-state ties for his own political purposes.[57] Interestingly, Weber's defence of individual freedom is brought out in his complex relation with Catholicism. Honigsheim makes this point well:

> Weber's respect for the conscience and for this individual calling was very great. Indeed, throughout his life, Max Weber considered Catholicism to constitute one of the gravest threats to the autonomous decision of the individual conscience and to the independence of scientific investigation.[58]

The perceived authoritarian nature of the Catholic Church, intensified after the 1870 declaration of papal infallibility, led Weber to distrust Catholicism as an institution bent on control and the quashing of individual freedom. Yet, as Honigsheim notes, it would be wrong to see this in too one-sided a way. He notes that Weber also opposed some of Bismarck's anti-Catholic laws on the grounds that they interfered with the religious freedom of the individual.[59] Clearly for Weber, whilst religious freedom was a Protestant principle, it also applied to Catholics. Honigsheim goes on to state his position on the depth of Weber's Protestant convictions:

> For Max Weber was not just a Protestant by birth; he was one by emotion and feeling. To be sure, he criticised German Lutheranism, but he distinguished forcefully between German Lutheranism conceived as a historically explainable aberration from the basic attitude of the founder, and the young monk from Wittenberg himself. If anyone is entitled to be brought into the neighbourhood of Luther, it is Max Weber. His tragic-consciousness has manifested itself not just in a theory emphasizing the tragic but also in a life determined by his own religiously conceived categorical imperative. This means nothing other than the realisation of a life conforming to Luther's words: "Here I stand. I cannot do otherwise, so help me God."[60]

The fact that Paul Honigsheim is, as Alan Sica has called him, "unique among those who knew Max Weber personally and decided to write about him,"[61] gives particular weight to this assessment of Weber's own religiosity and to the characterisation of Weber's scholarship and his commitment to the vocation of a modern scholar as part of his Protestant heritage.

In Honigsheim's assessment of the Neo-Kantian Protestant phase of Weber's life, some characteristic points particularly deepen and broaden this understanding of the importance of the Protestant heritage in Weber's work. For example, the Neo-Kantian group of the southern German School of Windelband, Rickert, Jellinek, Troeltsch, and their followers had a significant influence on Weber. The epistemological questions raised by this school reinforced a religious conviction in Weber that the matters of value judgement were to be based on the autonomous religio-ethical conscience of the individual. Honigsheim summarises this point:

> Weber combined these epistemological solutions with his Protestantism. This combination of Protestantism and Neo-Kantianism provided him with the tool to solve his own religious and ethical problems. The problems increasingly concerned the compatibility of the precepts of Jesus with the demands of modern society.[62]

The transition from the religio-ethical value judgements of the individual conscience to the relationship between Christian precepts and the demands of modern society, marks the second characteristic that Honigsheim identifies in his assessment of the importance of Weber's Protestant heritage in the second phase of his life, the phase of the Neo-Kantian Protestant. The tension between an ethic of conviction and an ethic of responsibility marks clearly the force field of this transition in Weber. Honigsheim suggests that three major factors influenced this transition in Weber's thought.

First, general discontent with the institutionalisation of the Protestant Church in Germany led some Germans to turn to Roman Catholicism and oriental mysticism as an alternative to the established religion (some Germans even became disciples of the anti-democratic Catholic poet Stephan George, who proposed the alternative of forming a spiritual aristocracy, an elite body that lived like Benedictine monks and rejected the institutionalised mediocrity and trivia of the democratic process).[63]

Second, the University of Heidelberg had become a centre for political and social dissenters from countries such as Russia. Weber earlier in his life had learnt Russian (in bed!) in order to follow closely the political and social developments in the country and, whilst in Heidelberg, he championed and defended Russian émigrés, as he did all students who had been persecuted for their convictions. This experience deepened his understanding of the politico-religious importance of Russian literature, especially in the works of Tolstoy and Dostoyevsky.

Finally, after the collapse of the Wilhelmine Empire and the revolution of 1918–1919, some German leaders advocated the use of violence in revolution but not in war. One of the most important advocates of this policy was Weber's Munich colleague Friedrich Wilhelm Foerster, who had proposed a form of state pacifism based on a Christian concept of natural law, and had insisted on the need for Germany to accept and own a sense of its own war guilt.[64] All these factors, argues Honigsheim, significantly influenced Weber's conviction that the ethics of the Sermon on the Mount could not and should not be applied to political ethics. On this point, he was also in the tradition of the distinction made by Luther and Calvin between the jurisdictions of secular and spiritual government.[65] For Weber, the one who cannot make this "intellectual sacrifice," who is not able to follow a vocation in politics or science, who cannot live with this degree of autonomy, should return to the churches since: "The arms of the old churches are opened widely and compassionately for him."[66] Further support for the view that Weber's Protestant heritage played a significant role in his work can also be found in the reminiscences of a number of his colleagues and friends. Thus, Helmuth Plessner, the Heidelberg professor, wrote:

> But nobody had ever doubted that he was a Protestant. A Lutheran with a sharp sense of the competition of Calvinism and the

> suffering of the split between the demands of conscience and the demands of responsibility. One sees this in the speeches given to the students in 1918 "Science as a Vocation" and "Politics as a Vocation," and in his heroic acceptance of the pluralism of a thoroughly rationalised society without any belief in an objective hierarchy of values or progress. One also sees it in his interpretation of science and methodology.[67]

Despite getting the dates of both the Munich speeches wrong, it is clear that Plessner judged it to be beyond reasonable doubt that Weber was a Protestant and that his intellectual work had been influenced by this fact. This is also stated by the feminist writer Gertrud Bäumer, who was a friend of both Max and Marianne Weber and frequent visitor to their house in Heidelberg. In her obituary of Max Weber, published in *Die Hilfe* in 1926, she wrote:

> For Max Weber, the Protestant cultural convictions are the remaining basis for the structure of his lifework, destiny, thoughts, formation, and view of the world. As broad and as much beyond the confessional dimension as his view of life was, it remains nevertheless underground in the heritage of his father and mother. A spiritual-moral structure, which firstly, and in a certain way, was not necessarily conscious, and yet in both his personal life and in his intellectual confrontation with the world remained decisive. We are in a spiritual sphere, in the sense that this morality defines a destiny. Not at all in a philistine sense of a limited morality of life, but on the contrary, that much more powerfully demonstrated itself as the demon which controlled and formed such a passionate and nervous personality.[68]

In the context of the influence of such a Protestant religious heritage, it is not out of place to pose the question which Werner Stark first posed in 1968, as to the place of Catholicism in Weber's work. Stark's answer to this question was uncompromising:

> Because Max Weber was a great man, a wreath of legends has tended to collect around his name, and one of them is to the effect that he always practiced what he preached, and in particular that he was as value-free, as unprejudiced and objective in his own scholarly work, as he demanded of any scholar at any time. It would have been nice to confirm this belief, but unfortunately

> the hard facts of the case force us rather to contradict it. The treatment which he metes out to Roman Catholicism in those parts of *Wirtschaft und Gesellschaft*, which Ephraim Fischoff has published under the title *The Sociology of Religion*, shows us Weber in the grip of prejudice. Not only does he display a surprising ignorance of what Catholicism is—surprising above all, because he was so careful in his discussion of, say, Confucianism or Taoism—but all he has to say is coloured by definite, if muted contempt.[69]

Stark suggests that Weber essentially charges Catholicism with two major faults: that it is really a form of polytheism; and that it is full of magical conceptions of reality and is thus the embodiment of a primitive and irrational world view.[70] He suggests that the basis of Weber's argument is a form of historicism which claims that, since Catholicism is older and thus nearer to the historically manifested polytheistic religions, Catholicism shares in this primitive worldview. As Stark points out, if this is the case, Weber committed a *non sequitur*. From being older it does not necessarily follow that Catholicism shared the traits of older polytheistic religions. Stark also suggests that Weber's Protestant individualism contrasts with his view of a collective and authoritarian Catholicism.

Following on from Werner Stark's work, Michael Zöllner considers the question of the possible effect that an anti-Catholic position may have had on the origins of the sociology of religion in the work of Weber and Troeltsch.[71] Zöllner suggests that Weber's attitude to Catholicism was based not on ignorance, but rather, on a form of implicit historicism. He suggests that both Weber and Troeltsch used the Protestant ethic as an index of the modernisation process and of the historical development of religions. Thus, Weber's notion about the magical impregnation of Catholicism was a hermeneutical principle designed to show the more advanced nature of Protestantism and, thus, the more primitive nature of Catholicism.[72]

Whether Weber was in the grip either of prejudice or of historicism, his anti-Catholicism seems to be influenced by his own Protestant heritage. As Zöllner puts it, he wrote his sociology of religion as a form of cultural Protestantism.[73]

Notes

1. For an excellent assessment of the relation of Protestantism to modern legal theory, see Witte (2002).

2. It will become clear in this section the extent to which religious confession has been insufficiently considered in all of these areas, resulting in a serious lack of appreciation for its importance in the formation of theories and methods. In this sense, one might say that a significant factor has been insufficiently thematised in the analysis of social, philosophical, legal, and historical phenomena until recently. In the area of English historiography, two recent books have questioned the writing of English history precisely on the lines of presumed confessional neutrality. This has been later shown to bear a strong anti-Catholicism that attempted to clothe itself in a scientific objectivity and confessional neutrality. See Eamon Duffy (1992) and Jones (2003). In the area of legal theory, the work of John Witte, Jr., has shown just how important the Lutheran Reformation was for the transformation of law and theology that occurred in the sixteenth century and beyond. Witte notes how most legal historians (following Troeltsch) have neglected the influence of this Protestant metanarrative shaping much of modern legal theory. See Witte (2002): 28–30.

3. For a Thomist critique of the Protestant heritage of Weber's work, see Midgley (1983).

4. See Stucki (1999): 9–15. These three characteristics of Protestantism are also noted by John Witte, Jr. Moreover, he notes that notions of the priesthood of all believers, and the distinctions between Law and Gospel and faith and works were central for the Lutheran Reformation. See Witte (2002): 298–299.

5. Lindberg (ed.) (2000): 43.

6. For the recent debate and agreement between the Catholic and Lutheran Churches on this question of justification, see Karl Lehmann (1998).

7. Lindberg (ed.) (2000): 40.

8. Stucki (1999): 62. "La thèse de la loi peut se formuler de la manière suivante: 'Dieu existe comme le Créateur qui a donné, sa loi aux hommes.' Elle se compose de deux éléments: 1) L'assertion de l'existence de Dieu, 2) La qualification de Dieu comme Créateur et donnateur de la loi. Il est nécessaire à la doctrine protestante de poser, cette thèse. Dans la conception de Luther, nous l'avons dit la loi est la première Parole de Dieu à laquelle l'homme est confronté. Ainsi, dans le protestantisme il ne s'agit pas d'admettre d'abord la thèse de la création, pour ensuite y ajouter que Dieu à donné sa loi aux hommes; il s'agit d'abord d'écouter la loi, laquelle implique que le donateur de la loi doit être compris aussi comme le Créateur. En d'autres termes, le protestantisme est d'abord une doctrine éthique, non pas une doctrine métaphysique."

9. The term *Kulturkampf* originated in an anti-Catholic address of 1873 and is used by historians to describe the conflict between Bismarck and the Roman Catholic Church in the period between 1871 and 1887. Bismarck was afraid that the decrees of the First Vatican Council, most especially the decree on papal infallibility issued in 1870 by Pope Pius IX, made a claim prior to the State on the obedience of the citizen. Bismarck was also concerned by Ludwig Windthorst's foundation of the Catholic Centre Party in 1871, which fought for the rights of Catholics and was vehemently anti-Prussian. The greatest conflict occurred in Prussia itself, because, even though throughout Germany priests had been forbidden from preaching on political matters and the Jesuits had been expelled, the Prussian "Falk Laws" of May 1873 led to a complete subordination of the Catholic Church to the State. Resistance to these laws was so great that many defiant priests were imprisoned, and Bismarck realised that such State control of religion was counterproductive. On the election of a new pope, Leo XIII, in 1878, Bismarck began negotiations with the Catholic Church to restore many of their rights, and by 1887 most had been restored.

10. See Graf (1992): 21–77.

11. It is interesting to note that the theology of Karl Barth, one of the greatest Protestant theologians of the twentieth century, is in great part a reaction against this nineteenth-century and early twentieth-century genre of Protestant theology. In his famous commentary on St. Paul's Letter to the Romans, written between 1916 and 1918, Barth stresses the fact that Christianity, which is not thoroughly eschatological, bears no relation to the preaching of the Gospel of Christ. Barth embodies the Protestant theological reaction against cultural Protestantism, which already in Weber's time was seen to be something of a "sell-out" to the *Zeitgeist*.

12. See Graf (1992): 24.

13. See Hübinger (1994): 112–113.

14. See ibid.: 157.

15. See Weiß (1992): 238.

16. Aldenhoff, (1987): 194.

17. See Thornhill (2000): 8–9.

18. See ibid.: 9.

19. One clearly sees the influence of Hegel here.

20. Münch (1995): 58–59.

21. It is interesting to note that in 1902 both Weber and Troeltsch fought against measures in Baden to reverse the ban on Catholic male religious orders originating in the *Kulturkampf* of the 1870s. See Graf (1995): 28.

22. Ibid.: 71.

23. On Weber's nationalism, see Liebersohn (1995): 123–131, and Lassman (ed.) (2006): Part IV.

24. As I mentioned with reference to Karl Barth's reaction against cultural Protestantism and also in the earlier consideration of Rudolf Sohm, the question of how much religion should bind itself to the modern secular culture was a major concern for Protestant theology. It is clear that this question was the major issue for Protestantism, and the inner tensions in Weber's views over his lifetime reflect these debates within Protestant theology. It is important to emphasise here that Weber's convictions are schooled in the force field of tensions occurring in this Protestant worldview at the end of the nineteenth century and early twentieth century.

25. Quoted by Graf (1995): 29–30 n. 11.

26. This is perhaps the reason why Weber had insisted that a theological response to his *PE* would be the most fruitful. On this point, see Graf (1995): 27.

27. Adolf von Harnack, "Protestantismus und Katholizismus in Deutschland," *Preußische Jahrbücher* 127 (1907): 295, quoted in Smith (1995): 13.

28. For a short and entertaining account of the history of the founding of the German Empire of 1848 and 1871, see Haffner (1989): 21–47.

29. See Elias (1978): 5.

30. Daniel Schenkel, "Die kirchliche Frage und ihre protestantische Lösung" (1862), quoted in Smith (1995): 22.

31. Wilhelm Scherer, "Die deutsche Spracheinheit" in Scherer, Geschichte des geistigen Lebens in Deutschland und Österreich" (1874): 55, quoted in Smith (1995): 23–24.

32. See Hartmann Tyrell (1995): 369.

33. Ibid.: 370–372.

34. For the best overall analysis of the fight of Durkheim's sociology to become established in the French Academy, see Lukes (1973). For the most comprehensive account of Durkheim's sociology of religion in English, see Pickering (1984).

35. On Durkheim's sociology as a legitimation of the secular French State, see Lukes (1973).

36. Blackbourn (1997): 293.

37. I am not suggesting here that one should reduce Weber's claims to their context. Rather, I wish simply to locate Weber's empirical and theoretical arguments within their social and cultural contexts of origin, because these have significantly shaped the very architecture of these arguments. Failure to locate Weber's arguments in such contexts has led scholars to overlook the importance of the Protestant metanarrative informing the architecture of Weber's argumentation.

38. Habermas criticises some postmodern theories for conflating the justified premise that there is no context transcendent reason, with the unjustified conclusion that the criteria of reason themselves changes in every new context. See Habermas (1998): 220.

39. For example, much of the Anglo-Saxon reception of Weber, most particularly through Talcott Parsons, has to a great extent been guilty of overlooking this culturally embedded context of Weber's thought. The neglect of the influence of Protestantism is one such example of this.

40. See Eliaeson (2002): 123–129.

41. See Smith (ed.) (2001): 4.

42. Ibid.: 4.

43. Ibid.

44. Ibid.: 4–5.

45. See Nipperdey (1988): 7–8.

46. See Smith (ed.) (2001): 5–6.

47. See Lucian Hölscher, "The Religious Divide: Piety in Nineteenth-Century Germany," in Smith (ed.) (2001): 45.

48. See Wolfgang Altgeld, "Religion, Denomination, and Nationalism in Nineteenth-Century Germany," in Smith (ed.) (2001): 55.

49. It is interesting to note that Altgeld suggests that the *Kulturkampf* was to a degree motivated by the need for religious homogeneity in order to forge the new nation-state in Germany. It is perhaps not too much of an exaggeration to suggest that Weber himself sought this homogeneity by defending the cultural superiority of Protestantism in his work. As we know from recent epistemological work of the natural sciences, facts come already theory laden. It seems unlikely that "social facts," to borrow a term from Durkheim, come any differently packaged than "natural facts."

50. In a similar vein, Peter L. Berger suggests that rather than funding such research on Iranian mullahs and various forms of religious fundamentalism, it might be more interesting to fund research on the secularism of the professors at the elite American universities, since they are a much more exceptional, curious, and difficult to understand phenomenon than the Iranian mullahs, when considered in the face of fervent global religiosity. See Peter L. Berger (1999): 2.

51. *Jugendbriefe*: 106–107. "So ist es gekommen, daß heutzutage alles, was wir unter dem Namen 'unsre Kultur' zusammenfassen, in erster Linie auf dem Christentum beruht, daß heute in den Einrichtungen und Ordnungen der ganzen menschlichen Gesellschaft, in ihren Denk- und Handlungsweisen, alles mit ihm zusammen und von ihm abhängt, so sehr sogar, daß wir selbst es gar nicht immer merken und gar nicht mehr uns bewußt sind, daß wir bei allem, was wir tun und denken, unter dem Einfluß der christlichen Religion stehen."

52. See Marianne Weber (1950): 408.

53. See Sica (ed.) (2000): ix.

54. Honigsheim (1950): 219.

55. See *Jugendbriefe*: 64, 106ff, 212.

56. See Honigsheim (1950): 223.

57. See *Jugendbriefe*: 294, 334.

58. Honigsheim (1950): 225. Cf. *Jugendbriefe*: 204, 234, 311.

59. Honigsheim (1950): 225.

60. Ibid.: 239.

61. See Sica (ed.) (2000): ix.

62. Honigsheim (1950): 228.

63. Ibid.: 229.

64. Ibid.: 230.

65. For an excellent account of the separation of jurisdictions in Weber's two-kingdoms theory, see Witte (2002): 87–117.

66. Wissenschaft: 155.

67. Helmuth Plessner's "Erinnerungen" of Max Weber in König and Winckelmann (eds.) (1963): 32. "Aber niemand hat je bezweifelt, daß er ein Protestant war, ein Lutheraner mit dem scharfen Blick für die Calvinistische Konkurrenz und dem Leiden am Zwiespalt zwischen den Forderungen des Gewissens und den Forderungen der Verantwortung. Man sieht das an den beiden nach 1918 vor Studenten gehaltenen Reden 'Wissenschaft als Beruf' und 'Politik als Beruf,' an seiner heroischen Bejahung des Pluralismus einer sich durchrationalisierenden Gesellschaft, einer Bejahung ohne Glauben an irgendeine objektive Hierarchie der Werte oder den Fortschritt, man sieht es an seiner Auffassung von Wissenschaft und seiner Methodologie."

68. Gertrud Bäumer, "Nekrologie," in König and Winckelmann (eds.) (1963): 117. "Für die Gestaltung von Lebenswerk, Schicksal, Gedanken, Bildung und für die Stellung zur Welt ist bei *Max Weber* die protestantische Gesinnungskultur die bleibende Grundlage. So weit und groß sich auch über das Konfessionsmäßige hinaus seine Lebensbetrachtung ausspant, es bleibt ihr derselbe tragende Untergrund—Väter- und Muttererbe. Eine geistig-sittliche Struktur, die zunächst—und in gewisser Weise immer—gar nicht einmal bewußt wird, aber doch im persönlichen Leben wie in der gedanklichen Auseinandersetzung mit der Welt maßgeblich bleibt. Wir sind in einer seelischen Sphäre, in der das *Sittliche* schicksalsbestimmend ist. Nicht und nirgends im philiströsen Sinne einer beschränkten Lebensmoral, sondern gerade deshalb um so mächtiger hervortretend, weil es die Dämonie einer leidenschaftlichen und zugleich nervös belasteten Persönlichkeit beherrscht und formt."

69. Stark (1968): 202.

70. Ibid.

71. See Zöllner (1996).

72. Ibid.: 595.

73. It is interesting to note in this regard the influence of the important historian Heinrich von Treitschke (1834–1896). At the age of fifteen, Weber commented that he was in overall agreement with the first volume of Treitschke's *Deutscher Geschichte im Neunzehnten Jahrhundert* published in 1879 (see *Jugendbriefe*: 29). Treitschke had argued in this work that German Catholicism was in basic conflict with the

spirit of the German nation (see Smith [2001]: 32). However, Weber was also strongly critical of Treitschke for using his academic post to sell his own political ideas, thus compromising what Weber considered the role of the academic to abide by the rule of value-freedom. Weber counted Treitschke, Theodore Mommsen, and Gustav Schmoller as guilty of this form of "Prophesorial-Prophecy." See Kaesler (1998): 245. For an excellent assessment of the importance of the influence of Treitschke's thought on Weber, see Sukale (2002): 108–121.

Conclusion

I began this work by using the analogy of architecture to describe the ways in which the theoretical edifice of Weber's work could be analysed as structured by a Protestant style. Now I would like to stand back from this building and survey the outlines that have been minutely observed in the previous chapters and suggest some areas that might fruitfully be developed in future research.

The central idea that this work has demonstrated is that Weber's theory of secularisation narrates a Protestant account of modernity. The task of exegetical reconstruction of Weber's works has grounded this central idea in a close reading of Weber's original works and has also supported this claim by reference to a wide range of secondary sources. The first task was to reconstruct Weber's theory of secularisation as a justifiable interpretation of his major texts. As I mentioned in Chapter 2, I make no claim that this interpretation exhausts the meaning of Weber's texts. Rather, I offer it as a legitimate reconstruction that can help to illuminate Weber's ideas and so lead to a better understanding of his purposes in writing on such diverse subjects as Neo-Kantian epistemology and the religions of China.

In reconstructing Weber's theory of secularisation, a number of central motifs have been observed—for example, the idea of the transformation of originally religious notions into secular form. Thus, the asceticism initially hidden behind monastery walls now emerges as rational ascetic action in the world. This "making worldly," a "*Verweltlichung*," of once-monastic practices into the secular domain of capitalist actions has propelled the Western world forward. As well as the transfer of ideas from one domain to another, Weber also identifies a shift in the valuation of specific practices that has empowered Western rationality. In the medieval period, he argues, contemplation of heavenly realities was valued as the highest goal of human life; modernity has transferred this valuation to rational action in the world. This transfer of energy has empowered the juggernaut of Western modernity, as it accelerates forwards in the race to dominate the world through purposive rational action. This motif of making worldly, or transfer from the sacred domain to the secular domain, is also found in the translation of the notion of a special religious vocation into the language of the universal vocation of all believers in a secular profession.

The complex notion of disenchantment (*Entzauberung*), a very powerful image of the world gradually being purified of the magical superstitions and practices that have dogged it for so long, forms another major contour of Weber's theory of secularisation. As Western reason emerges from its "self-imposed immaturity" and begins to stand on its own two feet, previously fused domains of society and culture emerge as separate and autonomously governed spheres, each with its own internal logic. This new ground is won through battle with the religious authorities who have policed these domains through theoretical domination and institutional power. Liberation of these spheres from the enchanted theories and practices of church control has left the world free to progress according to purposive rationality. This progress has led to the rationalisation of politics, the economy, the intellectual sphere, art, sexuality, and the erotic sphere. And, through this rationalisation, religion has been displaced and left on the sidelines as a mere spectator of the real affairs of life.

Yet, this progress has come at a price. The iron cage of an increasingly administered society will subject the new prophets of modernity to the cold wind of the dialectic of Enlightenment. Freedom from the enchanted theories and practices of a sacramental conception of existence will leave in its place a world orchestrated by the calculating logic of purposive rationality. This disenchantment is a secularisation of existence that has cleared the decks for the march of science and progress of reason, in a world no longer hijacked by the myths and magic of the priests and magicians. It has led to a mutual separation of grace from nature. Grace is no longer considered to be mediated through nature, and nature is no longer held to actively cooperate with grace.

Moreover, this disenchantment has also led to a privatisation of religion, another key dimension of secularisation for Weber, as religious influence and jurisdiction retreat from the public spheres of social life to the private piety of the individual. No longer will religion maintain the social rhythms of life from birth, through marriage, to death. Modernity will remove these functions from the previous monopolistic control of religions, and from now on these rites of passage will be registered and conducted by public servants of the state without any reference to religion. With this privatisation of religion, purposive rationality shifts religious experience into the private realm of individual experience, and so religion will be reduced to a matter of the heart, hidden safely away from the public domains of work and interaction.

Another feature of secularisation for Weber has been shown to be ingrained in the very structure of his sociological typologies. In opposing the ends of contemplation and action, Weber creates a secular theory of action. This typological distinction is crucial for his theory of rationality and attitudes to the world. It employs a purposive model of rational action that is emptied of any theological and metaphysical significance and incarnates a secular approach to the world. If, previously, action had been understood to have positive soteriological significance, Weber empties this significance into the reservoirs of the past, and in its place leaves the realisation of immanent goals. Following the Protestant tradition, ascetical action will now be a sign that one is already saved; it will no longer actively cooperate in the constitution of this salvation. In this sense, Weber's theory of action is a secularisation of the Catholic sacramental understanding of action and existence that dominated in the medieval period. In Weber's account, religions will be rational to the extent that they can generate "inner-worldly" ethics free from the "magical practices" of sacramental theories of action.

Emblematic of these sociological typologies has been the "Martha and Mary" motif, with Mary representing the ideal type of contemplation and Martha that of action. In choosing the way of Martha, the Western world has opted for rational action over against Mary's irrational contemplation, and so has paved the way for the development of capitalism and the progress of Western rationalism into all areas of modern life. In answering the question of theodicy through such means, Weber also finds Protestantism to have provided a rationalisation of the metaphysical image of God. This theoretical answer to the theodicy question complements the practical answer of ascetical action and provides a more rational account of God, exemplified in Luther's notion of the *Deus absconditus*.

Weber sees the rationalisation of natural law and the resulting formal positive law as an index of this process of secularisation. In providing the unique conditions for the emergence of formal positive law, a secular basis for Western society has emerged, which no longer requires legitimation from theological or metaphysical sources, but rather, grounds itself in its own rational objectivity.

The second task of this work has been to situate Weber's theory of secularisation within its Protestant heritage. This came to light in the very act of reconstructing Weber's theory of secularisation, as the two are so intimately connected. At the same time, in making explicit the confessional influences shaping the very architecture of Weber's theory of secularisation, further features of this theory have been illuminated.

The importance of the separation of grace and nature has been noted. The Catholic conception of grace present within nature, animating it with the life of the Holy Spirit, is replaced by the Protestant conception of grace as alien to nature, and only made present in the preaching of the Word of God when accepted in explicit faith, and not through institutional mediation by the sacraments. Thus, rather than the elevation of human nature to the level of being a son or a daughter of God, Weber follows Luther's conception of grace as centred on the forgiveness of sin, on the doctrine of Christian existence as being simultaneously a sinner and righteous (*simul justus et peccator*) and on the anti-Pelagian notion of salvation by faith alone. This Protestant conception of grace informs Weber's sociological typology of action and contemplation and has structured his theory of rational purposive action in the Western world. In this sense, the architecture of Weber's theory of action has been shown to be Protestant.

Here it is important to note that this is Weber's Protestantism, a Protestantism that he received from the theological sources of the time, as documented in many passages and footnotes in his works. That Protestantism itself is much more diverse, and that today it is the product of many theological changes, is not at issue here. The point is that in the construction of Weber's theory of secularisation he used the Protestant sources of his day, and it is these which shaped his arguments. This is the case in his differentiation of Lutheranism and Calvinism, in which he relies heavily on Matthias Schneckenburger's work, in his reliance on Julius Wellhausen's research on prophets in ancient Judaism, which he uses to speak of the type of person fit for a vocation in politics and scientific research, and in his conception of charisma, which was influenced by Rudolf Sohm. These are just some examples of the Protestant theological influences that have been shown to shape his conceptual formulations and, so, to situate Weber's theory of secularisation within a Protestant architecture. Weber was steeped in the Protestant theological literature of his day. He knew more than any other sociologist of the period about the important theological debates and issues that dominated German academic life. These theological discourses informed his reflections, from his writings on Protestantism and capitalism, through his sociology of religion and reflections on economy and society, right up to his Munich speeches at the end of his life. They provided a structure on which he could place his accounts of action, rationality, and society. The metaphor of a Protestant architecture is appropriate, as it figuratively depicts the structuring relationship between Weber's Protestantism and his theory of secularisation without reducing the one to the other.

My reflections on the *ora aut labora* (prayer or work) motif in the structuring of Weber's typologies have shown how this Protestant metanarrative of the separation of prayer and work has had decisive consequences for Weber's account of rational action and, consequently, for the historical development of the Western world. In eliminating the sociological significance of mysticism from his account of possible typologies of action, Weber closes off Catholic theories of action from having significance in the development of Western modernity. In this sense, Weber's account of Western rationality and its progress narrate a Protestant conception of modernity.

Given the influential nature of Weber's theories at both academic and popular levels, this Protestant account of modernity is of considerable consequence. In providing an account of Western progress that ignores the Catholic and, indeed, other types of "inner-worldly" mysticism, he has methodologically closed off alternative conceptions of modernity. In analytically linking asceticism to the historical development of the West and mysticism to that of the East, Weber also obscures the sociological significance of mysticism for rational theories of action. Whilst this separation is a possibility, it is neither logically necessary nor, in fact, historically accurate as a full account of action typologies. It betrays Weber's Protestant heritage at a crucial place in his work: his theory of action.

Furthermore, in following the Protestant view of eschatology as developed by the History of Religion school, Weber weaves a Protestant metanarrative into the fabric of his sociology of law. Using Johannes Johannes Weiß's conception of eschatology as being a purely future-oriented transcendent reality, Weber chooses to follow this Protestant separation of the realms of jurisdiction. This means that, whilst the gospel holds sway in the future world to come, secular rationality serves this world in the form of positive law. Weber follows Luther's highly influential Two-Kingdom theory, together with a more Calvinist-inspired eschatological framework, to narrate his account of the legal rationalisation of the Western world. These hermeneutical preferences situate his account within a Protestant conception of modernity and its legal rationalisation according to the secularisation of natural law as formal positive law.

Another central motif of the Protestant architecture of Weber's theory of secularisation is that of the Lutheran conception of the vocation of all believers. This universal understanding of vocation challenged the previously dominant

Catholic conception of the special vocation of the few. Weber follows Luther's rejection of this Catholic conception. He rejects the "spiritual aristocracy" it implies as being a type of traditionalism that has been manifest in various forms, such as the Catholic notion of the "contemplative" and even the Chinese notion of the "gentleman." In valuing the vocation of all believers, Protestantism affirmed ordinary life over against the special life of the contemplative few. This privileging of "inner-worldly" action over against "flight-from-the-world" contemplation provided a concrete example, for Weber, of how religious ideas have acted as carriers of the social impetus to change. This "democratisation of spiritual capital," which he found in different degrees in ancient Judaism and Protestantism, released the necessary energy for the masses to take forward the rationalisation of ordinary life on all levels. In transferring this spiritual capital from the monastery to the marketplace, capitalism gained a foothold in the West and would gradually expand, through increasing secularisation, to structure the economic life of the emerging Western nations of modernity.

In situating Weber's theory of secularisation in its Protestant heritage, the significance of the historical context of the then newly-formed German Empire for him has also been noted. Without wishing to reduce his ideas to this historical context, knowledge of it can help us understand just why he wrote as he did and also why he made particular hermeneutical judgments. An example may help to make the point here. If in, say, two thousand years, future generations of scholars were to come across some of Nelson Mandela's and Archbishop Tutu's speeches on South Africa without some knowledge of the history of apartheid, their interpretations of these speeches would be seriously hindered. Perhaps the scholars might also come across the multitude of books on post-apartheid South Africa that have appeared in recent years, and they would conclude that some important event or events must have triggered this interest, but would not know exactly what all the fuss was about. Was apartheid simply a collective national hysteria? Was it a new form of dialectical thinking? The interpretations would probably be even more fanciful than the many conspiracy theories of today. Knowledge of South Africa during the apartheid era helps one to interpret present day South Africa; without it, one can produce seriously fanciful theories.[1]

Reading Max Weber without a sense of the importance of German nationalism, of cultural Protestantism, of the *Kulturkampf*, of the confessionalisation of German scholarship and political life, is somewhat like the situation of such scholars. Clearly, not everything can be reduced to these historical realities, but knowledge of them enhances the scholar's understanding. As a passionate nationalist all his life, Weber was deeply concerned about the future and progress of his beloved German nation. As an intellectual involved in the public issues of his day, it would have been irresponsible for him to ignore his historical situation. The objectivity of the scientific observer of the facts, which Weber so much prided himself on being, demanded that an intellectual of any calibre know his age; and Weber certainly knew his age and the gravity of it for the future and progress of Germany.

The motif of freedom of conscience, which was of central importance to Weber, is also much more clearly understood in the context of his Protestant convictions of the opposition of faith and reason, the "intellectual sacrifice" demanded of the scientist, and of his suspicion of "Catholic authoritarianism" shaped by Protestant reactions to the 1870 declaration of papal infallibility. That the issue of objectivity and freedom of conscience was of confessional significance for Weber inscribes Protestantism on every aspect of his epistemological and methodical writings. If Catholics were bound by obedience to the pope, the notion of a Catholic scholar was an oxymoron. For Weber, tradition and modernity part company in Luther's rejection of papal authority, and he remained a lifelong defender of the independence and individual freedom of Protestant modernity.

In this elucidation of Weber's theory of secularisation and its Protestant heritage, I am also conscious that a number of interrelated questions have been raised that have not been adequately dealt with. The question of how an alternatively inspired social theory might differ from Weber's Protestant conception is clearly an important question. If Weber's theory of secularisation has taken shape within a Protestant architecture, then how would a social theory situated within a Catholic architecture differ from it? Of course, one might argue that social theory today has secularised to such an extent that confession no longer plays any significant role in theory formation. In fact, in many ways this position is itself consonant with Weber's social theory. Yet, even this secular position has been shown to originate in a Protestant metanarrative about the world.[2]

Charles Taylor's work on cultural and a-cultural theories of modernity is particularly relevant here.[3] Taylor points out that in formulating theories of modernity, one of two tendencies tends to predominate. Either a theory purports to be culturally neutral, not dependent upon particular cultural influences, or a theory is explicitly formulated within a particular cultural-hermeneutical horizon.[4] Clearly, Weber's intention in this regard is to produce an a-cultural theory, independent of particular cultural influences. However, I have demonstrated Weber's "a-cultural" social theory to be, in reality, a cultural theory of modernity, trading upon the assumptions of the cultural Protestantism of his day.

Clearly, this leaves me open to the charge of propounding simply another form of relativism. Yet, anyone aware of the debates within the social and natural sciences about the degree to which theories can be said to be objective or relative will realise that is not a simple matter. In fact, I am trying to steer a pathway between what Richard Bernstein has aptly called "objectivism and relativism."[5] In situating Weber's theory of secularisation within its Protestant framework, I am not suggesting that his social theory lacks rational validity. Rather, in so positioning Weber's theory, I am arguing that his rational arguments are structured by a Protestant tradition and hermeneutical framework.[6] Criteria of rational validity are not negated by the fact that reason is necessarily situated within a particular context.[7] Yet they do make the differentiation of universal claims to validity and particular hermeneutical options more challenging than either universalists or relativists would like to believe. Thus, for example, Weber's Protestant understanding of the grace-nature relationship does mean that his sociological typologies of action are dependent upon this particular hermeneutical option. This does not negate the validity of this option as a legitimate means of classifying various kinds of rational action. It does, however, qualify such validity by tying it to a particular hermeneutical option. That there are no hermeneutically-neutral options in the social sciences is a consequence of the fact of what Anthony Giddens has called their "double hermeneutic" nature.[8] This can, of course, be seen as an added value. That a theory of contemplative action, trading on a Catholic conception of the nature-grace relationship, might provide an interesting alternative pathway to modernity to those already spelled out by Weber in his action typology is one example of just such richness.[9]

If my argument about the Protestant heritage of Weber's theory of secularisation is correct, there are clear implications for the reception of his ideas in the work of later social theorists. Jürgen Habermas's social theory is a case in point. As Weber's theory of rationality plays a major role in his own conceptualisation of rationality and society, it would be interesting to analyse the importance of Weber's Protestant framework for his theoretical architecture. The extent to which Habermas's work bears traces of a Protestant metanarrative has not gone unnoticed by scholars, and a systematic enquiry into this could prove to be illuminating.[10]

Perhaps, to return to my starting point, one fruitful way of looking at differing theories of society might be to view them as buildings with particular architectural features. In coming to recognise particular shapes and structural features, one learns to appreciate both the beauty and the practical limitations of different styles of building, and to see the alternative possibilities opened up when one constructs with one style rather than another. Context, form, and function should be interrelated if harmony is to be achieved in a building. The rigorous standards of good architecture are no less exacting in the construction of the architecture of the theories of society. With skill and creativity, extraordinary edifices can be built that provide both aesthetic pleasure and functional purpose.

In exploring the architecture of Max Weber's theory, this work has aimed to help the reader observe the beauty and intricacy of his theoretical construction. It has also demonstrated some of the limitations of his way of theorising. Hopefully this analysis of particular features of this construction will help the reader better understand the function and purpose of his work. Sharing the beauty of what one has discovered is a wonderful aspect of life. If this work has communicated something of the beauty and intricacy of Max Weber's sociology, it will have been an exploration well worth making and sharing.

Notes

1. Here I am borrowing an idea from MacIntyre (1984): 1–5.

2. One might think of Marcel Gauchet's thesis about Christianity being "the religion of the exit from religion" as particularly applicable to Weber's Protestantism on this point.

3. See Taylor (1995) and (2007). In Taylor's latest work he traces the emergence of the modern secular age. Rather than seeing the secular as opposed to the religious, he finds the secular originating in the Protestant Reformation and leading to a plurality of worldviews of which the religious is one competing account.

4. I have developed this point in Hanvey and Carroll (2005): 75–83.

5. See Bernstein (1983).

6. See Gadamer (1990).

7. On this point, see Habermas (2005): 27–83.

8. See Giddens (1993): 9–10, 12–15, 166–167. Not only are the very "objects" of the social science themselves hermeneutical constructions, but also the theories that social scientists devise to understand and explain these "objects" are interpretations of these interpretations. Hence Giddens's phrase "double hermeneutic."

9. Historians have long noted that the Catholic contribution to modernity has often been overlooked. In the so-called "confessionalisation" debates within historical scholarship this lacuna has already been seriously questioned. See, for example, Reinhard (1977) and (1995), O' Malley (2000): 108–117, Rummel (2000), and Höpfl (2004).

In his account of passages to modernity, Louis Dupré makes the similar point that the Spiritual Exercises of St. Ignatius of Loyola were a particularly modern synthesis of freedom and grace, much more effective than the medieval theology of the time and one that contained an onto-theological synthesis of nature and grace untypical of the current Reformation understanding of grace. See Dupré (1993): 224–226. For an account of the intellectual foundations of the Enlightenment and its relationship to modernity, see Dupré (2004).

10. For a reading of Habermas's work as "Protestantism by other means," see Skinner (1982).

Bibliography

Weber's Works

References to a commonly available English translation follow the German version. I include in square brackets the date of the original publication.

"Antikritisches zum 'Geist' des Kapitalismus." In WINCKELMANN (ed.) (1972): 149–187 [1910].

English version: "Weber's First Reply to Felix Rachfahl, 1910." In CHALCRAFT and HARRINGTON (eds.) (2001): 61–85.

"Bermerkungen zu der vorstehenden 'Replik'." In WINCKELMANN (ed.) (1972): 44–56 [1908].

English version: "Weber's Second Reply to Karl Fischer, 1908." In CHALCRAFT and HARRINGTON (eds.) (2001): 43–51.

Das antike Judentum, *GARS* III, Tübingen: J. C. B. Mohr (Paul Siebeck). 1988 [1921].

English version: *Ancient Judaism*. In GERTH and MARTINDALE (eds.) (1952).

"Die drei reinen Typen der legitimen Herrschaft." Published posthumously by Marianne Weber. In *Preußische Jahrbuch*. Vol. clxxxvii (1922): 1–12. In *GAW*: 475–488.

"Die Objektivität sozialwissenschaftlicher und sozialpolitischer Erkenntnis." In *GAW*: 146–214.

English version: "Objectivity in Social Science and Social Policy." In SHILS and FINCH (eds.) (1973): 50–112.

Die protestantische Ethik und der "Geist" des Kapitalismus. Ed. and intro. Klaus Lichtblau and Johannes Weiß. Weinheim: Beltz Athenäum (2000).

English version: *The Protestant Ethic and the Spirit of Capitalism.* 2nd Roxbury ed. Trans. Talcott Parsons. Revised intro. Randall Collins. Los Angeles: Roxbury (1998) [1920 version only].

Die protestantischen Sekten und der Geist des Kapitalismus. In *GARS* I: 207–236.

English version: *The Protestant Sects and the Spirit of Capitalism.* In *The Protestant Ethic and the Spirit of Capitalism.* Second Roxbury ed. Trans. Talcott Parsons. Revised intro. Randall Collins. Los Angeles: Roxbury (1998): xiii–ixxiv.

Die Wirtschaftsethik der Weltreligionen. In *GARS* I: 237–573.

English version: The Religion of China, Translated by Hans H. Gerth. New York: The Free Press (1951). The "Zwischenbetrachtung" is the final part of *WEWR.* In *GARS* I: 536–573 (See below for English version).

Einleitung. In *GARS* I: 237–275.

English version: "The Social Psychology of the World Religions." In GERTH and MILLS (1958): 267–310.

Gesammelte Aufsätze zur Religionssoziologie. Vol. I. Tübingen: J. C. B. Mohr (Paul Siebeck) (1988) [1920].

Gesammelte Aufsätze zur Religionssoziologie. Vol. II. Tübingen: J. C. B. Mohr (Paul Siebeck) (1988) [1921].

English version: *The Religion of India. The Sociology of Hinduism and Buddhism.* Trans. and eds. Hans H. Gerth and Don Martindale. New York: The Free Press, (1967).

Gesammelte Aufsätze zur Religionssoziologie, Vol. III. Tübingen: J. C. B. Mohr (Paul Siebeck) (1988) [1921].

Jugendbriefe. Tübingen: J. C. B. Mohr (Paul Siebeck) (1926).

Max Weber Gesamtausgabe. Tübingen: J. C. B. Mohr (Paul Siebeck) (1984-continuing).

Politik als Beruf in *Gesammelte Politische Schriften.* Ed. Johannes WINCKELMANN, 5th edition. Tübingen: J. C. B. Mohr (Paul Siebeck) (1988): 505–560. [1921].

English version: "The Profession and Vocation of Politics." In LASSMAN and SPEIRS (eds.) (1994): 309–369.

Wirtschaft und Gesellschaft. 5th revised ed. student edition. Under the care of Johannes WINKELMANN. Tübingen: J. C. B. Mohr (Paul Siebeck) (1972) [1921/1922].

English version: *Economy and Society.* Edited by Günther Roth and Claus Wittich. Berkeley: University of California Press (1978).

Wissenschaft als Beruf. In Gesammelte Aufsätze zur Wissenschaftslehre (*GAW*). Edited by Johannes WINCKELMANN. 7th edition. Tübingen: J. C. B. Mohr (Paul Siebeck) (1988): 582–613 [1919].

English version: "Science as a Vocation." In GERTH and MILLS (eds.) (1958): 129–156.
Zwischenbetrachtung. In *GARS* I: 536–573.
English version: "Religious Rejections of the World and Their Directions." In GERTH and MILLS (1958): 323–359.

Secondary Works

ADORNO, Theodore and HORKHEIMER, Max (2001). *Dialektik der Aufklärung. Philosophische Fragmente.* 13th. Ed. Frankfurt am Main: Fischer Taschenbuch Verlag.
AGAMBEN, Giorgio (1998). *Homo Sacer. Sovereign Power and Bare Life.* Translated by Daniel Heller-Roazen. Stanford: Stanford University Press.
ALAND, Kurt (1983). *Die 95 Thesen Martin Luthers und die Anfänge der Reformation.* Gütersloh: Gütersloher Verlaghaus Gerd Mohn.
ALBROW, Martin (1990). *Max Weber's Construction of Social Theory.* New York: St. Martin's Press.
ALDENHOFF, Rita (1987). "Max Weber and the Evangelical-Social Congress." In Mommsen and Osterhammel (1987): 193–202.
ALEXANDER, Jeffrey C. (1996). "The Centrality of the Classics." In Turner, Stephen P. (ed.) (1996): 21–38.
ALT, Karin (1993). *Weltflucht und Weltbejahung. Zur Frage des Dualismus bei Plutarch, Numenios, Plotin.* Mainz: Akadamie der Wissenschaften und der Literatur, Franz Steiner Verlag.
ANDERSON, Margaret L. (1997). "Die Grenzen der Säkularisierung: Zur Frage des katholischen Aufschwungs im Deutschland des 19. Jahrhundert." In Lehmann (1997a): 194–222.
AN-NA'IM, Abdullahi A. (1990). "Political Islam in National Politics and International Relations." In Peter Berger (ed.) (1999): 103–121.
AQUINAS, St. Thomas (1991). *Summa Theologiae. A Concise Translation.* Edited by Timothy McDermott. Allen, Tx.: Christian Classics.
ARMSTRONG, Karen (2004). *The Battle for God. Fundamentalism in Judaism, Christianity and Islam.* London: Harper Perennial.
ARON, Raymond (1981). *La sociologie allemande contemporaine.* Paris: Quadrige, Presses Universitaires de France.
ASSMANN, Jan (2002). Herrscaft *und Heil. Politische Theologie in Altägypten, Israel und Europa.* Munich: Carl Hanser Verlag.
AUGUSTINE, St. (1998). *The City of God against the Pagans.* Ed. and Trans. R. W. Dyson. Cambridge: Cambridge University Press.
BAECHLER, Jean, HALL, John A. and MANN, Michael (eds.) (1988). *Europe and the Rise of Capitalism.* Oxford: Blackwell.

BAEHR, Peter (2000). "The 'Iron Cage' and the 'Shell as Hard as Steel': Parsons, Weber, and the *Stahlhartes Gehäuse* Metaphor in *The Protestant Ethic and the Spirit of Capitalism.*" *History and Theory* 40 (May): 153–169.

BARTH, Karl (1947). *Die Protestantische Theologie im 19. Jahrhundert.* Zurich: Evangelische Verlag.

BAUMGARTEN, Eduard (1964). *Max Weber. Werk und Person.* Tübingen: J. C. B. Mohr (Paul Siebeck).

BAUMGARTEN, Otto (1916). *Politik und Moral.* Tübingen: J. C. B. Mohr (Paul Siebeck).

BAUMGARTEN, Otto (1929). *Meine Lebensgeschichte.* Tübingen: J. C. B. Mohr (Paul Siebeck).

BEER, Theobald (1980). *Der Fröhliche Wechsel und Streit. Grundzüge der Theologie Martin Luthers.* Einsiedeln: Johannes Verlag.

BEETHAM, David (1974). *Max Weber and the Theory of Modern Politics.* London: George Allen and Unwin.

BELLAH, Robert (1970). *Beyond Belief.* Berkeley: University of California Press.

BENDIX, Reinhard, and ROTH, Guenther (1971). *Scholarship and Partnership. Essays on Max Weber.* Berkeley: University of California Press.

BENDIX, Reinhard (1977). *Max Weber: An Intellectual Portrait.* Berkeley: University of California Press.

BENJAMIN, Walter (1963). *Ursprung des deutschen Trauspiels.* Frankfurt am Main: Suhrkamp.

BERGER, Alan L. (1981). "Hasidism and Moonism. Charisma in the Counterculture." *Sociological Analysis* 41: 375–390.

BERGER, Peter (1963). "Charisma and Religious Innovation: The Social Location of Israelite Prophecy." *American Sociological Review* 28, 4–6: 940–950.

BERGER, Peter (1967). *The Sacred Canopy.* New York: Doubleday.

BERGER, Peter (ed.) (1999). *The Desecularization of the World. Resurgent Religion and World Politics.* Grand Rapids and Cambridge: Eerdmans.

BERGER, Peter (1999). "The Desecularization of the World: A Global Overview." In Peter Berger (ed.) (1999): 1–18.

BERNSTEIN, Richard (1983). *Beyond Objectivism and Relativism: Science, Hermeneutics and Praxis.* Philadelphia: University of Pennsylvania Press.

BERRY, Philippa, and WERNICK, Andrew (eds.) (1992). *Shadow of Spirit: Postmodernism and Religion.* London: Routledge.

BISER, Eugen (1991). *Glaubensprognose. Orientierung in postsäkularistischer Zeit.* Vienna: Styria.

BLACKBOURN, David (1997). *The Long Nineteenth Century*. London: Fontana Press.

BLOND, Philip (ed.) (1998). *Post-Secular Philosophy: Between Philosophy and Theology*. London: Routledge.

BLUMENBERG, Hans (1996). *Die Legitimität der Neuzeit*. Revised Ed. Frankfurt am Main: Suhrkamp.

BOURDIEU, Pierre (1990). *The Logic of Practice*. Translated by Richard Nice. Cambridge: Polity Press.

BOURDIEU, Pierre, and WACQUANT, Loïc J. D. (1992). *An Invitation to Reflexive Sociology*. Cambridge: Polity Press.

BOURETZ, Pierre (1996). *Les promesses du monde. Philosophie de Max Weber*. Paris: Gallimard.

BRETT, David (2004). *The Plain Style*. 2nd Ed. Cambridge: The Lutterworth Press.

BROWN, Callum G. (2001). *The Death of Christian Britain: Understanding Secularisation 1800–2000*. London: Routledge.

BRUCE, Steve (1996). *Religion in the Modern World: From Cathedrals to Cults*. Oxford: Oxford University Press.

BRUCE, Steve (2000). "The Supply-Side Model of Religion: The Nordic and Baltic States." *Journal for the Scientific Study of Religion* 39, 1: 32–46.

BRUCE, Steve (2001). "Christianity in Britain, R. I. P." *Sociology of Religion* 62, 2: 191–203.

BRUCE, Steve (2002). *God is Dead: Secularisation in the West*. Oxford: Blackwell.

BRUNNER, Otto, CONZE, Werner, and KOSELLECK, Reinhart (eds.) (1984). "Säkularisation, Säkularisierung." In *Geschichtliche Grundbegriffe: Historisches Lexikon zur politisch-sozialen Sprache in Deutschland*, 5. Stuttgart: Klett-Cotta.

BUCKLEY, Michael J. (1987). *At the Origins of Modern Atheism*. New Haven and London: Yale University Press.

BÜHLER, Andreas (1965). *Kirche und Staat bei Rudolf Sohm*. Zurich: EVZ-Verlag.

BURLEIGH, Michael (2005). *Earthly Power: Religion and Politics in Europe From The French Revolution To The Great War*. London: Harper Collins.

BYNUM, Caroline Walker (1988). "Mystik und Askese im Leben Mittelaltlicher Frauen. Einige Bemerkungen zu den Typologen von Max Weber und Ernst Troeltsch." In Schluchter (ed.) (1988b).

CAPLOW, Theodore (1985). "The 1984 Paul Hanley Furfey Lecture: Contrasting Trends in European and American Religion." *Sociological Analysis* 46, 2: 101–108.

CARLO, Antoni (1959). *From History to Sociology: The Transition in German Historical Thinking.* Translated by Hayden White. Detroit: Wayne State University Press.

CARR, William (1991). *A History of Germany: 1815–1990.* London: Arnold.

CARROLL, Anthony J. (2004). "Religious Symbols in Public Institutions." *The Way* 43, 4: 80–93.

CASANOVA, José (1984). "The Politics of the Religious Renewal." *Telos* 59, Spring: 3–33.

— (1994). *Public Religions in the Modern World.* Chicago: University of Chicago Press.

— (2003). "Beyond European and American Exceptionalisms: Towards a Global Perspective." In Davie, Heelas, and Woodhead (eds.) (2003): 17–29.

CAVALLI, Luciano (1987). "Charisma and Twentieth Century Politics." In Scott and Whimster (eds.) (1987): 317–333.

CHADWICK, Owen (1975). *The Secularisation of the European Mind in the 19th Century.* Cambridge: Cambridge University Press.

CHALCRAFT, David J. (1994). "Bringing the Text Back In: On Ways of Rendering the Iron Cage Metaphor in the Two Editions of 'The Protestant Ethic'." In Ray and Reed (eds.) (1994): 16–45.

CHALCRAFT, David J., and HARRINTON, Austin (eds.) (2001). *The Protestant Ethic Debate. Max Weber's Replies to his Critics, 1907–1910.* Trans. Austin Harrington and Mary Shields. Liverpool: Liverpool University Press.

CHAPMAN, Mark D. (2001). *Ernst Troeltsch and Liberal Theology. Religion and Cultural Synthesis in Wilhelmine Germany.* Oxford: Oxford University Press.

CHRÉTIEN, Jean-Louis, HENRY, Michel, MARION, Jean-Luc, and RICOEUR, Paul (eds.) (1992). *Phénomenologie et Théologie.* Presentation by Jean-François Chrétien. Paris: Criterion.

COLLEY, Linda (1996). *Britons. Forging the Nation 1707–1737.* London: Vintage.

COLLINS, Randall (1990). *Weberian Sociological Theory.* Cambridge: Cambridge University Press.

CONGAR, Yves (1973). "R. Sohm nous interroge encore." *Revue de science philosophique et théologique* 57: 263–294.

COQ, Guy (1995). *Laïcité et République. Le Lien Nécessaire.* Paris: Éditions du Félin.

CORETH, Emerich (1954). "In Actione Contemplativus." *Zeitschrift für Katholische Theologie* 76: 55–82.

COX, Harvey (1965). *The Secular City.* London: S. C. M.

CRAIB, Ian (1992). *Modern Social Theory. From Parsons to Habermas.* 2nd ed. London: Prentice Hall.

CRONE, Patricia (1987). "Max Weber, das islamische Recht und die Entstehung des Kapitalismus." In Schluchter (ed.) (1987a): 294–333.

DANIÉLOU, Jean. (1944). *Platonisme et théologie mystique.* Paris: Aubier.

DAVIE, Grace (1994). *Religion in Britain since 1945.* Oxford: Blackwell.

DAVIE, Grace (2001). "The Persistence of Institutional Religion in Modern Europe." In Woodhead, Heelas and Martin (eds.) (2001): 201–211.

DAVIE, Grace and HERVIEU-LÉGER, Danièle (1996). *Identités religieuses en Europe*, Paris: Éditions la Découverte.

DAVIE, Grace, HEELAS, Paul, and WOODHEAD, Linda (eds.) (2003). *Predicting Religion. Christian, Secular, and Alternative Futures.* Aldershot: Ashgate.

D'ENTRÈVES, Alexander P. (1994). *Natural Law. An Introduction to Legal Philosophy.* With a new Introduction by Cary J. Nederman. New Brunswick and London: Transaction Publishers.

DISSELKAMP, Annette (1994). *L'éthique protestante de Max Weber.* Paris: Presses Universitaires de France.

DOBBELAERE, Karel (1981). "Secularisation: A Multi-dimensional Concept." *Current Sociology* 29, 2: 1–216.

DOBBELAERE, Karel (1999). "Towards an Integrated Perspective of the Processes Related to the Descriptive Concept of Secularisation." *Sociology of Religion* 60, 3: 229–247.

DOMINGUES, José Maurício (2000). "The City. Rationalisation and Freedom in Max Weber." *Philosophy and Social Criticism* 26, 4: 107–126.

DRIJVERS, Han J. W. (1985). "Askese und Mönchtum im frühen Christentum." In Schluchter (ed.) (1985): 444–465.

DUFFY, Eamon (1992). *The Stripping of the Altars. Traditional Religion in England 1400–1580.* New Haven and London: Yale University Press.

DUFFY, Stephen J. (1992). *The Graced Horizon. Nature and Grace in Modern Catholic Thought.* Collegeville, Minnesota: The Liturgical Press.

DUFFY, Stephen J. (1993). *The Dynamics of Grace. Perspectives in Theological Anthropology.* Collegeville, Minnesota: The Liturgical Press.

DUPRÉ, Louis (1993). *Passage to Modernity: An Essay in the Hermeneutics of Nature and Culture.* New Haven and London: Yale University Press.

— (2004). *The Enlightenment and the Intellectual Foundations of Modern Culture.* New Haven and London: Yale University Press.

EBELING, Gerhard (1972). *Luther: An Introduction to his Thought.* Trans. R. A. Wilson. London: Collins.

EDEN, Robert (1983). *Political Leadership and Nihilism: the study of Weber and Nietzsche.* Tampa: University of South Florida Press.

EDER, Klaus (2002). "Europäische Säkularisierung—ein Sonderweg in die postsäkulare Gesellschaft?" *Berliner Journal für Soziologie.* Vol 3: 331–343.

EKSTRAND, Thomas (2000). *Max Weber in a Theological Perspective.* Leuven: Peeters.

ELIAESON, Sven (2002). *Max Weber's Methodologies.* Cambridge: Polity Press.

ELIAS, Norbert (1978). *The Civilising Process.* New York: Pantheon Books.

ESPOSITO, John L. (2000). "Islam and Secularism in the Twenty-First Century." In Esposito and Tamimi (eds.) (2000): 1–12.

ESPOSITO, John L. and TAMIMI, Azzam (eds.) (2000). *Islam and Secularism in the Middle East.* London: Hurst and Co.

FESTUGIÈRE, A. J. (1936). *Contemplation et vie contemplative selon Platon.* Paris: Vrin.

FISCHER, Hermann (2001). *Friedrich Schleiermacher.* Munich: Verlag C. H. Beck.

FISCHOFF, Ephraim (1972). "Die protestantische Ethik und der Geist des Kapitalismus." In Winckelmann (ed.) (1972): 346–371.

FRASER, Giles (2002). *Redeeming Nietzsche. On the piety of unbelief.* London and New York: Routledge.

GADAMER, Hans-Georg (1968). "Hans Blumenberg: Die Legitimität der Neuzeit." *Philosophische Rundschau* 15: 201–209.

GADAMER, Hans-Georg (1990). *Wahrheit und Methode. Grundzüge einer philosophischen Hermeneutik.* Tübingen: J. C. B. Mohr (Paul Siebeck).

GALBRAITH, John Kenneth (1987). *A History of Economics. The Past as Present.* London: Penguin.

GANE, Nicholas (2004). *Max Weber and Postmodern Theory. Rationalization versus Re-enchantment.* Basingstoke and New York: Palgrave MacMillan.

GARBER, Daniel and AYERS Michael (eds.) (1998). *The Cambridge History of 17th Century Philosophy.* Vol. 2. with the assistance of Roger Ariew and Alan Gabbey, Cambridge: Cambridge, University Press.

GAUCHET, Marcel (1985). *Le désenchantement du monde. Une histoire politique de la religion.* Paris: Gallimard.

GERTH, Hans. H., and MILLS, C. W. (1958). *From Max Weber: Essays in Sociology*. Trans. Ed. and Intro. by Gerth and Mills. New York: Oxford University Press.

GIDDENS, Anthony (1971). *Capitalism and Modern Social Theory. An Analysis of the Writings of Marx, Durkheim and Weber*. Cambridge: Cambridge University Press.

— (1993). *New Rules of Sociological Method*. 2nd Ed. with a new Introduction. Stanford: Stanford University Press.

— (1995) *Politics, Sociology and Social Theory. Encounters with Classical and Contemporary Social Thought*. Cambridge: Polity Press.

GILBERT, A. D. (1976). *Religion and Society in Industrial England: Church, Chapel and Social Change, 1740–1914*. London: Longman.

GILSON, Etienne (1952). *Les Metamorphoses de la Cité de Dieu*. Paris: Vrin.

GIRARD, René (1972). *La Violence et le Sacré*. Paris: Grasset and Fasquelle.

— (1978). *Des Choses Cachées depuis la Fondation du Monde*. Paris: Grasset and Fasquelle.

— (1982). *Le Bouc Émissaire*. Paris: Grasset and Fasquelle.

GOGARTEN, Friedrich (1952). *Der Mensch zwischen Gott und Welt*. Heidelberg: Verlag Lambert Schneider.

— (1953). *Verhängnis und Hoffnung der Neuzeit. Die Säkularisierung als theologisches Problem*. Stuttgart: Friedrich Vorwerk Verlag.

GOLDMAN, Harvey (1988). *Max Weber and Thomas Mann: Calling and the Shaping of the Self*. Berkeley: University of California Press.

GOLDSTEIN, Jürgen (1998). *Nominalismus und Moderne. Zur Konstitution neuzeitlicher Subjektivität bei Hans Blumenberg und Wilhelm von Ockham*. Freiburg and Munich: Karl Alber.

GOMBRICH, Ernst H. (1995). *The Story of Art*. 16th Ed. London: Phaidon.

GRAF, Friedrich Wilhelm (1987). "Max Weber und die protestantische Theologie seiner Zeit." *Zeitschrift für Religions- und Geistesgeschichte* 39: 122–147.

— (1987a). "Professional Friendship. Remarks on Max Weber and Ernst Troeltsch." In Mommsen and Osterhammel (eds.) (1987): 215–233.

— (1992). "Kulturprotestantismus. Zur Begriffsgeschichte einer theologiepolitischen Chiffre." In Müller (ed.) (1992): 21–77.

— (1995). "The German Theological Sources and Protestant Church Politics." In Lehmann and Roth (1995): 27–49.

GREELEY, Andrew (1972). *The Denominational Society*. Glenville: Scott Foresman and Co.

GREYERZ, Kaspar von (1997). "Secularisation in Early Modern England (1660–1750)." In Lehmann (1997): 86–100.

— (2000) Religion und Kultur. Europa 1500–1800. Göttingen: Vandenhoeck and Ruprecht.

GUNKEL, Hermann (1916). *Was bleibt vom Alten Testament?* Goettingen: Vandenhoeck and Ruprecht.

— (1917). *Die Propheten.* Goettingen: Vandenhoeck and Ruprecht.

GUTTANDIN, Friedhelm (1998). *Einführung in die "Protestantische Ethik" Max Webers.* Wiesbaden: Westdeutscher Verlag.

HAAKONSSEN, Knud (1998). "Divine/Natural Law Theories in Ethics." In Garber and Ayers (1998): 1317–1357.

HABERMAS, Jürgen (1968). *Technik und Wissenschaft als Ideologie.* Frankfurt am Main: Suhrkamp.

— (1976) *Zur Rekonstruktion des Histrorischen Materialismus.* Frankfurt am Main: Suhrkamp.

— (1981a) *Theorie des komminikativen Handelns.* I. Frankfurt am Main: Suhrkamp.

— (1981b) *Theorie des kommikativen Handelns.* II. Frankfurt am Main: Suhrkamp.

— (1981c) "Modernity versus Postmodernity." *New German Critique* 22: 3–14.

— (1983) *Moralbewußtein und kommunikatives Handeln.* Frankfurt am Main: Suhrkamp.

— (1986). "Entgegnung." In Honneth and Joas (eds.) (1986): 327–405.

— (1988). *Der philosophische Diskurs der Moderne. Zwölf Vorlesungen.* Frankfurt am Main: Suhrkamp.

— (1992). *Nachmetaphysisches Denken. Philosophische Aufsätze.* Frankfurt am Main: Suhrkamp.

— (1998). *Die postnationale Konstellation. Politische Essays.* Frankfurt am Main: Suhrkamp.

— (2005). *Zwischen Naturalismus und Religion.* Frankfurt am Main: Suhrkamp.

HABERMAS, Jürgen, and RATZINGER, Joseph (2005). *Dialektik der Säkularisierung. Über Vernunft und Religion.* Ed. and foreword Florian Schuller. Freiburg, Basel, and Vienna: Herder.

HAFFNER, Paul (1999). *The Sacramental Mystery.* Trowbridge: Gracewing.

HAFFNER, Sebastian (1989). *Von Bismarck zu Hitler.* Munich: Knaur.

HALEY, Peter (1980). "Rudolf Sohm on Charisma." *Journal of Religion* 60: 195–197.

HAMMOND, Philip E. (1985). *The Sacred in a Secular Age: Toward Revision in the Scientific Study of Religion.* Berkeley: University of California Press.

HANKE, Edith and MOMMSEN, Wolfgang J. (eds.) (2001). *Max Webers Herrschaftssoziologie.* Tübingen: J. C. B. Mohr (Paul Siebeck).

HANVEY, James, and CARROLL, Anthony J. (2005). *On The Way To Life.* London: Catholic Education Service.

HARDY, Peter (1987). "Islamischer Patrimonialismus: Die Mogulherrschaft." In Schluchter (ed.) (1987a): 190–216.

HARNACK, Adolf Von (1902). *Das Wesen des Christentums.* Leipzig: J. C. Hinrichs'sche Buchhandlung.

HARTWICK, Wolf-Daniel (1996). "Die Erfindung des Judentums. Antisemitismus, Rassenlehre und Bibelkritik in Friedrich Nietzsches Theorie der Kulture." *Trumah Zeitschrift der Hochschule für Jüdische Studien* 5: 179–200.

HEELAS, Paul, and WOODHEAD, Linda (2005). *The Spiritual Revolution. Why Religion is Giving Way to Spirituality.* Oxford: Blackwell.

HEGEL, G. W. F. (1994). *Vorlesungen über die Philosophie der Weltgeschichte.* I. Ed. J. Hoffmeister. Hamburg: Felix Meiner Verlag.

HEILBRON, Johan (1995). *The Rise of Social Theory.* Cambridge: Politiy Press.

HENKEL, Reinhard (2001). *Atlas der Kirchen und der anderen Religionsgemeinschaften in Deutschland-eine Religionsgeographie.* Stuttgart: Verlag W. Kohlhammer.

HENNIS, Wilhelm (1987). *Max Weber's Fragestellung. Studien zur Biographie des Werkes.* Tübingen: J. C. B. Mohr (Paul Siebeck).

HENRY, Michel (1996). *C'est moi la Vérité. Pour une philosophie du christianisme.* Paris: Seuil.

HERMELINK, Heinrich (1953). "Die Welt des freien Protestantismus." *Theologische Literaturzeitung* 78, 7: 385–392.

HERSKOVITS, M. (1947). *Man and His Works.* New York: Alfred Knopf.

HERVIEU-LÉGER, Danièle (1987). "Faut-il définir la religion." *Archives de science sociales des religions* 63, 1: 11–30.

— (1993). *La Religion pour Mémoire.* Paris: Les Éditions du Cerf.

— (2001). "The Two-fold limit of the notion of secularisation." In Woodhead, Heelas, and Martin (eds.) (2001): 112–125.

HERVIEU-LÉGER, Danièle, and WILLAIME, Jean-Paul (2001). *Sociologies et Religion: Approches Classiques.* Paris: Presses Universitaire de France.

HEUß, Theodor (1937). *Friedrich Naumann. Der Mann, das Werk, die Zeit.* 1st Ed. Stuttgart: Berlin.

HINTZE, Otto (1964). *Soziologie und Geschichte. Gesammelte Abhandlungen.* Vol. 2. Göttingen: Vandenhoeck and Ruprecht.

HOFFMANN, Joseph (1966). "Un canoniste dans la melée politique. Rudolf Sohm et l'association pour le socialisme nationale." *Revue de Droit Canonique* 16: 133–158.

HÖFFE, Otfried (2002). *Politische Gerechtigkeit. Grundlegung einer kritischen Philosophie von Recht und Staat.* Enlarged new Ed. Frankfurt am Main: Suhrkamp.

HONNEFELDER, Ludger (1988). "Die ethische Rationalität des mittelalterlichen Naturrechts. Max Webers und Ernst Troeltschs Deutung des mittelalterlichen Naturrechts und die Bedeutung der Lehre vom natürlichen Gesetz bei Thomas von Aquin." In Schluchter (ed.) (1988b): 254–275.

HONIGSHEIM, Paul (1950). "Max Weber: His Religious and Ethical Background and Development." *Church History* 19, 4: 219–239.

HÖPFL, Harro. (2004). *Jesuit Political Thought: The Society of Jesus and the State, c. 1540–1630.* Cambridge: Cambridge University Press.

HOPKINS, Gerard Manley (1970). *The Poems of Gerard Manley Hopkins.* 4th Ed. Revised, enlarged, and Ed. W. H. Gardner and N. H. MacKenzie. Oxford: Oxford University Press.

HÜBINGER, Gangolf (1994). *Kulturprotestantismus und Politik. Zum Verhältnis von Liberalismus und Protestantismus im wilhelminischen Deutschland.* Tübingen: J. C. B. Mohr (Paul Siebeck).

HUNTINGTON, Samuel P. (1997). *The Clash of Civilisations and the Remaking of World Order.* London: Touchstone Books.

— (2004). *Who Are We? America's Great Debate.* London: Simon and Schuster.

INWOOD, Michael (1992). *Hegel Dictionary.* Oxford: Blackwell.

JACOBI, E., and MOYER, O. (eds.) (1923). *Systematisches Handbuch der Deutschen Rechtswissenschaft.* 8th Section. II. Leipzig: Verlag von Ungleich.

JANICAUD, Dominique (1991). *Le tournant théologique de la phenomenologie française.* Paris: Éditions de l'éclat.

JASPERS, Karl (1946). *Max Weber. Politiker, Forscher, Philosoph.* 2nd Ed. Bremen: Johs Storm Verlag.

JENKINS, Philip (2002). *The Next Christendom. The Coming of Global Christianity.* Oxford: Oxford University Press.

JOAS, Hans (2000). "Social Theory and the Sacred: A Response to John Milbank," *Ethical Perspectives* 7: 233–243.

JONES, Edwin (2003). *The English Nation. The Great Myth.* 2nd Ed. Thrupp, Stoud: Sutton.

JÜNGEL, Eberhard (1992). *Gott als Geheimnis der Welt,* 6th revised Ed. Tübingen: J. C. B. Mohr (Paul Siebeck).

KAESLER, Dirk (1998). Max Weber. *Eine Einführung in Leben, Werk und Wirkung.* Frankfurt am Main: Campus.

— (ed.) (2002). *Klassiker der Soziologie.* 2 Vols. 3rd Ed. Munich: Verlag C. H. Beck.

KALBERG, Stephen (1994). *Max Weber's Comparative Historical Sociology.* Cambridge: Polity Press.

KANT, I. (1999). *Was ist Aufklärung? Ausgewählte kleine Schriften. Intro. Ernst Cassirer.* Ed. Horst D. Brandt. Hamburg: Felix Meiner Verlag.

KAUFMANN, Franz-Xaver (1989). *Religion und Modernität.* Tübingen: J. C. B. Mohr (Paul Siebeck).

KIPPENBERG, Hans G., and RIESEBRODT, Martin (eds.) (2001). *Max Webers Religionssystematik.* Tübingen: J. C. B. Mohr (Paul Siebeck).

KIRWAN, Michael (2004). *Discovering Girard.* London: Dart Longman and Todd.

KÖNIG, René, and WINCKELMANN, Johannes (eds.) (1963). *Max Weber zum Gedächtnis*, Cologne and Oplanden: Westdeutscher Verlag.

KRECH, Volkhard, and WAGNER, Gerhard (1994). "Wissenschaft als Dämon im Pantheon der Moderne. Eine Notiz zu Max Webers zeitdiagnostischer Verhältnisbestimmung von Wissenschaft und Religion." In Wagner, and Ziprian (1994): 755–779.

KRECH, Volkhard (2001a). "Religiosität." In Kippenberg, and Riesebrodt (eds.) (2001): 51–75.

KRECH, Volkhard (2001b). "Mystik." In Kippenberg and Riesebrodt, (eds.) (2001): 241–262.

KRECH, Volkhard, and TYRELL, Hartmann (eds.) (1995). *Religionssoziologie um 1900.* Würzburg: Ergon Verlag.

KROLL, Thomas (2001). "Max Webers Idealtypus der charismatischen Herrschaft und die zeitgenössische Charisma-Debatte." In Hanke, and Mommsen (eds.) (2001): 47–72.

KÜENZLEN, Gottfried (1980). *Die Religionssoziologie Max Webers. Eine Darstellung ihrer Entwicklung.* Berlin: Duncher and Humbolt.

KUHN, Thomas (1970). *The Structure of Scientific Revolutions.* 2nd Ed. Chicago: Chicago University Press.

LANGLOIS, Claude (1992). "La quantification en histoire religieuse. Un demi-siècle de pratique." In: *L'observation quantitative du fait religieux.* Lille: Colloque de l'Association Française d'Histoire Religieuse Contemporaine. (1992): 17–34.

LASH, Scott, and WHIMSTER, Sam (eds.) (1987). *Max Weber, Rationality and Modernity.* London: Allen and Unwin.

LASSMAN, Peter (ed.) (2006). *Max Weber* (International Library of Essays in the History of Social and Political Thought). Aldershot: Ashgate.

LASSMAN, Peter (2000). "The rule of man over man: Politics, power and legitimation." In Stephen Turner (ed.) (2000): 83–98.

LASSMAN, Peter, and VELODY, Irving, with MARTINS, Herminio (eds.) (1989). *Science as a Vocation*. London: Unwin Hyman.

LASSMAN Peter, and SPEIRS, Ronald (eds.) (1994). *Weber. Political Writings*. Cambridge Texts in the History of Political Thought. Cambridge: Cambridge University Press.

LEHMANN, Hartmut (1996) *Max Webers "Protestantische Ethik." Beiträge aus der Sicht eines Historikers*. Göttingen: Vandenhoeck and Ruprecht.

LEHMANN, Hartmut and ROTH, Guenther (eds.) (1995). *Weber's Protestant Ethic: Origins, Evidence, Contexts*. Cambridge: Cambridge University Press.

LEHMANN, Hartmut (ed.) (1997a). *Säkularisierung, Dechristianisierung, Rechristianisierung im neuzeitlichen Europa*. Göttingen: Vandenhoeck and Ruprecht.

LEHMANN, Hartmut (1997b). "Von der Erforschung der Säkularisierung zur Erforschung von Prozessen der Dechristianisierung und der Rechristianisierung im neuzeitlichen Europa." In Hartmut Lehmann (ed.) (1997): 9–16.

LEHMANN, Karl (1998). *Einig im Vertständnis der Rechtfertigungsbotschaft?* Bonn: Sekretariat der Deutschen Bischofskonferenz.

LICHTBLAU, Klaus, and WEIß, Johannes (eds.) (2000). *Die protestantische Ethik und der "Geist" des Kapitalismus*. Weinheim: Beltz Athenäum.

LIEBERSOHN, Harry (1995). "Weber's Concept of National Identity." In Hartmut, and Guenther (eds.) (1995): 123–131.

LIEBESCHÜTZ, Hans (1967). *Das Judentum im deutschen Geschichtsbild von Hegel bis Max Weber*. Tübingen: J. C. B. Mohr (Paul Siebeck).

LINDBERG, Carter (1996). *The European Reformations*. Oxford: Blackwell.

LINDBERG, Carter (ed.) (2000). *The European Reformations Sourcebook*. Oxford: Blackwell.

LITTLE, Lester K. (1988). "Laienbruderschaften in norditalienischen Städten." In Schluchter (ed.) (1988b): 383–409.

LOVE, John (2000). "Max Weber's Ancient Judaism." In Stephen Turner (2000): 200–220.

— (2000a). "Max Weber's Orient." In Stephen P. Turner (ed.) (2000): 172–185.

LÖWITH, Karl (1949). *Meaning in History*. Chicago: University of Chicago Press.

— (1968). "Hans Blumenberg: Die Legitimität der Neuzeit." *Philosophische Rundschau* 15: 195–201.

— (1995). *Von Hegel zu Nietzsche: Der revolutionäre Bruch im Denken des neunzehnten Jahrhunderts*. Hamburg: Felix Meiner Verlag.

LÖWITH, Karl (ed.) (1982). *Max Weber and Karl Marx*. Intro. Tom Bottomore and William Outhwaite. Trans. Hans Fantel. London: George Allen and Unwin.

LÜBBE, Hermann (1965). *Säkularisierung. Geschichte eines ideenpolitischen Begriffs*, Freiburg and Munich: Karl Alber.

LUCKMANN, Thomas (1967). *The Invisible Religion*. New York: MacMillan.

LUHMANN, Niklas (1977). *Funktion der Religion*. Frankfurt am Main: Suhrkamp.

— (1998). *Gesellschaftsstruktur und Semantik. Studien zur Wissenssoziologie der modernen Gesellschaft*. Vol. 3, 2nd Ed. Frankfurt am Main: Suhrkamp.

— (2000). *Die Religion der Gesellschaft*. Frankfurt am Main: Suhrkamp.

LUKES, Steven (1973). *Émile Durkheim. His Life and Work: A Historical and Critical Study*. London: Penguin.

LUTZ-BACHMANN, Matthias (2002). "Postmetaphysisches Denken? Überlegungenzum Metaphysikbegriff der Metaphysikkritik," *Zeitschrift für philosophische Forschung* 56, 3: 414–425.

LUTZ-BACHMANN, Matthias (ed.) (1995). *Metaphysik, Ethik, Religion*. Würzburg: Echter Verlag.

LYOTARD, Jean-François (1979). *La Condition Postmoderne*. Paris: Les Éditions de Minuit.

— (1988). *Le Postmoderne Expliqué aux Enfants*. Paris, Éditions Galilée.

MACINTYRE, Alasdair (1984). *After Virtue*. 2nd Ed. Notre Dame: University of Notre Dame Press.

MADDOX, Graham (2002). "The Secular Reformation and the Influence of Machiavelli." *The Journal of Religion* 82, 4: 539–562.

MANN, Golo (1958). *Deutsche Geschichte des 19. und 20. Jahrhunderts*. Frankfurt am Main: Büchergild Gütenberg.

MARKUS, R. A. (1970). *Saeculum: History and Society in the Theology of St. Augustine*. Cambridge: Cambridge University Press.

MARRAMAO, Giaccomo (1992). "Säkularisierung." In Ritter and Gründer (eds.) (1992), Vol. 8: 1133–1161.

— (1999). *Die Säkularisierung der westlichen Welt.* Trans. from Italian Günter Memmert. Frankfurt am Main: Insel Verlag.

MARTIN, David (1999). "The Evangelical Upsurge and its Political Implications." In Peter Berger (ed.) (1999): 37–49.

— (2003). "On Secularization and its Prediction." In Davie, Heelas, and Woodhead (eds.) (2003): 30–39.

— (2005a). "Secularisation and the Future of Christianity." *Journal of Contemporary Religion* 20, 2: 145–160.

— (2005b). *On Secularisation. Towards a Revised General Theory.* Aldershot: Ashgate

MARTY, Martin E. and APPLEBY, Scott R. (eds.). (1991) *Fundamentalism Observed.* Chicago: Chicago University Press.

— (1995). *Fundamentalisms Comprehended.* Chicago: Chicago University Press.

MARX, Karl and ENGELS, Friedrich (1927). *Marx/Engels.* Gesamteausgabe. Erste Abteilung. I. Erster Halbband, Marx–Engels Archiv. Frankfurt am Main: Vergesellschaft M. B. H.

MATUŠÍK, Martin J., and WESTPHAL, Merold (1995) (eds.). *Kierkegaard in Post/Modernity.* Bloomington and Indianapolis: Indiana University Press.

MCCARTHY, George E. (2001). *Objectivity and the Silence of Reason. Weber, Habermas, and the Methodological Disputes in German Sociology.* New Brunswick, New Jersey: Transaction Publishers.

— (2003). *Classical Horizons. The Origins of Sociology in Ancient Greece.* Albany, N. Y.: State University of New York Press.

MCCARTHY, Thomas (1991). *Ideals and Illusions. On Reconstruction and Deconstruction in Contemporary Critical Theory.* Cambridge, Mass.: MIT Press.

MCCORMICK, John P. (2007). *Weber, Habermas, and Transformations of the European State. Constitutional, Social, and Supranational Democracy.* Cambridge: Cambridge University Press.

MCGRATH, Alistair E. (1999). *Christian Spirituality. An Introduction.* Oxford: Blackwell.

MCLEOD, Hugh (2000). *Secularisation in Western Europe 1848–1914.* New York: St. Martin's Press.

MCMANNERS, John (ed.) (1990). *The Oxford History of Christianity.* Oxford: Oxford Universtiy Press.

MEHLHAUSEN, J. (ed.) (1995). *Pluralismus und Identität.* Gütersloh: Güttersloher Verlaghaus Gerd Mohn.

MERTON, Robert K. (1993). *Science, Technology, and Society in Seventeenth Century England.* New York: Howard Fertig.

METZ, Johann Baptist (1968). *Zur Theologie der Welt.* Mainz: Matthias-Grünewald-Verlag.

— (1992). *Glaube in Geschichte und Gesellschaft. Studien zu einer praktischen Fundamentaltheologie.* Mainz: Matthias-Grünewald-Verlag.

MIDGLEY, E. B. F. (1983). *The Ideology of Max Weber. A Thomist Critique.* Totowa, N. J.: Barnes and Noble Books.

MILBANK, John (1990). *Theology and Social Theory: Beyond Secular Reason.* Oxford: Blackwell.

MOMMSEN, Wolfgang J. (1974). *Max Weber und die deutsche Politik 1890–1920.* 2nd revised and enlarged Ed. Tübingen: J. C. B. Mohr (Paul Siebeck).

— (1974a). *The Age of Bureaucracy. Perspectives on the Political Sociology of Max Weber.* Oxford: Blackwell.

— (1989). *The Political and Social Theory of Max Weber.* Chicago: Chicago University Press.

— (1995). *Imperial Germany 1867–1918. Politics, Culture, and Society in an Authoritarian State.* Translated by Richard Deveson. London: Arnold.

— (1998). *Das Zeitalter des Imperialismus*, 21st Ed. Fischer Weltgeschichte. 28. Frankfurt am Main: Fischer Taschenbuch Verlag.

MOMMSEN, Wolfgang J. and OSTERHAMMEL, Jürgen (eds.) (1987). *Max Weber and his Contemporaries.* London: Allen and Unwin.

MONSMA, Stephen V., and SOPER, Christopher J. (1997). *The Challenge of Pluralism. Church and State in Five Democracies.* Lenham: Rowman and Littlefield Publishers.

MÜLLER, Hans Martin (ed.) (1992). *Kulturprotestantismus. Beiträge zu einer Gestalt des modernen Christentums.* Gütersloh: Gütersloher Verlaghaus Gerd Mohn.

MULLETT, Michael A. (1999). *The Catholic Reformation.* London: Routledge.

MÜNCH, Paul (1995). "The Thesis before Weber: An Archaeology." In Lehmann, and Roth (eds.) (1995): 51–71.

NIETZSCHE, Friedrich (1969). *Nietzsche Werke. Kritische Gesamtausgabe.* Eds. Giorgio Colli and Mazzino Montinare, 6th section, 3. Berlin: Walter de Gruyter and Co.

NIPPERDEY, Thomas (1986). *Nachdenken über die deutsche Geschichte.* Munich: Verlag C. H. Beck.

— (1988). *Religion im Umbruck. Deutschland 1870–1918.* Munich: Verlag C. H. Beck.

— (1993). *Deutsche Geschichte 1866–1918.* Vol. 1. Munich: Verlag C. H. Beck.

NORRIS, Pippa and INGLEHART, Ronald (2004). *Sacred and Secular. Religion and Politics Worldwide.* Cambridge: Cambridge University Press.

OAKES, Guy (1988). *Weber and Rickert. Concept Formation in the Cultural Sciences.* Cambridge, Mass.: MIT Press.

OEVERMANN, Ulrich (1995). "Ein Modell der Struktur von Religiosität. Zugleich ein Strukturmodell von Lebenspraxis und von sozialer Zeit." In Wohlrab-Sahr, Monika (ed.) (1995): 27–102.

OLLIG, Hans-Ludwig (1987). "Die Religionsphilosophie der Südwestdeutschen Schule." In Ollig (ed.) (1987): 428–457

OLLIG, Hans-Ludwig (ed.) (1987). *Materialien zur Neukantianismusdiskussion.* Darmstadt: Wissenschaftliche Buchgesselschaft.

O'MALLEY, John W. (1993). *The First Jesuits.* Cambridge, Mass. and London: Harvard University Press.

— (2000). *Trent And All That. Renaming Catholicism in the Early Modern Era.* Cambridge, Mass. and London: Harvard University Press.

OWEN, David (1994). *Nietzsche, Weber, Foucault and the Ambivalence of Reason.* London and New York: Routledge.

PAGLIA, Camille (1990). *Sexual Personae* New York: Vintage Books.

PANGLE, Thomas L. (1990). *The Spirit of Modern Republicanism. The Moral Vision of the American Founders and the Philosophy of Locke.* Chicago: University of Chicago Press.

PARKIN, Frank (2002) *Max Weber.* London: Routledge.

PARSONS, Talcott (1949). *The Structure of Social Action.* New York: The Free Press [1937].

PETERSON, Erik (1951). "Der Monotheismus als Politisches Problem." In *Theologische Traktate.* Munich: Hochland-Bücherei.

PICKERING, W. S. F. (1984). *Durkheim's Sociology of Religion. Themes and Theories.* London: Routledge and Kegan Paul.

PICKSTOCK, Catherine (1998). *After Writing: on the Liturgical Consummation of Philosophy.* Oxford: Blackwell.

PINKARD, Terry (2002). *German Philosophy 1760–1860: The Legacy of Idealism.* Cambridge: Cambridge University Press.

PLOTINUS (1962). *The Enneads.* Trans. Stephen MacKenna. London: Faber and Faber Ltd.

POGGI, Gianfranco (1996). "*Lego quia inutile*: An alternative justification for the Classics." In Stephen Turner (ed.) (1996): 39–47.

POPPER, Karl (1968). *The Logic of Scientific Discovery.* London: Hutchinson.

PULZER, Peter (1997). *Germany 1870–1945. Politics, State Formation and War.* Oxford: Oxford University Press.

RADKAU, Joachim (2005). *Max Weber. Die Leidenschaft des Denkens.* Munich and Vienna: Carl Hanser Verlag.

RAHNER, Karl (1967). "Theologische Reflexionen zum Problem der Säkularisation." In *Schriften zur Theologie.* 8. Zurich and Cologne: Benzinger Verlag.

RAULET, Gérard (ed.) (1997). *L'Éthique Protestante de Max Weber et l'esprit de la modernité.* Paris: Éditions de la maison des sciences de l'homme.

RAWLS, J. (1996). *Political Liberalism.* New York: Columbia University Press.

RAY, Larry, and REED, Michael (eds.) (1994). *Organizing Modernity: New Weberian Perspectives on Work, Organization and Society.* London: Routledge.

REINHARD, Wolfgang (1977). "Gegenreformation als Mondernisierung? Prologomena zu einer Theorie des konfessionellen Zeitalters." *Archive for Reformation History* 68: 226–252.

REINHARD, Wolfgang (1995) "Was ist katholische Konfessionalisierung?" In *Die katholische Konfessionalisierung: Wissenschaftliches Symposium der Gesellschaft zur Herausgabe des Corpus Catholicorum und des Vereins für Reformgeschichte, 1993,* Eds. Wolfgang Reinhard, and Heinz Schilling. Münster: Gütersloher Verlagshaus: 419–452.

— (2000). *Geschichte der Staatsgewalt. Eine vergleichende Verfassungsgeschichte Europas von den Anfängen bis zur Gegenwart.* Vol. 2. revised Ed. Munich: C. H. Beck.

RÉMOND, Réné (1999). *Religion and Society in Modern Europe.* Oxford: Blackwell.

RICHTER, Melvin (1995). *The History of Political and Social Concepts.* Oxford: Oxford University Press.

RICKERT, Heinrich (1902). *Die Grenzen der naturwissenschaftlichen Begriffsbildung. Eine logische Einleitung in die historischen Wissenschaften.* Tübingen and Leipzig: J. C. B. Mohr (Paul Siebeck).

RIESEBRODT, Martin (1980). "Ideen, Interessen, Rationalisierung: Kritische Anmerkungen zu F. H. Tennbrucks Interpretation des Werkes Max Webers." *Kölner Zeitschrift für Soziologie und Sozialpsychologie* 32: 111–129.

RINGER, Fritz (1997). *Max Weber's Methodology. The Unification of the Cultural and Social Sciences.* Cambridge, Mass. and London: Harvard University Press.

RITSCHL, Albrecht (1888). *Die christliche Lehre von der Rechtvertigung und Versöhnung.* III. 3rd Ed. Bonn: Adolf Marcus.

RITTER, J. GRÜNDER, K. (1992). *Historisches Wörterbuch der Philosophie.* 8. Basel: Wissenschaftliche Buchgesellschaft Darmstadt, Schwabe and Co A. G.

RODINSON, Maxime (1987). "Islamischer Patrimonialismus: Ein Hindernis für die Entstehung des modernen Kapitalismus." In Schluchter (1987a): 180–189.

ROODEN, Peter van (1997). "Secularisation, Dechristianisation and Rechristianisation in the Netherlands." In Lehmann (1997): 131–153.

RORTY, Richard (1980). *Philosophy and the Mirror of Nature.* Oxford: Blackwell.

ROTH, Guenther and SCHLUCHTER, Wolfgang (1979). *Max Weber's Vision of History Ethics and Methods.* Berkeley: University of California Press.

RUH, Ulrich (1980). *Säkularisierung als Interpretationskategorie. Zur Bedeutung des christlichen Erbes in der modernen Geistesgeschichte.* Freiburg: Herder.

RUMMEL, Erika (2000). *The Confessionalization of Humanism in Reformation Germany.* Oxford: Oxford University Press.

SCAFF, Lawrence A. (1991). *Fleeing the Iron Cage. Culture, Politics and Modernity in the Thought of Max Weber.* Berkeley: University of California Press.

SCHIEDER, Wolfgang (1997). "Konfessionelle Erneurung in den christlichen Parallelkirchen Deutschlands im 19. Jahrhundert." In Lehmann (1997): 223–228.

SCHLUCHTER, Wolfgang (1980). *Rationalismus der Weltbeherrschung. Studien zu Max Weber.* Frankfurt am Main: Suhrkamp.

— (1981b). "Altisraelitische religiöse Ethik und Okzidentaler Rationalismus." In Schluchter (1981a): 11–77.

— (1987). "Weber's Sociology of Rationalism and Typology of Religious Rejections of the World." In Lash, and Whimster (eds.) (1987): 92–115.

— (1988a). *Religion und Lebensführung.* 2 vols. Frankfurt am Main: Suhrkamp.

— (1995). "Zeitgemäße Unzeitgemäße. Von Friedrich Nietzsche Über Georg Simmel zu Max Weber." *Revue Internationale de Philosophie* 2: 107–126.

— (1998). *Die Entstehung des modernen Rationalismus. Eine Analyse von Max Webers Entwicklungsgeschichte des Okzidents.* Frankfurt am Main: Suhrkamp.

— (Ed.) (1981a). *Max Webers Studie über das antike Judentum. Interpretation und Kritik.* Frankfurt am Main: Suhrkamp.

— (Ed.) (1983). *Max Webers Studie über Konfuzianismus und Taoismus.* Frankfurt am Main: Suhrkamp.

— (Ed.) (1985). *Max Webers Sicht des antiken Christentums. Interpretation und Kritik.* Frankfurt am Main: Suhrkamp.

— (Ed.) (1987a). *Max Webers Sicht des Islams.* Frankfurt am Main: Suhrkamp.

— (Ed.) (1988b). *Max Weber's Sicht des okzidalen Christentums.* Frankfurt am Main: Suhrkamp.

SCHMITT, Carl (1934). *Politische Theologie. Vier Kapitel zur Lehre der Souveränität.* 2nd Ed. Berlin: Duncker and Humblot.

SCHMITT, Carl (1996). *Politische Theologie II: Die Legende von der Erledigung jeder Politischen Theologie.* 4th Ed. Berlin: Duncker and Humblot.

SCHMITT, Carl (1998). *Legalität und Legitimät.* 6th Ed. Berlin: Duncker and Humboldt.

SCHÖLLGEN, Gregor (1998). *Max Weber.* Munich: Verlag C. H. Beck.

SCHRAG, Calvin O. (1995). "The Kierkegaard-Effect in the Shaping of the Contours of Modernity." In Matušík, and Westphal (eds.) (1995): 1–17.

SCHROEDER, Ralph (1992). *Max Weber and the Sociology of Culture.* London: Sage.

SEBOTT, Reinhold (1993). *Fundamentalkanonistik. Grund und Grenzen des Kirchenrechts.* Frankfurt am Main: Knecht.

SEKIDA, Katsuki (1983). *Zen Training. Methods and Philosophy.* New York and Tokyo: Weatherhill.

SICA, Alan (ed.) (2000). *The Unknown Weber. Paul Honigsheim.* New Brunswick: Transaction Publishers.

SIEMANN, Wolfram (1995). *Vom Staatenbund zum Nationalstaat. Deutschland 1806–1871.* Frankfurt am Main: Büchergilde Gütenberg.

SIMMEL, Georg (1989). *Philosophie des Geldes.* Frankfurt am Main: Suhrkamp.

SKINNER, Quentin (1978a). *The Foundations of Modern Political Thought. Vol. 1. The Renaissance.* Cambridge: Cambridge University Press.

SKINNER, Quentin (1978b). *The Foundations of Modern Political Thought. Vol. 2. The Age of Reformation.* Cambridge: Cambridge University Press.

SKINNER, Quentin (1982). "Habermas's Reformation." *The New York Review of Books* 7 (October 29) 15: 35–38.

SMITH, Helmut Walser (1995). *German Nationalism and Religious Conflict: Culture, Ideology, Politics, 1870–1914.* Princeton: Princeton University Press.

SMITH, Helmut Walser (ed.) (2001). *Protestants Catholics and Jews in Germany 1800–1914.* Oxford: Berg.

SOCKNESS, Brent (1998). *Against False Apologetics. Wilhelm Herrmann and Ernst Troeltsch in Conflict, Beiträge zur historischen Theologie 105.* Tübingen: J. C. B. Mohr (Paul Siebeck).

SOHM, Rudolf (1892). "Kirchenrecht. 1. Die Geschichtlichen Grundlagen." In *Systematisches Handbuch der Deutschen Rechtswissenschaft.* 8th Section. I. Leipzig: Verlag von Ungleich.

SOHM, Rudolf (1912). *Wesen Und Ursprung Des Katholizismus.* 2nd Ed. Leipzig und Berlin: Verlag von B. G. Teubner.

SOHM, Rudolf (1923). "Kirchenrecht. Vol 2. Katholisches Kirchenrecht." In E. Jacobi and O. Moyer (eds.) (1923).

SOLIGNAC, Aimé and DONNAT, Lin (1980). "Marthe et Marie." In *Dictionnaire de Spiritualité. Ascetique et Mystique, Doctrine et Histoire.* Founded by M. Viller, F. Cavallera, and J. De Guibert, S. J., continued by A. Rayez, A. Derville and A. Solignac, S. J. Vol 10: 664–673, Paris: Mabille-Mythe, Beauchesne.

SOO, Chee (1984). *The Chinese Art of Tai Chi Ch'uan. The Taoist Way to Mental and Physical Health.* London: Harper Collins.

SPERBER, Jonathan (1984). *Popular Catholicism in Nineteenth Century Germany.* Princeton: Princeton University Press,.

STAMMEN, Theo, OBERREUTER, Heinrich, and MIKAT, Paul (eds.) (1996). *Politik-Bildung-Religion. Hans Maier zum 65. Geburtstag.* Padeborn: Ferdinand Schöningh.

STARK, Rodney (1998). "Explaining international variations in religiousness: The market model," *Polis.* Special Issue.

STARK, Rodney (1999) "Secularisation R. I. P." *Sociology of Religion* 60, 3: 249–273.

STARK, Rodney and BAINBRIDGE, William Sims (1987). *A Theory of Religion.* Bern and New York: Peter Lang.

STARK, Werner (1968) "The Place of Catholicism in Max Weber's Sociology of Religion." *Sociological Analysis* 29: 202–210.

STRÄTZ, Hans-Wolfgang (1984). "Säkularisation, Säkularisierung." In Brunner, Conze, and Koselleck (eds.) (1984): 789–809.

STRAUSS, Leo (1965). *Natural Right and History.* Chicago: Chicago University Press.

STROUMSA, Gedaliahu G. (1981). "Ascèse et Gnose: aux origins de la spiritualité monastique." *Revue Thomiste* 81: 557–573.

STROUMSA, Gedaliahu G. (1985). "Die Gnosis und die christliche 'Entzauberung der Welt." In Schluchter (ed.) (1985): 486–508.

STUCKI, Pierre-André (1999). *Le Protestantisme et La Philosophie: La Croisée des Chemins.* Geneva: Labor et Fides.

SUKALE, Michael (2002). *Max Weber—Leidenschaft und Disziplin. Leben, Werk, Zeitgenossen.* Tübingen: J. C. B. Mohr (Paul Siebeck).

SWEDBERG, Richard (ed.) (2005). *The Max Weber Dictionary. Key Words and Central Concepts.* With the assistance of Ola Agevall. Stanford: Stanford University Press.

TAYLOR, Charles (1989). *Sources of the Self. The Making of Modern Identity.* Cambridge: Cambridge University Press.

— (1995). "Two Theories of Modernity." *Hastings Center Report* 25, 2: 24–33.

— (2002). *The Varieties of Religion Today. William James Revisited.* Cambridge, Mass. and London: Harvard University Press.

— (2007). *A Secular Age.* Cambridge. Mass.: Belknap Press.

TENBRUCK, Friederich (1975). "Das Werk Max Webers." *Kölner Zeitschrift für Soziologie und Sozialpsychologie* 27: 663–702.

TENBRUCK, Friederich (1986). "Das Werk Max Webers. Methodologie und Sozialwissenschaften." *Kölner Zeitschrift für Soziologie und Sozialpsychologie* 38: 13–31.

TENBRUCK, Friedrich (1999). *Das Werk Max Webers. Gesammelte Aufsätze zu Max Weber.* Ed. Harald Homann. Tübingen: J. C. B. Mohr (Paul Siebeck).

THEINER, Peter (1987). "Friedrich Naumann and Max Weber: Aspects of a Political Partnership." In Mommsen and Osterhammel (eds.) (1987): 299–310.

THOMAS, Peter (2006). "Being Max Weber." *New Left Review* 41 (September–October): 147–158.

THORNHILL, Chris (2000). *Political Theory in Modern Germany: An Introduction.* Oxford: Blackwell.

TORRÓ, Lluis Oviedo (1990). *La Secularización Como Problema. Aportaciones al análysis de las relaciones entre fe cristiana y mundo moderno.* Valencia: Siftel.

TREIBER, Hubert (1985). "Elective Affinities Between Weber's Sociology of Religion and Sociology of Law." *Theory and Society* 14, 6: 809–861.

TREIBER, Hubert (1999). "Zur Genese des Askesekonzepts bei Max Weber." *Saeculum* 50, II: 245–295.

TREIBER, Hubert (2001). "Askese." In Kippenberg, and Riesebrodt (eds.) (2001): 262–278.

TROELTSCH, Ernst (1906). "Die Bedeutung des Protestantismus fű r die Entstehung der modernen Welt," *Historische Zeitschrift* 97: 1–66.

— (1913). "Zur Frage des religiösen Apriori." In *Gesammelte Schriften II.* Tübingen: J. C. B. Mohr (Paul Siebeck): 754–768.

— (1925). "Das Wesen des Modernen Geistes." In *Gesammelte Schriften IV.* Tübingen: J. C. B. Mohr (Paul Siebeck): 297–338.

— (1992). *The Social Teachings of the Christian Churches.* 2 Vols. Trans. Olive Wyon, with a Foreword by James Luther Adams. Louisville: Kentucky, Westminster and John Knox Press.

— (1994). *Die Sozialellehren der christlichen Kirchen und Gruppen.* 2 vols. Tübingen: J. C. B. Mohr (Paul Siebeck).

TUCK, Richard (1979). *Natural Rights Theories. Their Origin and Development.* Cambridge: Cambridge University Press.

TULLY, James (1980). *A Discourse on Property*. Cambridge: Cambridge University Press.

TURNER, Bryan S. (1974). *Weber and Islam. A Critical Study*. London: Routledge and Kegan Paul.

TURNER, Bryan S. (1977). "Confession and social structure." *The Annual Review of the Social Sciences of Religion* 1: 2–58.

TURNER, Bryan S. (1991). *Religion and Social Theory*, 2nd Ed. London: Sage.

TURNER, Bryan S. (1992). *Max Weber. From History to Modernity*. London: Routledge.

TURNER, Bryan S. (1996). *For Weber. Essays on the Sociology of Fate*. 2nd Ed. London: Sage.

TURNER, Bryan S. (ed.) (1990). *Theories of Modernity and Postmodernity*. London: Sage.

TURNER, Stephen P. (2000). *The Cambridge Companion to Weber*. Cambridge: Cambridge University Press.

TURNER, Stephen P. (ed.) (1996). *Social Theory and Sociology. The Classics and Beyond*. Oxford: Blackwell.

TURNER, Stephen P. and FACTOR, Regis A. (1994). *Max Weber. The Lawyer as Social Thinker*. London: Routledge.

TYRELL, Hartmann (1992). "Das Religiöse in Max Webers Religionssoziologie." *Saeculum* 43: 172–230.

TYRELL, Hartmann (1995). "Max Weber, Bismarck und der Kulturkampf." In Krech, and Tyrell (eds.) (1995): 365–77.

VAN LEEUWEN, Arendt Theodoor (1972). *Critique of Heaven*. New York: Charles Scribner's Sons.

VATTIMO, Gianni (ed.) (1986). *Filosophia '86*. Rome: Gius Laterza and Figlia.

VATTIMO, Gianni (1996). *Credere di Credere*. Rome: Garzanti.

VERDON, Timothy (2001). *L'Arte Sacra in Italia. L'Imaginazione Religiosa dal Palecristiano al Postmoderno*. Milan: Mondadori.

VILLIER, M., CAVALLARA, F., and DE GUIBERT, J. (eds.) (1953). *Dictionnaire de Spiritualité. Ascetique et Mystique, Doctrine et Histoire*. Vol 2. Cabasilas-Cyrille de Scythopolis. Paris: Beauchesne.

VOEGELIN, Eric (1995). *Die Grösse Max Webers*. Ed. and with a postscript by Peter J. Opitz. Munich: Wilhelm Fink Verlag.

VOIGT, Friedemann (2002). "Das protestantische Erbe in Max Webers Vorträgen über 'Wissenschaft als Beruf' und 'Politik als Beruf'." *Zeitschrift für Neuere Theologie Geschichte* 9, 2: 245–267.

WAGNER, Gerhard and ZIPRIAN, Heinz (1987). "Tenbruck, Weber und die Wirklichkeit. Eine Diskussionsbeitrag." *Kölner Zeitschrift für Soziologie und Sozialpsychologie* 39: 132–149.

WAGNER, Gerhard and ZIPRIAN, Heinz (eds.) (1994). *Max Webers Wissenschaftlehre. Interpretation und Kritik.* Frankfurt am Main: Suhrkamp.

WALLACE, Robert M. (1981). "Progress, Secularization and Modernity: The Löwith–Blumenberg Debate," *New German Critique* 21, Winter: 63–79.

WALZER, Michael (1976). *The Revolution of Saints: A Study in the Origins of Radical Politics.* New York: Atheneum.

WARD, W. R. (1987). "Max Weber and the Lutherans." In Mommsen and Osterhammel (eds.) (1987): 203–214.

WAX, Murray (1960). "Ancient Judaism and the Protestant Ethic." *American Journal of Sociology* 65, 5: 449–455.

WEBER, Marianne (1950). *Max Weber. Ein Lebensbild.* Heidelberg: Verlag Lambert Schneider.

WEHLER, Hans-Ulrich (1985). *The German Empire 1871–1918.* Oxford: Berg Publishers.

WEIGEL, George (1999). "Roman Catholicism in the Age of John Paul II." In Peter Berger (ed.) (1999): 19–35.

WEIß, Johannes (1992). "Troeltsch, Weber und das Geschichtsbild des Kulturprotestantismus." In Müller (ed.) (1992): 230–244.

WERNICK, Andrew (2001). *Auguste Comte and the Religion of Humanity. The Post-Theistic Program of French Social Theory.* Cambridge: Cambridge University Press.

WILSON, Bryan (1966). *Religion in Secular Society.* London: Watts.

WILSON, Bryan (1976). *Contemporary Transformations of Religion.* Oxford: Oxford University Press.

WINCKELMANN, Johannes (1980). "Die Herkunft von Max Webers 'Entzauberungs' Konzeption." *Kölner Zeitschrift für Soziologie und Sozialpsychologie* 32: 12–53.

WINCKELMANN, Johannes (ed.) (1972). *Max Weber. Die Protestantische Ethik II. Kritiken und Antikritiken.* 2nd revised and enlarged ed. Hamburg: Siebenstern Taschenbuch Verlag.

WINDELBAND, Wilhelm (1924). *Präludien, 2. Aufsätze und Reden zur Philosophie und ihrer Geschichte.* 9th Ed. Tübingen: J. C. B. Mohr (Paul Siebeck).

WITTE, John Jr. (2002). *Law and Protestantism. The Legal Teachings of the Lutheran Reformation.* Cambridge: Cambridge University Press.

WITTENBERG, Erich (1938). "The Crisis of Science in Germany in 1919." In Peter Lassman et al (eds.) (1989): 112–121.

WOHLRAB-SAHR, Monika (ed.) (1995). *Biographie und Religion.* Frankfurt am Main: Suhrkamp.

WOLF, Erik (1930). "Max Weber's Ethical Criticism and the problem of metaphysics." In Lassman et al (eds.) (1989): 122–137.

WOLIN, Sheldon S. (1981). "Max Weber: Legitimation, Method, and the Politics of Theory." *Political Theory* 9, 3: 410–424.

WOODHEAD, Linda, with HEELAS, Paul and MARTIN, David (2001) (eds.). *Peter Berger and the Study of Religion.* London and New York: Routledge.

WOODHEAD, L., HEELAS, P., and DAVIE, G. "Introduction." In Davie, Heelas, and Woodhead (eds.) (2003): 1–14.

YACK, Bernard (1997). *The Fetishism of Modernities. Epochal Self-Consciousness in Contemporary Social and Political Thought.* Notre Dame: University of Notre Dame Press.

ZABEL, Hermann (1968) *Verweltlichung/Säkularisierung. Zur Geschichte einer Interpretationskategorie.* Münster: PhD Dissertation (unpublished).

ZÖLLNER, Michael (1996) "Kulturprotestantismus als Religionssoziologie: Weber, Troeltsch und der Katholizismus." In Stammen, Oberreuter, and Mikat (eds.) (1996): 589–596.

Index